McGraw Hill Education | SMARTBOOK™

The first and only **adaptive reading exper** designed to transform the way students read.

Engages Students with a Personalized Reading Experience

SmartBook highlights what content a student needs to study by identifying what they know, what they don't know, and what they are most likely to forget.

Powerful Reports Pinpoint Specific Areas to Reinforce and Study

Students are able to study more efficiently because they are made aware of what they know and don't know. Instructor reports identify at-risk students and highlight the concepts the class as a whole struggles with the most.

Ensures Students Retain Knowledge

SmartBook detects the content a student is most likely to forget and brings it back to improve knowledge retention.

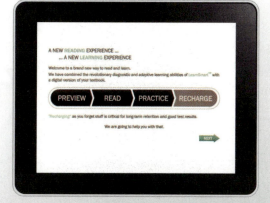

THE EVOLUTION OF LEARNING
learnsmartadvantage.com

Mc Graw Hill Education

Accounting
Information Systems

Accounting Information Systems

Vernon J. Richardson
University of Arkansas

C. Janie Chang
San Diego State University

Rodney Smith
California State University, Long Beach

Mc
Graw
Hill
Education

ACCOUNTING INFORMATION SYSTEMS

2 3 4 5 6 7 8 9 0 DOW/DOW 1 0 9 8 7 6 5 4

ISBN   978-0-07-802549-5
MHID   0-07-802549-4

Senior Vice President, Products & Markets: *Kurt L. Strand*
Vice President, Content Production & Technology Services: *Kimberly Meriwether David*
Director: *Tim Vertovec*
Executive Brand Manager: *Steve Schuetz*
Executive Director of Development: *Ann Torbert*
Managing Development Editor: *Gail Korosa*
Director of Digital Content: *Patricia Plumb*
Digital Development Editor: *Julie Hankins*
Marketing Manager: *Michelle Nolte*
Content Project Manager: *Angela Norris*
Senior Buyer: *Michael R. McCormick*
Design: *Jana Singer*
Cover Image: *(upper left)* © *The McGraw-Hill Companies, Inc./Jill Braaten, photographer; (upper right)* © *Rick Wilking/Reuters/Corbis; (middle)* © *Marijan Murat/dpa/Corbis; (bottom left)* © *Getty Images; (bottom right)* © *Eric Thayer/Reuters/Corbis*
Lead Content Licensing Specialist: *Keri Johnson*
Typeface: *10/12 Times Regular*
Compositor: *Laserwords Private Limited*
Printer: *R. R. Donnelley*
All credits appearing on page or at the end of the book are considered to be an extension of the copyright page.

Library of Congress Cataloging-in-Publication Data

Richardson, Vernon J.
    Accounting information systems / Vernon J. Richardson, C. Janie Chang, Rodney Smith.
        pages cm
    Includes index.
    ISBN 978-0-07-802549-5 (alk. paper)—ISBN 0-07-802549-4 (alk. paper)
    1. Accounting–Data processing. 2. Information storage and retrieval systems–Accounting.
    I. Chang, C. Janie. II. Smith, Rodney (Business writer) III. Title.
    HF5679.R53 2014
    657.0285'53–dc23
                                                                                        2013010595

www.mhhe.com

To my wife, Connie.

—Vern Richardson

To my students and my family who have inspired and supported me.

—Janie Chang

To my wife, Gayla.

—Rod Smith

About the Authors

Vernon J. Richardson *University of Arkansas*

Vernon J. Richardson is Professor of Accounting and the S. Robson Walton Distinguished Chair in the Sam M. Walton College of Business at the University of Arkansas. He currently serves as Accounting department chair. He received his BS, Masters of Accountancy, and MBA from Brigham Young University and a PhD in accounting from the University of Illinois at Urbana-Champaign. He has taught students at the University of Arkansas, University of Illinois, Brigham Young University, Aarhus University, University of Kansas, and the China Europe International Business School (Shanghai). He is a research fellow at the University of Technology Sydney.

Dr. Richardson is a member of the American Accounting Association. He has served as president of the American Accounting Association Information Systems section. He is currently editor at the *Accounting Review*. He has published articles in the *Accounting Review, Journal of Information Systems, Journal of Accounting and Economics, Contemporary Accounting Research, MIS Quarterly, Journal of Management Information Systems, Journal of Operations Management,* and the *Journal of Marketing.*

C. Janie Chang *San Diego State University*

C. Janie Chang is the Vern Odmark Professor of Accountancy at San Diego State University (SDSU). Currently, she serves as the William E. Cole Director of the Charles W. Lamden School of Accountancy at SDSU. She received her PhD from the University of California, Irvine. Before coming to SDSU, Dr. Chang served as Professor of Accounting Information Systems (AIS) at San Jose State University (SJSU). At SJSU, she established the undergraduate AIS program. She also taught at California State University, San Marcos. Dr. Chang's teaching interests in AIS include information systems audit, data modeling, issues in e-business, and business networks and controls.

Dr. Chang is active in research. She has studied issues in auditing, accounting, and information systems to investigate information processing of experts in addition to cross-cultural issues related to professional judgments and decisions in auditing and managerial accounting. Her studies have been published in *Abacus, Auditing: A Journal of Practice and Theory, Behavioral Research in Accounting, Data Base, International Journal of Accounting, Journal of Accounting Literature, Journal of Accounting and Public Policy,* among others.

Rod Smith *California State University, Long Beach*

Rod Smith is Professor of Accountancy at California State University, Long Beach. He received his BS in Mathematics from the University of Oregon, MS in Financial Management from the Naval Postgraduate School, Monterey, CA, and PhD in Management (Accounting) from University of California, Irvine. He previously taught at the University of Arkansas, University of California, Irvine, and University of Alaska.

Dr. Smith has published research in the *Accounting Review, Journal of Information Systems, Journal of Management Accounting Research, Journal of Accounting and Public Policy,* and *International Journal of Accounting Information Systems.* He is a certified public accountant (inactive), certified management accountant, and a retired captain in the U.S. Coast Guard.

His research interests include use of financial and nonfinancial measures to assess organizational performance; accounting information systems, enterprise systems, business processes, and business value; design science; and systems dynamics and business process simulation.

Preface

Whether accountants work in public accounting or in industry, they use a variety of technology tools. The International Federation of Accountants (IFAC) describes four roles for accountants with respect to information technology: **(1)** *users* **of technology and information systems, (2)** *managers* **of users of technology and related information systems, (3)** *designers* **of information systems, and (4)** *evaluators* **of information systems.** As users, managers, designers, and evaluators of technology and technology-driven business processes, accountants must understand the organization and how organizational processes generate information important to management. To ensure that processes and systems are documented—and to participate in improvements to processes and systems—accountants must be business analysts.

This textbook aims to provide students with a variety of technology and business analysis concepts and skills. It is intended for use in the first Accounting Information Systems course at both undergraduate and graduate levels. Ongoing changes in business technology, such as the move to Internet-based systems, software as a service, and mobile access to enterprise information, as well as increased security and control requirements, make technological skills more important than ever for accounting graduates. This textbook also aims to show how current changes in accounting and technology affect each of these roles. For example, the Sarbanes-Oxley Act affects financial reporting system controls, and XBRL changes system requirements and affects how companies develop and report financial information. The COBIT and COSO frameworks describe how organizations deal with risk management. In their roles as managers, designers, and evaluators, accountants must know how those frameworks affect their accounting and related information systems.

The core competencies of the American Institute of Certified Public Accountants (AICPA) emphasize accounting skills over content. This textbook emphasizes examples, problems, and projects through which students can develop the technological skills they need for their accounting careers. It uses real-world companies such as Starbucks, Walmart, Google, and Amazon that students can relate to. It takes a broad view of accounting information systems that emphasizes the accountants' roles in the use, management, design, and evaluation of the systems and the management information that they produce. To assist accounting students in experiencing the benefit of learning information technology/information services (IT/IS) concepts and using IT/IS skills in accounting, we focus on business processes, business requirements, how information technology supports those requirements, and how accountants contribute. In particular, this textbook helps students learn to:

- **Design business processes and represent them with standard documentation tools.** The role of the accounting function has evolved from stewardship and reporting to full partnership, supporting management decisions throughout the organization. As business analysts, accountants must be able to document business processes, identify potential improvements, and design and implement new business processes. Thus, this textbook helps develop business process modeling skills.
- **Design and implement well-structured databases to enable business processes.** Accountants must also understand how business processes generate data and how such data are structured, interrelated, and stored in a database system. To ensure that business processes and the database systems are documented and to participate in improvements to processes and systems, accountants must understand and be able to model such systems. Thus, this textbook helps develop data modeling and database implementation skills.

- **Query databases to provide insights about the performance of business operations.** Most organizational information resides in databases. To support management decisions throughout the organization, accountants must understand how those data are structured and how to retrieve information to support business management decisions. Thus, this textbook develops skills on the use of Microsoft Access and databases in general.

- **Evaluate internal control systems and apply business rules to implement controls and mitigate information systems risks.** Recent federal legislation—for example, the Sarbanes-Oxley Act of 2002, and COSO and COBIT guidance—emphasizes the importance of risk mitigation in modern organizations. Internal control systems must constantly evolve to meet a changing risk environment. Accountants are often the internal control experts and must, therefore, understand how internal controls should be implemented in business processes as part of the organization's overall risk mitigation and governance framework. Thus, this textbook presents specific material on internal control and accounting information systems, as well as general information about computer fraud and security. It also describes how to monitor and audit accounting information systems.

Accounting Information Systems, first edition, focuses on the accountant's role as business analyst in solving business problems by database modeling, database design, and business process modeling.

Chapter Maps

Chapter Maps provide a handy guide at the start of every chapter. These remind students what they have learned in previous chapters, what they can expect to learn in the current chapter, and how the topics will build on each other in chapters to come. This allows them to stay more focused and organized along the way.

Chapter-Opening Vignettes

Do your students sometimes wonder how the course connects with their future? Each chapter opens with a Vignette, which sets the stage for the rest of the chapter and encourages students to think of concepts in a business context.

A look at this chapter

A look back

A look ahead

Chapter-opening vignette

Chapter **Two**

Accountants as Business Analysts

A look at this chapter

As users, managers, designers, and evaluators of technology and technology-driven business processes, accountants must understand the organization and how organizational processes generate information important to management. To ensure that processes and systems are documented—and to participate in improvements to processes and systems—accountants must also be business analysts. This chapter defines business process modeling and describes how it supports the roles of accountants. It explains the potential value of business process modeling. Finally, it describes the types of business process models and introduces basic modeling tools to guide the student's development of modeling skills.

A look back

Chapter 1 discussed the importance of accounting information systems and the role accountants play in those systems. It further described how investments in information technology might improve the ability to manage business processes and create value for the firm.

A look ahead

Chapter 3 introduces data modeling. It describes how data modeling supports the design, implementation, and operation of database systems. It introduces basic modeling tools that will be used throughout the rest of the text.

One recent morning, I stopped at a very busy **Starbucks** in San Francisco. I looked at the line coming out of the door and immediately thought that it would take at least 20 minutes to get my morning coffee. Instead, I was pleasantly surprised at the efficiency of the employees who got me through that line in less than 2 minutes.

I watched closely as the **Starbucks** partners behind the counter executed the workflow of the process. One partner took my order and relayed my pastry order to another partner behind the pastry case. He also relayed my coffee order to the barista at the other end of the counter. As I moved through the line to the register, my order arrived just as I

26

did, and a fourth partner checked the order and took my payment. Within those 2 minutes, they had served at least a dozen other customers, too.

I thought about the number of options they had to deal with, the variety of hot and cold drinks, the pastries and other breakfast items, while also keeping a supply of freshly brewed coffee ready. I was sure that Starbucks had analyzed the process in detail to eliminate waste and enhance their partners' productivity. Then, they had to train all their partners in that process so they could work as one highly synchronized team. Finally, they delivered a hot cup of coffee to a grateful customer on a cool San Francisco morning.

Chapter Outline

Changing Roles of Accountants in Business
Business Process Documentation
Definitions
Purposes of Process Documentation
Value of Business Models
Types of Business Models
Activity Models
Business Process Modeling Notation
Building Blocks for BPMN Diagrams
Example of a Business Process Diagram
Identifying Participants in Business Process Diagrams
Messages in BPMN
Best Practices in Preparing BPMN Diagrams
Appendix A: Flowcharting
Appendix B: Data Flow Diagrams

Learning Objectives

After reading this chapter, you should be able to:

2-1 Describe the roles of the accounting/finance function in business and why those roles require knowledge of technology and business processes.

2-2 Understand the importance of business process documentation.

2-3 Recognize the value of business models.

2-4 Articulate the characteristics of activity models.

2-5 Understand and apply the building blocks for BPMN (activity) diagrams.

Learning Objectives

Learning Objectives are featured at the beginning of each chapter. The objectives provide students with an overview of the concepts they should understand after reading the chapter. These Learning Objectives are repeated in the margin of the text where they apply.

Chapter Outline

Each chapter opens with an Outline that provides direction to the student about the topics they can expect to learn throughout the chapter.

Learning Objectives

Chapter Outline

Integrated Project

Projects can generate classroom discussion or be the basis for good teamwork. This integrated project in Chapter 8 asks students to apply the different techniques they have learned in Chapters 5, 6, and 7 to a realistic situation. Students use a Microsoft Access relational database system.

> ### Chapter **Eight**
>
> ## Integrated Project
>
> **A look at this chapter**
>
> This chapter describes a business analysis and integrated systems development project. It is designed as a group assignment. To complete the assignment, each group must plan and execute a realistic systems design and development project. The finished product will include (1) activity and structure models of a company's business processes, (2) an analysis of the company's existing internal controls, (3) identification of opportunities for effective use of an accounting information system and related information technology to improve the company's performance, and (4) a Microsoft Access relational database system and appropriate queries necessary to prepare financial and managerial accounting reports.

Connection with Practice

Connection with Practice boxes highlight important and interesting real-world trends and practices.

> **"I like comprehensive problems that extend across multiple chapters so students can see how different components of a problem fit together."**
>
> —*Janice Benson, University of Wyoming*

> As another example, **Royal Bank** (formerly Royal Bank of Canada) considers CRM to be such an important part of its strategy that the stated objective of the bank is "to capture the full potential of our customer base through the use of customer information to deliver the right solutions in a consistent, professional manner at every point of contact".[8]
>
> ### Connection with Practice
>
> Salesforce.com is a popular vendor of CRM software. Note the explanation of CRM on the home page of their website:
>
> > Customer relationship management (CRM) is all about managing the relationships you have with your customers—including potential customers. CRM combines business processes, people, and technology to achieve this single goal: Getting and keeping satisfied customers. It's an overall strategy to help you learn more about your customers and their behavior so you can develop stronger, lasting relationships that will benefit both you and your customers. It's very hard to run a successful business without a strong focus on CRM. After all, it's all about the customer.
>
> Source: Accessed January 30, 2013, http://www.salesforce.com/assets/sw6/youtube_players/crm-sales.jsp

Photos

Unique to Accounting Information Systems textbooks, photos are included to highlight topics and generate student interest.

Hershey was not able to deliver Hershey Kisses for Halloween in 1999 right after the first attempt to implement its enterprise system.

1. **Hershey**
   Hershey spent $115 million on a failed enterprise system implementation attempt of SAP R/3, Siebel CRM, and Manugistics supply chain applications during Halloween season, which caused huge candy disruptions in 1999. This failed attempt prevented Hershey from delivering $100 million worth of Hershey Kisses for Halloween that year, causing a third-quarter sales drop of 12.4 percent. Earnings that year were off by 18.6 percent (compared with the previous year), and that caused the stock price to fall by 8 percent.

2. **Nike**
   In 2000, a $400 million i2 upgrade to Nike's supply chain and enterprise systems gave the shoe and athletic company $100 million in lost sales, a 20 percent stock dip, and a collection of class-action lawsuits.

3. **Hewlett-Packard (HP)**
   In 2004, HP's enterprise system implementation went awry. Gilles Bouchard, then-CIO of HP's global operations, said, "We had a series of small problems, none of which individually would have been too much to handle. But together they created the perfect storm." The project eventually cost HP $160 million in order backlogs and lost revenue—more than five times the project's estimated cost.

> "I really like the Quick Self Check box. It is a great tool for students' self assessment."
>
> —*Chih-Chen Lee, Northern Illinois University*

Progress Checks

These self-test questions and problems in the body of the chapter enable the student to determine whether he or she has understood the preceding material and to reinforce that understanding before reading further. Detailed solutions to these questions are found at the end of each chapter.

Progress *Check*

10. Give an example of how supply chain management software might work for **General Motors**. What type of information does General Motors need to share with its suppliers?

11. Using CRM techniques, what information could universities gather about their current and prospective customers, the students? What information might be most useful to them in recruiting future students?

LO 1-8
Assess the impact of AIS on firm profitability and stock prices.

AIS, FIRM PROFITABILITY, AND STOCK PRICES

Throughout this chapter, we have tried to make the case that AIS facilitates value-creating activities. This section presents a direct test of whether an investment in AIS, in fact, creates value by considering whether an AIS investment led to more profits or higher market value.

AIS and Firm Profitability

One way to consider how AIS creates value is to look at an income statement. Accountants understand that to make more profits, a firm either needs to increase revenues or decrease expenses (or both!). Figure 1.8 illustrates how AIS affects the income statement, making the case for how an AIS may increase profitability.

In a recent study,[9] a positive association was found between the level of the firm's annual IT investment and its subsequent accounting earnings (as measured by return on assets and return on sales), suggesting that IT investment does create value. In a completely different study,[10] ... found both an improvement in prof... as well as

Key Words

Key words are indicated in boldface the first time the term is used. The terms are also listed at the end of the chapter with page references for easy review.

Data Modeling and Microsoft Access

Chapter 3 describes how data modeling supports the design, implementation, and operation of database systems. Basic modeling tools are used throughout the rest of the text.

> "This textbook would be good when using the database approach. It provides the information needed to develop and use a database without getting into the details of transaction processing (activities, documents, and internal control)."
>
> —*Janice Benson, University of Wyoming*

Chapter **Three**

Data Modeling

A look at this chapter

Today's accountants must understand how business processes generate data and how those data are structured, interrelated, and stored in a database system. To ensure that business processes and the database systems are documented and to participate in improvements to processes and systems, accountants must understand and be able to model such data. This chapter describes data modeling. It explains how data models support database-driven systems. It introduces basic data modeling tools to guide the student's development of modeling skills. Finally, it discusses business rules and how the identification of relevant business rules supports both process and data modeling.

A look back

Chapter 2 described the roles of accountants as users, managers, designers, and evaluators of technology and technology-driven business processes. To perform in those roles, accountants need to ensure that processes and systems are documented—and to participate in improvements to processes and systems. Thus, accountants must be business analysts. The chapter continued to introduce types of business process models as well as the potential value of business process modeling.

End-of-Chapter Resources

End-of-chapter problem material is an integral part of any text. Good problems get students excited about the material and generate lively class discussions. The end-of-chapter material includes Answers to Progress Checks, Multiple Choice Questions, Discussion Questions, Problems, and Answers to Multiple Choice Questions

Discussion Questions

Discussion Questions not only ask students to apply concepts in the chapter to their own lives and experiences, but are intended to serve as a self-review or as class discussion starters.

Problems

Each chapter includes a set of problems for assignment. The problems are intended to be challenging but doable for students.

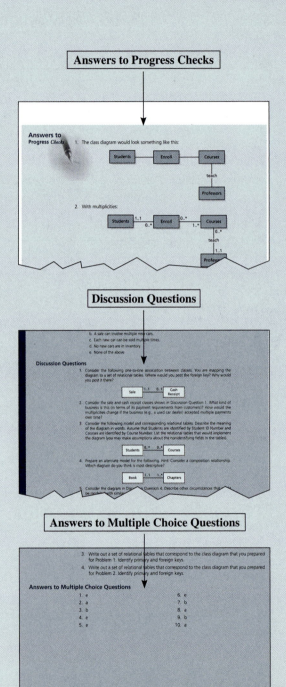

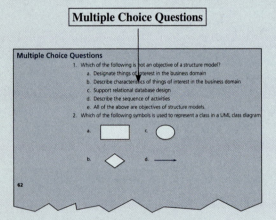

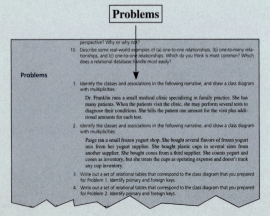

Glossary of Models

This glossary presents various structure and activity models to show modeling options. It is not intended to be all-inclusive, but rather to provide examples of how to model common situations. For the structure models, the basic assumption is that resources, agents, and type images are added to the database before they are linked to other classes, so the minimum multiplicity is zero. Otherwise, the models show the most common multiplicities. The glossary presents examples of structure models and then presents some generic activity models in the last section.

Glossary **of Models**

This glossary presents various structure and activity models to show modeling options. It is not intended to be all-inclusive, but rather to provide examples of how to model common situations. For the structure models, the basic assumption is that resources, agents, and type images are added to the database before they are linked to other classes, so the minimum multiplicity is zero. Otherwise, the models show the most common multiplicities.

The glossary presents examples of structure models in the following section and then presents some generic activity models in the last section. The models are presented in the following order: sales and cash receipts process, purchases and cash disbursements process, and the conversion process; for the structure models, it includes miscellaneous and integrated models.

Structure Models Using the REA Framework

1. Sales: Generic Model

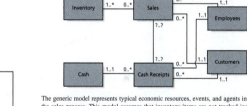

The generic model represents typical economic resources, events, and agents involved in the sales process. This model assumes that inventory items are not tracked individually (like high-value items such as automobiles and houses), but rather by UPC code, such that all products with the same UPC code are considered to be the same item.

313

2. Sales: With Invoice Tracking

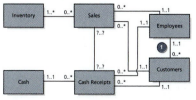

This model extends the generic model to track the invoices issued to each customer as shown in association 1 between Customers (Agent) and Invoices (Type Image).

3. Sales: Employees Assigned to Service Particular Customers

This model extends the generic model to represent assignment of employees to customers. Association 1 links customers to the assigned employee, such as when sales take place on commission. Similarly, employees can be assigned to inventory, when specific employees manage specific inventory items.

"The book does an excellent job of tying systems concepts to accounting/auditing concepts; the best I have seen at describing technical material like database design, foreign keys, cardinalities, business rules. Then technical material is connected to the accounting and auditing concepts."

—*Ken Henry, Florida International University*

Online Learning Center (www.mhhe.com/richardson1e)

The book's website (Online Learning Center) contains material for instructors and students. The password-protected instructor side houses all of the instructor resources to teach the course.

All of the supplements were prepared by the authors.

For the Instructor

- **Instructor's Solutions Manual** provides answers to all the end-of-chapter problem material.
- **Instructor's Resource Manual** includes assignment suggestions, brief topical outlines, comments and observations, course descriptions and objectives, and suggested team exercises.
- **Test Bank** provides true/false, multiple choice, and essay questions. Each question is tied to criteria, such as the example below, allowing instructors to choose the type of question for their needs.

  AACSB: Reflective Thinking
  AICPA BB: Industry
  AICPA FN: Decision Making
  Blooms: Remember
  Difficulty: 1 Easy
  Learning Objective: 09-01 Explain how data warehouses are created and used.
  Topic: Data Warehouse

- **Computerized Test Bank** utilizes McGraw-Hill's EZTest software to quickly create customized exams.
- **PowerPoint Presentations** comprise of two sets—one for instructors and one for students. Learning objectives from the chapter are included on each slide.
- **Figures from the Text** enable instructors to customize PowerPoint slides.
- **Databases for Chapter 4** cover Appendix A and Access Practices for end-of-chapter problems and solutions.
- **Text and Supplement Updates**

For the Student

- **PowerPoint Presentations** selected from the instructor PowerPoints.
- **Online Chapter Quizzes** provide students with instant feedback on short quizzes.
- **Databases for Chapter 4** cover Appendix A and Access Practices for end-of-chapter problems.
- **Links to Professional Resources**

LearnSmart

No two students are alike. McGraw-Hill's LearnSmart™ is an intelligent learning system that uses a series of adaptive questions to pinpoint each student's knowledge gaps. LearnSmart then provides an optimal learning path for each student, so that they spend less time in areas they already know and more time in areas they don't. The result is that LearnSmart's adaptive learning path helps students retain more knowledge, learn faster, and study more efficiently.

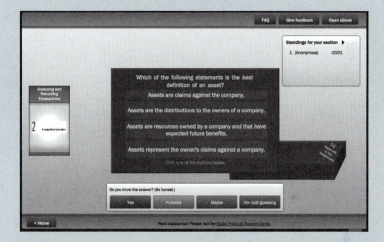

SmartBook

SMARTBOOK. THE FIRST AND ONLY ADAPTIVE READING AND LEARNING EXPERIENCE.

As the first and only adaptive reading experience, SmartBook is changing the way students read and learn. SmartBook creates a personalized reading experience by highlighting the most important concepts a student needs to learn at that moment in time. As a student engages with SmartBook, the reading experience continuously adapts by highlighting content based on what each student knows and doesn't know. This ensures that he or she is focused on the content needed to close specific knowledge gaps, while it simultaneously promotes long-term learning.

The end result? Students are more engaged with course content, can better prioritize their time and come to class ready to participate in thoughtful discourse.

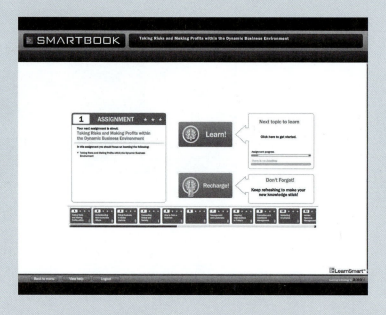

"SmartBook offers interactive learning as opposed to aimlessly reading page after page of a textbook... I am constantly driven to focus on new, important material and then asked questions to gauge my comprehension of it."

—*Annalee Ashley, Georgia Southern University*

"It seems a lot more helpful than a traditional textbook. The majority of the time I don't even read my entire textbook so it would be great to only have to focus on the vital information."

—*Kimberly Milner, University of Miami*

Acknowledgments

Throughout the development of this book, we were privileged to have the candid and valuable advice of our reviewers, survey and focus group participants. These reviewers provided us with priceless suggestions, feedback, and constructive criticism. The depth and sincerity of their reviews indicate that they are a devoted group of teacher-scholars. The content of the book over various versions was greatly enhanced because of their efforts.

T.S. Amer
Northern Arizona University
Janice Benson
University of Wyoming
Jennifer Blaskovich
University of Nebraska, Omaha
A. Faye Borthick
Georgia State University
Linda Bressler
University of Houston
Sandra Cereola
James Madison University
Siew Chan
Nova Southeastern University
Kim Church
Oklahoma State University
Ronald Clark
Auburn University
Curtis Clements
Abilene Christian University
Donna Free
Oakland University
Graham Gal
University of Massachusetts, Amherst
Andy Garcia
Bowling Green State University
David Gelb
Seton Hall University
Jan Gillespie
University of Texas
Terry Glandon
University of Texas, El Paso
Severin Grabski
Michigan State University
Gerry Grant
California State University, Fullerton
William Heninger
Brigham Young University
Kenneth Henry
Florida International University
Rani Hoitash
Bentley University

Diane Janvrin
Iowa State University
Nancy Jones
California State University, Chico
Grover Kearns
University of South Florida, St. Petersburg
Joseph Komar
University of St. Thomas
Don Kovacic
California State University, San Marcos
Brenda Lauer
Davenport University
Maria Leach
Auburn University
Chih-Chen Lee
Northern Illinois University
Picheng Lee
Pace University
Chan Li
University of Pittsburg
Tina Loraas
Auburn University
Lois Mahoney
Eastern Michigan University
James Mensching
California State University, Chico
Mike Metzcar
Indiana Wesleyan University
Bonnie Morris
West Virginia University
Johnna Murray
University of Missouri, St. Louis
Bruce Neumann
University of Colorado, Denver
Oluwakemi Onwuchekwa
University of Central Florida
Debra Petrizzo
Franklin University
Theresa Phinney
Texas A&M University

Ronald Premuroso
University of Montana
Helen Pruitt
University of Maryland
Jeffrey Pullen
University of Maryland
Austin Reitenga
University of Alabama
Paul San Miguel
Western Michigan University
Juan Manuel Sanchez
University of Arkansas
Arline Savage
Cal Poly, San Luis Obispo
George Schmelzle
Missouri State University
Dmitriy Shaltayev
Christopher Newport University
Lewis Shaw
Suffolk University
Robert Slater
University of North Florida
Kathleen Sobieralski
University of Maryland

Eileen Taylor
North Carolina State University
Barbara Uliss
Metropolitan State University of Denver
Linda Wallace
Virginia Tech
Marcia Watson
Mississippi State University
Darryl Woolley
University of Idaho
Al Chen Yuang-Sung
North Carolina State University

Much credit is due to Juan Manuel Sanchez of the University of Arkansas for class testing the book and detailing the student responses to the manuscript.

Vern Richardson

Janie Chang

Rod Smith

Brief Contents

Contents

AIS and the Business

Accounting Information Systems and Firm Value

A look at this chapter

Information plays a crucial role in today's information age. In this chapter, we discuss the importance of accounting information systems and the role accountants play in those systems. Firms invest in accounting information systems to create business value. In this chapter, we also describe investments in information systems to manage internal and external business processes and how they create value for the firm.

A look ahead

Chapter 2 examines the role of accountants as business analysts. The chapter defines business process modeling and describes how it supports the business analyst role of accountants. It explains the potential value of business process modeling and introduces basic modeling tools to guide the accountant's development of modeling skills.

 Walking in to **Starbucks** and ordering a latte, you notice the atmosphere and the quality and variety of its coffees and related offerings. What you may not immediately notice is the accounting information system that supports the recordkeeping, replenishment, financing, etc. To be sure, Starbucks has invested immense resources into planning, designing and developing a number of accounting information systems to track information needed to run an effective business and to report to its shareholders and regulators (e.g., Internal Revenue Service and Securities and Exchange Commission) on its performance. This accounting information system tracks information as diverse as the number of hours worked each day by each of its 142,000 employees throughout the world to the amount of sales taxes to be paid and remitted to tax authorities in each of those localities. This chapter focuses on the principles of information system planning needed for an effective accounting information system at a firm such as Starbucks.

Source: Hoover's Profile, 2010.

Chapter Outline

Introduction

Accountants as Business Analysts

Definition of Accounting
    Information Systems

A Simple Information System

Attributes of Useful Information

Data versus Information

*Discretionary versus Mandatory
    Information*

Role of Accountants in Accounting
    Information Systems

Specific Accounting Roles

*Certifications in Accounting Information
    Systems*

The Value Chain and Accounting
    Information Systems

AIS and Internal Business Processes

AIS and External Business Processes

The Supply Chain

Customer Relationship Management

AIS, Firm Profitability, and Stock
    Prices

AIS and Firm Profitability

AIS and Stock Prices

Learning Objectives

After reading this chapter, you should
be able to:

1-1 Define an accounting information
system, and explain characteristics
of useful information.

1-2 Distinguish among data,
information, and an information
system.

1-3 Distinguish the roles of
accountants in providing
information, and explain
certifications related to accounting
information systems.

1-4 Describe how business processes
affect the firm's value chain.

1-5 Explain how AIS affects firm value.

1-6 Describe how AIS assists the firm's
internal business processes.

1-7 Assess how AIS facilitates the
firm's external business processes.

1-8 Assess the impact of AIS on firm
profitability and stock prices.

INTRODUCTION

Information on business facts, numbers, and other useful indicators for business purposes is all around us. Most firms consider information to be a strategic asset and will use it to develop a competitive advantage to run their business better than their competitors. **Starbucks**, for example, uses information about its customers, suppliers, and competitors to predict how much coffee it will sell and how much coffee it will need to purchase. If the company predicts too many customers, it will have excess coffee and may incur extra carrying cost of inventory. If it predicts too few customers, perhaps the stores will run out of coffee and miss out on important sales. Information is considered a strategic asset if the firms know what information they need, develop systems to collect that information, and use that information to make critical decisions.

LO 1-1

Define an accounting information system, and explain characteristics of useful information.

ACCOUNTANTS AS BUSINESS ANALYSTS

As you've learned in your classes to date, accountants keep financial records, prepare financial reports, and perform audits. Increasingly, the role of an accountant is to help address business opportunities. These opportunities might include a decision whether to outsource a business function, produce one product or another based on which is most profitable, or pursue an attempt to minimize taxes. To address such a business opportunity, accountants need to decide what information is needed, build an information system to gather the necessary information, and then analyze that information to offer helpful advice to management.[1]

DEFINITION OF ACCOUNTING INFORMATION SYSTEMS

Of the many information systems used in a firm, one type of information system is used in almost every firm: an **accounting information system (AIS),** defined as a system that records, processes, and reports on transactions to provide financial and nonfinancial information to make decisions and have appropriate levels of internal controls (security measures to protect sensitive data) for those transactions. This is the focus of this book. Some might call an AIS just a financial reporting system. Others might include in their AIS a much broader set of data that includes nonfinancial information such as marketing activities. Viewed broadly, an AIS collects, processes, and reports information deemed useful in decision making.

The study of accounting information systems (AISs) lies at the nexus of two traditional disciplines: information systems and accounting. In this book, we will highlight knowledge from both of these disciplines to more fully understand AISs. While an AIS could take the form of a paper-and-pencil manual bookkeeping system, we will view AISs in this book as computerized systems.

A Simple Information System

An AIS, just like any system, can be explained using a general systems approach (as in Figure 1.1) with input, storage, processing, and output activities. We cover these activities in subsequent chapters, but the input may come in the form of sales recorded in a **Starbucks** cash register (or point of sale terminal). Processing may take the form of getting the input into storage (such as a database or a table). Processing might also query that database (e.g., using SQL queries) to produce the output in the form of a report for management use. As an example, Starbucks may query its sales database to see how much coffee it sells on Sundays to see if additional sales incentives need to be made to increase

---

[1]F. Borthick, "Helping Accountants Learn to Get the Information Managers Want: The Role of the Accounting Information Systems Course," *Journal of Information Systems* 10, no. 2 (1996), pp. 75–85.

Sunday sales in the future. Whether this report has information that is ultimately useful to management is covered in the next section.

FIGURE 1.1
A Simple Information System

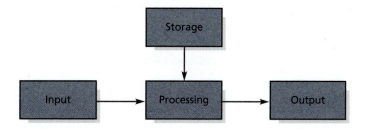

Attributes of Useful Information

To be most useful to decision makers, information from an AIS must be both relevant and reliable and have these attributes:

1. **Relevance**
   a. Predictive value (helps with forecasting the future).
   b. Feedback value (corrects or confirms what had been predicted in the past).
   c. Timeliness (available when needed or in time to have an impact on a decision).
2. **Reliability**
   a. Verifiable (can be confirmed by an independent party).
   b. Representational faithfulness (reports what actually happened).
   c. Neutrality (information is not biased).

Relevance

To be useful, information must be relevant to the decision maker. Information is relevant only if it would affect a business decision. In other words, information is relevant when it helps users predict what will happen in the future (predictive value) or evaluate how past decisions actually worked out (feedback value). It is also relevant if the information is received in time to affect their decisions (timeliness).

Reliability

Information is reliable if users can depend on it to be free from bias and error. Reliable information is verifiable by internal and external parties and faithfully represents the substance of the underlying economic transaction. If **Best Buy** sells a television for $4,000, it should be recorded and subsequently reported in its sales revenue account as $4,000. Reliable accounting information is also neutral, or free from bias. Accounting information should not be designed to lead users to accept or reject any specific decision alternative.

Sometimes there are trade-offs between information that is relevant and information that is reliable. The best information may be information that becomes reliable once an audit is complete. But waiting for an audit to be completed may take so long that it is no longer relevant. The most relevant information may require an estimate of the value of a building, but that estimate might be subject to bias of the appraiser limiting the reliability. Management often must make choices and trade off relevance and reliability.

AISs exist to provide useful information to decision makers. Considering the attributes of useful information helps AIS designers and users construct a system that delivers useful information.

LO 1-2
Distinguish among data, information, and an information system.

Data versus Information

Hal Varian, **Google's** chief economist, explains that while data are widely available, "what is scarce is the ability to extract wisdom from them." In that short statement, we learn that data and the information actually needed to make decisions may well have different definitions. **Data** are simply raw facts that describe the characteristics of an event that, in isolation, have little meaning.

Attributes of a simple sale of a U.S. flag at a **Walmart** store in Tempe, Arizona, may include the time, date, bar code number, price, and quantity purchased. However, to be most useful to Walmart, these data must be processed in a meaningful way to provide information useful to Walmart management. Thus, Walmart management would like the information to address such questions as:

- How many flags does Walmart need on hand to prepare for July 4 holiday each year?
- What is the right price to charge for flags to maximize Walmart's profits?
- Which size of U.S. flag sells the best in Tempe, Arizona, Stamford, Connecticut or Champaign, Illinois?

Information is defined as being data organized in a meaningful way to be useful to the user. Thus, data are often processed (aggregated, sorted, etc.) and then combined with the appropriate context. Decision makers typically require useful information to make decisions. As another example, while the sales prices of a particularly toy might be considered data, subtracting the cost of goods sold from the sales price to compute the net profit would be considered information if the data help a retailer decide whether to carry that particular toy in its inventory. To the extent that computers can process and organize data in a way that is helpful to the decision maker, it is possible that there may be so much information available to actually cause **information overload,** which we define as the difficulty a person faces in understanding a problem and making a decision as a consequence of too much information. Therefore, an AIS must be carefully designed to provide that information that is most useful without overwhelming the user.

The overall transformation from a business need and business event (like each individual sale of a U.S. flag) to the collection of data and information to an ultimate decision is called the **information value chain** and is reflected in Figure 1.2. If Walmart needs to know how many flags it should have at each location (i.e., business need), it will collect the information on flag sales (i.e., business event). Then it can take that data and turn them into useful information that might be used to make decisions on supply levels at each store. Certainly, the transformation from data to information is a key part of that value chain.

Useful Information or Just Data? On September 12, 2001, Walmart sold 88,000 U.S. flags, compared to only 6,400 that same day a year earlier.

Data are considered to be an input, whereas information is considered to be the output.

FIGURE 1.2
Information Value Chain

Source: Statements on Management Accounting, Institute of Management Accountants, 2008.

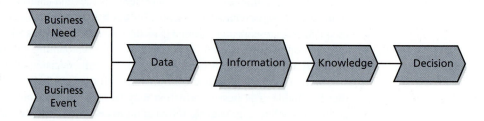

Discretionary versus Mandatory Information

Because you have already taken a few accounting classes, you understand the types of information that are recorded, processed, and subsequently reported for managerial, financial, or tax purposes. Managerial accounting information is generally produced for internal information purposes and would be considered to be **discretionary information** because there is no law requiring that it be provided to management. Management simply decides what information they need to track and build an information system to track it. For example, management may want an activity-based costing (ABC) system to figure out

As early as 1989, **Starbucks installed** a costly computer network and hired a specialist in information technology from **McDonald's** Corporation to design a point-of-sale (cash register) system for store managers to use. Every night, stores passed their sales information to the Seattle headquarters, which allowed managers to highlight regional buying trends almost instantly.

the true cost of making a product (like an **Apple iPad**). The value of information equals the difference between the benefits realized from using that information and the costs of producing it. Because discretionary information is not required, management must determine if the benefits of receiving that information are greater than the costs of producing it.

In contrast, much of the financial and tax accounting information is produced for external information purposes such as for investors, banks, financial ana-

An AIS must support the mandatory information required by tax returns.

lysts, and the Internal Revenue Service (IRS). This financial and tax accounting information would generally be considered to be **mandatory information.** As mentioned earlier, discretionary information should be produced if the value of the information it provides to management is worth more than the cost to produce it. However, mandatory information is usually produced at the lowest possible cost to comply with the laws of the regulators (e.g., Securities and Exchange Commission, IRS, state banking commission, state tax commission, etc.).

Progress *Check*

1. Propose useful information that is relevant to a college football coach. Also propose useful information that is reliable to a college football coach.
2. Give an example of data versus information at a Walmart store.
3. Provide two types of discretionary information and two types of mandatory information that might come from an accounting information system.

LO 1-3

Distinguish the roles of accountants in providing information, and explain certifications related to accounting information systems.

ROLE OF ACCOUNTANTS IN ACCOUNTING INFORMATION SYSTEMS

In today's age, technology is a key tool in creating information systems for today's businesses. As a result, accounting and information technology are now more closely linked than ever. As information technology (IT) has gained operational and strategic importance in the business world, the role of accountants, understandably, must change as well. The International Federation of Accountants (IFAC) notes:

> IT has grown (and will continue to grow) in importance at such a rapid pace and with such far reaching effects that it can no longer be considered a discipline peripheral to accounting. Rather, professional accounting has merged and developed with IT to such an extent that one can hardly conceive of accounting independent from IT.[2]

Indeed, accountants have a role as business analysts; that is, they gather information to solve business problems or address business opportunities. They determine what information is relevant in solving business problems, create or extract that information, and then analyze the information to solve the problem. An AIS provides a systematic means for

[2]"Information Technology Competencies in the Accounting Profession: AICPA Implementation Strategies for IFAC International Education Guideline No. 11," American Institute of Certified Public Accountants, 1996.

accountants to get needed information and solve a problem. Another illustration of the role of accountants in AIS comes from the Institute of Management Accounting. In this definition, note the role of devising planning and performance information systems:

> Management accounting is a profession that involves partnering in management decision making, devising planning and performance management systems, and providing expertise in financial reporting and control to assist management in the formulation and implementation of a firm's strategy.[3]

Specific Accounting Roles

Understanding the design, use, and management of information technology is of vital importance to not only management accountants, but to all of those within the accounting profession. To recognize the needed competencies for accountants with respect to information technology, it is important to recognize the potential role of accountants in accounting information systems, including the following:

1. The accountant as *user* of accounting information systems—whether it be inputting journal entries into an accounting system, using a financial spreadsheet to calculate the cost of a product, or using anti-virus software to protect the system, accountants use AISs.
   - As an example, accountants serving in an audit role should be able to understand how to access their client's AIS and how to use at least one major computer-assisted auditing package (such as ACL), an online or local database system, or a professional research tool.

2. The accountant as *manager* of accounting information systems (e.g., financial manager, controller, CFO).
   - Accountants serving as managers of AISs must be able to plan and coordinate accounting information systems and be able to organize and staff, direct and lead, and monitor and control those systems.

3. The accountant as the *designer* of accounting information systems (e.g., business system design team, producer of financial information, **systems analyst**).
   - Accountants serving in a design capacity must have significant practical exposure to some of the important techniques that are used in key phases of system analysis and design, such as the preparation of a feasibility analysis; information requirements elicitation and documentation techniques; data file design and documentation techniques; and document, screen, and report design techniques. In particular, accountants must understand business processes and the information requirements of other systems.

4. The accountant as *evaluator* of accounting information systems (e.g., IT auditor, assessor of internal controls, tax advisor, general auditor, consultant)
   - As will be discussed in Chapter 10, the **Sarbanes-Oxley Act of 2002 (SOX)** requires an evaluation of the internal controls in an AIS. As part of that act, and as part of a standard audit, accountants must be able to tailor standard evaluation approaches to an AIS and offer practical recommendations for improvement where appropriate. In addition, the accountant must be able to apply relevant IT tools and techniques to effectively evaluate the system.

In considering the information technology competencies in the accounting profession, the American Institute of Certified Public Accountants (AICPA) and International Federation of Accountants (IFAC) assumes that, at a minimum, all accountants will be proficient in

---

[3]Institute of Management Accountants, *Statements on Management Accounting,* 2008.

the AIS user role and at least one other of the listed roles (manager, designer, or evaluator). Accountants will be better users, managers, and evaluators of AIS if they understand the design of the system. Thus, throughout the text we touch on all of the roles that accountants have in the firms, but we particularly emphasize skills relevant to the designer role.

Certifications in Accounting Information Systems

In addition to the various roles that accountants play, accountants and related professionals may also seek various certifications to show they are proficient in specific areas of AISs. This will show their competence to specific employers or clients that need some specific services. There are three primary certifications that most directly apply to accounting and information systems (see Figure 1.3).

FIGURE 1.3
Certifications in Accounting Information Systems

Name	Certifying Body	Who They Are and What They Do	How to Qualify
Certified Information Systems Auditor (CISA)	Information Systems Audit and Control Association (ISACA) www.isaca.org	The CISA designation identifies those professionals possessing IT audit, control, and security skills. Generally, CISAs will perform IT audits to evaluate the accounting information system's internal control design and effectiveness.	To qualify as a CISA, a candidate must take an examination and obtain specialized work experience.
Certified Information Technology Professional (CITP)	American Institute of Certified Public Accountants (AICPA) www.aicpa.org	The CITP designation identifies accountants (CPAs) with a broad range of technology knowledge and experience. The CITP designation demonstrates the accountant's ability to leverage technology to effectively and efficiently manage information while ensuring the data's reliability, security, accessibility, and relevance. CITPs may help devise a more efficient financial reporting system, help the accounting function go paperless, or consult on how an IT function may transform the business.	A CPA can earn a CITP designation with a combination of business experience, lifelong learning, and an optional exam.
Certified Internal Auditor (CIA)	Institute of Internal Auditors (IIA) http://www.theiia.org/	The CIA designation is the only globally accepted certification for internal auditors and is the standard to demonstrate their competency and professionalism in the internal auditing field.	An individual can earn a CIA designation by having the required education, professional experience, and character references; the individual must also pass the CIA examination.

Progress *Check*

4. Would an IT auditor be considered to be a user, manager, evaluator, or designer of a client firm's accounting information system?
5. What would be the appropriate designation for someone who wants to be an IT auditor?
6. Let's suppose that **ConocoPhillips** is hiring accountants for an entry-level financial accounting position. Is it reasonable to expect accountants to be proficient in information technology?

LO 1-4
Describe how business
processes affect the
firm's value chain.

THE VALUE CHAIN AND ACCOUNTING INFORMATION SYSTEMS

Information technology (IT) is increasingly omnipresent! Worldwide spending on IT exceeded $1.4 trillion in 2010. IT capital spending has increased from 20 percent of corporate capital spending in 1995 to 50 percent of corporate capital spending in 2010.[4] Clearly, information technology is a huge investment that firms make, and they expect to create value through its use. How IT assists firms to carry out their internal and external business processes and, in turn, creates value is an important topic of this chapter.

A firm makes money by taking the inputs (e.g., raw materials, talented workers, buildings, equipment, etc.) and producing a more valuable output (e.g., iPhones available for sale, completed audit report, etc.). Take a university as an example. Universities admit students to the university (as inputs) and use their resources (curriculum, faculty, buildings, computers, etc.) to create a job-ready, educated graduate (the output). Arguably, the university creates value. If it is not creating value in one form or the other, it probably will not continue to survive.

Let's continue the discussion by defining **business value** as all those items, events, and interactions that determine the financial health and/or well-being of the firm. This value may come from suppliers, customers, or employees or even from information systems. Business value does not necessarily need to be determined by stock price or net income. A not-for-profit group like the **International Red Cross** may define business value as how many lives are saved or the number of children that are immunized.

To consider how value is created, we begin by looking at the business processes. A business process is a coordinated, standardized set of activities conducted by both people and equipment to accomplish a specific task, such as invoicing a customer. To evaluate the effectiveness of each of its business processes, a firm can use Michael Porter's value chain analysis. A **value chain** is a chain of business processes for a firm. Products pass through all activities of the chain in order; at each activity, the product is expected to gain some value. It is important not to confuse the concept of the value chain with the actual cost of performing those activities. One way of looking at this is by considering a rough diamond. Although the cutting activity of a diamond may have a very low cost, this cutting activity adds much of the value to the end product because a cut diamond is much more valuable than a rough diamond. And a diamond cut well adds more value than a diamond cut poorly.

The value chain illustrated in Figure 1.4 shows both primary activities and support activities. Primary activities directly provide value to the customer and include the following five activities:

1. **Inbound logistics** are the activities associated with receiving and storing raw materials and other partially completed materials and distributing those materials to manufacturing when and where they are needed.
2. **Operations** are the activities that transform inputs into finished goods and services (e.g., turning wood into furniture for a furniture manufacturer; building a house for a home builder).
3. **Outbound logistics** are the activities that warehouse and distribute the finished goods to the customers.
4. **Marketing and sales activities** identify the needs and wants of customers to help attract them to the firm's products and, thus, buy them.
5. **Service activities** provide the support of customers after the products and services are sold to them (e.g., warranty repairs, parts, instruction manuals, etc.).

---

[4]According to Gartner Inc. (2010), worldwide IT spending for 2010, not including telecommunications spending, is projected at $353 billion for computer hardware, $232 billion for software, and $821 billion for IT services, up more than 5 percent from 2009.

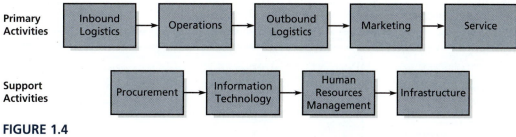

FIGURE 1.4
The Value Chain

These five primary activities are sustained by the following support activities:

1. **Firm infrastructure** activities are all of the activities needed to support the firm, including the CEO and the finance, accounting, and legal departments.
2. **Human resource management** activities include recruiting, hiring, training, and compensating employees.
3. **Technology** activities include all of the technologies necessary to support value-creating activities. These technologies also include research and development to develop new products or determine ways to produce products at a cheaper price.
4. **Procurement** activities involve purchasing inputs such as raw materials, supplies, and equipment.

LO 1-5

Explain how AIS affects firm value.

An AIS can add value to the firm by making each primary activity more effective and efficient. For example, AIS systems can assist with inbound and outbound logistics. Some of the greatest gains in efficiencies and cost savings in logistics (transportation and warehousing costs, etc.) are due to the use of AIS and geographic information systems to help identify the lowest cost of getting items from one location to another. AIS systems can make marketing, sales, and service activities more valuable by summarizing data about key customers to help manage and nurture a firm's interactions with its clients.

As an example, **Amazon.com** is one of the best at fostering its interaction with its customers by keeping a record of their past purchases and product searches and using that information to recommend other similar products for the customer to consider. As another example, as the loan officers at a bank learn more about the financial products currently being used by its bank's customers through its AIS, they will be able to help identify additional bank products (e.g., insurance, CDs, mutual funds, etc.) to sell to their clients.

As detailed here, AIS can add value to the firm by making each support activity more effective and efficient. An AIS:

- helps with the firm infrastructure by giving management information relevant to the decision makers.
- may also help provide the internal control structure needed to make sure the information is secure, reliable, and free from error (as discussed in Chapter 10).
- helps produce external and internal financial reports efficiently and helps decision makers get timely access to the processed information. This may give the information to the decision maker in time to influence the decision.
- supports the human resources function by assisting employees, who are arguably the most valuable asset of the firm. This assistance includes easy access to payroll information, compensation policies, benefits, tax benefits, and so on.
- assists procurement by improving the effectiveness and efficiency of the supply chain. This helps ensure that right product is at the right location at the right time, including receipts of raw material from suppliers to delivery of finished goods to the customers.

FIGURE 1.5
Amazon.com: "Recommendations, New for You and Customers with Similar Searches Purchased"

Progress *Check*

7. Consider the value chain for **Ford**. In your opinion, which primary activity is the most critical to creating value for the firm?
8. How does an AIS help **eBay** find the right marketing strategy?
9. An AIS adds value to the supporting activities by making access to financial results available on a more timely basis. Why does this matter?

LO 1-6
Describe how AIS assists the firm's internal business processes.

AIS AND INTERNAL BUSINESS PROCESSES

Our discussion now turns to how an AIS can assist the firm with its internal business processes. An AIS within a firm is usually the foundation for an **enterprise system (ES)**—also called an enterprise resource planning (ERP) system. An enterprise system is a centralized database that collects data from throughout the firm. This includes data from orders, customers, sales, inventory, and employees. These data are then accumulated in the centralized database and made available to all enterprise system users, including accounting, manufacturing (or operations), marketing, and human resources. As the data are integrated into one single, centralized database to become useful information, authorized employees throughout the firm (from the CEO all the way to the lowest-paid line worker) have access to the information they need to make a decision. For most firms, the informational benefits of these integrated data include enhanced completeness, transparency, and timeliness of information needed to effectively manage a firm's business activities.

As an example, an enterprise system can automate a business process such as order fulfillment. The enterprise system can take an order from a customer, fill that order, ship it, and then create an invoice to bill the customer. As an example, when a customer service representative receives a customer order into an enterprise system, she has all the information needed to approve and complete the order (e.g., the customer's credit rating and order history from the finance module of the centralized database, the firm's inventory levels to see if the product is available from the warehouse module of the centralized database, and the shipping dock's trucking schedule from the logistics module of the centralized database). Once the order is complete, the enterprise system routes the order to the warehouse and shipping department for order fulfillment and shipping and then to the finance department to make sure the customer is invoiced. During the process, all workers in the various departments can see the same information and update it as needed. As problems arise (e.g., backordered products, returned products, trucker strike, etc.), the enterprise system gives all within the firm the most current information to address these issues.

The enterprise system serves as the backbone of the firm's internal business processes and serves as a connection with the external business processes with external partners as discussed in the next section.

LO 1-7

Assess how AIS facilitates the firm's external business processes.

AIS AND EXTERNAL BUSINESS PROCESSES

Firms do not work in isolation. They are always connected to both their suppliers and customers and their wants and needs. As shown in Figure 1.6, the AIS assists in business integration with external parties such as suppliers and customers. The firm's interaction with the suppliers is generally called *supply chain management,* and the interaction with its customers is generally called *customer relationship management.*

FIGURE 1.6
AIS and External Business Processes

The Supply Chain

Supply chain refers to the flow of materials, information, payments, and services from raw materials suppliers, through factories and warehouses, all the way to the final customers of the firm's products. A supply chain also includes the firms and processes that create and deliver products, information, and services to the final customers. The supply chain refers to a network of processes that delivers a finished good or service to the final customer. Figure 1.7 reflects the sourcing, manufacturing (making), and delivering to the customer for each member of the supply chain (assuming the Procter and Gamble product is made in China, sold in Sam's Club and convenience stores and ultimately sold to an end customer). Handling the returns from the firm's customers and to the firm's suppliers also represent a significant process that requires substantial planning.

To make the supply chain function efficiently, supply chain tasks include processes such as purchasing, payment flow, materials handling, production planning and control, logistics and warehousing, inventory control, returns, and distribution and delivery.

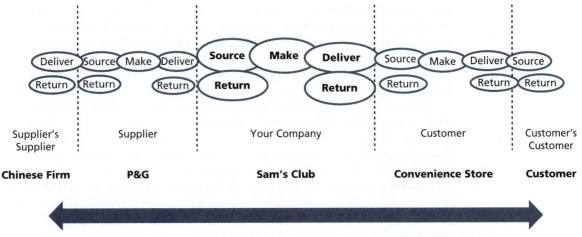

Supply Chain between Partners—Flow of Materials, Information, Payments, and Services

FIGURE 1.7
The Supply Chain

As an illustration, Michael Dell of **Dell Computer** explained one aspect of its use of supply chain management software with suppliers as follows:

> We tell our suppliers exactly what our daily production requirements are so it is not, "Well, every two weeks deliver 5,000 to this warehouse, and we'll put them on the shelf, and then we'll take them off the shelf." It is, "Tomorrow morning we need 8,562, and deliver them to door number seven by 7 am."[5]

The software used to connect the focal firm with its suppliers is generally referred to as **supply chain management (SCM) software.** This software addresses specific segments of the supply chain, especially in manufacturing scheduling, inventory control, and transportation. This SCM software is designed to facilitate decision making and optimize the required levels of inventory to be ordered and held in stock. It is expected that this inventory optimization will lower the required amount of raw materials and finished goods inventory the firm will have to hold and thus lower product costs.

A recent study[6] found that firms implementing SCM software are able to reduce the amount of raw materials inventory on hand and reduce selling, general, and administrative expenses. They are also able to increase their gross margins and overall inventory turnover. This suggests that supply chain management systems allow inventory to be optimized to lower inventory while not decreasing sales.

Walmart has long been regarded as having one of the best supply chain systems. One aspect of Walmart's supply chain management software is simply communicating the results of its retail sales to its top suppliers. Walmart's Retail Link database is one of the world's largest databases and allows many of its suppliers to view real-time sales data of its products for each store. This allows suppliers to assess the demand for their products and to optimize their own level of inventory and related logistics costs. In turn, the cost savings generated from this process is passed on to Walmart itself and its customers.

---

[5]A.A. Thompson, A.J. Strickland and J. Thompson, *Strategic Management: Concepts and Cases,* 11th ed. (New York: McGraw-Hill, 2006).

[6]B. Dehning, V.J. Richardson, and R.W. Zmud, "The Financial Performance Effects of IT-Based Supply Chain Management Systems in Manufacturing Firms," *Journal of Operations Management* 25 (June 2007), pp. 806–24.

Walmart uses its supply chain expertise to lower prices and fulfill its motto to "Save Money, Live Better."

Connection with Practice

One way of measuring the effectiveness of a supply chain is to calculate the fill rate. The fill rate is a calculation of the service level between two parties, generally a supplier and a customer. The fill rate is a measure of shipping performance usually expressed as a percentage of the total order. The fill rate is often calculated as the value of order lines shipped on the initial order divided by the total value of the order. If the fill rate increases over time, this means the overall service level is improving. Supply chain management software would be expected to improve the fill rate and, in turn, the overall service levels.

Customer Relationship Management

The more a company can learn about its customers, the more likely they will be able to satisfy their needs. **Customer relationship management (CRM)** is a term that describes the software used to manage and nurture a firm's interactions with its current and potential clients. CRM software often includes the use of database marketing tools to learn more about customers and to develop strong firm-to-customer relationships. CRM software also includes using IT to manage sales and marketing for current sales and customer service and technical support after the sale is done.

As mentioned in the opening vignette of this chapter, a good example of the need for CRM is **Starbucks**. After its quick expansion in the early 2000s, Starbucks felt like it had lost some of the original Starbuck's customer coffeehouse experience. This caused a desire within Starbucks to make sure it understood its customer and their coffeehouse needs. Therefore, a recent initiative at Starbucks was implemented to learn more about its customers. The new chief information officer, Stephen Gillett, argues that his most crucial duty is to enhance Starbucks' ability to mine its customer data to help "reignite our passion with our customers." Starbucks uses loyalty cards (Starbucks' Reward cards) and surveys to track its customers' purchases and build profiles of their customers.[7]

[7]T. Wallgum, "Starbuck's Next-Generation CIO: Young, Fast and In Control," *CIO Magazine*, January 2009, www.cio.com/article/474127/Starbucks_Next_Generation_CIO_Young_Fast_and_In_Control?page=3&taxonomyId=3123.

As another example, **Royal Bank** (formerly Royal Bank of Canada) considers CRM to be such an important part of its strategy that the stated objective of the bank is "to capture the full potential of our customer base through the use of customer information to deliver the right solutions in a consistent, professional manner at every point of contact".[8]

Connection with Practice

Salesforce.com is a popular vendor of CRM software. Note the explanation of CRM on the home page of their website:

> Customer relationship management (CRM) is all about managing the relationships you have with your customers—including potential customers. CRM combines business processes, people, and technology to achieve this single goal: Getting and keeping satisfied customers. It's an overall strategy to help you learn more about your customers and their behavior so you can develop stronger, lasting relationships that will benefit both you and your customers. It's very hard to run a successful business without a strong focus on CRM. After all, it's all about the customer.

Source: Accessed January 30, 2013, http://www.salesforce.com/assets/swf/youtube_players/crm-sales.jsp

Progress *Check*

10. Give an example of how supply chain management software might work for **General Motors**. What type of information does General Motors need to share with its suppliers?
11. Using CRM techniques, what information could universities gather about their current and prospective customers, the students? What information might be most useful to them in recruiting future students?

LO 1-8
Assess the impact of AIS on firm profitability and stock prices.

AIS, FIRM PROFITABILITY, AND STOCK PRICES

Throughout this chapter, we have tried to make the case that AIS facilitates value-creating activities. This section presents a direct test of whether an investment in AIS, in fact, creates value by considering whether an AIS investment led to more profits or higher market value.

AIS and Firm Profitability

One way to consider how AIS creates value is to look at an income statement. Accountants understand that to make more profits, a firm either needs to increase revenues or decrease expenses (or both!). Figure 1.8 illustrates how AIS affects the income statement, making the case for how an AIS may increase profitability.

In a recent study,[9] a positive association was found between the level of the firm's annual IT investment and its subsequent accounting earnings (as measured by return on assets and return on sales), suggesting that IT investment does create value. In a completely different study,[10] researchers found both an improvement in profitability as well as stock returns around the implementation of supply chain information systems.

---

[8]"CRM Case Study: The Analytics that Power CRM at Royal Bank (of Canada)," www.mindbranch.com.
[9]K. Kobelsky, V.J. Richardson, R. Smith, and R.W. Zmud, "Determinants and Consequences of Firm Information Technology Budgets," *The Accounting Review* 83 (July 2008), pp. 957–96.
[10]K.B. Hendricks, V.R. Singhal, and J.K. Stratman, "The Impact of Enterprise Systems on Corporate Performance: A Study of ERP, SCM and CRM System Implementations," *Journal of Operations Management* 25, no. 1 (January 2007), pp. 65–82.

FIGURE 1.8
The Potential Effect of AIS on an Income Statement

Income Statement	Effect of AIS on Income Statement
Revenues	Customer relationship management (CRM) techniques could attract new customers, generating additional sales revenue.
Less: Cost of Goods Sold	Supply chain management (SCM) software allows firms to carry the right inventory and have it in the right place at the right time. This, in turn, will lower obsolescence as well as logistics and procurement costs.
Gross Margin	
Less: Selling, General, and Administrative Expenses (SG&A)	An efficient enterprise system can significantly lower the cost of support processes included in sales, general, and administrative expenses.
Less: Interest Expense	SCM software allows the firm to carry less inventory. Less inventory leaves less assets to finance and may possibly reduce debt and its related interest.
Net Income	All combined, a well-designed and well-functioning AIS with investments in enterprise systems, SCM and/or CRM may be expected to improve net income.

AIS and Stock Prices

Every time a firm makes an investment, it expects a return of its original investment as well as a return on that investment. This is the case for AIS investments as well. When an investment is announced by a public firm, stock market participants assess whether the investment will pay off or not, either by enhancing revenues or reducing expenses or some combination of both. If the stock market participants believe the future cash flows from the investment will increase for the firm, the stock price of that firm is expected to increase. If the stock market participants believe the future cash flows from the investment will decrease for that firm, the stock price is expected to fall.

A recent study[11] divided up announcements of 315 firms making new AIS investments. The study broke these announcements into three groups, depending on what strategic role the technology was expected to fill within the firm. If AIS investments simply replace human labor to automate business processes, they are defined as automate AIS investments. The automate process will typically digitize (i.e., put in a digital form) the business processes. Once digitized, this information can be automatically and easily summarized in a usable form (i.e., reports, etc.) for management use (defined as the IT strategic role of informate-up) or in a usable form to employees across the firm (defined as IT strategic role of informate-down). IT can also change the basis of competition and redefine business and industry processes (defined as the IT strategic role of transform). As an example, **Fedex**, which allows its customers to track their own packages on the web, changed the basis of competition for the express transportation industry by fundamentally redefining business processes and relationships.

Using strategic role as a way to group the IT investments, the lowest strategic role for technology is to automate manual processes. The highest strategic role for technology is transform, with informate-up and informate-down having a medium strategic role. Here is a summary of these strategic roles:

- **Automate**—replace human labor in automating business processes.
- **Informate-up**—provide information about business activities to senior management.
- **Informate-down**—provide information about business activities to employees across the firm.
- **Transform**—fundamentally redefine business processes and relationships.

[11]B. Dehning, V.J. Richardson, and R.W. Zmud, "The Value Relevance of Announcements of Transformational Information Technology Investments," *MIS Quarterly* 27, no. 4 (2003), pp. 637–56.

Figure 1.9 shows how the stock market responded (adjusted for level of risk and overall market returns) on the day the AIS investment was announced. This analysis assumes there were no other significant news events at the firm on the same day of the AIS investment announcement. On average, the 172 "automate" AIS investments increased firm market value by 0.05 percent, and the 95 "informate" AIS investments increased firm market value by 0.40 percent. On average, the "transform" AIS investments increased firm market value by 1.51 percent. The authors found that those 48 AIS investments that transformed the business processes and changed the way business is done had the greatest impact on firm value. Automate and informate investments do have an impact, but they are substantially smaller than the value-enhancing impact of transform investments.

FIGURE 1.9
Stock Market Reaction to AIS Investments

Stock Market Increase around AIS Investment Announcements

AIS Investment Strategic Role

Automate	Informate*	Transform
0.05%	0.40%	1.51%

*Informate-up and Informate-down are consolidated in a single strategic role: Informate.

Progress *Check*

12. How does the use of supply chain management software reduce the cost of goods sold for a retailer like **Target**?
13. Many hospitals and doctor's offices are beginning to digitize the medical records of their patients. Would this be an example of an automate, informate, or transform IT strategic role?

Summary

Information plays a crucial role in the information age.

- Accountants play a critical role in recording, processing, and reporting financial information for decision making and control. An accounting information system (AIS) is defined as an information system that records, processes, and reports on transactions to provide financial information for decision making and control.
- The accounting profession (including the IFAC and the AICPA) recommends that accountants develop proficiency in at least two areas of information systems: as a user and as a manager, designer, or evaluator of information systems. Accountants often seek certification in information systems to show their level of proficiency to both prospective employers and clients.
- Firms invest in accounting information systems to create value. The value chain illustrates how, during each primary activity, the product should gain some value. An AIS serves an important role in providing value in each primary and supporting activity.
- An AIS creates value by managing internal and external business processes. Enterprise systems, sometimes called ERP or back-office systems, generally manage transactions within the firm. Supply chain management software is used to manage transactions with suppliers. Customer relationship management software is used to manage and nurture the relationship with current and potential customers.
- An AIS generally helps make business processes more efficient and effective. A well-designed and well-functioning AIS can be expected to create value by increasing revenues and reducing expenses.

Key Words

accounting information system (AIS) (4)   A system that records, processes, and reports on transactions to provide financial and nonfinancial information to make decisions and have appropriate levels of internal controls for those transactions.

automate (17)   The use of technology to replace human labor in automating business processes.

business value (10)   Items, events, and interactions that determine the financial health and well-being of the firm.

Certified Information Technology Professional (CITP) (9)   The CITP designation identifies accountants (CPAs) with a broad range of technology knowledge and experience.

Certified Information Systems Auditor (CISA) (9)   The CISA designation identifies those professionals possessing IT audit, control, and security skills. Generally, CISAs will perform IT audits to evaluate the accounting information system's internal control design and effectiveness.

Certified Internal Auditor (CIA) (9)   The CIA designation is the certification for internal auditors and is the standard to demonstrate competency and professionalism in the internal auditing field.

customer relationship management (CRM) (15)   Software used to manage and nurture a firm's interactions with its current and potential clients. CRM software often includes the use of database marketing tools to learn more about the customers and to develop strong firm-to-customer relationships.

data (6)   Raw facts or statistics that, absent a context, may have little meaning.

discretionary information (6)   Information that is generated according to one's own judgment.

enterprise system (ES) (12)   A centralized database that collects data from throughout the firm.

firm infrastructure (11)   Activities needed to support the firm, including the CEO and the finance, accounting, and legal departments.

human resource management (11)   Activities include recruiting, hiring, training, and compensating employees.

inbound logistics (10)   Activities associated with receiving and storing raw materials and other partially completed materials and distributing those materials to manufacturing when and where they are needed.

informate-down (17)   The use of computer technology to provide information about business activities to employees across the firm.

informate-up (17)   The use of computer technology to provide information about business activities to senior management.

information (6)   Data organized in a meaningful way to the user.

information overload (6)   The difficulty a person faces in understanding a problem and making a decision as a consequence of too much information.

information value chain (6)   The overall transformation from a business need and business event to the collection of data and information to an ultimate decision.

mandatory information (7)   Information that is required to be generated or provided by law or regulation.

marketing and sales activities (10)   Activities that identify the needs and wants of their customers to help attract them to the firm's products and buy them.

operations (10)   Activities that transform inputs into finished goods and services.

outbound logistics (10)   Activities that warehouse and distribute the finished goods to the customers.

procurement (11)   Activities involve purchasing inputs such as raw materials, supplies, and equipment.

relevance (5)   Information that is capable of making a difference in a decision.

reliability (5)   Information that is free from bias and error.

Sarbanes-Oxley Act of 2002 (SOX) (8)   A federal law in the United States that set new and enhanced standards for all U.S. public companies, management, and public accounting firms.

service activities (10)   Activities that provide the support of customers after the products and services are sold to them (e.g., warranty repairs, parts, instruction manuals, etc.).

supply chain (13)   The flow of materials, information, payments, and services from raw materials suppliers, through factories and warehouses, all the way to the final customers of the firm's products.

supply chain management (SCM) software (14)   Software that connects the focal firms with its suppliers. It generally addresses segments of the supply chain, including manufacturing, inventory control, and transportation.

systems analyst (8)   Person responsible for both determining the information needs of the business and designing a system to meet those needs.

technology (11)   Supports value-creating activities in the value change. These technologies also include research and development to develop new products or determine ways to produce products at a cheaper price.

transform (17)   The use of computer technology to fundamentally redefine business processes and relationships.

value chain (10)   A chain of critical business processes at a company that creates value.

Answers to
Progress *Checks*

1. Useful relevant information may include the number of sacks recorded or yards allowed by the upcoming opponent. Receiving this relevant information in a timely manner may help the team prepare for its upcoming football games. An example of useful reliable information might include the information collected and verified by an independent official keeping the score and statistics of a football game. This information might include the score of the game, the number of yards gained, and the number of fumbles lost. Having an unbiased source of information allows the coach to use the information received without having to worry about whether the information is biased.

2. Data at **Walmart** might be any random factoid without context. An example might be that one store in the United States had sales of $1.2 million yesterday. It is only when put in context that the data become useful. If we know that the store is in Lawrence, Kansas, and that on the same date a year earlier the store had sales of $0.8 million, the data become information.

3. Two types of discretionary information include the cost of manufacturing each **Apple iPad** or the type of pastry that sells best with hot chocolate at **Starbucks.** Two types of mandatory information might be the amount of sales taxes collected and remitted to the state tax collector or the number of common shares of stock outstanding reported to the Securities and Exchange Commission.

4. Generally, an IT auditor would be considered to be an evaluator of a client firm's accounting information system. In general, an IT auditor will assess the accounting information system to ensure the audit risk (the risk of reaching an incorrect conclusion based on the audit findings) will be limited to an acceptable level.

5. The Certified Information Systems Auditor (CISA) designation would be the most appropriate credential for an IT auditor. In some cases, the Certified Information Technology Professional (CITP) designation would also be an appropriate credential.

6. Most, if not all, entry-level financial accounting positions would expect some reasonable level of proficiency as a user of accounting information systems such as the ability to use a basic accounting/bookkeeping package (e.g., QuickBooks, Peachtree), **Microsoft Excel**, Microsoft Windows, etc. However, the International Federation of Accountants suggests accountants not only have proficiency as a user but also as an evaluator, manager, or designer of an accounting information system. Some of that proficiency will be gained in this textbook, so read carefully!

7. Clearly, all portions of the value chain have to be working well for **Ford** to be successful and create value for the firm and its shareholders. A case could be made for any and all of the primary activities. I will argue that marketing and sales are the most important because, to be successful, companies need to completely understand and then meet their customers' needs.

8. An AIS may help **eBay** find the right marketing strategy by figuring out where to advertise eBay's product offerings (e.g., banner ads, referral pages, etc.). AIS may also help eBay figure out which products sell best and which products have the biggest profit margins.

9. An AIS can add value to the firm by providing financial results in time to make a difference to the decision maker. As an example, if the firm finds out quickly that one of its products is too expensive to manufacture, the firm may choose to discontinue the product or choose a cheaper way to manufacture it. If that financial information is not received until weeks or months later, then the firm will have lost profits.

10. Let's suppose that **General Motors** will decide how many Chevrolet Malibus to produce at each plant. Once General Motors knows how many it will likely produce, the supply chain management software can immediately compute the specific parts needed and share this information with its suppliers. The suppliers can then plan and begin production of the parts they provide. For example, if General Motors plans to produce 100,000 Malibus at its Kansas City assembly plant, the tire suppliers can plan on producing and delivering 400,000 tires to meet those needs.

11. Universities are increasingly using CRM techniques to catalog information about their students from overall trends about the new millennials (who prefer more choices, experiential learning, flexibility, etc.) to archiving individual inquiries (i.e., e-mail, Facebook, Twitter, etc.) by each prospective student. Students generally don't like to be treated as one among the masses, so any information that might target a specific student need or interest would be particularly useful to recruiters.

12. Supply chain software can help reduce procurement, logistics, and inventory carrying costs. If the whole supply chain has a better idea of the final customer's demand of the product, it will reduce the need to order more inventory than is needed or to miss customer sales by not having enough products. This, in turn, will reduce procurement, logistics, and inventory carrying costs.

13. Digitizing medical records is an example of the automate IT strategic role.

Multiple Choice Questions

1. Accounting information systems are
   a. Always computerized
   b. Report only financial information
   c. An information system that records, processes, and reports on transactions to provide financial and nonfinancial information for decision making and control
   d. Require a CITP designation to understand

2. Which of the following is *not* a characteristic of useful information?
   a. Predictive value
   b. Timeliness
   c. Verifiable
   d. Expensive to generate

3. Which of the following is considered to be mandatory information required by a regulatory body?
    a. U.S. Tax Return
    b. The cost to produce a textbook
    c. The number of U.S. flags that are sold on July 4
    d. The cost to build an all-new Starbucks restaurant in Shanghai, China

4. The correct order of effects in the value chain is
    a. Inbound logistics → Operations → Service
    b. Inbound logistics → Outbound logistics → Marketing and Sales
    c. Inbound logistics → Operations → Outbound logistics
    d. Inbound logistics → Operations → Service

5. What designation would be most appropriate for those professionals possessing IT audit, control, and security skills?
    a. Certified Internal Auditor (CIA)
    b. Certified Public Accountant (CPA)
    c. Certified Information Technology Professional (CITP)
    d. Certified Information Systems Auditor (CISA)

6. A supply chain
    a. Supplies bicycle chains
    b. Refers to the flow of materials, information, payments, and services
    c. Is similar in function and purpose to the value chain
    d. Does not apply to a service firm like an accounting firm

7. Customer relationship management software does *not* include information about
    a. Current customers
    b. Prospective customers
    c. Former customers
    d. Current suppliers

8. IT strategic roles of AIS investments are classified as
    a. Automate, informate, transform
    b. Value creation, value destruction, value neutral
    c. Digitize, report, transform
    d. Automate, digitize, transportation

9. According to a recent study, the IT strategic role that has the greatest impact on shareholder value is
    a. Informate
    b. Digitize
    c. Automate
    d. Transform

10. The income statement account most likely affected by an AIS investment in supply chain management would be
    a. Revenues
    b. Cost of goods sold
    c. Selling, general, and administrative expenses
    d. Unearned revenue

Discussion Questions

1. Brainstorm a list of discretionary information that might be an output of an accounting information system and be needed by **Starbucks**. Prioritize which items might be most important, and provide support.

2. Explain the information value chain. How do business events turn into data, then into information, and then into knowledge? Give an example starting with the business event of the purchase of a CD at **Best Buy** all the way to useful information for the CEO and other decision makers.

3. Give three examples of types of discretionary information at your college or university, and explain how the benefits of receiving that information outweigh the costs.

4. After an NBA basketball game, a box score is produced detailing the number of points scored, assists made, and rebounds retrieved (among other statistics). Using the characteristics of useful information discussed at the beginning of the chapter, please explain how this box score meets (or does not meet) the characteristics of useful information.

5. Some would argue that the role of accounting is simply as an information provider. Will a computer ultimately completely take over the job of the accountant? As part of your explanation, explain how the role of accountants in information systems continues to evolve.

6. How do you become a Certified Information Technology Professional (CITP)? What do they do on a daily basis?

7. Explain the value chain for an appliance manufacturer, particularly the primary activities. Which activities are most crucial for value creation (in other words, which activities would you want to make sure are the most effective)? Rank the five value chain enhancing activities in importance for an appliance manufacturer.

8. Which value chain supporting activities would be most important to support a health insurance provider's primary activities? How about the most important primary activities for a university?

9. List and explain three ways that an AIS can add value to the firm.

10. Where does new-product development fit in the value chain for a pharmaceutical company? Where does new-product development for a car manufacturer fit in the value chain?

11. Customer relationship management software is used to manage and nurture a firm's interactions with its current and potential clients. What information would **Boeing** want about its current and potential airplane customers? Why is this so critical?

12. An enterprise system is a centralized database that collects and distributes information throughout the firm. What type of financial information would be useful for both the marketing and manufacturing operations?

Problems

1. A recent article suggests:

   > A monumental change is emerging in accounting: the movement away from the decades-old method of periodic financial statement reporting and its lengthy closing process, and toward issuing financial statements on a real-time, updated basis . . . real-time financial reporting provides financial information on a daily basis. Current technology allows for financial events to be identified, measured, recorded, and reported electronically, with no paper documentation. (Source: "Real-Time Accounting," *The CPA Journal,* April 2005).

   Would a shift toward real-time financial statements make the financial information more useful or less useful? More or less relevant? More or less reliable?

2. Consider the following bar chart of how accounting professionals' activities have changed over time. Comment on how information technology affects the role of accountants. In what respect is this a positive trend or a negative trend? What will this bar chart look like in 2020?

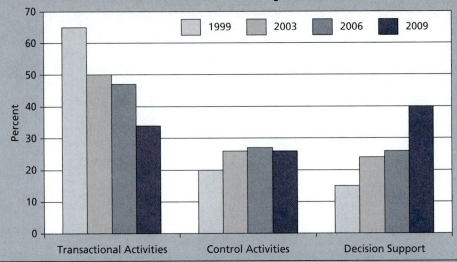

Continuous Evolution in Accounting Professional Activities

Legend: 1999, 2003, 2006, 2009

Source: *The Agile CFO: A Study of 900 CFOs Worldwide*, IBM, 2006.

3. In 2002, **John Deere's** $4 billion commercial and consumer equipment division implemented supply chain management software and reduced its inventory by $500 million. As sales continued to grow, the company has been able to keep its inventory growth flat. How did the supply chain management software implementation allow John Deere to reduce inventory on hand? How did this allow the company to save money? Which income statement accounts (e.g., revenue, cost of goods sold, SG&A expenses, interest expense, etc.) would this affect?

4. **Dell Computer** used customer relationship management software called IdeaStorm to collect customer feedback. This customer feedback led the company to build select consumer notebooks and desktops pre-installed with the Linux platform. Dell also decided to continue offering Windows 8 as a pre-installed operating system option in response to customer requests. Where does this fit in the value chain? How will this help Dell create value?

5. **Ingersoll Rand** operates as a manufacturer in four segments: Air Conditioning Systems and Services, Climate Control Technologies, Industrial Technologies, and Security Technologies. They installed an Oracle enterprise system, a supply chain system, and a customer relationship management system. The company boasts the following results. (Source: www.oracle.com/customers/snapshots/ingersoll-rand-financials-case-study.pdf)

   - Decreased direct product costs by 11 percent.
   - Increased labor productivity by 16 percent.
   - Increased inventory turns by four times.
   - Decreased order processing time by 90 percent and decreased implementation time by 40 percent.
   - Ensured minimal business disruption.
   - Streamlined three customer centers to one.

   Take each of these results and explain how the three systems (enterprise system, supply chain system, and customer relationship management system) affected these financial results and created value for the firm.

6. Using the accompanying explanations of each IT strategic role, suggest the appropriate IT strategic role (automate, informate or transform) for the following types of IT investments. Depending on your interpretation, it is possible that some of the IT investments could include two IT strategic roles.

   a. Digital health records
   b. Google Maps that recommend hotels and restaurants along a trip path

c. Customer relationship management software

d. Supply chain management software

e. Enterprise systems

f. Airline flight reservations systems

g. PayPal (www.paypal.com)

h. Amazon.com product recommendation on your homepage

i. eBay

j. Course and teacher evaluations conducted online for the first time (instead of on paper)

IT Strategic Roles[12]

Automate IT Strategic Role

- Replace human labor by automating business processes.
- Virtually no IT-driven transformation efforts.
- IT providing enhancements to existing processes or practices.

Informate-Up/-Down IT Strategic Role

- Provide new data/information to empower management, employees, or customers.
- An intermediate level of IT-driven transformation efforts.
- Gain clearer picture of cause–effect relationships, greater understanding of operating environment.

Transform IT Strategic Role

- Fundamentally alter traditional ways of doing business by redefining business capabilities and/or (internal or external) business processes and relationships.
- Strategic acquisition to acquire new capabilities or to enter a new marketplace.
- Use of IT to dramatically change how tasks are carried out recognized as being important in enabling firm to operate in different markets, serve different customers, and gain considerable competitive advantage by doing things differently.

---

7. Match the value chain activity in the left column with the scenario in the right column:

1. Service activities	A. Surveys for prospective customers
2. Inbound logistics	B. Warranty work
3. Marketing and sales activities	C. Assembly line
4. Firm infrastructure	D. Delivery to the firm's customer
5. Human Resource Management	E. New-product development
6. Technology	F. Receiving dock for raw materials
7. Procurement	G. CEO and CFO
8. Outbound Logistics	H. Buying (sourcing) raw materials
9. Operations	

Answers to Multiple Choice Questions

1. C	6. B
2. D	7. D
3. A	8. A
4. C	9. D
5. D	10. B

[12]B. Dehning, V.J. Richardson, and R.W. Zmud, "The Value Relevance of Announcements of Transformational Information Technology Investments," *MIS Quarterly* 27, no. 4 (2003), pp. 637–56.

Accountants as Business Analysts

A look at this chapter

As users, managers, designers, and evaluators of technology and technology-driven business processes, accountants must understand the organization and how organizational processes generate information important to management. To ensure that processes and systems are documented—and to participate in improvements to processes and systems—accountants must also be business analysts. This chapter defines business process modeling and describes how it supports the roles of accountants. It explains the potential value of business process modeling. Finally, it describes the types of business process models and introduces basic modeling tools to guide the student's development of modeling skills.

A look back

Chapter 1 discussed the importance of accounting information systems and the role accountants play in those systems. It further described how investments in information technology might improve the ability to manage business processes and create value for the firm.

A look ahead

Chapter 3 introduces data modeling. It describes how data modeling supports the design, implementation, and operation of database systems. It introduces basic modeling tools that will be used throughout the rest of the text.

One recent morning, I stopped at a very busy **Starbucks** in San Francisco. I looked at the line coming out of the door and immediately thought that it would take at least 20 minutes to get my morning coffee. Instead, I was pleasantly surprised at the efficiency of the employees who got me through that line in less than 2 minutes.

I watched closely as the **Starbucks** partners behind the counter executed the workflow of the process. One partner took my order and relayed my pastry order to another partner behind the pastry case. He also relayed my coffee order to the barista at the other end of the counter. As I moved through the line to the register, my order arrived just as I did, and a fourth partner checked the order and took my payment. Within those 2 minutes, they had served at least a dozen other customers, too.

I thought about the number of options they had to deal with, the variety of hot and cold drinks, the pastries and other breakfast items, while also keeping a supply of freshly brewed coffee ready. I was sure that **Starbucks** had analyzed the process in detail to eliminate waste and enhance their partners' productivity. Then, they had to train all their partners in that process so they could work as one highly synchronized team. Finally, they delivered a hot cup of coffee to a grateful customer on a cool San Francisco morning.

Chapter Outline

Changing Roles of Accountants in Business

Business Process Documentation
Definitions
Purposes of Process Documentation
Value of Business Models

Types of Business Models

Activity Models
Business Process Modeling Notation
Building Blocks for BPMN Diagrams
Example of a Business Process Diagram
Identifying Participants in Business Process Diagrams
Messages in BPMN
Best Practices in Preparing BPMN Diagrams

Appendix A: Flowcharting
Appendix B: Data Flow Diagrams

Learning Objectives

After reading this chapter, you should be able to:

2-1 Describe the roles of the accounting/finance function in business and why those roles require knowledge of technology and business processes.

2-2 Understand the importance of business process documentation.

2-3 Recognize the value of business models.

2-4 Articulate the characteristics of activity models.

2-5 Understand and apply the building blocks for BPMN (activity) diagrams.

LO 2-1
Describe the roles of
the accounting/finance
function in business
and why those roles
require knowledge
of technology and
business processes.

CHANGING ROLES OF ACCOUNTANTS IN BUSINESS

Over the past 15 years, a number of studies have highlighted the changing role of the accountant in business. Rapid changes in the global marketplace substantially affect the accounting profession. In the past, accountants typically focused on stewardship and reporting functions; they kept financial records, prepared financial reports, and performed audits. Now, they face the challenge of helping the enterprise to optimize its processes (financial, administrative, and operational) to achieve the competitive performance levels and maximize shareholder value.

Rapid changes in technology such as business intelligence (BI) and enterprise resource planning (ERP) systems have increased the availability of data throughout the organization. However, technology alone will not ensure good decision making. To be fully effective, the information produced by the technology must support the information requirements of the business's decision makers. Consequently, accountants are involved in supporting evidence-based decision making throughout the business. Although they continue to face the challenge of conducting their core transaction processing and reporting more efficiently, accountants must also act as business partners, involved in a host of business management activities—including strategic planning, process improvement, and compliance management—to produce better management information for both internal and external stakeholders. Table 2.1 summarizes the traditional stewardship and reporting and accounting management roles, as well as the increasingly important business management support roles.

TABLE 2.1
Roles of the Accounting/Finance Function in Business

Stewardship and Reporting	Accounting/Finance Operations	Business Management Support
Regulatory compliance	Finance and accounting processes (procure to pay, order to cash, record to report, payroll and treasury)	Management information
Tax returns	Financial close—completing period-end accounts	Planning, budgeting, and forecasting
Stakeholder assurance	Financial consolidation, reporting, and analysis	Performance measurement, reporting, and analysis
Investor relations	Providing comprehensive management information	Performance management
Raising capital and loans	People management	Risk management—from strategic to operational, including fraud risk
Board reports	Using IT to make finance and accounting processes more efficient and effective	Investment appraisal
Statutory reporting		Cost management
		Supply chain management
		Value-based management
		Project management
		Change management
		Capital structure and dividend policy
		Strategic planning
		Professional expertise (e.g., merger and acquisition or tax)

Source: Based on *Improving Decision Making in Organisations: The Opportunity to Transform Finance* (London: CIMA, 2007), Figure 3.

To perform all the roles described in Table 2.1 and be valuable business partners, accountants must first understand the business, as well as the various ways that the business collects data, summarizes, and communicates business information. They must understand how the business delivers value to its customers, interacts with other businesses, and meets requirements for good corporate citizenship. They must also understand the risks that the business faces and the internal controls in place to mitigate those risks. Finally, they must understand how accounting information systems collect, summarize, and report business process information. This highlights the need for good documentation of business processes and business systems. To ensure that processes and systems are documented—and to participate in improvements to business processes and systems—accountants must also be business analysts.

<table>
<tr><td>

LO 2-2

Understand the importance of business process documentation.

</td><td>

BUSINESS PROCESS DOCUMENTATION

Definitions

Before we describe how business analysis and business process modeling can support accountants' roles, we first present some definitions.

- **Business process:** A defined sequence of business activities that use resources to transform specific inputs into specific outputs to achieve a business goal. A business process is constrained by business rules.
- **Business analysis:** The process of defining business process requirements and evaluating potential improvements. Business analysis involves ascertaining, documenting, and communicating information about current and future business processes using business process modeling and related tools.
- **Business model:** A simple, abstract representation of one or more business processes.[1] A business model is typically a graphical depiction of the essential business process information.
- **Documentation:** Explains how business processes and business systems work. Documentation is "a tool for information transmission and communication. The type and extent of documentation will depend on the nature of the organization's products and processes."[2]

Purposes of Documentation

Documentation includes business process models, business rules, user manuals, training manuals, product specifications, software manuals, schedules, organization charts, strategic plans, and similar materials that describe the operation, constraints on, and objectives of business processes and systems. Although documentation has always been important for accounting information systems, the Sarbanes-Oxley Act of 2002 made documentation essential for businesses. That act requires managers to assess and attest to the business's internal control structure and procedures. The U.S. Securities and Exchange Commission (SEC) rules require "management to annually evaluate whether ICFR (internal control of financial reporting) is effective at providing reasonable assurance and to disclose its assessment to investors. Management is responsible for maintaining evidential matter, including documentation, to provide reasonable support for its assessment. This evidence will also allow a third party, such as the company's external auditor, to consider the work

</td></tr>
</table>

---

[1] In other contexts, the term "business model" is often used to describe the plan by which a company generates revenue.
[2] ISO 9001: 2008, International Standards Organization.

Documentation supports audits of business processes.

performed by management."[3] The act also requires external auditors to audit management's assessment of the effectiveness of internal controls and express an opinion on the company's internal control over financial reporting.[4] Thus, documentation is necessary for internal audit to support management's assertions as well as external auditors to evaluate management's assertions on internal control over financial reporting.

In addition to Sarbanes-Oxley compliance requirements, documentation is important for the following reasons:

- *Training.* User guides, employee manuals, and operating instructions help employees learn how business processes and systems operate.
- *Describing current processes and systems.* Documentation provides an official description of how business processes and systems, including AIS, work. Thus, documentation supports internal and external audit requirements, establishes accountability, and standardizes communications within the business and between the business and its customers, suppliers, and other stakeholders.
- *Auditing.* Documentation provides audit trails, which can assist auditors in determining the effectiveness of internal controls.
- *Accountability.* Documentation includes checklists, delegations of authority, and similar assignments of responsibility. Thus, documentation would specify who is authorized to approve orders or sign checks, for example.
- *Standardized interactions.* Documentation clearly describes the inputs and outputs of business processes and systems and thus provides a common language for all parties that interact with the process or system.
- *Facilitating process improvement.* Because it describes the way processes currently work, documentation is also the basis for determining what should be changed. Well-managed businesses regularly review all processes with a view to continuous improvement in four major areas:

    1. Effectiveness: Are the outputs of the process obtained as expected?
    2. Efficiency: Can the same outputs be produced with fewer inputs and resources?
    3. Internal control: Are the internal controls working?
    4. Compliance to various statutes and policies: Does the process comply with constantly changing local, state, federal, and international laws and regulations?

Value of Business Models

LO 2-3
Recognize the value of business models.

Imagine a map of a city like Los Angeles, California, or even a small city like Fayetteville, Arkansas. How many words would it take to provide the same information as the map? Undoubtedly, the graphical representation (map) presents the information more concisely and perhaps more clearly than a written description. Business processes and systems can also be difficult to describe concisely using words alone. Thus, business models allow us to depict the important features of business processes and systems clearly and concisely.

Business models are communication, training, analysis, and persuasion tools that are particularly suited for planning business transformations. Business transformations—including

[3]SEC interpretive guidance 33-8810, issued June 27, 2007.
[4]See the Public Company Accounting Oversight Board (PCAOB) Auditing Standard No. 5, *An Audit of Internal Control over Financial Reporting That Is Integrated with an Audit of Financial Statements.*

mergers, acquisitions, outsourcing, offshoring, product innovation, and continuous process improvement—are common. Business models allow managers to assess what needs to be changed and plan how to make the change.

- *Managing complexity.* Models are simpler than the processes and systems they depict, but they incorporate the essential elements.
- *Eliciting requirements.* Models offer a communications tool that can be used to interview involved parties and discuss the impact of possible changes.
- *Reconciling viewpoints.* Models can combine various local views into one integrated view. Some models can be used to simulate potential outcomes from a change to better assess the impact of the change.
- *Specifying requirements.* Models can be the basis for documentation of the changed process or system. Additionally, some models can be used to generate working software directly.

Progress *Check*

1. How would documentation help accountants perform some of the roles listed in Table 2.1?
2. From your own experience, describe how models (or pictures or maps) have helped you understand a complex issue.

LO 2-4
Articulate the characteristics of activity models.

TYPES OF BUSINESS MODELS

This textbook will focus on three different elements of business process models. To be complete, concise, and useful, business process models need to describe process activity, data structures, and the business rules that constrain and guide process operations (see Figure 2.1). This chapter focuses on activity models, and Chapter 3 introduces data models.

FIGURE 2.1
Business Process Models and Business Rules

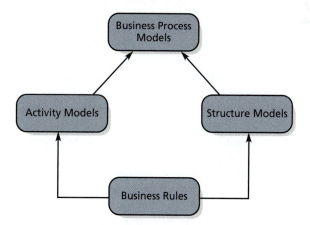

ACTIVITY MODELS

Activity models describe the sequence of workflow in a business process or processes. While the purpose of structure models is to create a blueprint for the development of a relational database to support the collection, aggregation, and communication of process information, the purpose of activity models is to represent the sequential flow and control logic of a set of related activities. They are tools for planning, documenting, discussing, and implementing systems; however, they also facilitate the use of those systems once implemented. Furthermore, they are important tools for analyzing and improving business processes.

Activity models, such as flowcharts, have been used to analyze business processes and design changes since well before 1920.[5] As technology changed, designers developed a variety of activity models, such as dataflow diagrams, business process maps, and IDEF0 functional modeling method,[6] to document and analyze business process workflow.

Regardless of the specific modeling notation, workflow models must be able to describe:

1. Events that start, change, or stop flow in the process.
2. Activities and tasks within the process.
3. The sequence of flow between tasks.
4. Decision points that affect the flow.
5. Division of activity depending on organizational roles.

Business Process Modeling Notation

LO 2-5

Understand and apply the building blocks for BPMN (activity) diagrams.

For this textbook, we employ **business process modeling notation (BPMN)** for activity models, although the concepts discussed also apply to other modeling notation, such as UML activity diagrams and data flow diagrams.[7] The Object Management Group also maintains the specifications for BPMN. The original specification for BPMN was issued in 2004. Since then, BPMN has been widely adopted because it was specifically designed for process modeling use and to be understood by businesspeople rather than software engineers (in contrast with UML activity diagrams). Additionally, there are free or inexpensive software products that support modeling and subsequent simulation of the process.

Building Blocks for BPMN Diagrams

Events include start, intermediate, and end events. Intermediate events affect the flow of a process, but do not start or end the process. Basic events are modeled as small circles, as shown in Figure 2.2. Start events have a single thin line circle. End events have a single thick line circle. Intermediate events have a double thin line circle. Categories of events can be defined with shapes inside the circles as we will explain later.

Activities represent specific steps in the business process. Basic activities are modeled as rounded rectangles, as shown in Figure 2.2. Each activity is described with a short verb phrase placed within the rectangle (e.g., process credit card payment or bill customer). An activity can depict a single action or some logical combination of actions depending on the required level of detail to achieve the objectives of the business process analysis.

Sequence flows are represented by arrows to indicate the progression of activity within the process, as shown in Figure 2.2. The diagram should show the sequence of activity from left to right and top to bottom.

Gateways show process branching and merging as the result of decisions. Basic gateways are depicted as diamonds. Usually, gateways appear as pairs on the diagram. The

---

[5]D. J. Couger, "Evolution of Business System Analysis Techniques," *Computing Surveys,* 5, no. 3 (1973), pp. 167–98. The article describes the use of flowcharts for industrial engineering by Frederick W. Taylor and others prior to 1920.

[6]See Federal Information Processing Standards Publication 183, www.idef.com.

[7]Data flow diagrams encompass elements of both activity and structure models, but they are primarily used to depict the sequence of data flows related to activities in a business process.

first gateway shows the branching, and the second gateway shows merging of the process branches.

Annotations allow the modeler to add additional descriptive information to the model. Annotations are modeled with text inside a bracket connected to other model symbols with a dashed line.

FIGURE 2.2
Basic Elements of Business Process Diagrams

Element	Description	Symbol
Events	Events are things that happen; they affect the flow of the business process when they occur. For example, a start event begins a process, an intermediate event may change the flow, and an end event signals the end of the process.	start intermediate end
Activities	Activities are where the work takes place; they can represent processes, subprocesses, or tasks depending on the diagram's level of detail.	Activity
Sequence Flows	An arrow shows the normal sequence flow—i.e., the order of activities—in a business process diagram.	Sequence Flow →
Gateways	Gateways control the branching and merging of flow paths in the business process.	Gateway
Annotations	Text annotations allow the analyst to add descriptive information to the diagram.	text annotation

Example of a Business Process Diagram

Figure 2.3 illustrates a simple business process activity diagram showing the checkout process at a retail store. In this process, the customer presents items for checkout. The clerk scans items and identifies payment method. Then, the process branches depending on the nature of payment. The payment is accepted, and the process branches merge. The clerk bags the items for the customer, and the process ends. Note that the start event can be labeled to explain the start event, and the gateway branches can be labeled to show the purpose of the branches (handling cash or credit payment in this case).

Progress *Check*

3. Draw a business process model (using BPMN) of a drive-through window at a fast-food restaurant. What starts the process? What ends the process? What are the important steps? Are there any decision points that would require gateways?

FIGURE 2.3
Sample Business
Process Diagram

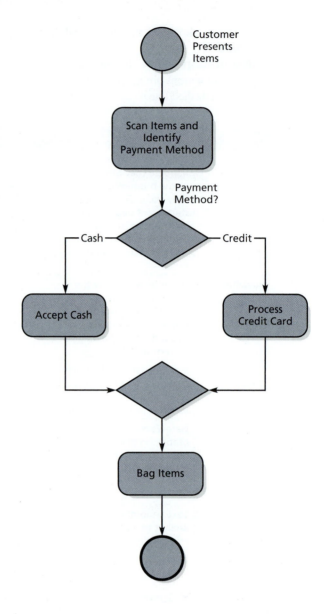

Identifying Participants in Business Process Diagrams

It is often important to identify who performs which activity in a business process. A participant is an actor or person that performs activities and interacts with other participants in a process. Participants include people, systems, organizations, and machines. Participants can also be identified by the role of the actor in the process. BPMN provides notation to identify both the organizations and the departments or individual actors participating in a process. The organization is identified by a **pool,** and the department is identified by **swimlanes** within the pool, as shown if Figure 2.4. Every diagram contains at least one pool, but if there is only one pool, the pool may be presented without a boundary. Activities can be assigned to only one participant, and thus may appear in only one pool or swimlane.

FIGURE 2.4
Pools and Swimlanes to Identify Participants

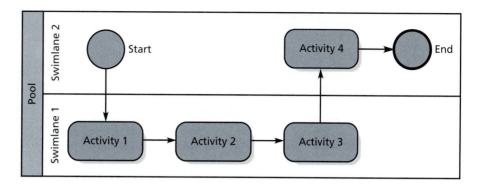

Messages in BPMN

BPMN represents exchanges between two participants (pools) in the same process as message flows. For example, in a sales process with a customer pool and a store pool, the customer order would be represented as a message flow. The activities within a pool are organized by sequence flow, but the interactions between pools are represented as **message flows.** A message flow is shown as a dashed arrow with a small circle at the starting end, as shown in Figure 2.5. Figure 2.6 presents an example of a message flow.

FIGURE 2.5
Message Flow Symbol

FIGURE 2.6
Message Flow Example

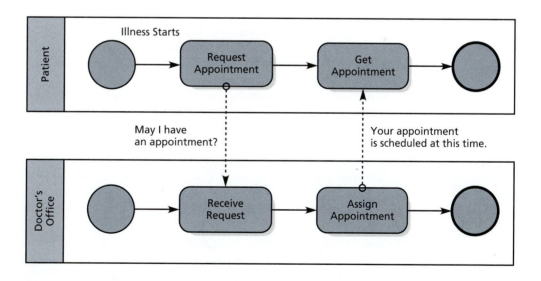

Progress *Check*

4. Using Figure 2.6 as a guide; draw a simple model of a customer interacting with **Amazon.com's** website to purchase an item. Assume the customer is an Amazon Prime™ member and can buy an item with 1-click (i.e., Amazon already has the credit card information). Use two pools and the associated message flows.

Best Practices in Preparing BPMN Diagrams

The primary objective of process activity modeling is to describe the important steps in a business process clearly, concisely, and accurately. Diagrams are tools to aid in planning, documenting, discussing, implementing, and using systems. Here are some modeling best practices that can enhance the use of models for these purposes.

1. Focus on one business process at a time.
2. Clearly identify the events that start and end the process.
3. Include essential elements, but avoid distracting detail.
4. Think about a token flowing from the start event through the process to the end event; the flow of the token should be clear for all paths through the process.
5. Label activities clearly with a verb and an object (e.g., pay invoice).
6. Model iteratively, getting feedback to improve accuracy and clarity.

Summary

Information plays a crucial role in the information age.

- Accountants' roles in business are evolving rapidly.
- Accountants are increasingly involved in business management support.
- Business process documentation is essential for training, describing current processes and systems to support internal and external audit, establishing accountability, and communicating among employees and various stakeholders.
- Business process documentation provides a starting point for business process improvement.
- Business models manage complexity, elicit requirements, reconcile viewpoints, and specify operating requirements for business processes.
- There are two major types of business process models: activity models and structure models.
- Activity models show the flow of work in a business process.
- BPMN provides a notation for specifying workflow.
- BPMN provides notation to identify events, activities, sequence flows, and gateways that allow process branching.
- BPMN allows the identification of participants in a process through the use of pools and swimlanes.
- BPMN message flows document exchanges between pools.

Key Words

activities (32)   In business process modeling, activities represent specific steps in a business process.

activity models (31)   Models that describe the sequence of workflow in a business process or processes.

annotations (33)   Model elements that allow the modeler to add additional descriptive information to the model. Annotations are modeled with text inside a bracket connected to other model symbols with a dashed line.

business analysis (29)   The process of defining business process requirements and evaluating potential improvements. Business analysis involves ascertaining, documenting, and communicating information about current and future business processes using business process modeling and related tools.

business model (29)   A simple, abstract representation of one or more business processes. A business model is typically a graphical depiction of the essential business process information.

business process (29)   A defined sequence of business activities that use resources to transform specific inputs into specific outputs to achieve a business goal.

business process modeling notation (BPMN) (*32*)   A standard for the description of activity models.

data flow diagram (DFD) (*42*)   Another type of activity model that graphically shows the flow of data through a system and also incorporates elements of structure models.

documentation (*29*)   An information transmission and communication tool that explains how business processes and business systems work.

events (*32*)   Important occurrences that affect the flow of activities in a business process. BPMN includes symbols to define start, intermediate, and end events.

flowcharts (*37*)   Visualizations of a process activity; they are activity models much like models using BPMN.

gateways (*32*)   Show process branching and merging as the result of decisions. Basic gateways are depicted as diamonds. Usually, gateways appear as pairs on the diagram. The first gateway shows the branching, and the second gateway shows merging of the process branches.

message flows (*35*)   BPMN represents exchanges between two participants (pools) in the same process as message flows, which are modeled as dashed arrows.

pools (*34*)   BPMN symbols used to identify participants, actors, or persons that perform activities and interact with other participants in a process.

process maps (*37*)   Simplified flowcharts that use a basic set of symbols to represent a business process activity.

sequence flows (*32*)   BPMN symbols that show the normal sequence of activities in a business process. Sequence flows are modeled as solid arrows, with the arrowhead showing the direction of process flow.

swimlanes (*34*)   BPMN symbols that provide subdivisions of pools to show, for example, functional responsibilities within an organization.

Appendix A

Flowcharting

WHAT IS A FLOWCHART?

Like business process models, **flowcharts** are visualizations of a process activity. Flowcharts have been widely used since they were first introduced in the 1920s. Modern techniques such as UML activity diagrams and BPMN are extensions of flowcharts. Flowcharts are useful tools for systems development, process documentation, and understanding internal controls. Three types of flowcharts are often used by accountants. These three types typically differ in the level of detail modeled.

1. *Systems flowcharts* provide an overall view of a system, including the inputs, activities, and outputs of the process.
2. *Process maps* use the basic set of flowchart symbols to provide a representation of the steps within a business process. **Process maps** are conceptually similar to business process diagrams created with BPMN.
3. *Document flowcharts* present the flow of documents through an entity, often describing the areas within the entity with responsibility for particular tasks.

BASIC BUILDING BLOCKS FOR FLOWCHARTS

The basic flowchart symbols shown in Figure 2.A1 are similar to, and serve the same basic functions as, the BPMN symbols for activity models.

- *Start/End.* Each flowchart should show the flow of process activities from one start to one or more logical ends. The start and end steps are drawn as ovals.
- *Tasks/Activities.* Tasks or activities represent specific steps in the business process. Basic activities are modeled as rectangles. Each activity is described with a short verb phrase placed within the rectangle (e.g., process credit card payment or bill customer). An activity can depict a single action or some logical combination of actions depending on the required level of detail to achieve the objectives of the business process analysis.
- *Sequence Flows.* Sequence flows are represented by arrows to indicate the progression of activity within the process. The diagram should show the sequence of activity from left to right and top to bottom.
- *Decisions.* Decisions are modeled as diamonds with multiple exits (sequence flows) based on the result of decisions.

FIGURE 2.A1
Basic Elements of Flowcharts

Element	Description	Symbol
Start/End	The Start/End steps indicate the beginning and ending of the process flow.	Start
Tasks/Activities	Tasks/Activities are the steps that describe the work; they can represent individual tasks or collections of tasks depending on the diagram's level of detail.	Task/Activity
Sequence Flows	An arrow shows the normal direction of flow—i.e., the order of activities—in a diagram.	Sequence Flow →
Decisions	Decision diamonds portray the nature of the decision and the exit options.	Decision

EXAMPLE OF BUSINESS PROCESS FLOWCHART

Figure 2.A2 shows a simple business process activity diagram showing the checkout process at a retail store. In this process, the customer presents items for checkout. The clerk scans items and identifies payment method. Then the process branches depending on the nature of payment. The payment is accepted, and the process branches merge. The clerk bags the items for the customer, and the process ends. Note that the start event can be labeled to explain the start event, and the gateway branches can be labeled to show the purpose of the branches (handling cash or credit payment in this case).

ADDITIONAL FLOWCHART SYMBOLS

The additional symbols shown in Figure 2.A3 are also widely used to depict specific operations within flowcharts. While none of these symbols are necessary for system flowcharts, they are often used in document flowcharts to differentiate manual and system operations and the media used in the process.

FIGURE 2.A2
Sample Business
Process Flowchart

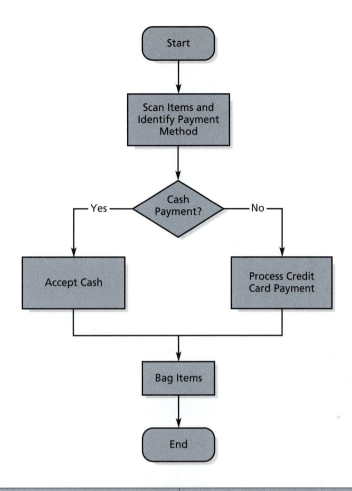

Element	Description	Symbol
Input/Output; Journal/Ledger	The parallelogram is a generalized symbol for input or output when the medium is not specified.	In/Out
Input/Output of Document(s) or Report(s)	The document symbol indicates hard-copy documents or reports coming into or going out of the process.	One Document / Multiple
Online Keying	This symbol indicates data entry using online devices such as a computer or a handheld device.	
Storage Offline	This symbol indicates storage, typically of documents, not accessible by computer. File-ordering sequence is indicated as follows: N = numerically, A = alphabetically, D = by date.	N
Magnetic Disc Storage	This symbol includes database (online) storage accessible by computer.	
Manual Task/Activity	This symbol indicates a manual task. If the flowchart differentiates between manual and computer operations, the basic task/activity symbol shown in Figure A1 then shows a computer operation.	Manual Task

FIGURE 2.A3
Additional Flowchart Symbols

(continued)

Element	Description	Symbol
On/Off Page Connectors	These symbols facilitate modeling by allowing a connection between two points on the same page or on different pages.	On Page / Off Page
Annotation	This symbol is to add descriptive comments or explanatory notes to clarify the process.	

FIGURE 2.A3
(continued)

SHOWING RESPONSIBILITY

Deployment flowcharts show both the sequence of steps in a process as well as the organizational responsibility for each step. Like business process models (BPMN), deployment flowcharts use swimlanes to represent different organizational units or functions. These flowcharts are particularly useful in identifying the multiple handoffs between organization units in a process. These handoffs can be sources of problems, and making these steps clear can help identify those problems. Additionally, deployment flowcharts are useful in documenting processes for activities such as employee training. The flowchart in Figure 2.A4 illustrates swimlanes and responsibilities.

FIGURE 2.A4
Flowchart with Swimlanes Showing Responsibility

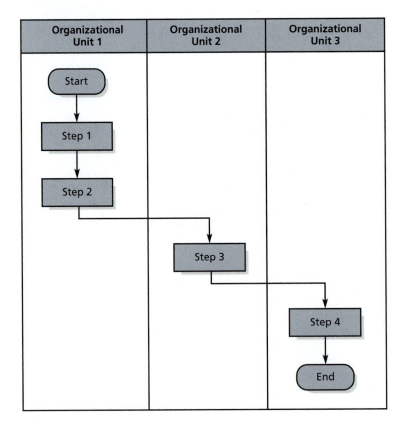

SHOWING OPPORTUNITY

Opportunity flowcharts highlight opportunities for improvement by, for example, separating value-added from cost-added activities within a process. Opportunity flowcharts use swimlanes to separate the activities that add value from those that add to the costs of the process, such as the costs of redoing work, waiting for information, waiting for parts, or correcting problems in general. Value-added activities are those that are essential to producing the process's product or service given the current state of technology, even if the process runs perfectly every time. Cost-added-only activities are those related to checking for defects, reworking, or supplying missing information.

For example, Figure 2.A5 shows the simple process of printing out and turning in an assignment document. If the process went as expected, we would select the printer, print the document, and turn in the assignment. The example assumes that, in some cases, the printer can be out of paper, which requires adding more paper before proceeding, or that the print cartridges could be out of ink, which requires replacing the cartridges and reprinting the document.

FIGURE 2.A5

Opportunity Flowchart Example of a Document Printing Process

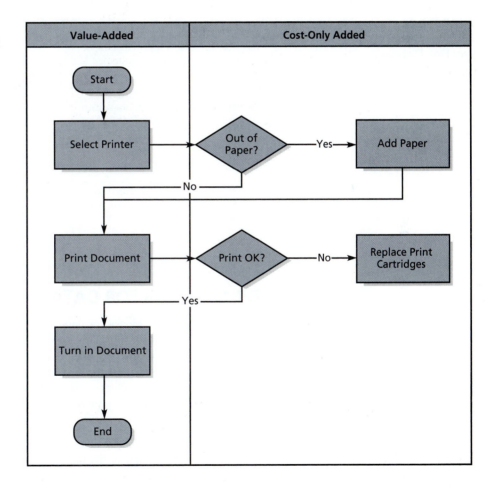

Data Flow Diagrams

WHAT IS A DATA FLOW DIAGRAM (DFD)?

A **data flow diagram (DFD)** represents graphically the flow of data through a system, such as one or more business processes. Data flow diagrams are often used to perform structured systems analysis and design, whereby a system is described at increasing levels of detail to facilitate new systems design. DFDs use a limited set of symbols (see Figure 2.B1) and are easily read and understood. Unlike most flowcharts, DFDs specifically represent the datastores—that is, the system files affected by or supporting the process—as well as the data that flow to and from the datastores. DFDs have no start and end symbols, which is also unlike flowcharts and BPMN business process diagrams. Instead, dataflow diagrams present the external sources of—or destinations for—the data.

FIGURE 2.B1

Basic Elements of Data Flow Diagrams

Element	Description	Symbol
Process	The activities within a system that use or generate data (e.g., Receive customer order).	Process
Data Source or Destination	The entities that interact with the system (e.g., customers, employees, or bank).	Source/ Destination
Data Stores	This symbol describes the physical or electronic data storage.	Datastore
Data Flows	This symbol shows the flow of data (e.g., an order coming from a customer); data flows are named to indicate the data content.	data flow 1

BASIC BUILDING BLOCKS FOR DATA FLOW DIAGRAMS

The following describes basic building blocks for data flow diagrams. The structure of these diagrams is substantially different from the structure of BPMN activity models.

Processes are activities that use or generate data. Depending on the software tools used to draw DFDs, processes may be represented with circles or rectangles with rounded corners. As with BPMN diagrams and flowcharts, processes are given names using short verb phrases (e.g., Receive customer order). A process must have at least one or more data flows coming in and going out.

- *Terminators* are external entities that are either sources or destinations for data. Terminators are typically represented with rectangles. Examples of terminators are customers, suppliers, or other entities external to the particular system being represented.

- *Data stores* represent the physical or electronic repositories of data within the system. Data stores are typically represented as rectangles with one or both ends open.

- *Data flows* represent the flow of physical or electronic data through the system. These are represented by arrows that show the direction of data flow.

EXAMPLE OF A DFD

Figure 2.B2 shows a simple example of a DFD showing the checkout process at a retail store. In this process, the customer (external source) presents items for checkout. The system includes scanning and bagging the items and accepting payment while updating sales and inventory records.

FIGURE 2.B2

Sample Level 0 DFD of Customer Checkout System

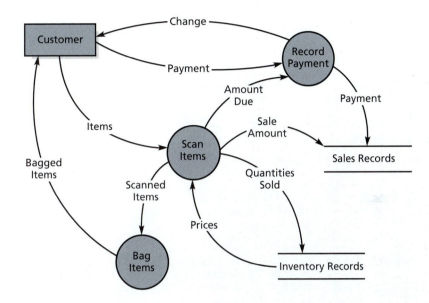

NESTING OR EXPLODING DFDs

DFDs describe a system at increasing levels of detail to facilitate new systems design. The context diagram shows the entire system as one process and identifies all relevant external sources and destinations for data, as well as the type of data coming from or going to those external entities. Then, subsequent models showing increasing detail would be identified as level 0, level 1, and level 2. Each process in a DFD is designated by the level and the number of the process. In Figure B2, for example, assuming that is the level 0 diagram, then *Scan Items* could be designated process 1.0. If any subprocesses of *Scan Items* are subsequently modeled, those would be designated 1.1, 1.2, and so on.

BEST PRACTICES FOR DFDs

There are several best practices to ensure that DFDs provide useful descriptions of systems. Similar to flowcharts and BPMN diagrams, DFDs are a communications tool. Thus, the names given to processes, data stores, data flows, and external entities are important. The names should be clear to the system users. With regard to modeling specific elements of the diagram, modelers should remember that processes do not spontaneously generate or absorb data. Processes only modify data; therefore, all processes should have at least one data flow coming in and out, and the data flow out of a process should be different than the data flow in. Data stores support the system's processing requirements, so every datastore should be connected to at least one process in the system. Finally, systems are developed to respond to inputs from external entities or to deliver information to external entities, so every external entity must be connected to at least one data flow.

USING DFDs FOR SYSTEM DOCUMENTATION

To form complete documentation for a system, the business analyst would augment the DFDs with additional information. For example, the analyst would define each datastore completely, specifying the fields, data types, data limits, and formats. The analyst would also define each element of a data flow in terms of the specific fields that it contains. Plus, the analyst would describe the business rules or logic for each process and confirm those with the process owners.

Answers to Progress *Checks*

1. Documentation is important to almost all accounting/finance functions listed.

2. The answer depends on the student, but all of us have used maps. Most of us have assembled a product from **IKEA**. Most of us have installed software on our computers.

3. Here's a simple business process model (without pools and swimlanes) for a fast-food drive-through:

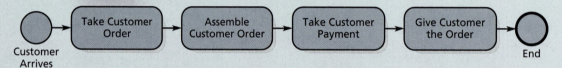

4. Here is one possible example of a process model using pools and message flows to show a customer interacting with **Amazon.com's** website to purchase an item.

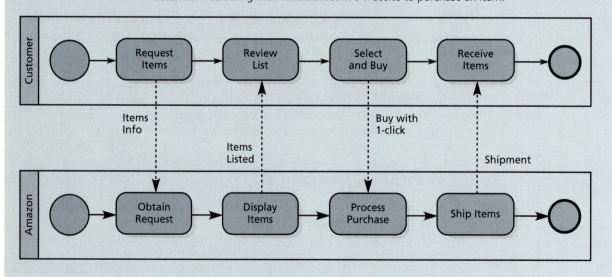

Multiple Choice Questions

1. Which of the following is not a role of the accounting function in business?
   a. Financial close
   b. Regulatory compliance
   c. Project management
   d. Using IT to make finance and accounting processes more efficient
   e. All of the above are roles of the accounting function.

2. Which of the following is not an example of business process documentation?
   a. Business process models
   b. Training manuals
   c. Organization charts
   d. Internal audit
   e. All of the above are examples of business process documentation.

3. Which of the following is not a purpose of business process documentation?
   a. Facilitating process improvement
   b. Specifying accountability
   c. Training
   d. Supporting internal audit
   e. All of the above are purposes of business process documentation.

4. Which of the following best describes the value of business models?
   a. A communication tool
   b. A planning tool
   c. A process improvement tool
   d. A tool for managing complexity
   e. All of the above

5. Which of the following describes how participants in a process are identified in BPMN?
   a. Message flows
   b. Swimlanes
   c. Pools
   d. Gateways
   e. Both b and c
   f. Both a and d

6. Which of the following symbols is used to represent a gateway in BPMN?

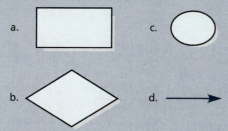

7. Which of the following symbols is used to represent sequence flow in BPMN?

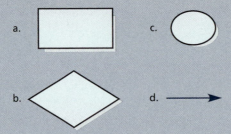

a.

c.

b.

d.

8. Which of the following statements about BPMN is not true?
    a. Arrows represent sequence flows.
    b. The BPMN specification is maintained by the Object Management Group (OMG).
    c. Events are modeled with a circle symbol.
    d. Annotations allow the modeler to add descriptive text.
    e. All of the above are true.

Discussion Questions

1. Do you think that your accounting education has prepared you for all roles of an accountant in business? Which roles do you feel best prepared for? Which roles do you feel least prepared for? Why?
2. How could a BPMN activity model support the Accounting/Finance Operations roles shown in Table 2.1?
3. Compare BPMN activity diagrams with flowcharts and DFDs. What is different? What is the same? When would one notation be better or worse than another?

Problems

1. Identify the start and end events and the activities in the following narrative, and then draw the business process model using BPMN:

    The **Starbucks** customer entered the drive-through lane and stopped to review the menu. He then ordered a Venti coffee of the day and a blueberry muffin from the barista. The barista recorded the order in the cash register. While the customer drove to the window, the barista filled a Venti cup with coffee, put a lid on it, and retrieved the muffin from the pastry case and placed it in a bag. The barista handed the bag with the muffin and the hot coffee to the customer. The customer has an option to pay with cash, credit card, or Starbucks gift card. The customer paid with a gift card. The barista recorded the payment and returned the card along with the receipt to the customer.

2. Draw a business process model using BPMN from the following narrative:

    Larry awoke to his alarm clock buzz. He got up and dressed for the day. Then, he ate a hearty breakfast of oatmeal, toast, orange juice, and coffee. He grabbed his books and prepared to leave for school. Before he left home, he checked the weather. If it looked like rain, he put on a jacket and took his umbrella, and he drove to school. If it looked sunny, he left his jacket and umbrella at home and walked to school. If he drove to school, he parked his car and walked to class. If he walked to school, he went straight to class.

Answers to Multiple Choice Questions

1. e
2. d
3. e
4. e
5. e
6. b
7. d
8. e

Data Modeling

A look at this chapter

Today's accountants must understand how business processes generate data and how those data are structured, interrelated, and stored in a database system. To ensure that business processes and the database systems are documented and to participate in improvements to processes and systems, accountants must understand and be able to model such systems. This chapter describes data modeling. It explains how data models support database-driven systems. It introduces basic data modeling tools to guide the student's development of modeling skills. Finally, it discusses business rules and how the identification of relevant business rules supports both process and data modeling.

A look back

Chapter 2 described the roles of accountants as users, managers, designers, and evaluators of technology and technology-driven business processes. To perform in those roles, accountants need to ensure that processes and systems are documented—and to participate in improvements to processes and systems. Thus, accountants must be business analysts. The chapter continued to introduce types of business process models as well as the potential value of business process modeling.

A look ahead

In the next several chapters, we use business process and data models to examine sales, acquisition, conversion, and related management processes.

Recently, **Starbucks** replaced a variety of systems with **Oracle's** application suite. According to Karen Metro, vice president of global business system solutions for **Starbucks**, "Many of our systems had grown up in silos and were loosely connected, and we were having a hard time keeping them upgraded or getting the functionality we needed out of those systems. **Accenture** came in to help us review the state of the environment and put together a global program to deploy standardized business processes and systems around the world." About 200 people from both **Accenture** and **Starbucks** worked full-time for 3 years on the project. The software was first implemented in Europe, then North America, and finally China. **Starbucks** expects a variety of performance benefits, including improved margins. In particular, the software will help **Starbucks** understand where its money is spent and "leverage that with our suppliers around the world."

Source: Information provided by Accenture case study posted on its website, www.accenture.com, 2009.

Chapter Outline

Structure Models
Unified Modeling Language Class Diagrams
Building Blocks for UML Class Diagrams
Best Practices in Preparing Class Diagrams
UML Class Models for Relational Database Design
Business Rules
Appendix A: Entity-Relationship Diagrams

Learning Objectives

After reading this chapter, you should be able to:

3-1 Understand the purpose of structure models.

3-2 Understand and apply the building blocks for UML class (structure) diagrams.

3-3 Describe multiplicities for a UML class diagram.

3-4 Understand how to implement a relational database from a UML class diagram.

3-5 Describe business rules and the various forms of rules.

STRUCTURE MODELS

Structure models describe the data and information structures inherent in a business process or processes. The primary purpose of these models is to create a blueprint for the development of a relational database to support the collection, aggregation, and communication of process information. They are tools for planning, documenting, discussing, and implementing databases; however, they also facilitate the use of databases after they are implemented.

For more than 50 years, **data models** have been used to represent the conceptual contents of databases to communicate with the users of those databases. For example, Charles Bachman developed data structure diagrams, also known as Bachman diagrams, in the 1960s. Using similar notation, Peter Chen developed entity-relationship modeling in 1975 to describe the entities (e.g., people, things, and events) and the relationships among entities in databases. Since then, a number of others have offered a variety of notations to describe the elements of databases, but the concepts in all variations are similar.

A model of logical database structures must be able to describe:

1. The entities or things in the domain of interest.
2. The relationships among those things.
3. The cardinalities that describe how many instances of one entity can be related to another.
4. The attributes or characteristics of the entities and relationships.

Unified Modeling Language Class Diagrams

This textbook employs the Unified Modeling Language (UML) class diagram notation for structure models, although the concepts also apply to other notation standards, such as entity-relationship modeling. The Object Management Group is a not-for-profit consortium of computer industry members that maintains and publishes the specification for the UML. **Class diagrams** are one type of diagram within UML and are similar in many ways to entity-relationship diagrams. They describe the logical structure of a database system.

Building Blocks for UML Class Diagrams
Classes

A **class** is any separately identifiable collection of things (objects) about which the organization wants to collect and store information. Classes can represent organization resources (e.g., trucks, machines, buildings, cash, investments), persons (e.g., customers, employees), events (e.g., sales, purchases, cash disbursements, cash receipts), and conceptual structures (e.g., accounts, product categories, budgets). Classes are typically implemented as tables in a relational database, where individual instances of objects are represented as rows in the table.

Each class is represented by a rectangle with three compartments, as shown in Figure 3.1. The top compartment shows the name of the class. The middle compartment shows the attributes (data elements) shared by all instances in the class. The bottom compartment describes operations that each instance in the class can perform. The attribute and operation compartments are optional. In this text, we will typically omit the attribute and operations compartments when depicting classes.

Cash disbursements represent events in a class. The class symbol would be name only such as bank account.

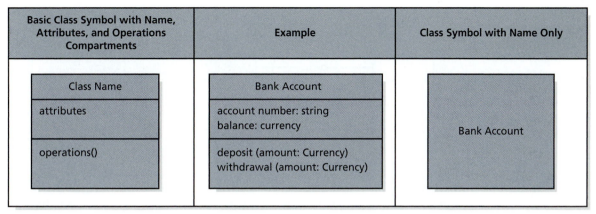

FIGURE 3.1
Class Notation

Associations

An **association** depicts the relationship between two classes. For example, customers (class) *participate* in sales (class); professors (class) *teach* courses (class); employees (class) *work for* organizations (class). It allows navigation between instances in one class and instances of another class, such as linking customer information to a particular sale. A generic association is drawn as a line connecting two classes. When the business purpose of the association is not clear, the association can be named by placing the text name on the line, as shown in Figure 3.2. Association names are verbs or verb phrases that indicate why instances of one class relate to instances of another class.

FIGURE 3.2
Classes with Associations

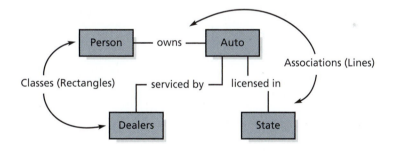

LO 3-3
Describe multiplicities for a UML class diagram.

Multiplicities

Multiplicities describe the minimum and maximum number of times instances in one class can be associated with instances in another class. Multiplicities for a class are represented by a pair of numbers placed on the opposite side of the association. In a binary association, there would then be two sets of multiplicities. Minimum values can be 0 or 1. The minimum values of multiplicities indicate whether participation in the relationship is optional (0) or mandatory (1). The maximum values can be 1 or many (*). In Figure 3.3, for example, it is optional for a person to own an automobile, but it is mandatory that each auto be owned by a person (assuming the auto class represents registered automobiles). The maximum values for a pair of multiplicities for a single association describe the nature of the relationship between classes: one-to-one, one-to-many, or many-to-many. In Figure 3.3, for example, a person could own many autos, so this is a one-to-many relationship.

FIGURE 3.3
Multiplicities
Each Person owns a minimum of 0 and a maximum of many Autos. Each Auto is owned by a minimum of 1 and a maximum of 1 Person.

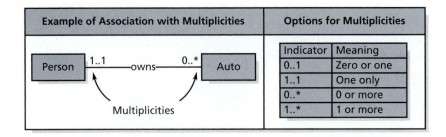

Attributes

Attributes are data elements that describe the instances in a class. Figure 3.4 lists the attribute names for the classes in a domain of interest (related to taking orders from customers) and identifies primary and foreign keys. The full specification of attributes would also include data type, default value (if any), **constraints** on the value (such as minimum and maximum possible values), and other descriptive information.

Primary Keys.   A **primary key (PK)** is an attribute or combination of attributes that uniquely identifies each instance in a class or row in a table. Primary keys can be modeled as part of the attribute list for each class on the UML class diagram; often, however, they are defined in the supporting documentation, such as the table listing shown in Figure 3.4, especially when using class symbols that only show the class name as shown earlier in Figure 3.2. The primary key is a unique identifier for each instance in the class. For example, the "State" class in Figure 3.2 collectively defines all the states. Each state is an instance in that class, and each state would be identified by a unique primary key, such as the abbreviations AR, CA, WA, and so on.

FIGURE 3.4
List of Tables with Attribute Names

Customers	[Customer_Number (PK), Customer_Name, Customer_City, Customer_State, Customer_Zip, Customer_Phone]
Orders	[Order_Number (PK), Order_Date, Delivery_Date, Order_Amount, Shipping_Cost, Customer_Number (FK)]
Order_Items	[Order_Number + Product_Number (PK), Quantity_Ordered, Price]
Inventory	[Product_Number (PK), Product_Description, Quantity_on_Hand (QOH), Unit_of_Issue, Current_List_Price, Standard_Cost]

There are often several candidates for the primary key of a class or database table. There are several important criteria that guide the selection of appropriate primary keys:

- The primary key must uniquely identify each instance of the class (or row of the table). Consequently, the designer should avoid anything that could be duplicated, such as names.
- The primary key cannot be null (blank) under any circumstances. For this reason, the designer should avoid using attributes for the primary key that are potentially unavailable for any instance of the class; for example, not everyone has a Social Security number.
- The primary key cannot change over time.
- The primary key should be controlled by the organization that assigns it. When the assigning organization does not control the primary key values, it becomes difficult to ensure uniqueness. For example, names are not good primary keys.
- A primary key with sequential values makes it easier to recognize gaps in the data.
- All else equal, shorter primary key values are better than longer ones, because shorter keys ease data entry, indexing, and retrieval.

Foreign Keys. A **foreign key (FK)** is an attribute or combination of attributes that allows tables to be linked together. A foreign key is linked *to the primary key of another table* to support a defined association. In Figure 3.3, for example, the Auto class would include a foreign key to match the primary key for the Person class to support the Owns association. In the table attribute listing shown in Figure 3.4, the primary key of the Customers Table is Customer_Number. The foreign key Customer_Number in the Orders Table allows rows in the Orders Table to be linked to the rows in the Customers Table.

Progress *Check*

1. Consider students enrolled in courses taught by professors. Draw a simple class diagram with associations that describes the registration process. *Hint:* Include courses, students, and professors.
2. Add multiplicities to your diagram. Can a student be enrolled in many courses? Can a course have many students enrolled?
3. Create a listing of the tables with attributes. What are the primary keys? What attributes do you think go with each table definition?

Other Relationships

The generic relationship between two classes is modeled as an *association* as described earlier. However, UML includes modeling notation for other types of relationships: **generalization** (or inheritance), **aggregation,** and **composition,** as shown in Figure 3.5. These special-purpose relationship notations should be used when it clarifies relationships in a particular model, but they can also be modeled using associations.

Other Useful UML Class Model Notation

UML is semantically rich; it provides notation that accommodates a wide variety of modeling situations. We have outlined the basic notation that should allow you to build most

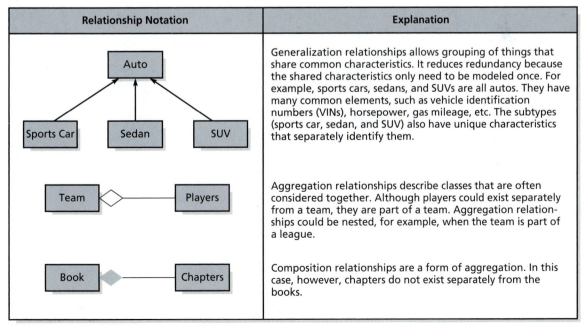

Relationship Notation	Explanation
Auto → Sports Car, Sedan, SUV	Generalization relationships allows grouping of things that share common characteristics. It reduces redundancy because the shared characteristics only need to be modeled once. For example, sports cars, sedans, and SUVs are all autos. They have many common elements, such as vehicle identification numbers (VINs), horsepower, gas mileage, etc. The subtypes (sports car, sedan, and SUV) also have unique characteristics that separately identify them.
Team ◇—— Players	Aggregation relationships describe classes that are often considered together. Although players could exist separately from a team, they are part of a team. Aggregation relationships could be nested, for example, when the team is part of a league.
Book ◆—— Chapters	Composition relationships are a form of aggregation. In this case, however, chapters do not exist separately from the books.

FIGURE 3.5
UML Notation for Other Relationships

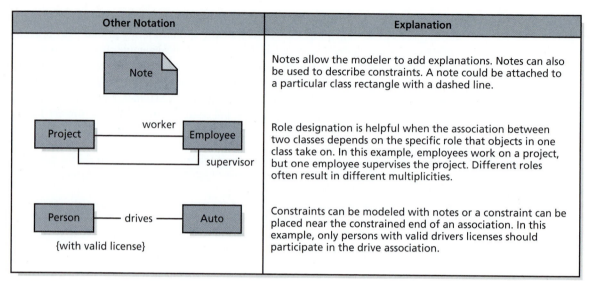

Other Notation	Explanation
Note	Notes allow the modeler to add explanations. Notes can also be used to describe constraints. A note could be attached to a particular class rectangle with a dashed line.
Project — worker — Employee — supervisor	Role designation is helpful when the association between two classes depends on the specific role that objects in one class take on. In this example, employees work on a project, but one employee supervises the project. Different roles often result in different multiplicities.
Person — drives — Auto {with valid license}	Constraints can be modeled with notes or a constraint can be placed near the constrained end of an association. In this example, only persons with valid drivers licenses should participate in the drive association.

FIGURE 3.6
Other Useful Class Diagram Notation

business process structural models. However, there are three other UML class model notations that can be particularly useful for modeling business processes from an accounting viewpoint. These three notations are described in Figure 3.6.

Best Practices in Preparing Class Diagrams

The primary objective of a class diagram is to describe the important elements of a domain of interest clearly, concisely, and accurately. As noted previously, class diagrams are tools to aid in planning, documenting, discussing, implementing, and using database systems. Here are some modeling best practices that can enhance the use of models for these purposes.

1. Use common terminology in the organization for class names (e.g., sales, orders, clients), and avoid confusing abbreviations.
2. Link classes on the diagram only when there is a clear business purpose for the relationship.
3. Avoid crossing lines where possible, because that increases the potential for misreading the diagram.
4. Use consistently sized class rectangles to avoid an unwanted emphasis on a larger symbol.
5. Avoid running association lines close together, because they may be hard to follow.
6. Opt for simplicity; show only what you need to show.
7. Focus first on the accuracy of the content, then address appearance.
8. Use notes to explain more complex situations.

LO 3-4
Understand how to implement a relational database from a UML class diagram.

UML CLASS MODELS FOR RELATIONAL DATABASE DESIGN

As we noted at the beginning of this chapter, the primary purpose of structure models is to create a blueprint for the development of a relational database to support the collection, aggregation, and communication of process information. They are tools for planning, documenting, discussing, and implementing databases. This section describes basic processes

FIGURE 3.7
**Mapping Classes
to Tables**

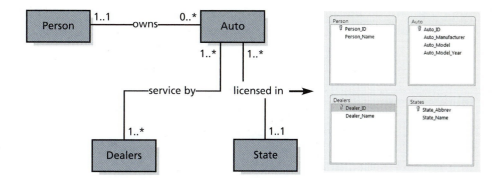

for mapping a UML class diagram to a relational database schema, which defines the tables, fields, relationships, keys, etc., in the database.[1]

1. *Map classes to tables.* The first step is to map the classes to tables. In Figure 3.7, for example, the UML class diagram (shown earlier in Figure 3.2 without multiplicities) would map to four tables in the relational database. Each instance of the class maps to a row in the corresponding table.
2. *Map class attributes to table fields and assign primary keys.* Map the attributes for each class to fields in the corresponding relational table. If the primary keys have not been designated, determine an appropriate primary key for each relational table. In the example shown in Figure 3.7, the primary keys are indicated by **Microsoft** Access's primary key symbol.
3. *Map associations to foreign keys.* Each association in Figure 3.7, except the "serviced by" association between Dealers and Auto, will be implemented by adding foreign keys. The multiplicities determine the foreign key placement. The figure indicates that one person owns a minimum of 0 and a maximum of many autos. This is an example of a one-to-many relationship. Thus, the primary key for Person is posted in Auto as a foreign key. Table 3.1 provides general rules for posting foreign keys based on the type of association between two classes.
4. *Create new tables to implement many-to-many relationships.* A many-to-many relationship is when the maximum multiplicity is "*" on both ends of the association, regardless of the minimum multiplicities. In this situation, the database designer creates a new table to implement the association. The default primary key for the new table is the combination of the two primary keys for the associated tables. In Figure 3.7, for example, each Auto can be serviced by many Dealers, and each Dealer can service many Autos. Thus, the "serviced by" association is implemented by creating a new table with a primary key that includes both Auto_ID and the Dealer_ID (called concatenated or composite key), as shown in Figure 3.8.
5. *Implement relationships among tables.* Create relationships among the relational tables to match the associations shown on the class diagram. After the foreign keys are posted and the linking tables created for the many-to-many relationships, the database designer can implement the relationships as shown in Figure 3.9. Note that each half of the composite primary key for the Serviced_By table acts as a foreign key; Auto_ID in the Serviced_By table links to Auto_ID in the Auto table and Dealer_ID in Serviced_By links to Dealer_ID in the Dealers table.

---

[1]Schemas can also define other database requirements, such as levels of access, but this section focuses on designing the basic elements.

TABLE 3.1
Posting Foreign Keys[a]

[a] The foreign key is the primary key of the related table; however, foreign keys may be assigned different names if it improves understanding.
[b] Foreign keys can be posted in either table, but the minimum multiplicity of 0 indicates an optional association for that table and general rule provides the most efficient option for posting the foreign key.

Multiplicity for A	Multiplicity for B	Relationship Type	General Rules for Posting Foreign Keys
0..1	0..1	One-to-one [b]	Post foreign key in either A or B but not both
0..1	1..1	One-to-one	Post foreign key in A
0..1	0..*	One-to-many	Post foreign key in B
0..1	1..*	One-to-many	Post foreign key in B
1..1	0..1	One-to-one	Post foreign key in B
1..1	1..1	One-to-one	Post foreign key in either A or B but not both
1..1	0..*	One-to-many	Post foreign key in B
1..1	1..*	One-to-many	Post foreign key in B
0..*	0..1	One-to-many	Post foreign key in A
0..*	1..1	One-to-many	Post foreign key in A
0..*	0..*	Many-to-many	Create linking table
0..*	1..*	Many-to-many	Create linking table
1..*	0..1	One-to-many	Post foreign key in A
1..*	1..1	One-to-many	Post foreign key in A
1..*	0..*	Many-to-many	Create linking table
1..*	1..*	Many-to-many	Create linking table

FIGURE 3.8
Implementing a Many-to-Many Relationship
In theory, every relationship type can be implemented with a linking table as shown in this figure.

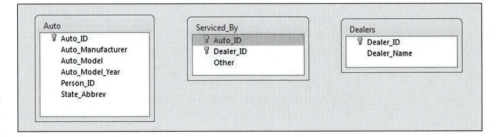

FIGURE 3.9
Mapping Class Diagram Associations to Relationships

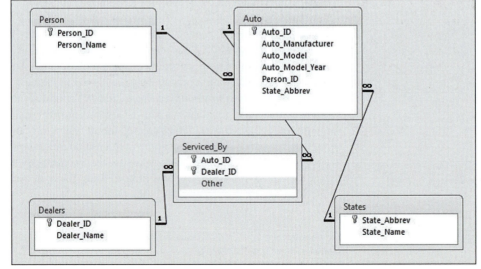

The set of relational tables shown in Figure 3.9 then implements the class diagram shown in Figure 3.4. In other words, the class diagram is the blueprint from which the database is built. Just as inadequate plans result in substandard buildings, an incomplete or erroneous class diagram will result in an ineffective database. It is easier to change the blueprint than change the building, and it is easier to change the class diagram (and ensure that it is correct) than to change the database.

LO 3-5

Describe business rules and the various forms of rules.

BUSINESS RULES

A **business rule** is a succinct statement of a constraint on a business process. It is the logic that guides the behavior of the business in specific situations. Business rules are typically written in text, not modeled; however, they influence the structure and flow of models. Business rules establish multiplicities in class models, and they set criteria for branching in activity models.

There are several forms for business rules. To put these in context, let's consider a simple example of customer payments at a restaurant. Suppose the restaurant accepts cash or credit card payments as long as the credit card is American Express. Additionally, the restaurant only accepts payments in U.S. dollars, not foreign currency, and it does not accept checks. These payment constraints involve the following rule forms:

Rule: Credit card payments are allowed if the card is American Express.

- *Obligatory.* This rule form states what should occur: Payment should be made in U.S. dollars.
- *Prohibited.* This rule form states what should not occur: No payments by check.
- *Allowed.* This rule form says what is allowed under what conditions: Credit card payments are allowed if the card is American Express.

Rules are stated in short sentences as described earlier. In an attempt to formalize the statement of rules, the Object Management Group published a standard, titled "Semantics of Business Vocabulary and Business Rules" (SBVR) in 2008.[2] SBVR sets standards for stating business rules using natural language. The standard describes operative business rules, such as the three forms just described: obligatory, prohibited, and allowed. It also describes similar structural rules that describe fundamental characteristics, such as, "It is necessary that each sale be made to a customer," rather than operating policy rules that are stated in terms of preferred outcomes.

Rules must be enforceable. So, there must be related enforcement-level information that describes how to deal with potential violations. Enforcement levels include strict enforcement, pre-override, and post-override. If a rule is strictly enforced, violations are not authorized. If a rule is subject to pre-override, violations are allowed if authorized in advance. If a rule is subject to post-override, violations are allowed if authorized after the violation. When rules are subject to override, there should also be a statement of who can

---

[2]For further information on SBVR, see www.omg.org/spec/SBVR/1.0/.

authorize a violation. Additionally, certain rules can be considered guidelines, which are generally followed but not enforced. The enforcement level can vary for different parts of the organization.

Rules are valuable because they make modeling business processes easier. They limit the number of options to those allowed by business policy. The rules for a business process establish systems requirements when acquiring new technology. However, rules can also inhibit process improvements because they can be tied to outdated technology. Thus, a close examination of business rules—and the business reasons for them—can reveal unnecessary constraints. In most situations, however, business rules are not stated formally; they are implicit. The process analysis should, therefore, elicit important business rules.

Summary

- Structure models, such as UML class models, describe the information structures of one or more business processes.
- Structure models allow communication about database design.
- Structure models support the design, implementation, and use of databases.
- The building blocks for UML class diagrams include classes, associations, multiplicities, and attributes.
- Attributes for each class include the primary key, foreign keys, and other attributes describing characteristics of the class.
- Primary keys uniquely define each instance of a class (and each row in a relational database table).
- Foreign keys allow tables to be linked together.
- Foreign keys are primary keys of other tables posted in the current table to allow linking.
- Other class diagram relationships include generalizations, aggregations, and compositions.
- Associations model the business purpose of a relationship between two classes, such as the role that members of one class have with respect to the other class.
- UML class models can be used to create tables by mapping classes to tables, mapping class attributes to table fields, mapping associations to foreign keys depending on the multiplicities of the association, and creating new tables to implement many-to-many relationships.
- Business rules establish business policies and constrain business processes.

Key Words

aggregation relationship (53)   A special-purpose UML notation representing the relationship between two classes that are often considered together, such as when a sports league is made up of a collection of teams.

association (51)   UML symbol that depicts the relationship between two classes; it is modeled as a solid line that connects two classes in a model.

attributes (52, 60)   Data elements that describe instances in a class, very much like fields in a database table.

business rule (57)   Succinct statements of constraints on business processes; they provide the logic that guides the behavior of the business in specific situations.

cardinalities (60)   *See* multiplicities.

class (50)   Any separately identifiable collection of things (objects) about which the organization wants to collect and store information. Classes can represent organization resources (e.g., trucks, machines, buildings, cash, investments), persons (e.g., customers, employees), events (e.g., sales, purchases, cash disbursements, cash receipts), and conceptual structures (e.g., accounts, product categories, budgets). Classes are typically implemented as tables in a relational database, where individual instances of the class are represented as rows in the table.

class diagrams (*50*)   Structure models prepared using UML notation.

composition relationship (*53*)   A special-purpose UML notation representing the relationship between two classes that are often considered together, similar to aggregation relationships, except in composition relationships, one class cannot exist without the other, such as a book and the chapters that compose the book.

constraints (*52*)   Optional or mandatory guidance about how a process should perform in certain situations.

data models (*50*)   A graphic representation of the conceptual contents of databases; data models support communication about database contents between users and designers of the database.

entities (*60*)   The people, things, and events in the domain of interest; in UML notation, entities are modeled as classes.

foreign key (FK) (*53*)   Attribute that allows database tables to be linked together; foreign keys are the primary keys of other tables placed in the current table to support the link between the two tables.

generalization relationship (*53*)   A special-purpose UML symbol that supports grouping of things that share common characteristics; it reduces redundancy because the shared characteristics need only be modeled once.

multiplicities (*51*)   UML symbols that describe the minimum and maximum number of times an instance of one class can be associated with instances of another class for a specific association between those two classes; they indicate whether the two classes are part of one-to-one, one-to-many, or many-to-many relationships.

primary key (PK) (*52*)   An attribute or a combination of attributes that uniquely identifies an instance of a class in a data model or a specific row in a table.

relationship (*60*)   The business purpose for the association between two classes or two database tables; *see* association.

structure model (*50*)   A conceptual depiction of a database, such as a UML class model or an entity-relationship model.

Appendix A

Entity-Relationship Diagrams

WHAT IS AN ENTITY-RELATIONSHIP DIAGRAM?

An entity-relationship diagram (ERD) represents graphically the logical data structure of a system, such as a database supporting one or more business processes. ERDs were originally proposed in a 1976 paper[3] by Peter Chen as a tool to capture the conceptual design (schema) of a relational database system, and ERD modeling techniques have evolved over time. Fundamentally, ERDs and UML class models are equivalent tools for modeling data structures.

[3] P. P. Chen, "The Entity-Relationship Model: Toward a Unified View of Data," *ACM Transactions on Database Systems* 1 (1976), pp. 9–36.

BASIC BUILDING BLOCKS OF ERDS

Not surprisingly, the basic building blocks of ERDs include entities and relationships. Each entity has attributes that describe its characteristics. Entities correspond to tables in a relational database where the attributes are the fields in the table. Each relationship indicates a business purpose for connecting two or more entities. Relationships correspond to the links between tables. Cardinalities (i.e., multiplicities) define how one entity links to another. See Figure 3.A1.

Entities represent separately and uniquely identifiable things of interest in a system, for example, customers, employees, sales, inventory, and cash receipts. Entities are modeled as rectangles. Entities correspond to classes in UML class models.

Relationships represent associations between entities, for example, customers (entity) *participate in* (relationship) sales (entity). Relationships are modeled as diamonds. Relationships correspond to associations in UML class models.

Attributes are characteristics of entities; for example, customer attributes could include name, address, city, state, zip code, and credit limit. Attributes correspond to fields in a relational table, so the selection of attributes for an entity should reflect efficient table design as discussed within Chapter 3.

Cardinalities describe the nature of the relationship between two entities; they describe how many instances of an entity relate to one instance of another entity, for example each *customer* may *participate in* many *sales*. Cardinalities correspond to multiplicities in UML class diagrams.

FIGURE 3A.1

Basic Elements of Entity-Relationship Diagrams

Element	Description	Symbol
Entity	Separately and uniquely identifiable things of interest in a system.	Entity
Relationship	Associations between two entities reflecting a business purpose (Chen's notation).	Relationship
Relationship with Cardinalities	Associations between two entities reflecting a business purpose (information engineering style), where the ends indicate the cardinalities.	

ERD EXAMPLE USING CHEN'S NOTATION

Figure 3.A2 shows a simple ERD using min-max cardinality notation. The two entities are Singers and Songs. The relationship between the two entities shows that we are modeling the singers that recorded the songs. This example uses min-max notation to describe the cardinalities. The cardinalities next to the Singers entity indicate the minimum (0) and maximum (N) number of songs that each singer recorded. The cardinalities next to the Songs entity indicate the minimum (1) and maximum (1) number of singers that recorded each song.

FIGURE 3.A2

ERD Example Using Chen's Notation

ERD EXAMPLE USING INFORMATION ENGINEERING NOTATION

Figure 3.A3 shows the same example as Figure 3.A2 using information engineering notation. Again, the two entities are Singers and Songs. In this case, however, the purpose of the relationship between the two entities is not as clearly identified. The "crow's feet" markings on the relationship line indicate the cardinalities. The cardinality notation next to the Singers entity indicates there is one singer for each song. Note that a double line symbol (—⊪—) is sometimes used to indicate one and only one (mandatory). The cardinality notation next to the Songs entity indicates a singer can record many songs (optional). Thus, there may be singers in the database who did not record any songs, but each song must be recorded by one singer.

FIGURE 3.A3
ERD Example
Using Information
Engineering Notation

CARDINALITY OPTIONS

In general, there are four options for each cardinality. The minimum can be zero (the relationship is optional) and the maximum can be either one or many, or the minimum can be one (the relationship is mandatory) and the maximum can again be either one or many. Considering the cardinalities at each end of the relationship between two entities (entity A and entity B), there are three basic types of relationships (see Figure 3.A4):

- *One-to-one (1:1).* One instance of entity A is related only to one instance of entity B. For example, each sale earns one cash receipt.
- *One-to-many (1:N).* One instance of entity A is related to many instances of entity B (or vice versa). For example, a customer participates in many sales.
- *Many-to-many (M:N).* Many instances of entity A are related to each instance of entity B and many instances of entity B are related to entity A. For example, a sale can include many inventory items, and each inventory item could be sold on many sales.

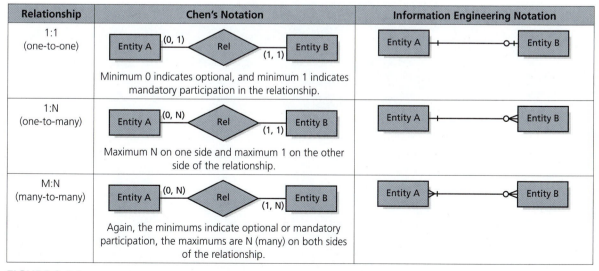

FIGURE 3.A4
Examples of Cardinality Options Using Both Chen's Notation and Information Engineering Notation

Answers to
Progress Checks

1. The class diagram would look something like this:

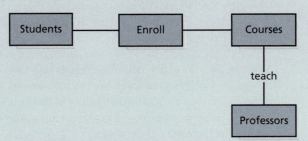

2. With multiplicities:

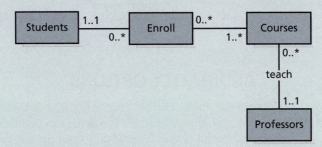

   Note that this assumes that each course only has one professor teaching it and students have not yet enrolled in some courses.

3. The table structure would look something like this:

   Students   [Student ID (PK), Student Name, Student Address, Student email, . . .]

   Enroll   [Enrollment transaction number (PK), Enrollment date, Student ID (FK), . . .]

   Courses   [Course number (PK), Course Name, Course Description, Professor ID (FK), . . .]

   Professors [Professor ID (PK), Professor Name, Professor Department, . . .]

Multiple Choice Questions

1. Which of the following is not an objective of a structure model?
   a. Designate things of interest in the business domain
   b. Describe characteristics of things of interest in the business domain
   c. Support relational database design
   d. Describe the sequence of activities
   e. All of the above are objectives of structure models.

2. Which of the following symbols is used to represent a class in a UML class diagram?

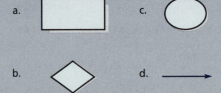

3. Which of the following statements concerning this class diagram with multiplicities is not true?

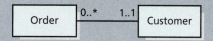

    a. An order can involve only one customer.

    b. A customer can place only one order.

    c. A customer can place many orders.

    d. A customer may not have ordered yet.

    e. All of the above are true.

4. Which of the following statements is true about the following class diagram?

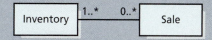

    a. A sale can involve zero inventory items.

    b. A sale can involve one inventory item.

    c. A sale can involve many inventory items.

    d. A and C are true.

    e. B and C are true.

5. Which of the following is an example of an *obligatory* business rule?

    a. Customers must provide a valid credit card number.

    b. Customers must enter a shipping address.

    c. Customers may not enter a post office box as a shipping address.

    d. Customers may use VISA or MASTERCARD.

    e. Both a and b are obligatory business rules.

6. Which of the following is not an enforcement level for a business rule?

    a. Strict enforcement

    b. Optional enforcement

    c. Pre-override enforcement

    d. Post-override enforcement

    e. Guideline

7. Contrast the UML class diagrams with the entity-relationship diagrams shown in Appendix A. Which of the following pairs are not equivalent?

    a. Class and Entity

    b. Class and Relationship

    c. Association and Relationship

    d. Multiplicity and Cardinality

    e. All of these are equivalent.

8. Which of the following best describes the meaning of this diagram?

    a. Each sale can result in many subsequent cash receipts.

    b. Each cash receipt can apply to many sales.

    c. All sales must have cash receipts.

    d. Each sale can result in one cash receipt.

    e. None of the above

9. Which of the following best describes the meaning of this entity-relationship diagram?

   a. Every student is enrolled in many classes.

   b. Every class must have at least one student enrolled.

   c. Every student must be enrolled in at least one class.

   d. No students are enrolled in any classes.

   e. None of the above

10. Which of the following best describes the meaning of this UML class diagram?

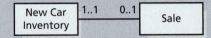

   a. Each new car can be sold once.

   b. A sale can involve multiple new cars.

   c. Each new car can be sold multiple times.

   d. No new cars are in inventory.

   e. None of the above

Discussion Questions

1. Consider the following one-to-one association between classes. You are mapping the diagram to a set of relational tables. Where would you post the foreign key? Why would you post it there?

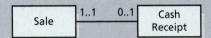

2. Consider the sale and cash receipt classes shown in Discussion Question 1. What kind of business is this (in terms of its payment requirements from customers)? How would the multiplicities change if the business (e.g., a used car dealer) accepted multiple payments over time?

3. Consider the following model and corresponding relational tables. Describe the meaning of the diagram in words. Assume that Students are identified by Student ID Number and Courses are identified by Course Number. List the relational tables that would implement the diagram (you may make assumptions about the nonidentifying fields in the tables).

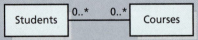

4. Prepare an alternate model for the following. *Hint:* Consider a composition relationship. Which diagram do you think is most descriptive?

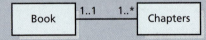

5. Consider the diagram in Discussion Question 4. Describe other circumstances that might be modeled with similar models.

6. Think about the process you went through to enroll in this class. What business rules do you think applied to the enrollment process? Are all of these rules written? Why or why not?

7. Think about the last time that you purchased something over the Internet. What did the checkout page look like? What business rules applied?

8. Compare the UML class diagram shown in Figure 3.7 with the entity-relationship diagram shown in Figure 3.A2. Describe the differences and the similarities.

9. In your college career, you may have attended several universities. Draw a simple UML class diagram or an entity-relationship diagram showing your relationship with those universities. Now add the multiplicities or cardinalities. Would the multiplicities/cardinalities be different if the diagram was drawn from the university's perspective rather than your perspective? Why or why not?

10. Describe some real-world examples of (a) one-to-one relationships, (b) one-to-many relationships, and (c) many-to-many relationships. Which do you think is most common? Which does a relational database handle most easily?

Problems

1. Identify the classes and associations in the following narrative, and draw a class diagram with multiplicities:

   Dr. Franklin runs a small medical clinic specializing in family practice. She has many patients. When the patients visit the clinic, she may perform several tests to diagnose their conditions. She bills the patient one amount for the visit plus additional amounts for each test.

2. Identify the classes and associations in the following narrative, and draw a class diagram with multiplicities:

   Paige ran a small frozen yogurt shop. She bought several flavors of frozen yogurt mix from her yogurt supplier. She bought plastic cups in several sizes from another supplier. She bought cones from a third supplier. She counts yogurt and cones as inventory, but she treats the cups as operating expense and doesn't track any cup inventory.

3. Write out a set of relational tables that correspond to the class diagram that you prepared for Problem 1. Identify primary and foreign keys.

4. Write out a set of relational tables that correspond to the class diagram that you prepared for Problem 2. Identify primary and foreign keys.

Answers to Multiple Choice Questions

1.	e	6.	e
2.	a	7.	b
3.	b	8.	a
4.	e	9.	b
5.	e	10.	a

Relational Databases and Enterprise Systems

A look at this chapter

Databases serve as a means of organizing information. We focus on relational databases that store information in tables. We explore relational database principles, including primary and foreign keys, basic requirements of database design, and data retrieval using Structured Query Language (SQL). We also explain enterprise systems (or ERP systems) using a relational database system and their relevance to the organization.

A look back

Chapter 3 described data modeling, explaining how data models support database-driven systems. It introduced basic data modeling tools to guide the student's development of modeling skills. The chapter also provided a discussion of business rules and how identifying relevant business rules supports both process and data modeling.

A look ahead

Chapters 5 through 8 use data models to describe business processes such as sales to cash collection, procurement to pay, and product conversion.

As **Starbucks'** main competitor in the northeast United States, **Dunkin' Donuts** looks to use relational database technology to help determine who ends up on the corner of your block first!

To help it win this race, **Dunkin' Donuts** is using a new system that helps it more quickly close deals with its new franchisees. Franchisees apply to run a **Dunkin' Donuts** franchise, pay the franchise fee after the approval process, and then pay royalties on each dollar of sales thereafter. **Dunkin' Donuts'** management uses the system to manage information about these potential franchisees, including the status of each potential deal and the status of the franchisee financing. This is particularly important in the competition against **Starbucks**, which doesn't franchise its stores, so its growth isn't delayed by issues with finding suitable franchise operators and getting them signed up to sell coffee in a timely fashion.

Dunkin' Donuts' managers use this dashboard-type system to get a geographic view of regions where deals are stalling; it then has the ability to drill down to see which specific item is slowing down the process. It can identify potential deals in locations that are too close in proximity. Key metrics the company is tracking and monitoring include the average cycle time to complete a franchise deal and the expected size of those deals.

Source: *Informationweek,* 2007, www.informationweek.com/news/global-cio/showArticle.jhtml?articleID=199001001; www.betheboss.ca/franchise_news_april_2007%5Cdunkin-donuts-crm161.cfm.

Chapter Outline

Learning Objectives

After reading this chapter, you should be able to:

4-1 Describe the advantages of relational databases.

4-2 Explain basic relational database principles.

4-3 Describe how to query using Structured Query Language (SQL).

4-4 Understand the purpose and basic framework for an enterprise system.

4-5 Assess how cloud computing facilitates enterprise systems.

INTRODUCTION

A **database** is a collection of related data for various uses. Databases used in a business setting often maintain information about various types of objects (e.g., raw materials inventory), events (e.g., sales transactions), people (e.g., customers), and places (e.g., retail store). In databases today, three types of data models are used: the hierarchical model, the network model, and the relational model.

Hierarchical data models were widely used in mainframe database management systems. Hierarchical data models organize data into a tree-like structure that allows repeating information using defined parent/child relationships. One example of a tree-like structure is financial statements, where a financial statement element (parent) can be decomposed into finer elements (child). More specifically, assets (parent) can be decomposed into current assets (child 1) and noncurrent assets (child 2). Current assets (parent) could be further decomposed into cash and cash equivalents (child 3), accounts receivable (child 4), and inventory (child 5). You can see how the hierarchical relationships define the relationships among the data elements associated with a balance sheet in a tree-like structure. In a hierarchical data model, data elements are related to each other using a notation known as 1:N mapping (one parent: more than one child), also known as one-to-many relationships.

A **network data model** is a flexible model representing objects and their relationships. The network model allows each record to have multiple parent and child records or M:N mapping, also known as many-to-many relationships. These form a lattice structure (often looking like a big net) connecting parent and child records together.

LO 4-1
Describe the advantages of relational databases.

The **relational data model** is a data model that stores information in the form of related two-dimensional tables. It allows designers and users to identify relationships at the time the database is created or much later whenever new informational requirements from the data model are desired. While hierarchical and network data models require relationships to be formed at the database creation, relational data models can be made up as needed.

Relational data models are the dominant data model form in use today, likely because they offer many advantages over other data models, including:

1. *Flexibility and scalability.* As business and informational requirements change, relational data models are able to handle these changes quickly and easily. For this flexibility, the relational data model for databases is the most popular data model today. In fact, most enterprise system-vendors (e.g., SAP, Oracle, Microsoft, etc.) use the relational data model as their foundation.
2. *Simplicity.* A relational data model is a relatively simple model that is easy to communicate to both database users and database developers.
3. *Reduced information redundancy.* A relational data model requires each piece of data to be recorded only in one place, eliminating the need for information to be stored in multiple places in the organization. This also helps keep the information updated because the information only has to be updated once in one database, which can help avoid data inconsistency.

For the remainder of the chapter, we focus on the use of relational databases.

Definitions for Databases

Before we get into the details of how relational databases are created and used in an organization, it is useful to define a few terms related to databases.

- **Database management system (DBMS)**—The DBMS is defined as a computer program that creates, modifies, and queries the database. Specifically, the DBMS is designed to manage a database's storage and retrieval of information.

- **Data dictionary**—The data dictionary describes the data fields in each database record such as field description, field length, field type (e.g., alphanumeric, numeric), and so on.
- **Database administrator**—The database administrator is responsible for the design, implementation, repair, and security of a firm's database.

Progress *Check*

1. A database is an organized collection of data for various uses. Name three uses for a sales database at **Bed Bath & Beyond**.
2. Relational data models allow changes to the data model as information needs change. **General Motors** has recently expanded into China and been very successful. How does the use of a relational data model help **General Motors'** database designers and database users?

FUNDAMENTALS OF RELATIONAL DATABASES

LO 4-2

Explain basic relational database principles.

Entities and Attributes

First, it is important to describe entities and attributes of a relational database. As introduced in Chapter 3, a class in the relational database model could be a person, place, thing, transaction, or event about which information is stored. Customers, sales, products, and employees are all examples of classes. Classes could be grouped into resources (R), events (E), and agents (A) in data modeling.[1] *Resources* are those things that have economic value to a firm, such as cash and products. *Events* are the various business activities conducted in a firm's daily operations, such as sales and purchases. *Agents* are the people who participate in business events, such as customers and salespeople.

Attributes are characteristics, properties, or adjectives that describe each class. Attributes for customer may include the Customer ID, Customer Last Name, Customer First Name, and Customer Address. Attributes for sales could be Invoice Number, Customer ID, Date, and Product Number. Attributes for products may include Product Number, Product Name and Product Price.

There are three main constructs in a relational database: tables, attributes, and records. The primary construct is called a table or relation for data storage, with rows and columns much like a spreadsheet. Each table in a database represents either a class or a relationship among classes. Tables need to be properly linked to make a relational database. The columns in a table are called fields and represent the attributes or characteristics of the class or relationship. The rows in a table are called records or tuples. A record represents all the specific data values that are associated with one instance.

Keys and Relationships

Logical relationships within a relational database model are created by using primary keys and foreign keys. A simplistic illustration of a relational database for Gizmos and Gadgets (a reseller of smartphones) appears in Figure 4.1. As defined in Chapter 3, a **primary key (PK)** is an attribute or combination of attributes that uniquely identify a specific row in a table. Notice the Customer ID in the Customer table is the primary key that uniquely identifies the customer. In this case, the telephone number of the customer serves as the Customer ID. In Figure 4.1, the primary key that uniquely identifies a sale in the Sales table is the invoice

---

[1]The REA model was first conceptualized by William E. McCarthy in 1982. See W.E. McCarthy, "The REA Accounting Model: A Generalized Framework for Accounting Systems in a Shared Data Environment," *The Accounting Review,* July 1982, pp. 554–78.

Products of Gizmos and Gadgets.

number, and the primary key that uniquely identifies each product in the product table is the product number.

A **foreign key (FK)** in the relational database model serves as an attribute in one table that is a primary key in another table. A foreign key provides a logical relationship, or a link, between two tables. For example, notice the link between the Customer table and the Sales table by use of the foreign key, Customer ID, in Figure 4.1. Also, notice the link between the Sales table and the Product table by use of the foreign key Product No. in the Sales table.

FIGURE 4.1
Illustration of a Relational Database Using Primary keys and Foreign Keys for Gizmos and Gadgets, a Phone Reseller

Gizmos and Gadgets   June 17, 2014
Sales Invoice
Invoice #13131

To: Mark Wagstaff
168 Apple Rd., Rockville, MD 20852
602-966-1238

Product No.	Description	Price	Amount
1233	Apple iPhone 5g	399.00	399.00

Order Total   399.00

Customer Table			
Customer ID	**Customer Last Name**	**Customer First Name**	**Customer Address**
602-966-1238	Wagstaff	Mark	168 Apple Rd., Rockville, MD 20852
602-251-7513	Waite	Seth	2500 Campanile Dr., NY, NY 10001

Primary Key

Foreign Key

Sales Table			
Invoice No.	**Customer ID**	**Date**	**Product No.**
13131	602-966-1238	10/17/13	1233
13945	602-966-1238	12/28/13	1334
11995	602-251-7513	2/21/14	1233
12123	602-251-7513	3/11/14	5151
13127	602-251-7513	5/12/14	3135

Primary Key   Foreign Key

Primary Key

Product Table		
Product No.	**Product Name**	**Product Price**
1233	Apple iPhone 5g	399.00
1334	Motorola Droid	299.00
1233	Apple iPhone 5g	399.00
5151	iPhone cover	32.00
3135	Apple Charger	23.00

Basic Requirements of Tables

The approach of relational database imposes requirements on the structure of tables. If these basic requirements are not fulfilled or if data redundancy exists in a database, anomalies may occur. The requirements include the following:

- The **entity integrity rule**—the primary key of a table must have data values (cannot be null).
- The **referential integrity rule**—the data value for a foreign key must either be null or match one of the data values that already exist in the corresponding table.
- Each attribute in a table must have a unique name.
- Values of a specific attribute must be of the same type.
- Each attribute (column) of a record (row) must be single-valued. This requirement forces us to create a relationship table for each many-to-many relationship.
- All other nonkey attributes in a table must describe a characteristic of the class (table) identified by the primary key.

Progress *Check*

3. Describe how primary keys and foreign keys link tables in a relational database. (*Hint:* Use Figure 4.1 to help describe how they work.)

USING MICROSOFT ACCESS TO IMPLEMENT A RELATIONAL DATABASE

Introduction to Microsoft Access

Microsoft Access is a program in the Microsoft Office Suite. Access is a simple database management system that can be used to run databases for individuals and small firms. In practice, many larger firms choose more complicated database systems like MySQL server or Microsoft SQL Server. The Access system is composed of seven objects that are used to implement relational databases.

The basic building block of a database is the *table*. A table is used to store data, which consist of a series of rows (records) and columns (attributes) connected by relationships (links between tables). All data stored in the database will be stored in tables. Tables are linked by the use of foreign keys, forming an interconnected network of records that taken together are the relational database.

When users want to find answers to questions in the database, such as "how many customers do I have?" they use **queries.** Queries are a tool used to retrieve and display data derived from records stored within the database. This can range from listing all customers who live in Oregon, which is a subset (dynaset) of records in the customer table, to the balance in Accounts Payable, which must draw data from multiple tables. Calculations and data sorting are often performed with queries.

Forms are utilized by users to enter data into tables and view existing records. In viewing existing records, forms are powered by queries that allow data from multiple tables to be displayed on each form. Often, a firm that uses a fully electronic accounting information system will allow end users to directly update the database through the use of forms.

Reports are used to integrate data from one or more queries and tables to provide useful information to decision makers. Unlike a form, the report does not allow users to edit database information. In an accounting database, reports might consist of a sales invoice to be mailed to customers or the year-end balance sheet to show stakeholders the financial position of the firm. The applications of reports are limited only by data that have been stored in the database.

Access also allows for web-based forms, called **pages,** which allow data to be entered into the database in real time from outside of the database system. This type of application might be used to allow customers to place orders through the firm's website.

For more advanced users, Access offers **macros.** Macros are defined by users to automate processes such as opening a specific form.

Finally, Access's code can be altered by the use of **modules.** Some Microsoft applications come with modules built in that will be automatically added onto access, like the **PayPal** module that facilitates integration with the organization's **PayPal** account. Other modules can be coded using visual basic script to alter the fundamental processes at the heart of Access.

Steve's Stylin' Sunglasses

Steve's Stylin' Sunglasses (SSS) is a retail store that designs and manufactures custom sunglasses. Every pair of sunglasses Steve creates is unique and is therefore fairly expensive to buy. The excellent reputation for quality products and the stellar customer service provided by SSS have attracted new and returning customers.

To promote sales, Steve, the owner, allows payments to be made periodically over time based on a zero-interest installment plan. However, a down payment is required. Though most customers pay for their sunglasses in full with either cash or credit card, some choose to take advantage of the payment plan option. Steve has noticed that the installment plan is utilized most frequently by customers buying multiple pairs of sunglasses at one time. Steve's policy on installment sales is that each payment from a customer must be clearly marked for one specific sale.

Because Steve is directly supervising two salespeople, who are paid on commission, he prefers to keep all sales separate to facilitate oversight of the revenue cycle. Steve does not collect any data on his customers until they make their first purchase at the store. However, he insists on storing data on every customer, because each customer is entitled to free cleanings and adjustments.

Steve handles the bulk of the behind-the-scenes work at the store, including designing the sunglasses. As a result, he employs two salespeople – Frank and Sandra – who deal with the customers. When a customer walks through the door, the first available salesperson greets and assists that customer from the beginning to the end of the transaction, including helping select the best pair of sunglasses and ringing up the sale on the cash register. To that point, Frank and Sandra also act as the company's cashiers, and in that capacity they take turns making weekly trips to Bank of America to deposit the cash receipts. The company has a few bank accounts with Bank of America.

A Data Model and Attributes for
Steve's Stylin' Sunglasses' Sales Process

In Figure 4.2, we use a UML class diagram to draft a data model for the sales process of Steve's Stylin' Sunglasses (SSS). Notice that an REA data model presents classes in the UML diagram in three general categories: resources, events, and agents.

The central column in Figure 4.2 includes two events (i.e., business activities)—Sales and Cash Receipt. The Sales event conducted by SSS involves one resource (Inventory) and two agents (Salesperson and Customer). The Cash Receipt event involves one resource (Cash) and two agents (Cashier and Customer). The two events are related. One would decrease the resource of SSS (selling inventories), which leads to the other that

FIGURE 4.2
The Data Model for Sales Process of Steve's Stylin' Sunglasses

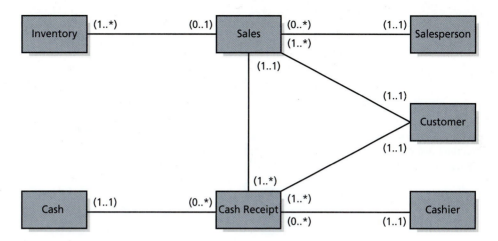

would increase the recourse of SSS (collecting cash). They are economic events involving exchanging resources with external agents (i.e., customers).

Please notice that the class Cash contains information of the bank accounts that SSS has. You can consider Cash as Bank Accounts in the diagram. To simplify, you may also consider each record in the Cash Receipt event as a check from a customer.

Multiplicities in Steve's Stylin' Sunglasses' Data Model

Figures 4.3, 4.4, and 4.5 explain the multiplicities regarding the sales event of Steve's Stylin' Sunglasses.

FIGURE 4.3
Explanations on Multiplicities Related to the Sales Event

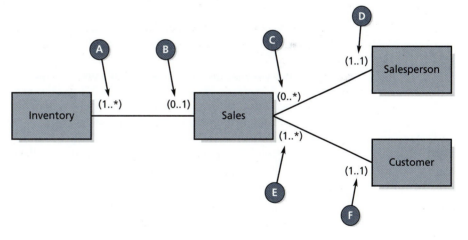

A   SSS may sell more than one pair of sunglasses to a customer at one time.

B   Every pair of sunglasses SSS creates is unique and could be sold once only. Zero means a pair of sunglasses could be designed but not yet sold.

C   The shop employs two employees who can act as salespersons. A salesperson (new) may not handle any sale transaction yet, and at most, each salesperson could handle many sale transactions.

D   One and only one salesperson greets and assists a customer from the beginning to the end of the sale transaction.

E SSS has repeat customers. Customer data are recorded after the first purchase.

F Each sale involves one and only one customer.

FIGURE 4.4
Explanations on Multiplicities Related to the Cash Receipt Event

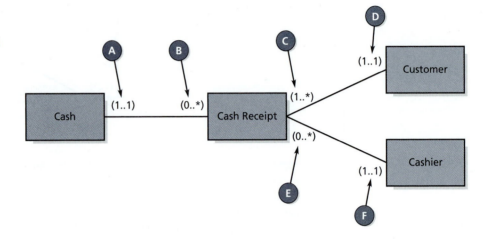

A Each cash receipt is deposited in one and only one bank account.

B Each bank account could have no deposit or many deposits from the cash receipt event.

C Each customer has the option for an installment plan (i.e., SSS will have many cash receipts from one customer). The "1" means a down payment is required.

D Each cash receipt is from one and only one customer.

E The shop employs two employees who can act as cashier. A cashier (new) may not handle any cash receipt yet, or a cashier could take charge of many cash receipts.

F Each cash receipt (e.g., a check from a customer) is handled by one and only one cashier.

FIGURE 4.5
Explanations on Multiplicities between the Sales and Cash Receipt Events

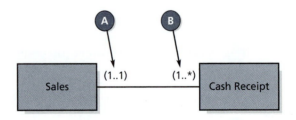

A Each cash receipt is for one and only one sale transaction.

B Each sale transaction may have at least one cash receipt (i.e., a down payment is required), and at most many cash receipts from customers (i.e., installment sales).

Given the data model in Figure 4.2, we assume the following attributes for each table.

Customer	[Customer_Number (PK), Customer_First_Name, Customer_Last_Name, Customer _Address, Customer_City, Customer_State, Customer_Zip, Customer_Email]
Salesperson	[Salesperson_Number (PK), Salesperson_First_Name, Salesperson_Last_Name, Salesperson_SSN]
Cashier	[Cashier_Number (PK), Cashier_First_Name, Cashier_Last_Name, Cashier_SSN]
Sales	[Sale_Number (PK), Sale_Date, Sale_Amount, Payment_Type, Customer_Number (FK), Salesperson_Number (FK)]
Cash_Receipt	[Receipt_Number (PK), Receipt_Date, Receipt_Amount, Customer_number (FK), Cashier_Number (FK), Sale_Number (FK), Account_Number (FK)]
Cash	[Account_Number (PK), Bank_Name, Bank_Address, Bank_Contact_Person, Balance]
Inventory	[InventoryID_Number (PK), Description, Completion_Date, Cost, Price, Sale_Number (FK)]

Using Access to Implement a Simple Database for Steve's Stylin' Sunglasses

Getting Started in Access

Step 1. Open Access.

Step 2. Access will ask you to choose from available templates. Select "Blank database" (see Figure 4.6).

FIGURE 4.6
Starting Access

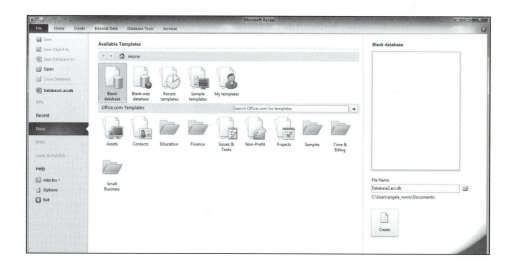

Step 3. To change the name of the database, click File → Save Database As; then save the database as "SSS." You will likely get a message saying "All objects must be closed before you save the database" (see Figure 4.7). Click "Yes."

Step 4. Ensure that the ribbon marked "Enable content" is enabled.

FIGURE 4.7
Save a Database in Access

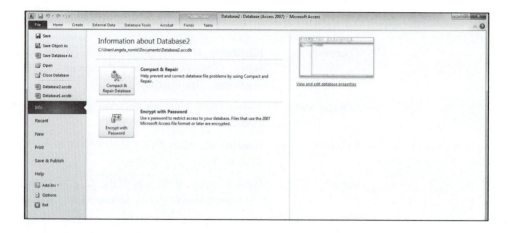

Creating New Tables in Access

Refer to the tables and attributes designed based on the data model (Figure 4.2). This is the database we will be constructing. The first table is the Customer table.

Step 1. Click the tab Create ➔ Table (see Figure 4.8). (Note: The Table Design button will create a table and open it in Design View. See Figure 4.9)

FIGURE 4.8
Create a Table in Access

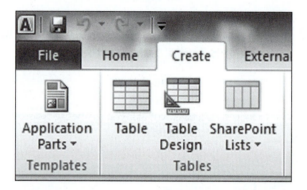

FIGURE 4.9
Create a Table in Design View

Step 2. Click the tab Home ➜ View (dropdown menu) ➜ Design View (see Figure 4.9).
Step 3. You will be promoted to Save As, so save the table as "Customer." This table will contain the records of Steve's Stylin' Sunglasses' customers. Note the Field Name, Data type, Description columns. You will use these to configure the Customer table (see Figure 4.10).

FIGURE 4.10
The Design View of
the Customer Table

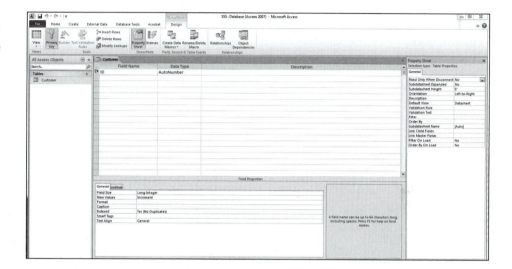

Step 4. The first attribute of the Customer table will be its primary key. Currently, the primary key is named ID. Highlight ID in the Field Name column and change it to "Customer Number." A field name names an attribute in a table. It may contain 64 characters and may not contain periods, exclamation points, or brackets because they are used in Visual Basic scripts. You should see a key icon next to the Customer Number (see Figure 4.11). If it is not there, right click and select "Primary Key" or look for the primary key button on the design tab of the ribbon.

FIGURE 4.11
Create the Primary
Key of the Customer
Table

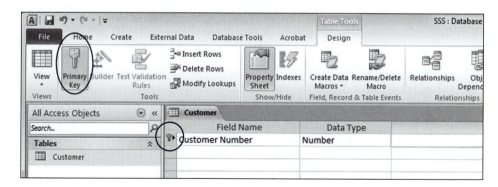

Step 5. Click on the dropdown button for the Data Type and select Number. Take some time to familiarize yourself with the options on this menu. This will force any data entered into this field to be in the form of a number. The Description field, when used, allows useful information about the attribute to be provided to users.

Step 6.   It is a good practice to set Field Properties for each attribute. For example, for Customer Number, we would set the Field Size to Long Integer, the Validation Rule to Like "######". By doing so, we will ensure that all Customer Numbers are six digits long (i.e., six pond signs). The Validation Text of "Customer Number should be 6 digit" provides an error message to tell users what they did wrong. Because this is a primary key, choose the Required field as "Yes" and the Indexed field as "Yes (No Duplicates)" (see Figure 4.12).

FIGURE 4.12
Field Properties for the Primary Key of the Customer Table

Field Properties	
General Lookup	
Field Size	Long Integer
Format	
Decimal Places	Auto
Input Mask	
Caption	
Default Value	
Validation Rule	Like "######"
Validation Text	Customer# should be 6 numbers
Required	Yes
Indexed	Yes (No Duplicates)
Smart Tags	
Text Align	General

Step 7.   For some fields, it is appropriate to use an Input Mask. For example, Customer Zip should have an Input Mask. To do this, select the attribute Customer Zip and click in the Input Mask area in the Field Properties box. You will see to the right a button with ". . ." on it. Click this button to bring up the Input Mask Wizard window as shown in Figure 4.13. Select Zip Code from the menu and click Next and Finish.

FIGURE 4.13
Input Mask for Customer Zip Field

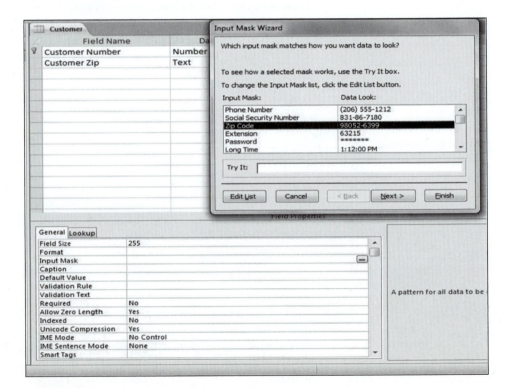

Step 8.   Create the rest of the tables and attributes given before, using appropriate data types and properties. Generally, validation rules are used for primary keys. The attributes of the Sales table are as follows (see Figure 4.14). For other fields such as Sales Date in the Sales table, you will also use Input Masks.

FIGURE 4.14
Attributes of the
Sales Table

	Field Name	Data Type
🔑	Sale Number	Number
	Sale Date	Date/Time
	Sale Amount	Currency
	Payment Type	Text
	Customer Number	Number
	Salesperson Number	Number

Creating Relationships in Access

In order to implement a relationship in Access, you must use a foreign key. Note that the names of the two fields (the primary key in one table and the foreign key in the other table) do not have to be the same. You will create links between these similar fields in Access's Relationship window.

Step 1.   To pull up the Relationship window, click Database Tools ➜ Relationships (see Figure 4.15).

FIGURE 4.15
Open the Relationship
Window in Access

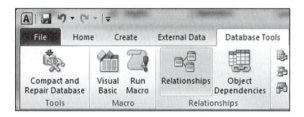

Step 2.   Click the Show Table button in the Design tab to pull up a list of all your tables. Select all your tables and press the Add button. Arrange the tables in the form similar to the data model.

Step 3.   Click each primary key that you want to link, and drag it to its respective foreign key in another table. Be sure to check the "Enforce Referential Integrity" box for each relationship (see Figure 4.16).

FIGURE 4.16
Enforce Referential
Integrity in Linking
Tables

Step 4. When you have completed this process for all relationships among your tables, your Relationship window should look like Figure 4.17. You have created a referential database in Access for Steve's Stylin' Sunglasses.

FIGURE 4.17
A Database for Steve's Stylin' Sunglasses

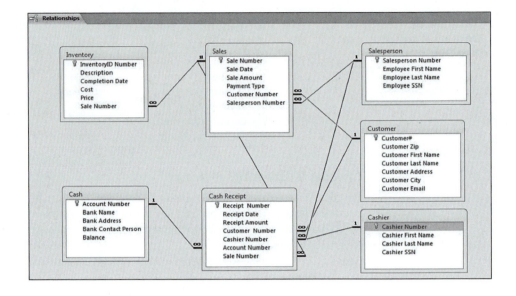

STRUCTURED QUERY LANGUAGE (SQL)

LO 4-3
Describe how to query using Structured Query Language (SQL).

SQL (usually pronounced "Sequel") stands for **Structured Query Language** and is a computer language designed to query data in a relational database. SQL is based on relational algebra and allows a user to query and update the database. In a database, while queries allow the user to access, read, and report on desired data, the responsibility of actually making physical changes to the relational database belongs to the database management system (DBMS).

The SELECT statement is used to begin a query. The SELECT statement tells the query which columns (or attributes) of a table should be included in the query result. A query includes a list of columns in the final result immediately following the SELECT keyword. An asterisk ("*") can also be used to specify that the query should return all columns of the queried tables. SELECT is the most complex statement in SQL, with optional keywords and clauses that include the following:

1. The FROM clause to the SELECT statement indicates the name of table(s) from which to retrieve data.

> **SQL Example 1:** Given the attributes in the Customer table in Figure 4.18, how is a query used to find the salesperson for each customer?

FIGURE 4.18

Customer#	Name	A/R Amt	SP#
C-1	Bill	345	E-12
C-2	Mick	225	E-10
C-3	Keith	718	E-10
C-4	Charlie	828	E-99
C-5	Ron	3,200	E-10

If we use the following SQL commands, we are asking SQL to select the Customer#, Name and SP# attributes from the Customer Table:

SELECT Customer#, Name, SP#

FROM Customer;

We will get the following query result (Figure 4.19):

FIGURE 4.19

Customer#	Name	SP#
C-1	Bill	E-12
C-2	Mick	E-10
C-3	Keith	E-10
C-4	Charlie	E-99
C-5	Ron	E-10

2. The WHERE clause states the criteria that must be met to be shown in the query result. There are many search criteria that you can specify for the final result. Search criteria using relational operators, the between operator, and the like operator are very common in SQL commands (Figure 4.20).

SQL Example 2:

FIGURE 4.20
Cash Receipt

Remittance Advice#	Amount	Bank Account#	Date	Customer Number	Cashier Number
RA-1	1,666	BA-6	25-JUL-2014	C-2	E-39
RA-2	10,000	BA-7	26-JUL-2014	C-2	E-39
RA-3	72,000	BA-7	15-AUG-2014	C-1	E-39
RA-4	32,600	BA-7	15-AUG-2014	C-5	E-39
RA-5	1,669	BA-6	25-AUG-2014	C-2	E-39

If we use the following SQL command, we are asking SQL to retrieve all cash receipt information for customer C-2 from the table called "Cash Receipt."

SELECT *

FROM [Cash Receipt]

WHERE [Customer Number] = 'C-2';

Please note that the asterisk (*) following the SELECT SQL statement is a wild card indicating all columns should be selected. The brackets are needed following the FROM and WHERE clauses because there are spaces in the table and attribute names. In addition, if any table name or attribute name contains a space(s), we have to use brackets such as [Cash Receipt] to make sure it is considered as one table or one attribute in SQL.

We will get the following query result (Figure 4.21):

FIGURE 4.21

Remittance Advice#	Amount	Bank Account#	Date	Customer Number	Cashier Number
RA-1	1,666	BA-6	25-JUL-2014	C-2	E-39
RA-2	10,000	BA-7	26-JUL-2014	C-2	E-39
RA-5	1,669	BA-6	25-AUG-2014	C-2	E-39

Notice the WHERE command eliminated those rows that did not have Customer Number equal to C-2.

SQL Example 3: Assume you would like to use a query to find the salesperson for each customer, and you would like to show the name of each salesperson as part of the result. Data are presented in Figures 4.22 and 4.23.

Customer#	Name	A/R Amt	SP#
C-1	Bill	345	E-12
C-2	Mick	225	E-10
C-3	Keith	718	E-10
C-4	Charlie	828	E-99
C-5	Ron	3,200	E-10

FIGURE 4.22
Customer

SP#	SP_Name
E-10	Howard
E-12	Pattie
E-34	Stephanie
E-99	David

FIGURE 4.23
Salesperson

If we use the following SQL commands, we are asking SQL to select the Customer#, Name, SP#, and SP_Name attributes from the Customer table and Salesperson table:

SELECT Customer#, Name, SP#, SP_Name

FROM Customer, Salesperson

WHERE Customer.SP#=Salesperon. SP#;

It is critical that we include WHERE here to link two tables. SP# is a foreign key in the Customer table. We use it to link Salesperson table with the Customer table.

We will get the following query result (Figure 4.24):

FIGURE 4.24

Customer#	Name	SP#	SP_Name
C-1	Bill	E-12	Pattie
C-2	Mick	E-10	Howard
C-3	Keith	E-10	Howard
C-4	Charlie	E-99	David
C-5	Ron	E-10	Howard

3. The GROUP BY operator is used with aggregate functions on the query results based on one or more columns.

SQL Example 4: Refer to the Cash Receipt table in SQL Example 2. Assume you would like to know the total cash receipt amount from each customer. If you use the following SQL command, you can get the result.

SELECT [Customer Number], SUM(Amount)

FROM [Cash Receipt]

GROUP BY [Customer Number];

The query results will be (Figure 4.25):

FIGURE 4.25

Customer Number	Amount
C-2	13,335
C-1	72,000
C-5	32,600

4. The ORDER BY clause identifies which columns are used to sort the resulting data. If there is no ORDER BY clause, the order of rows returned by an SQL query will not be defined.

> **SQL Example 5:** Refer to the Cash Receipt table in SQL Example 2. if we use the following SQL commands instead, the amount of cash receipt would be ordered in ascending amount (ASC) or descending amount (DESC). The result (Figure 4.26) is different from that of Example 2.
>
> SELECT *
>
> FROM [Cash Receipt]
>
> WHERE [Customer Number] = 'C-2'
>
> ORDER BY Amount ASC;

FIGURE 4.26

Remittance Advice#	Amount	Bank Account#	Date	Customer Number	Cashier Number
RA-1	1,666	BA-6	25-JUL-2014	C-2	E-39
RA-5	1,669	BA-6	25-AUG-2014	C-2	E-39
RA-2	10,000	BA-7	26-JUL-2014	C-2	E-39

5. The INSERT INTO operator inserts data into a SQL table. For example, you can insert a row into the Cash Receipt table with the following SQL command:

> INSERT INTO [Cash Receipt]
>
> VALUES ('RA-6', 5000, 'BA-7', '28-AUG-2014', 'C-2', 'E-39');
>
> After insertion, the Cash Receipt table will have one more row and the result of the execution is as follows (Figure 4.27):

FIGURE 4.27
Cash Receipt

Remittance Advice#	Amount	Bank Account#	Date	Customer Number	Cashier Number
RA-1	1,666	BA-6	25-JUL-2014	C-2	E-39
RA-2	10,000	BA-7	26-JUL-2014	C-2	E-39
RA-3	72,000	BA-7	15-AUG-2014	C-1	E-39
RA-4	32,600	BA-7	15-AUG-2014	C-5	E-39
RA-5	1,669	BA-6	25-AUG-2014	C-2	E-39
RA-6	5,000	BA-7	28-AUG-2014	C-2	E-39

6. The UPDATE operator is for updating data in a SQL table. For example, you can use the following SQL UPDATE command to change the Amount value from 5000 to 6000 for the inserted entry of RA-6. You often need to use the command SET for the updated data value.

> UPDATE [Cash Receipt]
>
> SET Amount = 6000
>
> WHERE [Remittance Advice#] = 'RA-6';

7. The DELETE FROM operator deletes data from a SQL table. For example, to delete the entry previously inserted, you can use the following SQL commands:

> DELETE FROM [Cash Receipt]
>
> WHERE [Remittance Advice#] = 'RA-6';

After executing the DELETE command, the record of Remittance Advice# 'RA-6' will be deleted from Cash Receipt table, and the table will look the same as the original one.

8. The SELECT DISTINCT clause selects a column without showing repetitive values.

   SQL Example 6: Refer to the Cash Receipt table in SQL Example 2. You can retrieve each customer number once from the Cash Receipt table with the following command:

   SELECT DISTINCT [Customer Number]

   FROM [Cash Receipt];

   You will get the following query result (Figure 4.28):

FIGURE 4.28

Customer Number
C-2
C-1
C-5

9. The BETWEEN operator can be used to specify the end points of a range. Possible criteria can be "WHERE Amount BETWEEN 1000 AND 2000" or "WHERE Date BETWEEN '01-JAN-2014' AND '31-DEC-2014'." Assuming that you are interested in finding out cash receipt entries made in July, then you can issue the following SQL command to retrieve those entries.

   SELECT *

   FROM [Cash Receipt]

   WHERE Date BETWEEN '01-JUL-2014' AND '31-JUL-2014';

   The query result will be (Figure 4.29):

FIGURE 4.29

Remittance Advice#	Amount	Bank Account#	Date	Customer Number	Cashier Number
RA-1	1,666	BA-6	25-JUL-2014	C-2	E-39
RA-2	10,000	BA-7	26-JUL-2014	C-2	E-39

10. Membership Operator (IN) allows you to test whether a data value matches the specified target values.

    SQL Example 7: Refer to the Cash Receipt table in SQL Example 2. Assume you would like to know the total cash receipt amount from customers C-1 and C-2. If you use the following SQL command, you can get the result shown in Figure 4.30, which is different from that of Example 4.

    SELECT [Customer Number], SUM(Amount)

    FROM [Cash Receipt]

    WHERE [Customer Number] IN ('C-1', 'C-2')

    GROUP BY [Customer Number];

    The query results will be:

FIGURE 4.30

Customer Number	Amount
C-1	72,000
C-2	13,335

In addition, there are six relational operators in SQL. Their definitions are listed here:

Relational Operators	Meaning
=	equal
! = or < >	not equal
<	less than
< =	less than or equal to
>	greater than
> =	greater than or equal to

Given the data in Figure 4.20, if you are interested in those entries with an amount ≥10000, you can use the following SQL commands.

SELECT *

FROM [Cash Receipt]

WHERE Amount > = 10000;

You will get the following query result back (Figure 4.31):

FIGURE 4.31

Remittance Advice#	Amount	Bank Account#	Date	Customer Number	Cashier Number
RA-2	10,000	BA-7	26-JUL-2014	C-2	E-39
RA-3	72,000	BA-7	15-AUG-2014	C-1	E-39
RA-4	32,600	BA-7	25-AUG-2014	C-5	E-39

SQL language provides several convenient aggregate functions to be used in SQL commands. These aggregate functions include AVG, SUM, MAX, MIN, and COUNT. Their definitions are as follows:

- AVG(X): gives the average of column X.
- SUM(X): gives the summation of all rows that satisfy the selection criteria for column X.
- MAX(X): gives the maximum value of column X.
- MIN(X): gives the minimum value of column X.
- COUNT(X): gives the number of rows that satisfy the given condition.

To query the total amount and average amount from the Cash Receipt table, use

SELECT SUM(Amount), AVG(Amount)

FROM [Cash Receipt];

To query the largest amount entry from the Cash Receipt table, use

SELECT MAX(Amount)

FROM [Cash Receipt];

To query the total amount that occurred in July from the Cash Receipt table, use

SELECT SUM(Amount)

FROM [Cash Receipt]

WHERE Date BETWEEN '01-JUL-2014' AND '31-JUL-2014';

SQL create commands, update commands, and many other SQL query commands as well as SQL functions are beyond the scope of this textbook. See for example, www.w3schools.com/sql/ for a list of popular SQL query commands.

Progress *Check*

4. What does the SQL command SELECT * do?
5. What SQL command would you use to order an amount in descending order?
6. What SQL commands would you use if you wanted to query transactions made in July from the "Cash Receipt" table?

ENTERPRISE SYSTEMS

LO 4-4

Understand the purpose and basic framework for an enterprise system.

Before enterprise systems were developed, each function within the organization (finance, accounting, human resources, procurement, manufacturing, etc.) had its own information system that met its own needs. However, imagine the challenge for a company like **General Motors** to predict, budget, and manage its costs for producing a new Corvette! The company would have to get production information from the manufacturing database, costs from the accounting database, and labor information and costs from the human resources database and attempt to integrate them. Because of these types of problems and the power of integrated information, enterprise systems were developed, including major, commercial enterprise systems such as SAP/ERP, Oracle ERP, and Microsoft Dynamics.

In fact, for a popular ERP product (SAP/ERP) installation, there are 10,000 tables that are all linked to each other!

Enterprise systems (ESs), also known as enterprise resource planning (ERP) systems, are commercialized information systems that integrate and automate business processes across a firm's value chain located within and across organizations. Typically, an enterprise system uses a relational data model as a basis for the information system. The use of primary and foreign keys links the hundreds of tables that form the basis for the enterprise system.

As mentioned in Chapter 1, ESs accommodate the integration and support of the various business processes and information needs of a company by integrating multiple modules to help a manufacturer or other business manage the important parts of its business, including product planning, parts purchasing, inventory maintenance, supplier interaction, customer service, and order tracking. ESs can also include application modules for the accounting, finance, and human resources aspects of a business. ESs are applicable to all types of businesses. In fact, most universities now use enterprise systems to manage course registration and student accounts (including the payment of library fines and parking tickets!).

Figure 4.32 offers a list of potential modules available from SAP. You can quickly see the breadth of the offering that would come from a typical enterprise systems vendor.

Managers (and auditors) can trace the creation of information throughout business processes and also identify the participants in each process. Therefore, ES has a higher level of internal transparency compared to the typically isolated legacy systems. For example, once one user from the sales department enters a customer order, users from the inventory department can see this information immediately and begin to process the customer order. At the same time, users from the accounting department can use this information to prepare the customer invoice and recognize revenue once it has been earned. Database transactions in ES are often designed to track specific details of any given business transaction, including who entered the data into the system, who modified it, and who actually used it.

The purported informational benefits of an enterprise system include enhanced completeness, transparency, and timeliness of information needed to manage effectively an organization's business activities.[2]

[2]H. Klaus, M. Rosemann, and G.G. Gable. "What is ERP?" *Information Systems Frontiers* 2, no. 2, (2000), p. 141.

FIGURE 4.32
List of Modules
Available from SAP

List of SAP Modules Available for Implementation
Financial Applications
FI   Financial Accounting
CO Controlling
EC Enterprise Controlling
IM Investment Management
PS Project System
Human Resources
PA Personnel Administration
PT Personnel Time Management
PY Payroll
Logistics Applications
SD Sales and Distribution
MM Materials Management
PP Production Planning and Control
LE Logistics Execution
QM Quality Management
CS Customer Service

The enterprise system serves as the backbone of the company's internal business processes and serves as a connection with the external business processes for supply chain and customer relationship management systems.

Challenges of Enterprise System Implementation

Although the standard enterprise system software is packaged and technically sound, all types of challenges emerge both from a technical and organizational perspective when it comes time to custom-fit the software to a particular organization's needs. More specifically, organizations face many challenges in implementing enterprise systems, including the following:

1. Integrating various modules within the enterprise system.
2. Integrating with external systems such as the information system of a supplier and/or customer.
3. Integrating with the firm's own existing legacy systems.
4. Converting data from existing legacy systems to the enterprise system.
5. Getting any big project implemented at a firm. This might include scope creep (i.e., increasing the number of changes to the software initially planned), cost overruns, time delays, and so on. In addition, getting adequate training for employees and getting them to actually adopt the new software when they might feel their old system seemed to meet their needs just fine.

These challenges can be overwhelming and some are specifically addressed in Chapter 15. Here, we provide an illustration of a few of the high-profile examples of firms that have had failed or challenged enterprise system implementations, as well as the resulting damage inflicted on the firm:

Hershey was not able to deliver Hershey Kisses for Halloween in 1999 right after the first attempt to implement its enterprise system.

1. **Hershey**

   Hershey spent $115 million on a failed enterprise system implementation attempt of SAP R/3, Siebel CRM, and Manugistics supply chain applications during Halloween season, which caused huge candy disruptions in 1999. This failed attempt prevented Hershey from delivering $100 million worth of Hershey Kisses for Halloween that year, causing a third-quarter sales drop of 12.4 percent. Earnings that year were off by 18.6 percent (compared with the previous year), and that caused the stock price to fall by 8 percent.

2. **Nike**

   In 2000, a $400 million i2 upgrade to Nike's supply chain and enterprise systems gave the shoe and athletic company $100 million in lost sales, a 20 percent stock dip, and a collection of class-action lawsuits.

3. **Hewlett-Packard (HP)**

   In 2004, HP's enterprise system implementation went awry. Gilles Bouchard, then-CIO of HP's global operations, said, "We had a series of small problems, none of which individually would have been too much to handle. But together they created the perfect storm." The project eventually cost HP $160 million in order backlogs and lost revenue—more than five times the project's estimated cost.

4. **Enterprise System Failure at a University**

   During fall semester 2004, more than 27,000 students at the University of Massachusetts, Stanford University, and Indiana University were unable to find their classes and unable to collect their financial aid checks due to a flawed ERP system. However, after a couple of frustrating days and weeks, everyone eventually got their checks and class schedules![3]

5. **Fox Meyer**

   Fox Meyer, once the nation's fourth-largest distributor of pharmaceuticals, blamed its enterprise system fiasco as the reason for its bankruptcy in 1996.

6. **Shane Co.**

   Shane Co., the family-owned jewelry retailer that sought bankruptcy in 2009, told a U.S. judge that the company's decline was triggered partly by delays and cost overruns for a $36 million SAP AG enterprise system.

Enterprise Systems Computing in a Cloud

LO 4-5

Assess how cloud computing facilitates enterprise systems.

Providing sufficient computing power in an organization to run an enterprise system can be challenging. In recent years, **cloud computing** has emerged as a potential alternative to host enterprise systems and other firm computing needs. Cloud computing is Internet-based computing, where shared resources, software, and information are provided to firms

[3]Source: www.cio.com/article/486284/10_Famous_ERP_Disasters_Dustups_and_Disappointments.

on demand. Just like an electrical grid can handle electricity needs on the fly, cloud computing can handle computing needs on the fly. Cloud computing is simply a set of pooled computing resources that are delivered over the Internet.

Cloud Computing can easily host enterprise system applications. Enterprise system applications can quickly scale to the requirements of the computing task by making hundreds of servers and related resources available when they are required. When using cloud computing, firms do not need to worry about buying more computers to meet increasing computing traffic demands or about huge computing traffic spikes. They will simply pay for the computing power they use, much like you pay for the amount of electricity you use in your home or work.

Cloud computing, of course, has disadvantages as well. Ensuring that any sensitive data are secure and backed up frequently by the host is often a concern of cloud computing clients. Making sure the host has minimal down time and adequate processing speed at all times are also concerns. But perhaps the biggest concern is that cloud computing requires the client to have a constant Internet connection. If, for some reason, the Internet connection goes down, the system will not function. This represents an obvious downside on a firm's business that uses cloud computing for its interfaces with their enterprise system.

Progress *Check*

7. Why are enterprise systems so much better than legacy systems that firms are willing to invest the time, money, and effort to risk implementing such systems?
8. From Figure 4.32, which SAP modules would an accounting firm implement to track its billable hours for the audit staff?

Summary

- Relational databases offer efficient, effective databases for a firm. Their flexibility and scalability along with their simplicity offer powerful advantages for a firm and its information systems.
- Relational databases rely on primary and foreign keys to link tables.
- Structured Query Language (SQL) is used with relational databases to query the database.
- Enterprise systems are based on relational databases and link many different modules and functions of the firm to give integrated information to the firm's management and workers throughout the firm.
- Cloud computing is a recent innovation that could host a firm's enterprise systems such as SAP's cloud-based ERP software Business ByDesign.

Key Words

attributes (69)   Characteristics, properties, or adjectives that describe each class.

cloud computing (88)   Internet-based computing, where shared resources, software, and information are provided to firms on demand.

data dictionary (69)   Describes the data fields in each database record such as field description, field length, field type (e.g., alphanumeric, numeric), etc.

database (68)   A shared collection of logically related data for various uses.

database administrator (69)   The person responsible for the design, implementation, repair, and security of a firm's database.

database management system (DBMS) (68)   A computer program that creates, modifies, and queries the database. Specifically, the DBMS is designed to manage a database's storage and retrieval of information.

enterprise system (ES) (86)   Commercialized information system that integrates and automates business processes across a firm's value chain located within and across organizations.

entity integrity rule (71)   The primary key of a table must have data values (cannot be null).

foreign key (FK) (70)   Attribute that allows database tables to be linked together; foreign keys are the primary keys of other tables placed in the current table to support the link between the two tables.

form (71)   Forms are utilized by users to enter data into tables and view existing records.

hierarchical data model (68)   Organizes data into a tree-like structure that allows repeating information using defined parent/child relationships.

macro (72)   Macros are defined by Access users to automate processes such as opening a specific form.

module (72)   Some Microsoft applications come with modules built in that will be automatically added onto Access.

network data model (68)   A flexible model representing objects and their relationships; allows each record to have multiple parent and child records or M:N mapping, also known as many-to-many relationships.

pages (72)   Access pages allow data to be entered into the database in real time from outside of the database system.

primary key (PK) (69)   An attribute or a combination of attributes that uniquely identifies an instance of a class in a data model or a specific row in a table.

query (71)   Query in Access is a tool used to retrieve and display data derived from records stored within the database.

referential integrity rule (71)   The data value for a foreign key must either be null or match one of the data values that already exist in the corresponding table.

relational data model (68)   Stores information in the form of related two-dimensional tables.

report (71)   Reports in Access are used to integrate data from one or more queries and tables to provide useful information to decision makers.

Structured Query Language (SQL) (80)   A computer language designed to retrieve data from a relational database.

Answers to Progress *Checks*

1. There could be different answers for this question. Three possible answers are as follows:
   a. Which **Bed Bath & Beyond** products are selling the best.
   b. Which products the company needs to advertise or which it needs to lower the price of.
   c. How many of which product to order for tomorrow, next week, and next month from its suppliers.
2. If relational data models are not used, database designers and database users have to predict information uses in the future, even when their business model (the way they make money) changes. This is one of the key reasons relational data models (and relational databases) are used.
3. The primary key of one table serves as a foreign key in another table. When they are matched together, they are able to link two distinct tables in preparation for querying, updating, or modifying.
4. The SQL statement "SELECT *" requests that all columns in a table be selected for use in the query.
5. The SQL clause "ORDER BY Amount DESC" would be used.

6. The following SQL commands should be used.

    SELECT *

    FROM [Cash Receipt]

    WHERE Date BETWEEN '01-JUL-2014' AND '31-JUL-2014';

7. The power of integration of the various modules and functions (e.g., accounting, marketing, procurement, manufacturing, etc.) across the organization make an enterprise system particularly valuable to not only management, but also to workers throughout the enterprise.

8. The SAP module PT Personnel Time Management appears to be the most applicable module for tracking billable hours for the audit staff.

Appendix A

Creating a Form for Data Entry and Display

Forms are utilized to enter data into tables and view existing records. This appendix provides a tutorial to create a simple form for Steve's Stylin' Sunglasses (SSS) to enter customer information into the Customer table and display the customer records one by one.

Step 1. Open the SSS database in Microsoft Access.

Step 2. Display all the tables on the left-hand side of database window, and highlight the Customer table. Click on the Form Wizard icon in the form section of the Create tab (Figure 4.A1).

FIGURE 4.A1

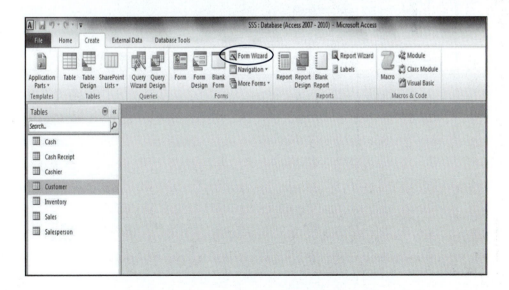

Step 3. In the pop-up Form Wizard window, select Customer table from the Table/Queries pull-down menu, and select all seven fields for inclusion in the form (Figure 4.A2).

FIGURE 4.A2

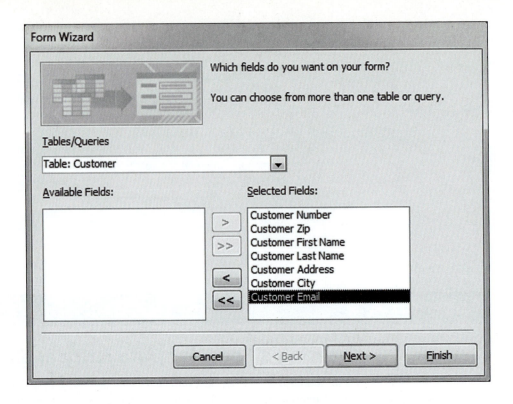

Step 4.   Click the Next button. You will see four types of form layouts. Choose "Columnar" as the form layout (Figure 4.A3).

FIGURE 4.A3

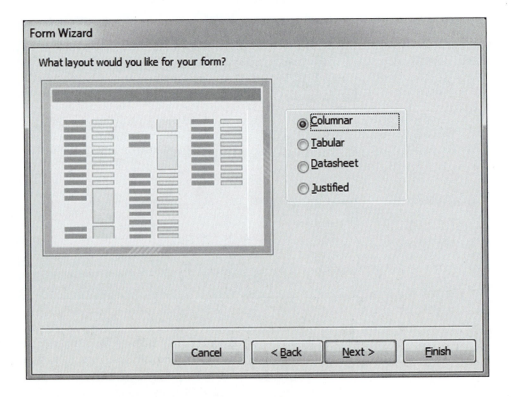

Step 5. Click the Next button. Name the title of the form as "Customer Form," and select "Modify the form's design" as indicated in Figure 4.A4. Click Finish and a screen resembling Figure 4.A5 will appear.

FIGURE 4.A4

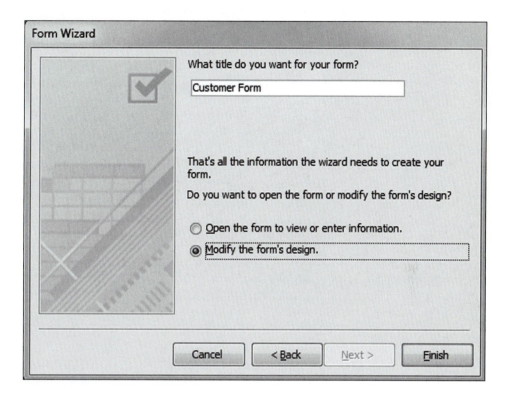

FIGURE 4.A5

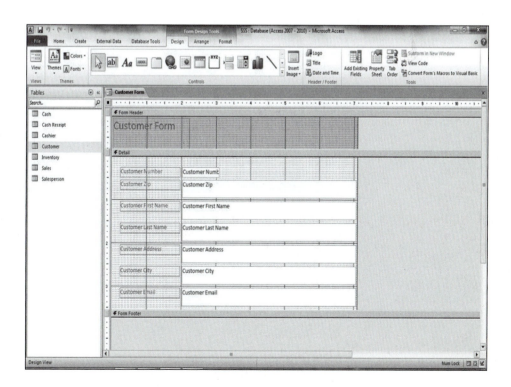

Step 6. Figure 4.A5 is the design view of the Customer Form in which you can format the form. The customer zip text field looks too wide. Select the customer zip field and resize it (Figure 4.A6).

FIGURE 4.A6

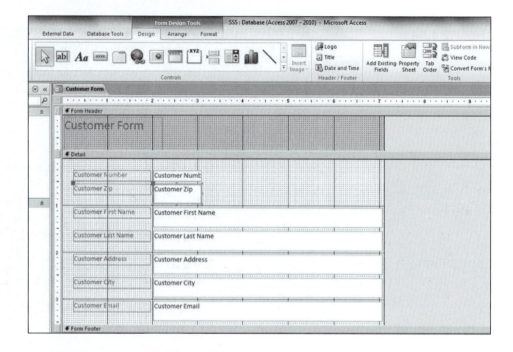

Step 7. Adjust the size of the text field for Customer First Name, Customer Last Name, Customer City, Customer Address, and Customer Email. Make the form look like Figure 4.A7.

FIGURE 4.A7

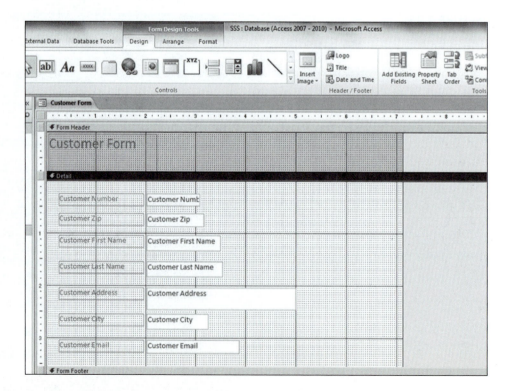

Step 8. In order to enter data using the form, we need to switch to Form View. Click on the Form View icon in the View section of the File tab (Figure 4.A8).

FIGURE 4.A8

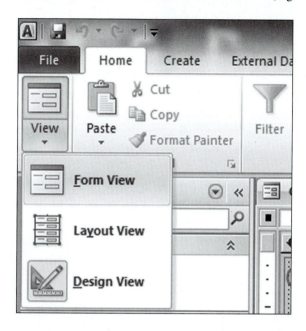

Step 9. In Form View, enter a new customer record as follows—Customer Number: 100001, Customer First name: John, Customer last name: Smith, Customer Address: 2105 East Main Street, Customer zip 80202-4781, Customer city: Denver, Customer Email: Joh_S@gmail.com. If you would like to add the second record using this form, click on the triangle symbol icon on the record line at the bottom of the Customer Form. It will display another blank page for data entry.

Step 10. Close and save the Customer Form. Double click on the Customer Table on the left-hand side of the database window to open the table. You will see the new record has already been entered into the Customer Table (Figure 4.A9).

FIGURE 4.A9

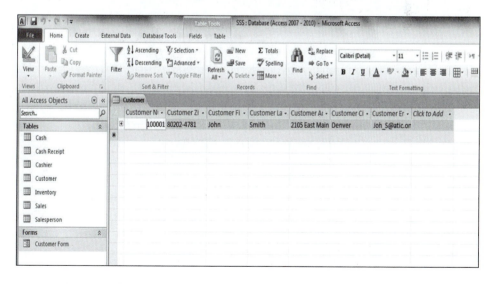

Step 11. Save and close the SSS file.

In this exercise, you learned how to create a form to enter customer information into the Customer table (steps 2 to 7) and how to review customer information one by one using the form (step 9).

Multiple Choice Questions

1. The hierarchical data model, the mapping from parent to child is:
   a. 1:1 (one-to-one)
   b. 1:N (one-to-many)
   c. N:N (many-to-many)
   d. N:1 (many-to-one)

2. Advantages of relational data models generally include:
   a. Flexibility and scalability
   b. Low cost
   c. Ease of implementation
   d. Most reliable

3. A class in a relational database model is defined as:
   a. The sum of a whole
   b. Characteristics or properties of a table
   c. Person, place, thing, transaction, or event about which information is stored
   d. Being or existence, especially when considered as distinct, independent, or self-contained

4. Which statement about enterprise systems is correct?
   a. Most the enterprise systems are designed mainly for accounting and finance functions.
   b. SAP, Oracle, and Microsoft all offer products for enterprise systems.
   c. Most enterprise systems are designed for the service industry.
   d. Small companies do not use enterprise systems at all.

5. Refer to Figure 4.2, if Steve's Stylin' Sunglasses accepts installments without requiring a down payment, the multiplicities between Sales and Cash Receipts should be changed to:
   a. Sales (0..1) − (1..*) Cash Receipts
   b. Sales (1..1) − (0..*) Cash Receipts
   c. Sales (1..1) − (1..1) Cash Receipts
   d. Sales (0..*) − (1..1) Cash Receipts
   e. None of the above is correct.

6. The FROM clause to the SELECT statement used in SQL indicates:
   a. The name of the table(s) from which to retrieve data
   b. The name of the column(s) from which to retrieve data
   c. The name of the database(s) from which to retrieve data
   d. The name of the query from which to retrieve data

7. The WHERE clause to the SELECT statement used in SQL states the criteria that must be met:
   a. To run a query
   b. To be included as an attribute in the table
   c. To be included in the database
   d. To be shown in the query result

8. The "ORDER BY Amount ASC" clause to the SELECT statement used in SQL suggests that the:
   a. Amount of the query result will be listed in ascending order
   b. Amount of the query result will be listed in descending order

c. The data attribute ASC be shown in order

   d. None of the above

9. SAP modules available for implementation include:

   a. Payroll, Personnel Time Management, and Enterprise Management

   b. Payroll, Financial Accounting, and Enterprise Management

   c. Financial Accounting, Payroll, Sales and Distribution

   d. Sales and Distribution, Financial Accounting, and Procurement

10. Cloud computing:

   a. Takes energy from the sun and clouds

   b. Is Internet-based computing, where shared resources, software, and information are provided to firms on demand

   c. Requires a firm to make an extensive investment in hardware and software to meet firm needs

   d. Can meet computing needs today but is not expected to meet tomorrow's computing needs

Discussion Questions

1. Explain the differences among hierarchical, network, and relational data models. What makes the relational data model the most popular data model in use today?

2. What are the basic requirements of a relational database?

3. Structured Query Language (SQL) is used to retrieve data from a database. Why would an accountant need to learn SQL?

4. Figure 4.32 lists the modules available from SAP. List and explain which modules would be most appropriate for either **Maytag** or a manufacturing company you are familiar with.

5. Given the description of **Hershey's** failed enterprise system implementation from the chapter, which of the four challenges of the enterprise described in the chapter seem to best explain what happened? Use **Google** or **Yahoo!** to get more details on this case to help answer this question.

Problems

1. Using the following Cash Table, show the output if the following SQL command is given:

   Select Account#, Balance

   From Cash

   Where Balance < 50000;

   Cash

Account#	Type	Bank	Balance
BA-6	Checking	Boston5	253
BA-7	Checking	Shawmut	48,000
BA-8	Draft	Shawmut	75,000
BA-9	Checking	Boston5	950

2. Using the following Cash Table, show the output if the following SQL command is given:

   SELECT Account#, Balance

   FROM Cash

   WHERE Bank = 'Boston5'

   ORDER BY Amount DESC;

Cash

Account#	Type	Bank	Balance
BA-6	Checking	Boston5	253
BA-7	Checking	Shawmut	48,000
BA-8	Draft	Shawmut	75,000
BA-9	Checking	Boston5	950

3. If Steve's Stylin' Sunglasses (SSS) sells famous, brand-name sunglasses, not custom sunglasses, modify the UML diagram in describing Steve's sales process.

4. List three classes whose information is stored in database that might be used by **NetFlix**.

   a. What are five possible attributes that might be associated with each class (table)?

   b. Can you describe the data dictionary associated with these attributes, including field description, field length, field type, etc.?

   c. Why would **NetFlix** be interested in storing and tracking these five attributes in a table (i.e., to enhance customer service or future customer sales, to sell more affiliated products to customers, etc.)?

5. Cloud computing has plenty of appeal for many firms, especially those that have immense computing needs. Why do you think some might be reluctant to have their data and computing power originating from the cloud?

6. Using the following Cash Table, show the SQL command that will return Type with only checking accounts.

Cash

Account#	Type	Bank	Balance
BA-6	Checking	Boston5	253
BA-7	Checking	Shawmut	48,000
BA-8	Draft	Shawmut	75,000
BA-9	Checking	Boston5	950

7. Using the following Cash Table, show the SQL command that will return the sum of balance.

Cash

Account#	Type	Bank	Balance
BA-6	Checking	Boston5	253
BA-7	Checking	Shawmut	48,000
BA-8	Draft	Shawmut	75,000
BA-9	Checking	Boston5	950

8. Use the *Access_Practice.accdb* database to complete the following tasks in Access.

   a. The database contains three tables containing information about this company's sales process: Inventory, Sales, and SalesItems. Use the Relationships window to link the tables together.

   b. The SalesItems table records the quantity and price of each item sold on each sale (sales may include more than one item). Calculate the extended amount of sale (call it Amt) for each item (Quantity * UnitPrice). Include InvoiceID, InventoryID, Quantity, and UnitPrice in the query. Name the query Item_Extension_Calculation.

c. Calculate the total dollar amount of *each sale*. Include InvoiceID, InvoiceDate, CustomerID, and EmployeeID from the Sales table and the Amt from the Item_Extension_Calculation query. Name the query Sale_Amount_Calculation.

d. Calculate total sales for *each inventory item*.

e. Calculate *total sales*.

f. Calculate the month in which each sale occurred. Include InvoiceID and InvoiceDate from the Sales table. Name the query Sales_Months. (*Hint:* Look for the Month function in the expression builder.)

g. Calculate the sum of sales for each month.

9. This problem continues Problem 8. Use the **Access_Practice.accdb** database that you have been working on to complete the following tasks.

a. Go to the Relationships screen and connect the five tables, enforcing referential integrity.

b. Calculate the total sales for each customer. Include CustomerID and CompanyName from the Customer table and the calculated sale amount from the Sale_Amount_ Calculation query. Name the query Total_Customer_Sales.

c. Generate an e-mail user name for each employee using the first letter of the employee's first name and the first five letters of the employee's last name, e.g., Rod Smith = > rsmith. Include EmployeeID, EmployeeFirstName, and EmployeeLastName in the query. Name the query Employee_Email_Generator.

d. Calculate the total sales for each month.

e. Determine which customer had the highest average sales amount. (*Hint:* Sort in descending order.)

f. Assume the employees earn a 5 percent commission on sales. Calculate the total commission due to each employee. Use two queries to do these calculations.

Answers to Multiple Choice Questions

1.	b	6.	a
2.	a	7.	d
3.	c	8.	a
4.	b	9.	c
5.	d	10.	b

Part Two

Business Processes

Chapter **Five**

Sales and Collections Business Process

A look at this chapter

This chapter examines the sales and cash collection process. We use a comprehensive example to develop activity and structure models of the process. We show how the activity model in conjunction with business rules can be used to develop, implement, and monitor control activities. We show how the structure model can be used to develop a relational database to support information processing requirements. The chapter includes a comprehensive exercise in which students prepare UML class models and then develop the corresponding Microsoft Access database to prepare specific financial information.

A look back

Chapters 2 and 3 described types of business process models and introduced basic modeling tools to guide the student's development of modeling skills. Chapter 4 introduced relational databases and Microsoft Access. We use those skills to examine activity and structure models for the sales and collection process.

A look ahead

In the next chapter, we examine the purchasing and cash disbursement process. We again use the basic modeling tools from Chapters 2, 3, and 4 to examine activity and structure models and corresponding database structures for the process.

In April 2008, **Starbucks** started offering additional benefits to registered **Starbucks** Card holders when they use their cards at **Starbucks** stores in the United States and Canada:

1. Complimentary customization on select syrups and milk alternatives (e.g., soy milk).
2. Complimentary Tall beverage of choice with the purchase of one pound of whole bean coffee.
3. Free refills on brewed coffee during the same visit.
4. Two hours daily of free, in-store Wi-Fi.
5. The opportunity to join **Starbucks** in supporting charitable causes.

Speaking about this sales initiative, **Starbucks** CEO Howard Schultz said, "Already, one in seven customers uses the **Starbucks** Card, and now we are taking the first steps toward recognizing these customers by providing them value beyond any other coffeehouse. It is the personal relationship our customers have with our brand, our stores and our baristas that is the foundation of our success. Through this initiative, we are making it even easier to make the **Starbucks** Experience your own."

At the same time, **Starbucks** introduced its Pike Place Roast aimed at providing its customers a "unique, consistent, and fresh brewed coffee experience." It also began making coffee in smaller batches to ensure that its coffee is always fresh.

Starbucks' senior management clearly recognizes the importance of its sales process, and the continuing improvement of its customers' experiences, to its success and long-term growth. What kinds of information do you think Starbucks needs to manage and improve its sales process?

Chapter Outline

Learning Objectives

After reading this chapter, you should be able to:

5-1 Describe the business activities that comprise the sales and collection process.

5-2 Develop an activity model of the sales and collection process using BPMN.

5-3 Understand and apply different activity modeling options.

5-4 Develop business rules to implement controls for the sales and collection process.

5-5 Develop a structure model for the sales and collection process using UML class diagrams.

5-6 Use multiplicities to implement foreign keys in relational tables.

5-7 Implement a relational database from the UML class diagram of the sales and collection process.

LO 5-1
Describe the business
activities that comprise
the sales and collection
process.

SALES AND COLLECTION PROCESS

The sales and collection process includes business activities related to selling products and services, maintaining customer records, billing customers, and recording payments from customers. It also includes activities necessary to manage accounts receivable, such as aging accounts and authorizing credit. Certainly, the sales and collection processes generate accounting transactions to record revenue, accounts receivable, and cash receipts. They also affect cost of goods sold and inventory for companies that sell merchandise.

Figure 5.1 describes typical accounting transactions resulting from the sales and collection process. **Sales** are typically made in exchange for **cash** or credit. The transaction may also require collection of sales tax. A cash sale increases cash. A credit sale results in an account receivable. **Accounts receivable** are monies owed to the firm from the sale of **products** or services. A sale of goods also results in a corresponding recognition of cost of goods sold expense and reduction of inventory. When the customer subsequently pays for the goods or services sold on credit, cash is increased and accounts receivable are reduced.

We apply the tools introduced in Chapters 2, 3, and 4 to a comprehensive example of the sales and collection process. For this example, we take on the role of business analysts helping a small business, Sunset Graphics Inc., document its business processes. In this chapter, we first describe the sales and collection activities using BPMN, and then we define the typical information structure using UML class diagrams. Finally, we use the UML class diagrams to build a database to collect and report sales and collection information. Throughout, we describe business rules that establish potential process controls.

FIGURE 5.1
Accounting
Transactions for the
Sales and Collection
Process

Oct 1	Accounts Receivable		1,350.54	
	Sales Tax Payable			100.04
	Sales			1,250.50
	Sold products on credit to Smith, Inc. Invoice No. 459			
Oct 1	Cash		1,452.87	
	Sales Tax Payable			107.62
	Sales			1,345.25
	Sold products for cash			
Oct 1	Cost of goods sold		750.30	
	Inventory			750.30
	Recording cost of sales			
Oct 31	Cash		1,350.54	
	Accounts Receivable			1,350.54
	Received payment from Smith, Inc. for Invoice No. 459			

SUNSET GRAPHICS EXAMPLE

Company Overview

Virgil and Linda B (their family name is Bartolomucci, but everyone calls them Mr. and Mrs. B) started their company more than 20 years ago and have grown it into a successful graphic design and printing business. They design and sell signs and banners, lettering and vinyl graphics for vehicles and boats, corporate promotional items, and silk-screened T-shirts and embroidered gear, among other products. Recently, Virgil and Linda decided that they wanted to try and step back from the day-to-day operations. Before they did that, they decided that it was time to review their business processes to develop better documentation, improve processes, and establish consistency in customer service. They also wanted to be sure that effective internal controls were in place, because they wouldn't be on site as often.

Sunset Graphics' Sales and Collection Process Description

Because most of its products are designed to customer specifications, Sunset usually prepares a **quote** for the **customer** that carefully describes the products and services it will provide. If the customer likes the quote, he or she will place the **sales order** for all or part of the quoted products and services. At that point, Sunset may

Designing for customer specifications.

order any products not in inventory from its suppliers. When it receives the products, Sunset then applies the graphics. When the entire order is complete, Sunset delivers the products to the customer. In some cases Sunset applies the graphics or installs the products at the customer's site. When the job is complete, it bills the customer and either collects payment immediately or allows the customer to pay within 30 days, depending on the customer's credit.

LO 5-2
Develop an activity model of the sales and collection process using BPMN.

SUNSET GRAPHICS' ACTIVITY MODELS

Basic Sales Activity Model

After talking with Virgil and Linda B about their sales and collection process, our first task was to draw a simple activity model using BPMN. As shown in Figure 5.2, the start of the process occurs when the customer requests a quote. Then, a series of tasks takes place in sequence until the customer pays for the products and services and the process ends. Sunset records sales when the products and services are delivered to the customer. Although some customers do not place orders after getting a quote, Virgil allowed that most do.

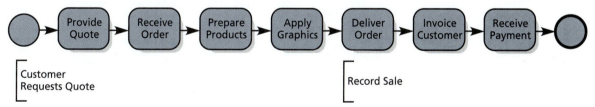

FIGURE 5.2
Basic Sales Activity Model

LO 5-3
Understand and apply different activity modeling options.

Refining the Model to Show Collaboration

Business process analysis is an iterative process. After thinking about the basic model, Linda remarked that much of their business involved interaction with customers, and the basic model doesn't really show that interaction. We agreed, but said that BPMN also allows *pools* that show different participants in a process. *Message flows* (shown by dashed arrows) between pools describe the interaction between participants. To illustrate, we prepared Figure 5.3 that shows the customer's activities in one pool and Sunset Graphics' activities in the other pool. We explained that each pool needs a start and end event, and the *sequence flow* (shown by the solid arrows) within a pool continues from the start event to the end event without a break. This type of activity model is called a **collaboration** model in BPMN, and the interaction between participants is called **choreography.**

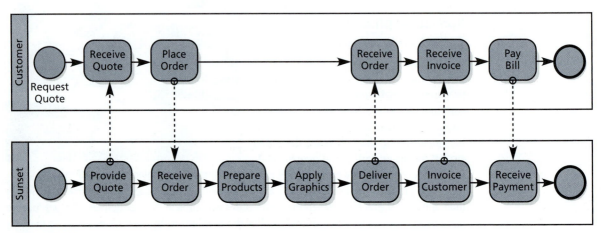

FIGURE 5.3
Collaboration Sales Activity Model

Linda said that this model more clearly shows the interactions, but she really did not care about the customers' activities. She was just concerned about the choreography of interactions between the pools and the orchestration of Sunset's activities (the sequence of activities within one pool is called an **orchestration**). We understood and changed the model. Figure 5.4 now hides the customer's activities, but it shows the important message flows between participants. We told Linda that we could also hide Sunset's activities and just show the choreography between participants, but she liked this model.

Progress *Check*

1. What information does the collaboration model in Figure 5.4 tell you that is different from the basic model shown in Figure 5.2?
2. From your own experience, describe how you would change Figure 5.4 to reflect another sales and collection process.

Refining the Model to Consider Exceptions

Virgil then asked how we would model potential exceptions to the typical process flow. For example, he said that sometimes Sunset's suppliers don't have the products that Sunset needs to complete the job, and it has to notify the customer and cancel the job. We weren't ready to model details of the purchasing process, yet, but we could model it generally as a *collapsed* **subprocess** and also allow for the exception. A collapsed subprocess contains a series of steps that are hidden from view. Because this was getting more complicated, we temporarily dropped the pools and revised the basic sales model.

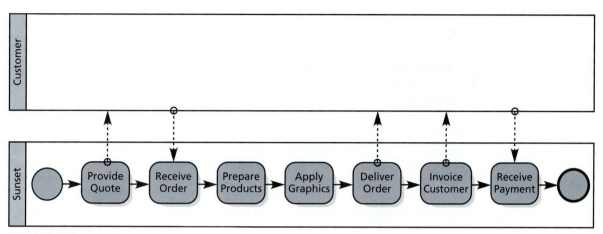

FIGURE 5.4
Collaboration Sales Activity Model

Figure 5.5 now models the purchasing exception when products are not available. We show the exception that occurs when the product is not available as an *intermediate* **error event** attached to the subprocess. When the exception occurs, the customer is notified and the process ends. Under normal conditions, the process continues as before.

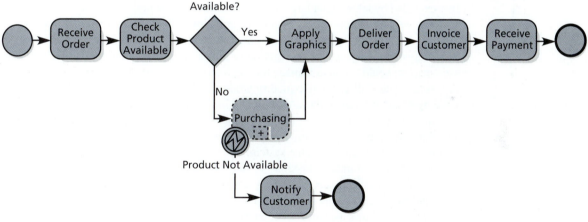

FIGURE 5.5
Sales Activity Model with Exception

LO 5-4
Develop business rules to implement controls for the sales and collection process.

BUSINESS RULES AND SUNSET GRAPHICS' SALES AND COLLECTION PROCESS CONTROLS

Next, we wanted to talk about controls over the sales and collection process, because Virgil and Linda planned to step back from the day-to-day operations. We said that we would like to implement controls by developing business rules for the process. We explained to Virgil and Linda that a business rule is a compact statement that constrains some aspect of business activity. Business rules help ensure that information systems operate in a consistent and effective manner to achieve organizational objectives.

Virgil remarked that business rules seemed similar to internal controls. He quickly pulled out his laptop and went to the COSO website, www.coso.org.[1] He paraphrased its definition,

[1]See Chapter 10 for more complete explanation of COSO (Committee of Sponsoring Organizations of the Treadway Commission) and internal control elements.

"Internal control is broadly defined as a process designed to provide reasonable assurance regarding the effectiveness and efficiency of operations, reliability of financial reporting, and compliance with applicable laws and regulations." We answered that business rules are not processes; they are constraints on the process. However, you could think of business rules as control activities. COSO describes control activities as including approvals, authorizations, verifications, reconciliations, reviews of operating performance, security of assets, segregation of duties, and other activities designed to address risks to achievement of the entity's objectives. After thinking about it, Virgil agreed. He understood that business rules implement specific control activities for a particular business process. He just wasn't sure how to do it.

We explained that the first step is to identify important business events. We need to know your intention or objective for each event. Then, we determine the appropriate actions to take based on the conditions. For example, we've already listed important business events in the activity models, so let's examine Sunset's sales and collection process in Figure 5.4 and develop some possible business rules.

Both Virgil and Linda were now involved, so we started with the first step in the process: provide quote. We asked what their intention was for this step. They replied that they wanted to provide quotes accurately and promptly because the quote was extremely important in winning the customer's business. We then asked about the constraints that should be applied to the activity because a Sunset partner would prepare the quotes in the future. Virgil responded that the partner should provide the quote to the customer within one day of the customer's request. Linda added that they wanted to control approvals so that a manager approved large value quotes. That way, they could be sure that Sunset would not be overextended by taking on a large job that it could not accomplish on time.

Next, we asked about the accounting information system controls over the process. We explained that **access controls** limit who can use and change records in the system. This helps implement appropriate segregation of duties. Virgil said that the partners who provide quotes should not also manage the inventory and set prices, so they should not have access that would allow them to modify product and price information. Finally, we said we need **application controls** to ensure data integrity and an audit trail. For example, we need to control the assignment of quote numbers to make sure all of them are accounted for. Plus, we need to establish appropriate ranges or limits for each value that Sunset's partners can add or change in the system.

With Virgil and Linda's direction, we were able to develop an initial set of business rules for the sales and collection process. They articulated their intentions for every step in the process, and then we set business rules to segregate duties and limit partner authority appropriately. Table 5.1 shows the initial set of business rules for Sunset's sales and collection process.

Process Steps	Intention	Partner Authority/Action	Access Controls	Application Controls
Provide Quote	Provide quotes promptly and accurately.	Partner must provide quote within 1 business day of request; manager must approve quotes >$5,000.	Partners preparing quotes cannot modify established product and service prices.	System must provide quote number control, default values, range and limit checks, and create audit trail.
Receive Order	Record order promptly and accurately; ensure customer credit is authorized.	Partner must record order within 1 hour of receipt; manager must approve orders >$5,000; credit manager must approve credit order >$1,000.	Partners accepting orders cannot modify established product and service prices; partners accepting orders cannot approve request for customer credit >$1,000.	System must provide order number control, default values, range and limit checks, and create audit trail; system links quote to order.

TABLE 5.1
Using Business Rules to Implement Internal Controls

Process Steps	Intention	Partner Authority/Action	Access Controls	Application Controls
Prepare Products and Apply Graphics	Prepare products promptly; ensure products match order; ensure quality products.	Partner must check all products for defects and show defective products/graphics to manager; partner must prepare products and apply graphics to meet required delivery schedule.	Partners preparing products cannot modify order.	System must allow the partner to modify only the status information; system must assign current date by default.
Deliver Order	Deliver order on date requested; ensure customer accepts delivery.	Partner delivering order must verify that delivery matches order.	Partners delivering products cannot modify order.	System must supply delivery information and not allow modification.
Invoice Customer	Invoice customer promptly; monitor until paid.	Partner must invoice customer no later than 3 business days after delivery.	Partner preparing invoice cannot modify order; before preparing the invoice, make sure the product has been delivered.	System must supply invoice number; invoice information must be filled in automatically from order.
Receive Payment	Record and deposit receipt promptly.	Partner receiving payment must record receipt immediately and deposit intact on same day.	Partner receiving payment cannot modify order or invoice.	System must supply receipt number, default to current date, default payment value to order amount.

TABLE 5.1
(continued)

LO 5-5
Develop a structure model for the sales and collection process using UML class diagrams.

SUNSET GRAPHICS' STRUCTURE MODELS

We proceeded to examine Sunset Graphics' information requirements by preparing UML class diagrams that describe their sales and collection process. As described in Chapter 3, the primary purpose of a UML model of the sales and collection process is to create a blueprint for the development of a relational database to support the collection, aggregation, and communication of process information. To develop UML class diagrams, we follow the **REA** framework (resources, events, and agents) as a proven approach to describing business processes in a way that meets both accounting and broad management information requirements.

UML Class Model for Quotes

Virgil and Linda B outlined Sunset's process for preparing quotes for customers. They call their employees partners. In this case, a Sunset partner works with the customer to document how Sunset will meet the customer's requirements. The Sunset partner will prepare the quote, and the customer will confirm the quote. The quote specifies the prices and quantities of Sunset's products and services to be delivered. So, our preliminary model shows Sunset's **resources** (products), the Quote **event,** and the two **agents** (Sunset Partner and Customer) that participate in the event.

In Figure 5.6, we've numbered the three relevant associations: (1) the Sunset Partner to Quote event association, (2) the Customer to Quote event association, and (3) the Quote events to Products resource association. The multiplicities for association number 1 indicates that each Sunset Partner may participate in a minimum of zero Quotes and a maximum of many Quotes, but each Quote involves only one Sunset Partner.[2] Similarly, for

[2]When describing multiplicities, we refer to the instances of the class—for example, Quotes refers to the individual quotes that are instances of the Quote class (or rows in the Quote table).

association number 2, each Customer may participate in zero to many Quotes and each Quote is prepared for only one Customer. For association number 3 each Quote specifies prices and quantities for at least one product (minimum of one and maximum of many). Each product may be listed on many quotes (but some products may not yet be listed on quotes). Associations 1 and 2 represent **one-to-many relationships** between classes. Association number 3 represents a **many-to-many relationship.** As we discuss later, the nature of these relationships determines how the associations are implemented in the relational database.

FIGURE 5.6
UML Class Diagram for Quotes

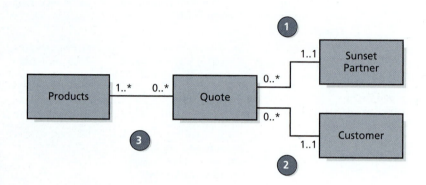

UML Class Model for Adding Orders

Next, Virgil and Linda B described how Sunset's quotes typically result in one or more orders from the customer. Of course, the same customer is involved in both the quote and the order, but a different Sunset partner could take the order. Sunset does not always prepare quotes prior to taking an order because some of its products are ready for delivery and do not need to be customized. When the customer places the order, Sunset has a formal commitment from the customer that will result in a sale when Sunset completes the delivery. Sunset does not deliver products and services until the order is complete, so there is a one-to-one relationship between orders and subsequent sales.

Figure 5.7 adds the Order event. We highlight association 4, because it links the Customer's order to the previous quote. Other associations with Order are similar to associations with Quote. The multiplicities for association 4 indicate that each Quote is related to a minimum of zero Orders, which may happen if the Customer does not place an order but also indicates that orders follow quotes in time (i.e., there can be delay between the quote and the customer order). Each Quote may be related to more than one Order if the Customer places partial orders, such as when the customer needs certain products and services immediately but others can wait. Orders are related to a minimum of zero Quotes and a maximum of one Quote.

FIGURE 5.7
UML Class Diagram for Orders and Quotes

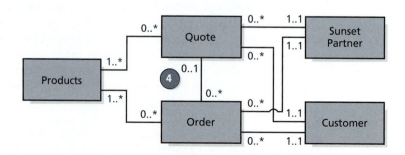

UML Class Model for Adding Cash Receipts

Linda B then remarked that some customers pay Sunset as soon as they deliver the products and services. However, Virgil said that Sunset's business and government customers are usually offered credit terms. In some situations, the customers may send one check for several orders. In any case, a Sunset partner records the **cash receipt** from the customer. All cash receipts are deposited in their primary bank account daily.

Figure 5.8 adds the Cash Receipt event and the Cash resource (e.g., bank accounts) to the UML class diagram. As with Orders and Quotes, a Sunset Partner and Customer both participate in the Cash Receipt event, and the multiplicities for these associations are similar to the earlier associations between agents and events. We've highlighted the association between Orders and Cash Receipts *events* (number 5) and the association between the Cash Receipts event and the Cash resource (number 6). For association number 5, the multiplicities indicate that each Cash Receipt is linked with a minimum of one Order and a maximum of many Orders (one customer payment for multiple orders), and each Order is linked to a minimum of zero (not paid yet) and a maximum of one (paid in full) Cash Receipt. Thus, the delivered Orders for which there are no Cash Receipts define Sunset's accounts receivable. For association number 6, the multiplicities indicate that each Cash Receipt is deposited into one account (Cash resource), and each account could have many Cash Receipts.

Progress *Check*

3. Describe when a sales/order might be preceded by the quote activity.
4. Could the order event be divided into two events: orders and sales? If so, when does this make sense?

FIGURE 5.8
UML Class Diagram for Orders and Cash Receipts

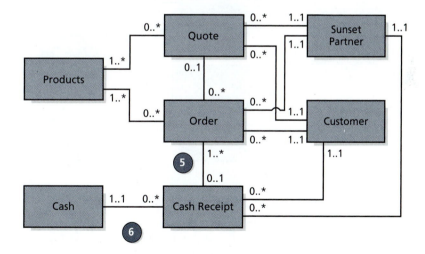

UML Class Model for Adding Categorical Information

Both Virgil and Linda now agree that the model generally represents their sales and collection process, but they wondered how to include product categories and order status information that they use for management. For example, they categorize their products into t-shirts and gear for silk screening and embroidery, lettering material for vehicles and boats, sign and banner material, customer artwork, and printing materials (card stock and stationary items). Additionally, they have a number of different categories for their promotional products. They also track the status of their orders (e.g., waiting for supply, pending graphic application, ready for delivery, and delivered).

We replied that companies often apply guidelines, constraints, and descriptive information to their resources, events, and agents to help manage the business process. Additionally, companies need to summarize the economic activity to support management's information requirements. Generically, these other classes can be called **type images**.[3] For Sunset, we can model product category and order status information by adding two classes to the basic model as shown in Figure 5.9.

In Figure 5.9, the Product Category and Order Status classes allow Sunset to establish appropriate categories for the related classes (i.e., Products for Product Categories and Orders for Order Status). The number 7 highlights the two associations between the underlying class and its type image. The multiplicities for both associations reflect that each category/status can apply to many instances of the underlying class. For example, each Product Category comprises many Products. Once implemented in a relational database, these type images allow process information to be summarized by category.

Type images could also support control activities by designating responsibilities. For example, a Sunset Partner could be assigned inventory management responsibility for one or more Product Categories, as shown by association number 5. The multiplicities for association number 8 indicate that one Sunset Partner is assigned to each Product Category, but some Sunset Partners could be assigned to manage multiple Product Categories.

FIGURE 5.9
UML Class Diagram for Orders and Cash Receipts with Type Images

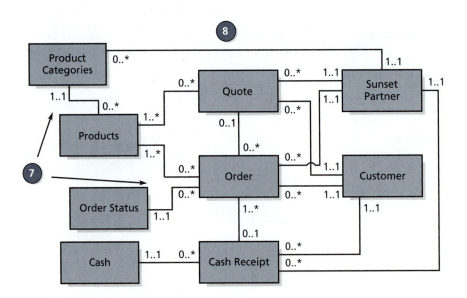

LO 5-6

Use multiplicities to implement foreign keys in relational tables.

UML Class Model for Supporting Relational Database Planning

Virgil B had no more questions about the UML class diagrams of Sunset's sales and collection process, but he did wonder how the model would be implemented in the relational database. He knew that relational databases implement links between tables through foreign keys.[4] "How do you know where to put the foreign keys," he asked.

We said that once you understand the multiplicities, it is pretty easy to determine where to put the foreign keys. Let's use some of the associations that we've already discussed as examples. Figure 5.10 shows the one-to-many relationship between Customers and Orders. We've included some sample attributes for the classes. The <<pk>> notation indicates the

---

[3]See, e.g., G. Geerts and W. McCarthy, "Policy Level Specifications in REA Enterprise Information Systems," *Journal of Information Systems* 20, no. (2006), pp. 37–63.
[4]See Chapter 4 for a complete discussion of foreign keys and referential integrity.

FIGURE 5.10
**Using Multiplicities
to Determine Foreign
Key Implementation
for One-to-Many
Relationships**

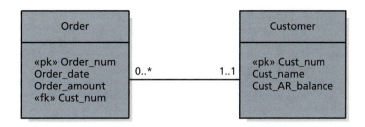

primary keys; the <<fk>> notation indicates the foreign keys. Thus, *cust_num* (customer number) is the primary key for the Customer table, and *order_num* (order number) is the primary key for the Order table. The multiplicities indicate that each Customer can be linked with multiple Orders, but each Order only involves one Customer. Foreign keys are primary keys of linked tables, so either the *cust_num* is a foreign key in the Orders table or the *order_num* is the foreign key in the Customer table. Remember that properly designed relational tables cannot have multi-valued fields. Thus, the *order_num* cannot be a foreign key in the Customer table because each Customer can participate in multiple Orders. Instead, the *cust_num* must be placed in the Orders table as the foreign key as shown in Figure 5.10.

Next, we have to determine what to do with the many-to-many relationships as shown between Order and Products in Figure 5.11. In this case, we need to turn the many-to-many relationship into two one-to-many relationships that can be easily implemented in a

FIGURE 5.11
**Implementing
Many-to-Many
Relationships**

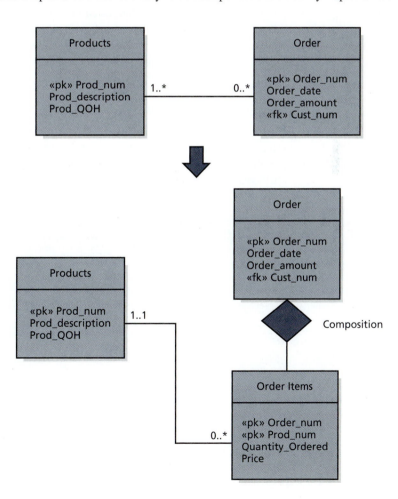

relational database. To do that, we define the Order Items class and model a *composition* association between Orders and Order Items as shown in Chapter 4. Note that the primary key of Order Items is the combination of *order_num* and *prod_num* (called concatenated key or composite key): *order_num* in Order Items links to *order_num* in Orders and *prod_num* in Order Items links to *prod_num* in Products. The Order Items table will include *quantity ordered* and *price* attributes because those attributes depend on both the Order and the Product ordered.[5] Although we could have modeled Order Items on the original UML class diagram, identifying the many-to-many relationship serves the same purpose because, in either case, the Order Items table would have to be defined when the model is implemented.[6]

Progress *Check*

5. Refer to Figure 5.9. Where does the foreign key go for the Customer to Cash Receipt association?
6. Where would the foreign keys go in the Order to Cash Receipt association?

LO 5-7

Implement a relational database from the UML class diagram of the sales and collection process.

SUNSET GRAPHICS' RELATIONAL DATABASE

Virgil and Linda B were now interested in seeing how the structure model would be implemented in a relational database for Sunset. For this example, we use Microsoft Access, but the process would be similar for any database-driven system. We encourage students to use the following description to implement a relational database to support information requirements for the sales and collection process.

Relational Database Planning for Attributes

During the model development process, we reviewed Sunset's existing documents to determine specific data requirements for each class/table. We then followed the guidance in the previous section to determine allocation of foreign keys. This resulted in a list of tables, attributes, data types, field sizes and primary and foreign keys as shown in Table 5.2.

PK/FK	Attribute Name	Type	Size		PK/FK	Attribute Name	Type	Size
	Table: tblBankAccounts					**Table: tblCashReceipts**		
PK	Account_number	Text	10		PK	Receipt_number	Text	10
	Bank_routing_number	Text	10			Receipt_date	Date/Time	8
	Bank_balance	Currency	8			Receipt_amount	Currency	8
	Bank_name	Text	15		FK	Customer_number	Text	10
	Bank_branch	Text	15			Customer_check_number	Text	10
	Bank_phone_number	Text	15		FK	Received_by	Text	10

TABLE 5.2
Sunset Database Table and Attribute Definitions

---

[5]Think about your cash register receipt at the grocery store; one sale includes many items.
[6]Additionally, the Order Items class cannot exist without the Order class, and because it can be derived from other classes, some argue that it should not be modeled.

PK/FK	Attribute Name	Type	Size
FK	Bank_account_number	Text	10
	Receipt_deposit_date	Date/Time	8
	Table: tblCustomers		
PK	Customer_number	Text	15
	Customer_name	Text	30
	Customer_address	Text	30
	Customer_address_2	Text	30
	Customer_city	Text	20
	Customer_state	Text	2
	Customer_zip	Text	5
	Customer_contact	Text	30
	Customer_phone	Text	15
	Customer_established_date	Date/Time	8
	Customer_last_activity	Date/Time	8
	Customer_balance	Currency	8
	Table: tblOrderItems		
PK	Order_number	Text	10
PK	Product_number	Text	10
	Order_quantity	Integer	2
	Order_price	Currency	8
	Table: tblOrders		
PK	Order_number	Text	10
	Order_date	Date/Time	8
FK	Customer_number	Text	10
FK	Quote_number	Text	10
FK	Order_taken_by	Text	10
	Order_required_by	Date/Time	8
	Order_delivered	Date/Time	8
	Order_total_amount	Currency	8
	Order_instructions	Memo	
FK	Receipt_number	Text	10
FK	Order_status	Text	10
	Table: tblOrderStatus		
PK	Order_status_code	Text	10
	Order_status_description	Text	255
	Table: tblPartners		
PK	Partner_number	Text	10
	Partner_first_name	Text	15

PK/FK	Attribute Name	Type	Size
	Partner_last_name	Text	15
	Partner_hire_date	Date/Time	8
	Partner_SocSecNo	Text	11
	Partner_Address	Text	50
	Partner_Address2	Text	50
	Partner_City	Text	20
	Partner_State	Text	2
	Partner_Zip	Text	10
	Partner_phone	Text	14
	Partner_cellphone	Text	14
	Table: tblProductCategory		
PK	Product_category_number	Text	10
	Product_category_description	Text	255
	Product_category_manager	Text	10
	Product_category_notes	Memo	
	Table: tblProducts		
PK	Product_number	Text	10
	Product_description	Text	255
	Product_price	Currency	8
	Product_unit_of_sale	Text	10
	Product_category	Text	10
	Product_quantity_on_hand	Integer	2
	Product_notes	Memo	–
	Table: tblQuoteItems		
PK	Quote_number	Text	10
PK	Product_number	Text	10
	Quote_quantity	Integer	2
	Quote_price	Currency	8
	Quote_notes	Text	255
	Table: tblQuotes		
PK	Quote_number	Text	10
	Quote_date	Date/Time	8
FK	Customer_number	Text	10
FK	Quote_by	Text	10
	Quote_amount	Currency	8

TABLE 5.2
(continued)

Create Database and Define Tables

The next step is to create a new, blank Microsoft Access database and create the tables described in Table 5.2 with the following steps:

1. Create the Table Design as shown in Figure 5.12 by selecting the CREATE tab; then select the Table Design icon on the ribbon bar.
2. Define each attribute listed for the table in Table 5.1 by typing the field name, selecting the data type, and setting the field size as shown in Figure 5.13.
3. Set the primary key by selecting the appropriate field and clicking the primary key icon on the ribbon bar as shown in Figure 5.14.
4. Save the table.
5. Repeat until all the tables are defined.

FIGURE 5.12
Create the Table Design

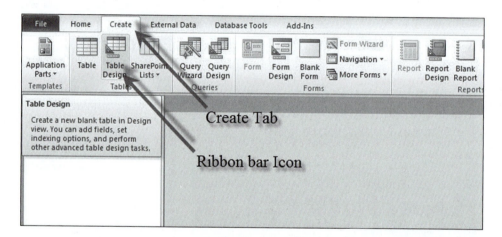

FIGURE 5.13
Define the Fields in the Table

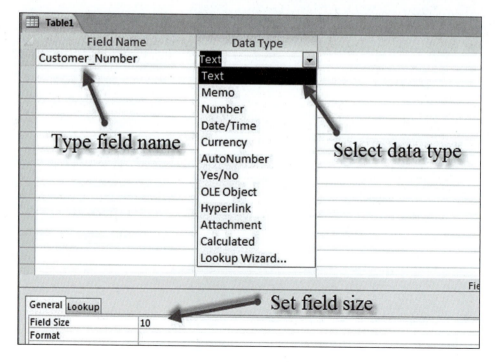

FIGURE 5.14
Set the Primary Key
for the Table

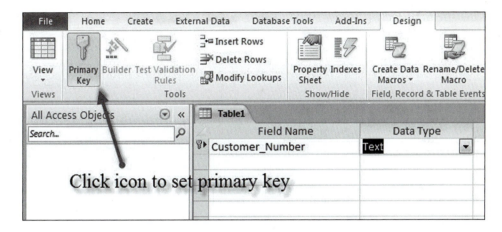

Set Relationships

After the tables are defined, the next step is to establish the links between tables. Click on the DATABASE TOOLS tab and select the RELATIONSHIPS icon on the ribbon bar as shown in Figure 5.15. Then, as shown in Figure 5.16, add all the tables to the relationships screen and connect foreign keys to primary keys so that the relationships mimic the UML class diagram shown in Figure 5.8.

FIGURE 5.15
Set Relationships

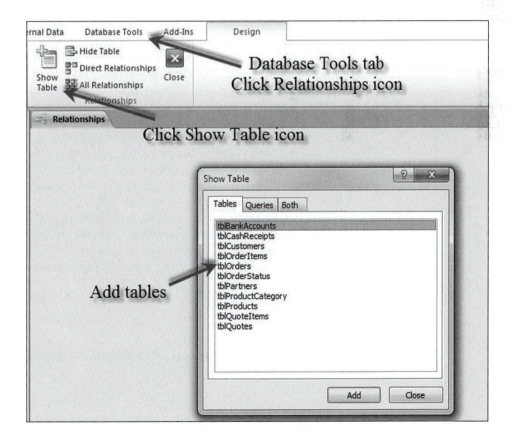

FIGURE 5.16
Partially Linked
Tables with
Referential Integrity
Enforced

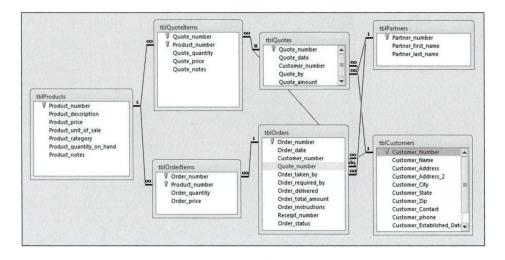

COMPREHENSIVE EXERCISE: BAER BELLY BIKINIS' SALES TO RETAILERS

Baer Belly Bikinis Inc. (BBB) is a small business located in Santa Monica, California. It sells swimwear and related products to specialty stores throughout the United States. It also sells its products to individuals over a company website. Paige Baer founded BBB almost 10 years ago after she graduated from the Fashion Institute of Design and Merchandising. She recognized the need for swimsuits sold as separates. Her business has grown rapidly, and now BBB has a large following of customers who want to be able to mix and match to find their ideal swimsuit. Currently, BBB products are carried in more than 1,000 specialty swimwear boutiques and online retailers.

During an initial interview with Paige Baer, she outlined BBB's business processes. She acknowledged that she doesn't know much about accounting and information technology. As the business grew, her accounting suffered and information systems were added piecemeal. So, she is looking forward to an assessment of her requirements and recommendations that would position BBB for substantial further growth.

This case examines BBB sales to independent boutique retailers. BBB uses a group of independent sales representatives to sell its products to boutique retailers around the country. These sales representatives are not BBB employees. They are paid commissions based on the dollar volume of sales. After working with the sales representatives, individual retailers call BBB to place their order for the upcoming season. BBB will then ship the products when they become available. The retailers are expected to pay for shipments within 30 days. BBB offers a prompt payment discount for payment within 10 days.

The following material summarizes BBB's activities to prepare for and conduct the sales process:

- Summer
  - BBB finalizes designs for next year's products and prepares catalog materials with information on its future products.
- Fall to Spring
  - BBB sales representatives (independent agents working on commissions) visit retailers to develop sales. BBB's payment of commissions to sales representawtives is outside the scope of this case, although you should include the Sales Reps in your model and database.

- BBB's retailer customers place orders for one of two deliveries in season: (1) early spring (April) and (2) early summer (May/June). BBB records information on its retailers before they place any orders.
- Upon receipt of finished goods from their manufacturer in April and May, BBB ships products to retailers.
- Retailers' payments are due 30 days after shipment and include shipping costs. Some retailers pay late. Some take advantage of the prompt payment discounts.

BBB Finished Goods Inventory

BBB tracks its inventory by catalog number (catalog#). Each product is identified by color code, use (e.g., tops or bottoms), and type (e.g., the specific design of the piece). The color codes reflect the color and fabric design options, and they can change each year. At the beginning of the season, the quantity on hand of each item is zero. The quantity on hand increases when BBB gets deliveries from its manufacturer (outside the scope of this case) and decreases as it ships the products to the retailers to fill orders.

BBB Shipments

BBB makes one shipment for each retailer order and records revenue when the products are shipped. Warehouse employees prepare the shipments. All shipments are made under BBB's contract with a shipping company. BBB charges customers for the cost of the shipment, so the amount due from the retailers depends on the wholesale price of each item, the quantity shipped, and the shipping cost for the shipment. Payments to the shipping company are outside the scope of this case.

BBB Cash Receipts

Retailer customers send payment by check according to the payment terms (BBB standard payment terms are 2% 10 days net 30). The payment from the retailer customer always applies to only one order, but sometimes the retailers send multiple checks for that order. A BBB employee (accounts receivable) logs cash receipts from retailers. At the end of the day, the cash receipts are deposited intact into one bank account (BBB's main account). Each cash receipt is tracked by unique sequential cash receipt number.

Exercise Requirements

1. Based on the preceding information and the following attributes list, prepare a UML class model and corresponding table listing describing BBB's sales to retailers. List the tables in following order: resources, events, agents, type images, and linking tables. Identify the primary keys and foreign keys in each table.
2. [optional] Based on the preceding information, prepare a BPMN activity model that describes BBB's Sales to Retailers process. The model should begin with retailers placing orders and end when BBB collects payments for the sales to the retailers.
3. Your instructor will provide an Excel spreadsheet with the BBB information. Create a new Access database, and import each worksheet in the spreadsheet into the database. Set appropriate primary keys.
4. After importing all the data, create relationships among tables to implement your data model.
5. Prepare queries to answer the following questions:
   a. What was BBB's total revenue?
   b. What is BBB's account receivable balance for each retailer customer as of the end of June?
   c. Which BBB product generated the largest sales volume? (List all products in descending order of sales dollars).

Attribute Listing for BBB

Bank Name	Finished Inventory Quantity on Hand
Cash Account Balance 4/1/13	Flat Rate Ship Charge
Cash Account Description	Inventory Type Use
Cash Account#	Order Date
Cash Receipt#	Order Date
Customer Address	Order Employee#
Customer City State Zip	Order#
Customer Name	Quantity Ordered
Customer Phone	Receipt Amount
Customer#	Receipt Date
Delivery Date	Requested Date
Employee Address	Retail Price
Employee City	Sales Rep Area
Employee Department	Sales Rep Email Address
Employee First Name	Sales Rep Name
Employee Hire Date	Sales Rep Phone
Employee Last Name	Sales Rep#
Employee Pay Amount	Ship Date
Employee Phone	Shipping Employee#
Employee Salary/Wage	Shipping Cost
Employee Zip	Size of Inventory Item
Employee#	Standard Cost of Inventory Item
Fabric Color Code	Supervisory Employee#
Fabric Color Name	Type Code
Fabric Cost per Yard	Wholesale Price
Finished Inventory Catalog#	Yards Fabric Required for this Inventory Type
Finished Inventory Description	

Summary

- From an accounting standpoint, we must account for sales, accounts receivable, and cash collection in the sales and collection process.
- Sunset Graphics Inc. provides an ongoing example of how to model the sales and collection process.
- Activity models can show the basic steps in the process and the collaborations between the company and its customers, as well as exceptions to the process.
- Business rules implement internal control activities.
- There is a standard structure model pattern for the sales and collection process that shows the economic reality of the process.
- The standard pattern is tailored to a specific organization by adding type images to collect management information.
- The structure model provides a blueprint for a relational database that will collect, store, and report sales and collection information.
- The comprehensive exercise reinforces the concepts presented in the chapter.

Key Words

access controls (*108*)   Limit who can use and change records in the system; for example, passwords control who can use an application.

accounts receivable (*104*)   Monies owed by customers for prior sales of goods or services. In a data modeling context, accounts receivable are calculated as each customer's sales less corresponding cash receipts.

agents (*109*)   The people or organizations who participate in business events, such as customers and salespeople.

application controls (*108*)   Ensure data integrity and an audit trail; for example, new invoices are assigned sequential numbers.

cash (*104*)   The organization's monies in bank or related accounts. The instances of the class are individual accounts. This is considered a resource.

cash receipts (*111*)   Record receipts of cash from external agents (e.g., customers) and the corresponding deposit of those receipts into cash accounts. This is considered an event.

choreography (*106*)   The interaction (message flows) between two participants (modeled as pools) in a process modeled using BPMN.

collaboration (*106*)   A BPMN model showing two participant pools and the interactions between them within a process.

customer (*105*)   The external agent in the sales and collection process.

error event (*107*)   An intermediate event in a BPMN model showing processing for exceptions to the normal process flow.

events (*109*)   Classes that model the organization's transactions, usually affecting the organization's resources, such as sales and cash receipts.

many-to-many relationship (*110*)   Exists when instances of one class (e.g., sales) are related to many instances of another class (e.g., inventory) and vice versa. These relationships are implemented in Access and relational databases by adding a linking table to convert the many-to-many relationship into two one-to-many relationships.

one-to-many relationship (*110*)   Exists when instances of one class are related to multiple instances of another class. For example, a customer can participate in many sales, but each sale involves only one customer.

orchestration (*106*)   In BPMN, the sequence of activities within one pool.

product (*104*)   Class representing the organization's goods held for sale, that is, the organization's inventory. This is considered a resource.

quote (*105*)   Description of the products and/or services to be provided to a customer if ordered.

REA (*109*)   Resource-event-agent framework for modeling business processes, originally developed by William McCarthy.

resources (*109*)   Those things that have economic value to a firm, such as cash and products.

sales (*104*)   Events documenting the transfer of goods or services to customer and the corresponding recognition of revenue for the organization.

sales order (*105*)   Event documenting commitments by customers to purchase products. The sales order event precedes the economic event (sale).

subprocess (*106*)   Represent a series of process steps that are hidden from view in BPMN. The use of subprocesses in modeling helps reduce complexity.

type image (*112*)   Class that represents management information (such as categorizations, policies, and guidelines) to help manage a business process. Type image often allows process information to be summarized by category.

Generic REA Model with Multiplicities for the Sales and Collection Process

GENERIC PATTERN WITH MULTIPLICITIES

Figure 5.A1 shows a generic sales and collection process UML diagram. There are two resources, *inventory* and *cash;* there are two events, *sales* and *cash receipts;* and, there are two agents, *employees* (internal agent) and *customers* (external agent). In this example, let's assume that the inventory is something tracked by universal product code (UPC). UPC codes are those bar codes you see on literally millions of products, such as soap, breakfast cereal, and packages of cookies. The cash resource represents the various bank accounts that would make up this enterprise's cash balance on its balance sheet. The sales event records information about individual sales transactions (e.g., transaction number, date, total dollar amount). The cash receipt event records information about payments received from customers and deposited into one of the bank accounts (e.g., receipt number, receipt date, receipt dollar amount, customer check number). The employees agent records information about the enterprise's employees, including those employees who handle sales transactions. The customers agent records information about actual and potential customers (let's assume that customer information is recorded in some cases when customers ask for product information and before they participate in their first sale, and let's also assume that the company only receives cash from customers).

FIGURE 5.A1

Generic Sales and Collection UML Diagram

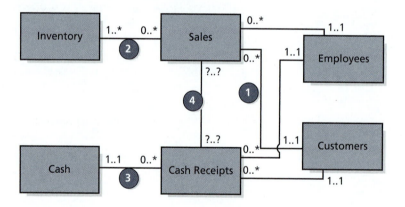

Consider association 1 between *customers* and *sales.* The multiplicities indicate that each customer participates in a minimum of zero and a maximum of many sales. Does this seem reasonable? The minimum of zero means that we can record information about customers before they participate in any sale. On the other side of the association, the multiplicities indicate that each sale involves one and only one customer. Again, does this seem reasonable? Notice that the multiplicities for the other associations between agents and events are the same. In fact, these are the typical multiplicities for those associations. There are circumstances where they might be different, but those circumstances occur infrequently.

Next, consider association 2 between the *sales* event and *inventory* resource. The multiplicities indicate that each sale involves a minimum of one and a maximum of many inventory items. For example, you visit your local **Starbucks** and buy one coffee, a tea for your friend, plus two scones. The multiplicities also indicate that each inventory item can be sold zero times or many times. For example, **Starbucks** has to put an item on its menu before it can be sold, so it could have inventory items that have not yet been sold. But, the same inventory item can be sold many times—as long as the quantity on hand is greater than zero. The multiplicities on this association are typical when the inventory is carried at a type of product level, such as when the inventory is identified by UPC code. If the company sells high-value items, the multiplicities would differ. (How?)

Now, consider association 3 between the *cash receipt* event and the *cash* resource. These multiplicities indicate that each cash receipt (e.g., one check from a customer) is deposited into one and only one account, and each account is associated with a minimum of zero cash receipts and a maximum of many cash receipts. These multiplicities reflect typical business practices. Cash receipts are deposited into one account (when you deposit money via an ATM, you are putting it in one account, right?).

Finally, consider the duality association 4 between the *sales* and *cash receipt* events. The question marks indicate that these multiplicities depend on the nature of the business. Some businesses require payment at the time of the sale. Some allow payment terms. Some provide revolving accounts for their customers. Some collect payments in advance of the sale (e.g., magazine subscriptions). So, there are no typical multiplicities for this association.

Although we discourage memorization of data modeling elements, students often find that multiplicities are easier to understand once they see the typical sets for particular associations. We therefore recommend that students recognize and use the standard patterns for multiplicities as shown in Figure 5.A1, remembering that those standard multiplicities could change depending on the particular circumstances of the business.

Answers to Progress *Checks*

1. The collaboration model shown in Figure 5.4 highlights the interactions between Sunset Graphics and its customers. Figure 5.2 shows the sequence of activities for the sales process without identifying information coming into or out of each activity.

2. The answer depends on the choice of firm. Take **Amazon.com** for example. **Amazon** collects payments at the time of the order and does not invoice customers.

3. Companies that provide quotes typically build or tailor their products to the specific customer requirements compared to companies that simply sell available products.

4. The order event could be separated into orders and sales when one order could result in multiple sales or one sale could involve multiple orders.

5. The foreign key for the Customer to Cash Receipt association in Figure 5.8 would be posted in the Cash Receipt table.

6. The foreign key for the Order to Cash Receipt association in Figure 5.8 would be posted in the Order table.

Multiple Choice Questions

1. Which of the following is not an activity within the sales and collection process?
   a. Selling products and services
   b. Billing customers
   c. Managing inventory
   d. Recording payments from customers
   e. All of the above are sales and collection activities.

2. The sales and collection process is the point of contact between the firm and which set of external business partners?
   a. Investors
   b. Customers
   c. Employees

d. Vendors

e. All of the above

3. Which of the following sales and collection process activities can result in the creation of an account receivable?

    a. Receiving a sales order from a customer

    b. Shipping ordered products to the customer

    c. Billing the customer

    d. Recording payment from the customer

    e. None of the above

4. Which of the following describes message flows between pools?

    a. Orchestrations

    b. Sequence flows

    c. Choreography

    d. Intermediate events

    e. None of the above

5. Which of the following statements is(are) not true?

    a. Each pool must have a start event.

    b. Sequence flows are shown by arrows with a solid line.

    c. Message flows are shown by arrows with a solid line.

    d. Each pool must have more than one swimlane.

    e. Both c and d are not true.

6. Which of the following is not a purpose of a subprocess in BPMN?

    a. Reducing complexity

    b. Presenting higher-level process descriptions

    c. Creating alternative activities

    d. Developing a reusable model

    e. All of the above are purposes of subprocesses in BPMN.

7. What is the purpose of an intermediate error event?

    a. Indicates a change in flow due to a process exception

    b. Indicates the end of a process

    c. Indicates the start of a collapsed subprocess

    d. Describes the activities that will occur when there is not an error

    e. None of the above

8. Which of the following is an example of a business rule implementing access controls?

    a. The warehouse containing inventory must be locked when the inventory manager is not present.

    b. User's recording collections cannot modify sales records.

    c. The computer system shall generate an audit trail.

    d. Internal auditors shall be used.

    e. Both a and b are business rules implementing access controls.

9. Which of the following is not part of the REA framework?

    a. Agents

    b. Type images

    c. Resources

    d. Events

    e. All of the above are part of the REA framework.

10. How do you implement a one-to-many relationship in a relational database?
    a. Post a foreign key.
    b. Create a new table.
    c. Combine two fields to create a primary keys.
    d. Create an association.
    e. None of the above

Discussion Questions

1. The sales and collection process generates revenue, accounts receivable, and cash flow information for a firm's financial statements. What other information do you think managers would like to collect?

2. What kinds of businesses collect cash before recording the corresponding sales? How would that different sequence affect internal control requirements?

3. Draw a basic sales activity model using BPMN for a fast-food restaurant. Draw a second basic sales activity model using BPMN for a traditional restaurant. Discuss similarities and differences. How would you add taking reservations to the second model?

4. Now draw a collaboration diagram that shows two pools and the message flows between a fast-food restaurant and its customers. How would you change that diagram for a traditional restaurant?

5. Draw UML class diagrams for fast-food and traditional restaurants. Discuss similarities and differences. How would you add taking reservations to the second model?

6. Using **Amazon.com** as an example, prepare a collaboration sales activity model. What is the difference between an online process and a traditional brick-and-mortar store process?

7. From your experience, describe some business rules that implement internal controls for a sales process.

8. What classes and associations would be included in a model that describes the information needed for a query that calculates the accounts receivable balance for each customer? Describe differences in the information for the *open-invoice method,* where customers pay according to specific invoices, versus the *balance-forward method,* where customers pay balances on monthly statements.

Problems

1. The Beach Dude (BD) employs a legion of current and former surfers as salespeople who push its surfing-oriented products to various customers (usually retail outlets). This case describes BD's sales and collection process.

   Each BD salesperson works with a specific group of customers throughout the year. In fact, they often surf with their customers to try out the latest surf gear. The BD salespeople act laid-back, but they work hard for their sales. Each sale often involves hours of surfing with their customers while the customers sample all the latest surf wear. Because BD makes the best surfing products, the customers look forward to the visits from the BD salespeople. And, they often buy a lot of gear. Each sale is identified by unique invoice number and usually involves many different products. Customers pay for each sale in full within 30 days, but they can combine payments for multiple sales.

   BD manages its clothing inventory by item (e.g., XL BD surfer logo T-shirts), identified by product number, but it also classifies the items by clothing line (the lines are differentiated by price points as well as the intended use of the clothing, e.g., surfing products, casual wear, etc.).

   a. Draw a UML class diagram that describes the Beach Dudes sales and collection process.

   b. Using Microsoft Access, implement a relational database from your UML class diagram. Identify at least three fields per table.

   c. Describe how you would use the relational database to determine the Beach Dude's accounts receivable.

2. The Bob White Karate Studio has been a local fixture for almost 40 years. The studio offers training in American Kenpo Karate to students from 3 years old to 80 years old. Students select one of several programs: (a) monthly payments, (b) semi-annual payments, or (c) the black belt program. Each of these programs allows them to take group classes as well as one or more private lessons with a qualified black belt instructor, depending on the program selected. For example, the monthly program includes one private lesson, the semi-annual program includes three private lessons, and the black belt program includes one lesson per week until the student attains black belt rank. Additionally, students may purchase additional private lessons, as well as uniforms, sparring gear, and various studio insignia and clothing items. The additional half-hour private lessons are priced as packages, which include 5, 10, 20, 40, or 60 lessons, and the price also varies depending on whether the lessons are provided by senior or junior instructors. When students purchase a package, they are assigned to a particular instructor for the duration of the package. Students typically pay for anything that they buy at the time of their purchase, but established students are sometimes allowed to purchase on credit. In that case, they generally must pay within 2 weeks. While all studio employees are also instructors, only a few employees handle sales transactions and accept payments.

   a. Draw a BPMN activity diagram that describes the Bob White Karate Studio's sales and collection process.

   b. Prepare a UML class diagram with classes, associations, and multiplicities.

   c. Using the preceding information and the following attributes list, prepare a listing of the relational tables necessary to support this sales and collection process. List the tables in the following order: resources, events, agents, type images, and linking tables.

   Attributes:

Cash account#	Program#
Cash account balance	Program description
Credit card number for this sale	Program price
Date sale paid	Quantity of instructors of this type
Employee/instructor#	Quantity of this inventory item purchased on this sale
Employee name	
Employee rank	Sale#
Instructor type	Sale amount
Inventory item#	Sale date
Inventory item description	Sale paid (Y/N)
Inventory item price	Student#
Inventory item quantity on hand (QOH)	Student current rank
Private lesson package#	Student name
Private lesson package description	Student original enrollment date
Private lesson package price	

3. Beach Rentals (BR) maintains an inventory of rental houses near universities and leases those houses to student renters. This case describes their rental business process. BR agents—former marketing majors renowned for their fast-talking and flamboyant lifestyles—work with potential renters and sign the rental contracts for BR.

   BR tracks its houses by city, neighborhood, and distance from campus. BR assigns one specific BR agent to each neighborhood to manage rentals for all houses in that neighborhood, but each BR agent may be assigned to multiple neighborhoods. BR cashiers collect the rent and are bonded for security purposes. Because cashiers never become agents (or vice versa), BR tracks BR cashiers separately from BR agents, although both are identified by employee numbers.

   BR sets rental rates to its student customers by considering such matters as number of bedrooms and age of the house. Additionally, BR applies a monthly rental surcharge to each house that depends solely upon its neighborhood designation; for example, upscale neighborhoods have higher surcharges and less desirable neighborhoods have lower surcharges.

The same surcharge applies for the life of the lease. Every house has rental surcharge, and all houses in a particular neighborhood have the same surcharge.

Prospective renters, usually students, contact BR to inquire about renting a house. When a potential renter contacts BR, a BR agent is assigned to assist him or her. That BR agent remains the person's point of contact for as long as he or she continues to deal with Beach Rentals. BR records information on each potential renter as soon as he or she contacts BR to inquire about a house.

BR agents negotiate the rental contracts with the students. Each rental contract must last at least 6 months, and 12-month contracts get a 5 percent discount. BR also charges a damage fee that is due along with the first month's rent when the rental contract is signed. The BR agent earns a 10 percent commission on each rental contract, and BR tracks the year-to-date (YTD) commission earned for each of the BR agents. Of course, the BR agents compete with one another to see who earns the highest commissions, and BR fosters the competition by giving an annual award to its "best" agent.

When multiple students want to rent one house, BR requires that they designate the primary renter—the one who will be responsible for paying the rent. BR also gathers information about all the other occupants of the house and designates them as secondary renters. All the student renters, however, sign the rental contract, and BR assigns a unique renter number to each occupant. The students may not change primary renter for the term of a contract. BR cashiers collect the rental payments monthly from the primary renters. BR records information concerning employees, house owners, bank accounts, and neighborhoods in the database before the renters are involved in any events.

a. Prepare a UML class diagram with classes, associations, and multiplicities.

b. Using the preceding information and the following attributes list, prepare a listing of the relational tables necessary to support this sales and collection process. List the tables in the following order: resources, events, agents, type images, and linking tables.

c. Using the list of relational tables and Microsoft Access, define the relational tables and establish the relationships among tables necessary to implement the Beach Rentals sales and collection process in Access.

Attributes:

agent employee#	monthly rent
agent name	neighborhood name
agent real estate license status	number of bedrooms
bank account#	number of houses this city
bank account balance	rent discount for 12 month contract
bank name and address	rental contract#
cash receipt $ amount	rental contract begin date
cash receipt#	rental contract duration in months
cashier employee#	rental surcharge amount
cashier name	renter bank and routing numbers
city name	renter name
damage fee	renter number#
house street address	YTD rental commissions
house zip code	

Answers to Multiple Choice Questions

1. e		6. e	
2. b		7. a	
3. b		8. e	
4. c		9. e	
5. e		10. a	

Purchases and Payments Business Process

A look at this chapter

This chapter examines the purchases and payments process. We continue the comprehensive example to develop activity and structure models of the process. We show how the activity model in conjunction with business rules can be used to develop, implement, and monitor control activities. We show how the structure model can be used to develop a relational database to support information processing requirements.

A look back

Chapter 5 examined the sales and collection processes. It began the comprehensive example that we use to examine typical process activities and data structures.

A look ahead

In the next chapter, we examine the conversion process, whereby companies transform raw material into finished goods. We again use the basic modeling tools from Chapters 2 and 3 and database design methods presented in Chapter 4 to examine activity and structure models for the process.

In a 2002 interview,[1] David Norton, **Starbucks** vice president of logistics, talked about its global supply chain: "Rapid global growth requires comprehensive, integrated strategies focused on the needs of our retail stores, license and joint venture partners. We have a formal process for developing both strategic and operating plans which ensures we link manufacturing, procurement, and logistics to the needs of the business."

Norton went on to describe the role of technology: "Technology has become increasingly a staple of the supply chain rather than a driver. There have been few significant advances on the physical distribution side of the supply chain in years. In the information arena, the pattern seems to be over-commit and under-deliver. Systems are generally harder, more costly, and take longer to implement than has been the promise. The evolution of systems over the past 15 years might be even characterized as a journey from homegrown proprietary systems through best-of-breed/homegrown combinations, and finally to monolithic ERP environments. And my experience is that the integrated, monolithic ERP environments simply lack the flexibility to meet unique business requirements. We believe the best place to be today is

[1]Reported January 1, 2002, www.SupplyChainBrain.com.

combining the best of different applications. And, our IT professionals here at **Starbucks** are comfortable with this because of advances in business integration systems/tools that enable this approach."

Finally, describing what it takes to design and operate integrated supply chain management tools, Norton noted, "A lot of folks come into the business and don't understand that you need a solid item master, a solid price master, a solid customer master, a solid order management system, a solid inventory system—all tied in nicely with AP [accounts payable] and AR [accounts receivable]—and if you don't have any of that stuff right, you can just about forget everything else."

Clearly, technology is important to **Starbucks** for the management of its supply chain. What kinds of information do you think **Starbucks** needs to manage and improve its supply chain?

Chapter Outline

Purchases and Payments Process
Sunset Graphics Example
Company Overview
*Sunset Graphics' Purchases and
  Payments Process Distribution*
Sunset Graphics' Activity Models
Basic Purchases Activity Model
Refining the Model to Show Collaboration
Business Rules and Sunset Graphics'
  Purchases and Payments Process
  Controls
Sunset Graphics' Structure Models
*Basic UML Class Diagram for Purchases
  and Payments*
*Refining the UML Class Diagram for
  Purchases and Payments*
Sunset Graphics' Relational Database
*Relational Database Planning for
  Attributes*
Create Database and Define Tables
Comprehensive Exercise: Baer Belly
  Bikinis' Purchases of Fabric
Appendix A: Generic REA Model
  with Multiplicities for the
  Purchases and Payments Process

Learning Objectives

After reading this chapter, you should be able to:

6-1   Describe the business activities that comprise the purchase and payment process.

6-2   Develop an activity model of the purchase and payment process using BPMN.

6-3   Understand and apply different activity modeling options.

6-4   Develop business rules to implement controls for the purchase and payment process.

6-5   Develop structure models for the purchase and payment process using UML class diagrams.

6-6   Implement a relational database from the UML class diagram of the purchase and payment process.

LO 6-1
Describe the business
activities that comprise
the purchase and
payment process.

PURCHASES AND PAYMENTS PROCESS

The purchases and payments process includes business activities related to buying inventory from **suppliers,** maintaining supplier records, and making payments to suppliers for trade accounts payable while taking appropriate **purchase discounts.** The purchases and payments process generates accounting transactions to record **purchases, accounts payable,** and **cash disbursements.** The process also affects inventory values as purchases are added to inventory. Figure 6.1 describes typical transactions resulting from the purchases and payments process.

We will apply the tools introduced in Chapter 2, 3, 4, and 5 to a comprehensive example of the purchases and payments process. We first describe the process activities using BPMN, and then we define the typical information structure using UML class diagrams. Finally, we use the UML class diagrams to build a database to collect and report relevant process information. We also describe business rules that establish potential process controls.

FIGURE 6.1
Accounting
Transactions for
Purchases and
payments Process

Oct 1	Purchases (or Inventory)*	1,495.50	
	Accounts Payable		1,495.50
	Purchased inventory on credit from Richardson & Sons, Inc.		
	Invoice 1125 dated Oct 1, terms 2/10, net 30		
Oct 11	Accounts Payable	1,495.50	
	Purchase Discounts		29.91
	Cash		1,465.59
	Paid Richardson & Sons, Inc. for Invoice 1125 dated Oct 1		
	less 2% discount		
	* Debit to Purchases or Inventory accounts depend on whether the company uses a periodic or perpetual inventory system.		

SUNSET GRAPHICS EXAMPLE

Company Overview

As described in Chapter 5, Virgil and Linda B own and operate Sunset Graphics. They design and sell signs and banners, lettering and vinyl graphics for vehicles and boats, corporate promotional items, and silk-screened T-shirts and embroidered gear, among other products. Recently, they decided that it was time to review their business processes to develop better documentation, improve processes, and establish consistency in customer service. They also wanted to be sure that effective internal controls were in place. This comprehensive example assumes that we are business analysts who are helping Virgil and Linda accomplish these goals.

Sunset Graphics' Purchases and Payments Process Description

Linda B does most of the buying and also pays most of the bills for Sunset, so she explained the process. When Sunset needs to purchase items, it usually follows a straightforward process:

1. Research prices and product availability.
2. Select the best price and availability combination, and send a **purchase order** to the supplier.

3. Receive the items from the supplier (and record the purchase and accounts payable).
4. Pay the supplier according to the credit terms.

LO 6-2

Develop an activity model of the purchase and payment process using BPMN.

SUNSET GRAPHICS' ACTIVITY MODELS

Basic Purchases Activity Model

After talking with Linda B about their purchases and payments process, our first task was to draw a simple business process model using BPMN. As shown in Figure 6.2, the start of the process occurs when Sunset needs to purchase items to fulfill a customer order or to replenish inventory. Then, a series of tasks takes place in sequence until Sunset pays for the items and the process ends. Sunset records purchases and updates inventory when it receives the items.

FIGURE 6.2
Basic Purchases Activity Model

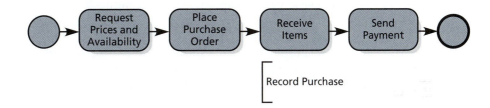

LO 6-3

Understand and apply different activity modeling options.

Refining the Model to Show Collaboration

After reviewing models for the sales and collection process in Chapter 5, Linda was starting to understand these models. She remarked that she liked the **collaboration** model better, because it shows the interactions with the external parties that Sunset relies on. So, she asked if we could prepare a collaboration model of the purchases and payments process. Of course, we said we could. In this case, the *pools* would show suppliers and Sunset, with *message flows* (shown by dashed arrows) between pools describing the interaction between participants. In fact, if you are primarily interested in the interactions, you don't need to model the **orchestration** within either pool. To illustrate, we prepared Figure 6.3 that shows the two pools for the suppliers and Sunset Graphics and the **choreography** between them.

FIGURE 6.3
Collaboration Purchases Activity Model

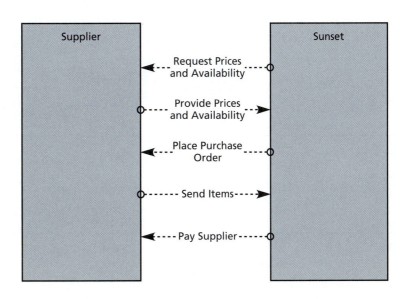

Linda thought that this model offered a good overview of their typical purchase and payment process. It showed the choreography of interactions between the pools. However, she reminded us that she would not be doing most of Sunset's buying and bill paying in the future. Because she was delegating those jobs, she thought that she should separate the buying duties from the payment duties for better internal control. She wondered if we could prepare a model that shows the process while highlighting different jobs within Sunset. We said that we could, and we reminded her about swimlanes in BPMN that allow us to model those different jobs.

Linda thought that showing the different jobs would provide better process documentation. However, she also noted that sometimes they do not get acceptable items from the supplier and have to send them back. She asked if we could also allow for that in the model. We prepared Figure 6.4 to show her a model with swimlanes that also allows for the return of deficient items.

In Figure 6.4, we included swimlanes for the buyer, receiving, and accounts payable (A/P) jobs that will exist at Sunset after Linda delegates her duties. We combined the Request Prices and Availability and Place Purchase Order activities in the original model shown in Figure 6.2 with a **subprocess,** because we want to expand on those activities later. We also added another step to assess the items after receiving them from the supplier. Then, we included a **gateway** to branch into two possible courses of action. If the items are not acceptable, Sunset returns them to the supplier and the process ends. If

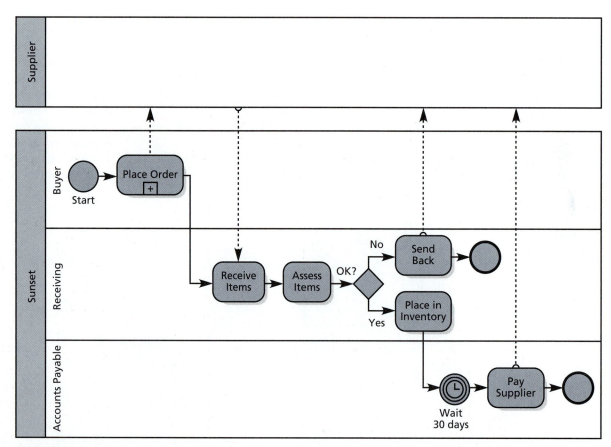

FIGURE 6.4
Expanded Collaboration Purchases Activity Model with Swimlanes

the items are acceptable, they are placed in inventory; 30 days later (depending on credit terms), Sunset sends a payment to the supplier. Because there are two possible paths that do not reconnect, we include two end events.

Because we added some new notation, we explained what the new symbols mean. The gateway is modeled with the diamond. In this case, the gateway branches into two exclusive paths. We noted that with BPMN 2.0, gateways don't represent activities, so we needed to include the assessment activity, Assess Items, before the gateway. We also included an **intermediate timer event** (the **intermediate event** symbol with clock hands) to represent the time delay, Wait 30 days, before payment. **Timer events** represent a delay in the flow of a process. They can indicate a delay to (1) a specific date, such as December 31; (2) a relative time, such as 30 days; or (3) a relative repetitive date, such as next Friday at 5:00 p.m.

Progress *Check*

1. In Figure 6.4, at what point would Sunset record the purchase?
2. From your own experience, describe how you would change Figure 6.4 to reflect another purchases and payments process. What if the customer purchased over the Internet and paid by credit card?

LO 6-4
Develop business rules to implement controls for the purchases and payments process.

BUSINESS RULES AND SUNSET GRAPHICS' PURCHASES AND PAYMENTS PROCESS CONTROLS

Next, we wanted to talk about planning controls over the purchases and payments process to give Virgil and Linda more confidence in the integrity of the process when they stepped back from the day-to-day operations. As with the sales and collection process, we want to define controls by developing business rules for the process. First, we need to identify important business events and define Sunset's intention or objective for each event. Then, we determine the appropriate actions to take based on the conditions. For example, we've already listed important business events in the business process models, so let's examine Sunset's purchases and payments process in Figure 6.4 and develop some possible business rules.

Again, Virgil and Linda summarized their objectives for the steps in the process. Of course, their overall goal was to purchase needed items from reliable suppliers at the best possible prices to meet required delivery schedules. They also wanted to be sure that these suppliers were paid on time, taking prompt payment discounts were appropriate, so they could maintain positive, long-term relationships. Because they were not going to directly supervise the process anymore, they wanted to be sure that effective controls were applied.

We outlined some standard controls over the purchases and payments process, suggesting segregation of ordering, receiving, and payment duties. We reiterated that *access controls* limit

Adding new purchases to inventory.

Process Steps	Intention	Partner Authority/ Action	Access Controls	Application Controls
Place Order	Order products from reliable suppliers at the best available prices to meet required delivery time.	Manager approval required for orders >$5,000; partner ordering products must not manage inventory.	Partners preparing purchase orders cannot modify product inventory records, receive items, or pay suppliers.	System must provide purchase order number control, default values, and range and limit checks and must create an audit trail.
Receive Items	Record receipt of items promptly and accurately.	Partner receiving items must not be same partner who ordered the items.	Partners receiving items cannot modify purchase orders or inventory records; they cannot view purchase order quantity ordered information.	System must only allow partner to enter the number of items received, subject to range and limit checks on quantities received; date of receipt defaults to current date.
Assess Items	Reject defective items; record acceptance promptly and accurately.	Partner assessing items must not be same partner who ordered the items.	Partners assessing items cannot modify purchase orders or inventory records.	System must only allow partner to record the assessment; date of assessment defaults to current date.
Place in Inventory	Place accepted items in proper inventory locations promptly.	Partner placing the items in inventory must not be same partner who ordered the items.	Partners placing items in inventory cannot modify purchase orders.	System must specify where items are to be placed.
Send Items Back	Return defective items to suppliers promptly.	Manager approval required for defective items return.	Partner returning items cannot modify supplier information.	System must supply supplier return address.
Pay Supplier	Pay suppliers accurately, taking cost-effective discount terms.	Partner making payment must not be partner who ordered items or received/ accepted items.	Partner making payments cannot modify purchase orders and receipt/ acceptance records.	System must supply supplier payment information and amount of payment; payment date defaults to current date.

TABLE 6.1
Using Business Rules to Implement Internal Controls

which of their partners can view and change records in the system and help implement appropriate segregation of duties. We also need *application controls* to ensure data integrity and an audit trail. For example, we need to control the assignment of purchase order and receiving report numbers to make sure all of them are accounted for. Plus, we need to establish appropriate ranges or limits for each value that Sunset's partners can add or change in the system.

With Virgil and Linda's direction, we developed an initial set of business rules for the purchases and payments process. They articulated their intentions for every step in the process, and then we set business rules to segregate duties and limit partner authority appropriately. Table 6.1 shows the initial set of business rules for Sunset's purchases and payments process. We noted that we would need to set application controls for almost every attribute updated during data entry.

LO 6-5

Develop structure models for the purchases and payments process using UML class diagrams.

SUNSET GRAPHICS' STRUCTURE MODELS

Linda B seemed pleased with the business process models so far. However, Virgil B was more interested in planning Sunset's new database. He'd already set up the sales and collection tables in Access, and he was waiting for the purchases and payments model so he could set up these tables, too. So, we proceeded to examine Sunset Graphics' purchases and payments information requirements. As described in Chapter 3, the primary purpose of our UML class diagram of the purchases and payments process is to create a blueprint for the development of a relational database to support the collection, aggregation, and communication of process information. As in Chapter 5, we follow the **REA** framework (**resources, events,** and **agents**) as a proven approach to describing business processes in a way that meets both accounting and broad management information requirements.

Basic UML Class Diagram for Purchases and Payments

We quickly reviewed what Linda B had told us about the purchases and payments process with Virgil B. In this case, a Sunset Partner (agent) selects the Supplier (agent) and issues a Purchase Order (event) as indicated by the number 1 on Figure 6.5. The Purchase Order specifies the prices and quantities of Products (resource) ordered. The Supplier (agent) sends and a Sunset Partner (agent) receives (Receipts event) the products (resource) as indicated by the number 2 on Figure 6.5. The **receipt** triggers the recognition of the purchase and the corresponding account payable in the accounting records. Then, when the payment is due, a Sunset Partner (agent) pays (cash disbursement event) the Supplier (agent) from a Cash account (resource) as indicated by the number 3 on Figure 6.5.[2] The payment reduces accounts payable.

   We showed Virgil the basic model, and he noticed that this model looked very similar to the sales and collection process model. Although the events were different, the resources and the Sunset Partner agent were the same. We said that this was a typical purchases and payments process. We always start with this basic diagram when we model the purchases and payments process, and then we modify it to reflect the unique information structure of a particular company. The Purchase Orders event represents Sunset's commitment to purchase **products** and pay the supplier, although commitments do not affect the financial statements. The Receipts event does affect the financial statements because it records the purchase for those items received and accepted and records the increases to accounts payable. The Cash Disbursement event also affects financial statements because it records decreases to **cash** and decreases to accounts payable.

FIGURE 6.5
Basic UML Class Diagram for Purchases and Payments

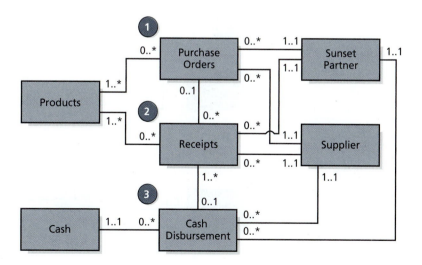

[2]Note that UML class diagrams reflect data structure and do not necessarily reflect the sequence of events.

Virgil said that he thought he understood multiplicities pretty well from our sales and collection process models, but he wanted to review a couple of them to make sure. For example, the multiplicities for the association between Purchase Orders and Products specify a **many-to-many relationship.** Each purchase order requests a minimum of one and a maximum of many products, and each product might have not yet been ordered and could be ordered many times.[3] We said that was correct but asked Virgil to explain the multiplicities for the Purchase Orders to Receipts association. He thought about it for a minute, because he was not sure why a Purchase Order could be associated with multiple Receipts or why a Receipt could be related to a minimum of 0 Purchase Orders. We answered that we thought some Receipts were purchased over-the-counter from suppliers without first issuing a Purchase Order. Additionally, we thought that some Purchase Orders could result in partial shipments from the Supplier. Virgil responded that he could see how the model reflected those assumptions, but our assumptions were not correct. He said that Sunset always records a Purchase Order, even for over-the-counter purchases, and does not accept partial shipments.

Refining the UML Class Diagram for Purchases and Payments

Because Virgil said that Sunset always records Purchase Orders for a purchase and never accepts partial shipments, we revised the diagram. Because there is always **one-to-one relationship** between Purchase Orders and Receipts, we can collapse the two classes into one and simplify the diagram (even though receipts happen after the orders). The new Purchases (event) class in Figure 6.6 would record purchase orders and include an attribute to indicate that the products were received. This is similar to the way we modeled Orders in the sales and collection process. Each Purchase is associated with a minimum of 0 and a maximum of 1 Cash Disbursement, because Sunset usually pays for purchases 30 days after receipt and pays in full. Each Cash Disbursement is associated with a minimum of 0 and a maximum of many Purchases, because Sunset writes checks for other purposes and combines payments for multiple purchases from the same supplier when possible.

FIGURE 6.6
Revised UML Class Diagram for Purchases and Payments

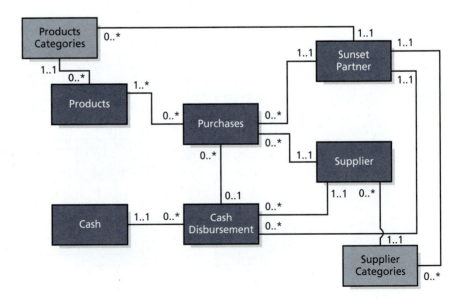

[3]We assume that products are identified before they are ordered.

Because we were refining the diagram, we added the **type image** for Product Categories that we also identified in the sales and collection process. Virgil then said that they also categorize their suppliers, so he suggested that we add a type image for Supplier Categories. He was really starting to understand UML class diagrams. We also added the association between Sunset Partners and Product Categories to reflect the assignment association that we identified in the sales and collection process.

Virgil agreed that Figure 6.6 accurately reflected their purchases and payments process. He was anxious to get started on defining the database. He recognized the composition association between Purchases and Purchase Items reflected by the many-to-many relationship between Purchases and Products. He said he understood how to post the foreign keys (see Chapters 3 and 4).

Progress *Check*

3. Describe when you would define two events—purchase orders and purchases—instead of combining them.
4. Review Figure 6.6 and explain when you might consider an association between Product Categories and Supplier Categories.

LO 6-6

Implement a relational database from the UML class diagram of the purchases and payments process.

SUNSET GRAPHICS' RELATIONAL DATABASE

Virgil and Linda B were both interested in implementing the purchases and payments UML class diagram in a relational database for Sunset. Again, we use Microsoft Access, but the process would be similar for any database-driven system. We encourage students to use the following description to implement a relational database to support information requirements for the purchases and payments process.

Relational Database Planning for Attributes

During the model development process, we reviewed Sunset's existing documents to determine specific data requirements for each class/table. We then followed the guidance in Chapter 3 to determine allocation of foreign keys. This resulted in a list of tables, attributes, data types, field sizes, and primary and foreign keys as shown in Table 6.2.

PK/FK	Attribute Name	Type	Size
	Table: tblBankAccounts		
PK	Account_number	Text	10
	Bank_routing_number	Text	10
	Bank_balance	Currency	8
	Bank_name	Text	15
	Bank_branch	Text	15
	Bank_phone_number	Text	15
	Table: tblCashDisbursements		
PK	Check_Number	Text	10
	Check_Amount	Currency	8
	Check_Date	Date/Time	8
FK	Supplier_Number	Text	10

PK/FK	Attribute Name	Type	Size
FK	Account_Number	Text	10
FK	Partner_Number	Text	10
	Table: tblPartners		
PK	Partner_number	Text	10
	Partner_first_name	Text	15
	Partner_last_name	Text	15
	Partner_hire_date	Date/Time	8
	Partner_SocSecNo	Text	11
	Partner_Address	Text	50
	Partner_Address2	Text	50
	Partner_City	Text	20
	Partner_State	Text	2

TABLE 6.2
Sunset Database Table and Attribute Definitions

(continued)

PK/FK	Attribute Name	Type	Size
	Partner_Zip	Text	10
	Partner_phone	Text	14
	Partner_cellphone	Text	14
	Table: tblProductCategory		
PK	Product_category_number	Text	10
	Product_category_description	Text	255
	Product_category_manager	Text	10
	Product_category_notes	Memo	–
	Table: tblProducts		
PK	Product_number	Text	10
	Product_description	Text	255
	Product_price	Currency	8
	Product_unit_of_sale	Text	10
	Product_category	Text	10
	Product_quantity_on_hand	Integer	2
	Product_notes	Memo	–
	Table: tblPurchaseItems		
PK	Purchase_Order_number	Text	10
PK	Product_number	Text	10
	Purchase_Order_quantity	Integer	2
	Purchase_Order_price	Currency	8
	Received_quantity	Integer	2
	Accepted_quantity	Integer	2
	Table: tblPurchases		
PK	Purchase_Order_Number	Text	10
	Purchase_Order_Date	Date/Time	8

PK/FK	Attribute Name	Type	Size
FK	Prepared_by	Text	10
FK	Supplier_Number	Text	10
	Received_Date	Date/Time	8
	Purchase_Order_Amount	Currency	8
	Required_by	Date/Time	8
FK	Check_Number	Text	10
	Memo	Memo	–
	Table: tblSupplierCategory		
PK	Supplier_category_number	Text	10
	Supplier_category_description	Text	255
	Supplier_category_purchases_YTD	Currency	8
	Supplier_category_notes	Memo	–
	Table: tblSuppliers		
PK	Supplier_Number	Text	15
	Supplier_Name	Text	25
	Supplier_Contact_Name	Text	20
	Suppllier_Address	Text	30
	Supplier_Address_2	Text	30
	Supplier_City	Text	20
	Supplier_State	Text	2
	Supplier_Zip	Text	5
	Supplier_phone	Text	15
	Supplier_web_site	Hyperlink	–
FK	Supplier_Category	Text	10

TABLE 6.2
(continued)

Create Database and Define Tables

The next step is to create a new, blank Microsoft Access database and create the tables described in Table 6.2. Then, establish *relationships* between the tables as shown in Figure 6.7 and as described in Chapter 5. At that point, Sunset's purchases and payments process database is set up.

COMPREHENSIVE EXERCISE: BAER BELLY BIKINIS' PURCHASES OF FABRIC

As outlined in Chapter 5, Baer Belly Bikinis, Inc. (BBB) is a small business located in Santa Monica, California. It sells swimwear and related products to specialty stores throughout the United States. It also sells its products to individuals over a company website. Paige Baer founded BBB almost 10 years ago after she graduated from the Fashion Institute of Design and Merchandising. She recognized the need for swimsuits sold as separates. Her business has grown rapidly, and now BBB has a large following of customers who want to

FIGURE 6.7
Linked Tables with Referential Integrity Enforced

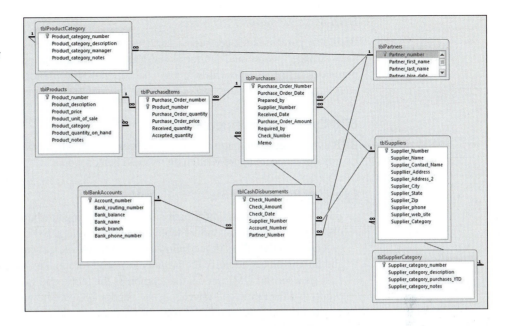

be able to mix and match to find their ideal swimsuit. Currently, BBB products are carried in more than 1,000 specialty swimwear boutiques and online retailers.

During an initial interview with Paige Baer, she outlined BBB's business processes. She acknowledged that she doesn't know much about accounting and information technology. As the business grew, her accounting suffered and information systems were added piecemeal. So, she is looking forward to an assessment of her requirements and recommendations that would position BBB for substantial further growth.

This case examines BBB purchases of fabric. BBB's production staff selects the fabric and materials for the swimsuits. This case also examines BBB purchases of and miscellaneous supplies and services.

BBB Purchases of Fabric

BBB works closely with local fabric vendors to determine the color themes for each season's products. When BBB has received enough orders from the retailer customers to estimate the quantity of swimsuits and products to manufacture, BBB then orders the required quantities of fabric and related materials from the fabric vendors. BBB pays each fabric vendor at the end of the month for all purchases

Assessing fabric purchase requirements.

during the month. For each fabric order, there is one receipt. For each receipt of fabric, there is one order. Consequently, the order and purchases (receipts) can be modeled as one event.

Details of the Fabric Purchase Process

1. The Production supervisor places an order for fabric according to internal estimates of production quantities (the estimates are not part of the project).
2. Fabric vendors ship fabric in bulk to BBB usually within 2 weeks of the order.
3. A Shipping and Warehouse employee receives the bulk fabric and verifies quantities received.

BBB Miscellaneous Purchases

BBB also purchases miscellaneous services and supplies, such as electricity, water, sewage, garbage, phone, and janitorial services. It also pays monthly rent on the building, purchases office supplies, hires photo shoot models and photographers, and so on. BBB pays its miscellaneous suppliers at the end of the month for all purchases during the month.

BBB Cash Disbursements

BBB assigns sequential numbers to each check issued. All checks for purchases (both fabric and miscellaneous) are written on its main bank account.

Exercise Requirements

1. Based on the preceding information and the following attributes list, prepare a UML class model and corresponding table listing describing BBB's purchases and payments process. List the tables in the following order: resources, events, agents, type images, and linking tables. Identify the primary keys and foreign keys in each table. [optional] Prepare a second UML model that combines the fabric and miscellaneous purchases events and the fabric and miscellaneous vendor agents. Show how you might model a way to differentiate among the types of vendors.
2. [optional] Based on the preceding information, prepare a BPMN activity model that describes BBB's purchases and payments process. The model should begin with BBB placing orders with its vendors and end when BBB makes payments for the purchases to the vendors.
3. Your instructor will provide an Excel spreadsheet with the BBB information. Create a new Access database, and import each worksheet in the spreadsheet into the database. Set appropriate primary keys.
4. After importing all the data, create relationships among tables to implement your data model.
5. Prepare queries to answer the following questions:
   a. What were BBB's total purchases of fabric in the second quarter (April to June)?
   b. What is BBB's accounts payable balance for each fabric as of April 15?
   c. Based on the information available, what is the quantity on hand in yards for each fabric color code as of April 15?

Attribute Listing for BBB

Bank Name	Employee Last Name
Cash Account#	Employee Pay Amount
Cash Account Description	Employee Phone
Cash Account Balance 4/1/13	Employee Salary/Wage
Check Amount	Employee Zip
Check Pay Date	Fabric Color Code
Check#	Fabric Color Name
Employee Department	Fabric Cost per Yard
Employee#	Fabric Inventory Quantity on Hand
Employee Address	Fabric Purchase Total Amount
Employee City	Fabric Purchase Quantity in Yards
Employee First Name	Fabric Purchase Received By
Employee Hire Date	Fabric Purchase Date Received

Fabric Purchase Order Date	Miscellaneous Vendor Company
Fabric Purchase Order#	Miscellaneous Vendor Item Number
Fabric Vendor Address1	Miscellaneous Vendor State
Fabric Vendor Address2	Miscellaneous Vendor#
Fabric Vendor Company	Miscellaneous Vendor Zip
Fabric Vendor Item Number	Order Employee#
Fabric Vendor State	Pay Employee#
Fabric Vendor Type	Miscellaneous Purchase#
Fabric Vendor#	Miscellaneous Purchase Amount
Fabric Vendor Zip	Miscellaneous Purchase Date
Miscellaneous Vendor Address1	Miscellaneous Purchasing Employee#
Miscellaneous Vendor Address2	Vendor Type

Summary

- From an accounting standpoint, we must account for purchase orders, the receipt of goods and services (purchases), accounts payable, and cash disbursements (payments) in the purchases and payments process.
- Sunset Graphics Inc. provides a continuing example of how the purchases and payments process is modeled.
- BPMN activity diagrams can provide the basic sequence of tasks or can be extended to describe specific organizational responsibilities for tasks.
- Business rules implement controls over the purchases and payments process.
- UML class diagrams for the purchases and payments process are built on the standard REA pattern and look very similar to sales and collection process structure diagrams.
- Type images categorize information about agents and resources and show assignments.
- The structure models are the blueprint from which relational databases are designed and implemented.
- A comprehensive example reinforces the concepts presented in the chapter.

Key Words

accounts payable (*130*)   Amounts owed to suppliers for goods and services received. In a data modeling context, accounts payable are calculated based on receipts (purchases) from each supplier less the corresponding payments (cash disbursements) to those suppliers.

agents (*135*)   The people or organizations who participate in business events, such as customers and salespeople.

cash (*135*)   The organization's monies in bank or related accounts. The instances of the class are individual accounts. This is considered a resource.

cash disbursements (*130*)   Record payments of cash to external agents (e.g., suppliers) and the corresponding reduction in cash accounts. This is considered an event.

choreography (*131*)   The interaction (message flows) between two participants (modeled as pools) in a process modeled using BPMN.

collaboration (*131*)   A BPMN model showing two participant pools and the interactions between them within a process.

events (*135*)   Classes that model the organization's transactions, usually affecting the organization's resources, such as sales and cash receipts.

gateway (132) Shows process branching and merging as the result of decisions. Basic gateways are depicted as diamonds. Usually, gateways appear as pairs on the diagram. The first gateway shows the branching, and the second gateway shows merging of the process branches.

intermediate event (133) Occurs between start and end events and affects the flow of the process.

intermediate timer event (133) Intermediate events that indicate a delay in the normal process flow until a fixed amount of time has elapsed.

many-to-many relationship (136) Exists when instances of one class (e.g., sales) are related to many instances of another class (e.g., inventory) and vice versa. These relationships are implemented in Access and relational databases by adding a linking table to convert the many-to-many relationship into two one-to-many relationships.

one-to-one relationship (136) Exists when instances of one class (e.g., sales) are related to only instance of another class (e.g., cash receipts) and each instance of the other class is related to only one instance of the original class.

orchestration (131) In BPMN, the sequence of activities within one pool.

product (135) Class representing the organization's goods held for sale, that is, the organization's inventory. This is considered a resource.

purchase discount (130) An offer from the supplier to reduce the cost of a purchase if payment is made according to specified terms, usually within a specified time.

purchase order (130) A commitment event that precedes the economic purchase event. It records formal offers to suppliers to pay them if the supplier complies with the terms of the purchase order.

purchases (130) Records the receipt of goods or services from a supplier and the corresponding obligation to pay the supplier. These are considered events.

REA (135) Resource-event-agent framework for modeling business processes, originally developed by William McCarthy.

receipt (135) Same as the purchases event.

resources (135) Those things that have economic value to a firm, such as cash and products.

subprocess (132) Represent a series of process steps that are hidden from view in BPMN. The use of subprocesses in modeling helps reduce complexity.

suppliers (130) In the UML diagram of the purchases and payments process, the external agents from whom goods and services are purchased and to whom payments are made.

timer events (133) Indication of a delay in the flow of a process to a specific date, an elapsed time (for example, 30 days), or a relative repetitive date, such as every Friday.

type image (137) Class that represents management information (such as categorizations, policies, and guidelines) to help manage a business process. Type image often allows process information to be summarized by category.

Appendix A

Generic REA Model with Multiplicities for the Purchases and Payments Process

GENERIC PATTERN WITH MULTIPLICITIES

Figure 6.A1 shows a generic purchases and payments process UML diagram. There are two resources, *inventory* and *cash;* there are two events, *purchases* and *cash disbursements;* and there are two agents, *employees* (internal agent) and *suppliers* (external agent).

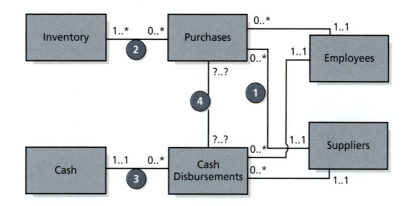

FIGURE 6.A1

Generic Purchases
and Payments UML
Diagram

In this example, let's assume that the inventory is something tracked by universal product code (UPC). UPC codes are those bar codes you see on literally millions of products, such as soap, breakfast cereal, and packages of cookies. The cash resource represents the various bank accounts that would make up this enterprise's cash balance on its balance sheet. The purchases event records information about individual purchase transactions (e.g., transaction number, date, total dollar amount). The cash disbursement event records information about payments made to suppliers from one of the bank accounts (e.g., check number, check date, check dollar amount). The employees agent records information about the enterprise's employees, including those employees who handle purchases transactions. The suppliers agent records information about actual and potential suppliers (let's assume that supplier information is recorded in some cases before the firm orders anything from them, and let's also assume that the company only writes checks to suppliers).

Figure 6.A1 shows the generic REA model. You should immediately notice the similarity with the sales and collection process diagram shown in Appendix A of Chapter 5. Consider association 1 between *suppliers* and *purchases*. The multiplicities indicate that each supplier participates in a minimum of zero and a maximum of many sales. Does this seem reasonable? The minimum of zero means that we can record information about suppliers before they participate in any sale. On the other side of the association, the multiplicities indicate that each purchase involves one and only one supplier. Again, does this seem reasonable? Notice that the multiplicities for the other associations between agents and events are the same. In fact, these are the typical multiplicities for those associations. There are circumstances where they might be different, but those circumstances occur infrequently.

Next, consider association 2 between the *purchases* event and *inventory* resource. The multiplicities indicate that each purchase involves a minimum of one and a maximum of many inventory items. The multiplicities also indicate that each inventory item can be purchased zero times or many times. The multiplicities on this association are typical when the inventory is carried at a type of product level, such as when the inventory is identified by UPC code.

Now, consider association 3 between the *cash disbursement* event and the *cash* resource. These multiplicities indicate that each cash disbursement (e.g., one check) is paid from one and only one account, and each account is associated with a minimum of zero cash disbursements and a maximum of many cash disbursements. These multiplicities reflect typical business practices. Think about paying bills using your bank's online banking feature. You log on, select the account, and then pay the bill. The amount of the payment is subtracted from that one account.

Finally, consider the duality association 4 between the *purchases* and *cash disbursement* events. The question marks indicate that these multiplicities depend on the nature of the business as well as the terms of the particular purchase. Payments could be made before, after, or at the same time of the purchase. One payment could be made for several purchases, or one purchase could involve several payments. So, there are no typical multiplicities for this association.

We recommend that students recognize and use the standard patterns for multiplicities as shown in Figure 6.A1, remembering that those standard multiplicities could change depending on the particular circumstances of the business.

Multiple Choice Questions

1. Which of the following is not an activity in the purchases and payments process?
   a. Request prices
   b. Receive items
   c. Pay for items
   d. Bill customers
   e. All of the above are activities in the purchases and payments process.

2. Which activity results in an increase to accounts payable?
   a. Request prices
   b. Place purchase order
   c. Receive items
   d. Return rejected items
   e. Send payment

3. *Choreography* describes which of the following?
   a. Sequence of activities in a process
   b. Message flows between pools
   c. Process gateways
   d. Both a and c
   e. Both b and c

4. Which of the following is not an example of an application control?
   a. Range checks ensure that purchases are limited to valid amounts.
   b. Employee making disbursements cannot modify purchase orders.
   c. System supplies supplier address for the payment.
   d. System creates audit trail documenting all changes.
   e. All of the above are examples of application controls.

5. Which of the following describes the purpose of an intermediate timer event?
   a. Indicates receipt of a message
   b. Indicates branching

c. Indicates delay

d. Both a and c

e. Both b and c

6. Which of the following is a resource in a purchases and payments structure model?

    a. Employee labor

    b. Receipt of goods

    c. Paying by check

    d. Inventory

    e. Supplier

7. Which of the following is an agent in a purchases and payments structure model?

    a. Employee labor

    b. Receipt of goods

    c. Cash disbursement

    d. Inventory

    e. Supplier

8. Which of the following is an event in a purchases and payments structure model?

    a. Cash

    b. Inventory

    c. Employee

    d. Cash disbursement

    e. None of the above

9. Which of the following events would indicate recording of a purchase in the AIS?

    a. Issue Purchase Order

    b. Receive Goods

    c. Make Payment

    d. Transfer Inventory

    e. None of the above

10. In a typical relational database supporting the purchase and payment process, which of the following tables is likely to have the most foreign keys?

    a. Employee table

    b. Supplier table

    c. Inventory table

    d. Cash disbursement table

    e. Cash table

Discussion Questions

1. Business rules implement internal controls. Review Table 6.1 and describe which business rules implement segregation of duties. Classify each of those business rules as obligatory, prohibited, or allowed as described in Chapter 3.

2. **Walmart** uses a vendor-managed inventory process, where the inventory is owned and managed by the vendor until it is delivered from **Walmart's** distribution center to the stores. What implications does this process have for **Walmart's** purchases and payments process?

3. Draw an activity model using BPMN for the process that you used when you purchased your textbooks for the current semester.

4. Refer to Figure 6.5. Describe the types of businesses that would employ a similar diagram for their purchases and payments processes. What other options are there? Describe some businesses that would use other options for the purchases and payments process structure.

5. Recall that type images apply guidelines, constraints, and descriptive information, as well as categorizing the economic resources, events, and agents for a business process. Figure 6.6 shows two examples of type images for Sunset Graphics. Are there other possible type images that could be added to the diagram to help Sunset's managers manage the purchases and payments process?

6. Some larger companies and government entities issue contracts for major purchases and then issue specific purchase orders to their contractors according to the terms of the contract. The contract can specify prices and payment terms as well as other administrative procedures. How would the use of contracts affect the standard process flow as shown in Figure 6.2? How would it affect the UML class diagram for the purchases and payments process?

7. Sunset Graphics often buys inventory after receiving a sales order from the customer. Suppose you are asked to prepare one UML class diagram that combines both the sales and collection process and the purchases and payments process. What would be shared among those processes? What would be unique to each process? Why?

8. What classes and associations would be included in a model that describes the information needed for a query that calculates the accounts payable balance for each supplier? Describe the logic of that query. (In other words, how would you compute that balance?)

Problems

1. The Tablet Store recently opened to sell iPads and other tablet computing devices. It purchases its tablets directly from the manufacturers (e.g., **Apple**, **Samsung**, and **Dell**). This problem describes its purchases and payments process. To order tablets, a Tablet Store employee submits a purchase order to the manufacturer electronically. Each purchase order could stipulate several different models of tablets from one manufacturer. The manufacturers typically deliver the tablets to the store within 2 weeks after they receive the purchase order. The Tablet Store pays for each shipment within 30 days after receipt. If there are multiple orders to the same manufacturer, the Tablet Store occasionally combines payments, issuing one check for multiple receipts. All of the Tablet Store checks are drawn on one bank account.

   a. Draw a UML class diagram that describes the Tablet Store's purchases and payments process.

   b. Using Microsoft Access, implement a relational database from your UML class diagram. Identify at least three fields per table.

   c. Describe how you would use the relational database to determine the Tablet Store's accounts payable.

2. Quick Jet Inc. provides air taxi service to the wealthy, including celebrities, sports stars, and business executives. This case describes how Quick Jet leases and maintains its planes. Quick Jet employees negotiate long-term leases with airplane leasing companies. Each lease involves one plane. Quick Jet categorizes its planes according to passenger capacity and normal flying range. Quick Jet makes monthly lease payments for its planes. If it leases multiple planes from the same lease company, it combines payments.

   ### Maintenance
   The company has no maintenance staff of its own, so it also contracts with a number of airplane maintenance companies to perform the routine maintenance required to keep its fleet airworthy. It issues orders against the contracts for specific maintenance required for the planes. To comply with FAA regulations, it tracks the details of the specific maintenance performed on each plane. To facilitate the tracking, each maintenance order specifies the maintenance services for one plane. Quick Jet pays for all the maintenance performed by each maintenance contractor within 15 days, according to the terms of the contracts, and may combine payments.

   ### Miscellaneous Purchases
   Quick Jet also provides each of its pilots with credit cards so they can purchase fuel and miscellaneous supplies at the various airports they use. The pilots turn in detailed lists of

their purchases that identify the supplier, the date, the amount purchased, and the prices, as well as the plane for which the items were purchased. Each list is assigned a miscellaneous purchase number. Quick Jet pays the credit card bills in full each month upon receipt from the credit card company.

Other Information

Quick Jet keeps information about the plane leasing companies, the plane maintenance contractors, miscellaneous suppliers, and the credit card companies in one vendor file. However, it tracks plane leases, maintenance contracts, maintenance orders, and miscellaneous purchases separately (separate events). Quick Jet categorizes its employees according to their job assignments (e.g., pilots, purchasing employees, A/P clerks). It also categorizes vendors according to the services/goods they provide. It puts information about its agents, resources, and type images in the database before linking to other classes.

a. Draw a BPMN activity diagram that describes Quick Jet's purchases and payments process.

b. Prepare a UML class diagram with classes, associations, and multiplicities.

c. Using the preceding information and the following attributes list, prepare a listing of the relational tables necessary to support this sales and collection process. List the tables in the following order: resources, events, agents, type images, and linking tables.

Attributes:

Cash account#	Plane#
Cash account balance	Plane maintenance contract#
Check#	Plane maintenance contract date
Check amount	Plane maintenance contract duration
Check date	Plane maintenance item performed on this order for this plane
Date this misc. purchase billed by credit card company	Plane maintenance order#
Employee#	Plane maintenance order date
Employee hire date	Plane miles since last maintenance
Employee Name	Plane type
Employee type	Plane type passenger capacity
Employee type description	Plane type range in miles
Lease#	Vendor#
Lease date	Vendor Name
Lease monthly payment amount	Vendor type
Misc. supply purchase#	Vendor type description
Misc. supply purchase date	Year-to-date (YTD) purchases from this vendor type
Number of vendors of this type	

3. BR Management Company (BRMC) operates apartment complexes and earns revenues by renting out the apartments in those complexes. BRMC assigns an agent/manager to each complex (one manager can manage several complexes) to handle day-to-day operations, such as maintaining the property and signing rental contracts. This case describes the maintenance and rental processes.

Complexes and Apartments

BRMC has acquired 15 and built several more apartment complexes over the past 2 years. It identifies complexes by address and apartments by the combination of address and apartment number. BRMC categorizes each apartment according to a number of factors, including the quality of its furnishings, number of rooms, and size. There are 27 apartment categories at present, each identified by unique category number. Because each complex presents a unique set of luxury appointments and amenities, BRMC determines the standard monthly rental fee by considering both the apartment category and complex; for example, 2 bedroom 1 bath apartments (category 21) rent for $850 per month in the Broadway complex, but the same category apartments rent for $1,450 per month in the Naples complex.

Maintenance

BRMC keeps its apartments and complexes in top condition. The BRMC agents monitor the condition of the facilities. Whenever the condition falls below BRMC standards, the agents hire contractors to bring the apartment back up to specifications. BRMC classifies each maintenance job by job type, and it matches the job type to the contractor type that can best perform the job. The BRMC agent then selects one specific contractor for the job from that contractor type. Each contractor may belong to several contractor types. Each maintenance job involves either one apartment or the common areas of the complex. BRMC tracks the maintenance performed on apartments and complex common areas.

Rentals

BRMC agents negotiate rental contracts with tenants. Each rental contract governs one year-long lease of an apartment. Although there is a standard monthly rental fee for each apartment in each building, agents may negotiate higher or lower rents if they see the need to do so. It is important to have a full record of the actual rent for all apartments. When there is more than one tenant per apartment, every tenant must sign the rental contract. BRMC assigns a unique tenant ID number to each tenant and issues them ID cards to control access.

Cash Receipts and Disbursements and Other Information

To simplify the case, the cash resource, the cashier agent, and the cash receipt and disbursement events (although they would certainly exist) are eliminated. You should *not* model those in your solution. All agents, resources, and types are put into the database before they are linked to other classes.

a. Prepare an integrated UML class diagram with classes, associations, and multiplicities.

b. Using the preceding information and the following attributes list, prepare a listing of the relational tables necessary to support BRMC's processes. List the tables in the following order: resources, events, agents, type images, and linking tables.

Attributes:

employee#	actual cost of this job
apartment square footage	apartment category#
apartment#	number of available apartments in this category
date complex was constructed	
total complex square footage	count of rooms in apartment
contractor#	vendor#
contractor name	actual monthly rent
contractor quality rating	tenant ID#
contractor phone number	tenant name
contractor type	rental contract#
apartment complex address	rental contract date
job type	tenant credit rating
standard cost for this job type	year to date (YTD) advertising $ for this vendor
YTD $ spent on this job type	
count of this type of contractor	agent monthly salary
actual completion date of job	agent name
maintenance job#	standard monthly rent
projected completion date of job	YTD $ spent on this job type in this complex

Answers to Multiple Choice Questions

1. d
2. c
3. b
4. e
5. c

6. d
7. e
8. d
9. b
10. d

Conversion Business Process

A look at this chapter

This chapter examines the conversion process whereby manufacturing companies convert raw material into finished goods. We continue our comprehensive example to develop activity and structure models of the process. We show how the activity model in conjunction with business rules can be used to develop, implement, and monitor control activities. We show how the structure model can be used to develop a relational database to support information processing requirements.

A look back

Chapter 6 examined the purchases and payments processes. It continued the comprehensive example that we are using to examine typical process activities and data structures.

A look ahead

Chapter 8 provides a hands-on project to review Chapters 5, 6, and 7.

Starbucks roasts its coffee in roasting plants distributed around the United States. One plant is a nondescript, 320,000-square-foot warehouse building located in Kent, Washington. Other roasting plants are located in Carson Valley, Nevada; York, Pennsylvania; and Amsterdam, Netherlands. The coffee beans are stacked in 150-pound burlap bags, and each bag is marked to identify the country of origin.

The bags of green coffee beans are stacked over a large metal grate in the floor. A worker cuts open the bag and the beans pour through the grate. They are pulled into a washer that separates foreign material. After washing, the beans are weighed, sorted, and stored for roasting. They are transferred into large roasters that can hold up to 600 pounds of beans. The roasting process is carefully computer-controlled. As the beans roast, they slowly turn brown. When the beans pop, the flavor is released.

The beans are transferred to cooling vats that turn and toss them to stop further roasting. Workers test the roasted beans. Soon, they are bagged and boxed for shipment. On average, the roasted beans will be in stores within 3 days.

To keep a constant flow of quality product to their worldwide network of stores, Starbucks needs to monitor its conversion process closely. In addition to the cost information that affects its financial statements, what other information is necessary for Starbucks' management of this process?

Chapter Outline

Learning Objectives

After reading this chapter, you should be able to:

7-1 Describe the business activities that comprise the conversion process.

7-2 Develop an activity model of the conversion process using BPMN.

7-3 Understand and apply different activity modeling options.

7-4 Develop business rules to implement controls for the conversion process.

7-5 Develop a structure model for the conversion process using UML class diagrams.

7-6 Implement a relational database from the UML class diagram of the conversion process.

LO 7-1

Describe the business
activities that comprise
the conversion process.

CONVERSION PROCESS

The conversion process is inherently more complicated than the sales and collections
and purchases and payments processes described in the previous two chapters, primarily
because of increased recordkeeping requirements and variations in the sophistication of the
process itself among companies. Many types of businesses employ conversion processes,
including bakeries, wineries, breweries, restaurants, car repair shops, construction companies, equipment manufacturers, automobile manufacturers, and so on.[1] The conversion
process includes business activities related to maintaining inventories of raw material and
finished goods, producing finished goods from raw material, tracking direct labor, direct
equipment costs, and applying overhead.

The conversion process generates accounting transactions to record the transfer of raw
material to work-in-process and work-in-process inventory to finished goods. In addition
to the cost of raw materials, the conversion process must also account for direct labor and
other direct costs incurred in determining the cost of goods manufactured. The allocation
of overhead and indirect costs to work-in-process is typically based on direct labor-hours,
although overhead could be allocated based on a number of cost drivers in an activity-
based costing system. More specifically, conversion costs are typically accounted for at
standard, where the standard is based on management estimates, and then the costs are
updated to reflect actual costs incurred. Figure 7.1 describes typical transactions resulting
from the conversion process. In addition to the accounting transactions, the specific details
of the conversion process are often tracked to the individual job.

In this chapter, we continue to apply the tools introduced in Chapters 2 through 6
to a comprehensive example of the conversion process. We first describe the process
activities using BPMN, and then we define the typical information structure using UML
class diagrams. Finally, we use the UML class diagrams to build a database to collect and
report relevant process information. We also describe business rules that establish potential process controls.

SUNSET GRAPHICS EXAMPLE

Company Overview

As described in Chapters 5 and 6, Virgil and Linda B own and operate Sunset Graphics.
They design and sell signs and banners, lettering and vinyl graphics for vehicles and boats,
corporate promotional items, and silk-screened T-shirts and embroidered gear, among
other products. Recently, Virgil and Linda decided that it was time to step back from the
day-to-day operations. Before they did, they wanted to review their business processes to
develop better documentation, improve processes, and establish consistency in customer
service. They also wanted to be sure that effective internal controls were in place, since
they wouldn't be on site as often.

Sunset Graphics' Conversion Process Description

Until recently, Sunset didn't track its conversion costs. If labor was involved in preparing
products for a customer's order, Sunset simply billed the customer a flat rate for the service. The company didn't assign any labor or overhead costs to its products. However,
that changed when it signed a major contract to provide a variety of signs and banners to
state agencies. The terms of the contract required that Sunset include direct labor, direct

---

[1]We focus on companies that use job cost accounting methods, although the models could apply
generally to companies that also use process costing methods.

FIGURE 7.1

Typical Conversion Process Accounting Transactions

Sep 1	Work-in-Process Inventory	2,875,50			
	Raw Material Inventory		2,875.50		
	Record transfer of raw material to Work-in-process				
Sep 2	Manufacturing Wages	4,650.00			
	Cash		4,650.00		
	To record manufacturing payroll				
Sep 2	Work-in-Process Inventory	3,250.00			
	Manufacturing Wages		3,250.00		
	To record direct labor				
Sep 2	Manufacturing Overhead	1,400.00			
	Manufacturing Wages		1,400.00		
	To record indirect labor				
Sep 2	Manufacturing Overhead	1,945.25			
	Utilities Payable		1,945.25		
	To record manufacturing overhead costs				
Sep 2	Work-in-Process Inventory	4,062.50			
	Manufacturing Overhead		4,062.50		
	To allocate manufacturing overhead to				
	work-in-process at 125% of direct labor				
Sep 3	Finished Goods	10,188.00			
	Work-in-Process Inventory		10,188.00		
	Record transfer work-in-process to finished goods				

equipment costs, and overhead in the cost of its products. Although Sunset used job costing for this contract, Virgil and Linda B began to wonder if job costing could be used to provide better information about the real costs of their products.

Virgil and Linda B explained their conversion process. Demand for products under the state contract fluctuated but often required short delivery times, so they decided to keep a safety stock of those products (**finished goods inventory**) on hand. When inventory levels dropped below certain levels, they then authorized production to replenish the inventory. To reduce delays, they also decided to maintain a **raw materials inventory,** although they wanted to keep those inventory levels as low as possible. It required some planning, but they created bills of material that identified the raw material required for each product and estimated the required inventory levels to keep production smooth and meet demand.

They summarized Sunset's conversion process as follows:

1. When the quantity on hand of a product dropped below the minimum level, the item manager authorized production to increase the quantity on hand.
2. Based on the bill of material for that item, they issued material into work-in-process.
3. Sunset partners then constructed the items.
4. Upon completion, the products were placed in inventory.

LO 7-2
Develop an activity
model of the
conversion process
using BPMN.

SUNSET GRAPHICS' ACTIVITY MODELS

Basic Purchases Activity Model

After talking with Virgil and Linda B about their conversion process, our first task was to draw a simple activity model using BPMN. As shown in Figure 7.2, the start of the process occurs when Sunset needs to replenish finished goods inventory. Then, the production authorization starts production activities, including the issue of raw material (R/M) and the use of direct labor. Work continues until the required quantity of the finished good item is prepared. At that point, production is complete, and the finished goods inventory is updated.

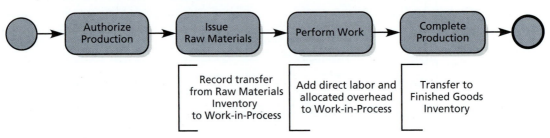

FIGURE 7.2
Basic Conversion Activity Model

LO 7-3
Understand and apply
different activity
modeling options.

Refining the Model

Virgil remarked that a collaboration model would not make much sense here. All the work is within Sunset. We agreed, but we said that swimlanes could show the different functions within Sunset to help clarify responsibilities. Both Virgil and Linda thought that, yes, it would clarify responsibilities. Virgil then added that sometimes they performed the work in a series of batches to make the process more manageable. Plus, they didn't necessarily issue all the raw materials at once. Sometimes, they started a batch, issued some raw materials, worked on those, and then issued more raw materials. They repeated these steps until they finished production.

We said that it would be pretty easy to add those refinements to the model, but wondered if there was anything else to consider. Linda then added that they always inspect the work before it is added to the finished goods inventory, and if it doesn't meet quality standards, they discard the bad items and replace them. Finally, while partners place the finished items in inventory, the inventory manager updates the records.

We then proposed the model shown in Figure 7.3. This model showed two swimlanes: (1) for the inventory manager and (2) for the Sunset employees who perform the work. This model shows the inventory manager authorizing production. Then, the conversion partners set up the batch, issue raw materials, and perform work making the finished good item. At that point, a partner inspects the work and if the work does not meet quality standards, the **intermediate error event** directs the process flow to the "discard items" activity. The sequence then loops back to issue more raw materials. If the batch is not finished, the **gateway** also directs the sequence flow back to issue more raw materials, and the steps are repeated until the batch is done. Then, a second gateway branches, depending on whether all batches are complete. If not, the sequence flow is directed back to the "set up batch" activity and the steps repeat until all batches are done. The conversion partners complete production by placing the finished items in inventory, and the inventory manager updates the inventory records.

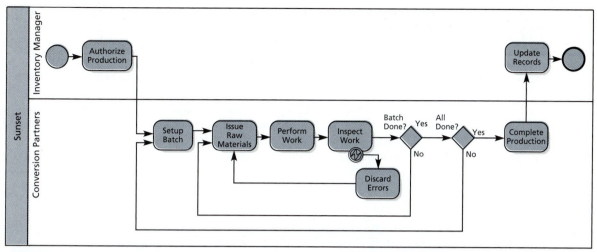

FIGURE 7.3
Conversion Process with Swimlanes and Loops

Both Virgil and Linda agreed that this model accurately describes their process. We noted that for internal control, we probably should have identified a third swimlane to show the separate "inspect work" function. The same partners who perform the work should not inspect the work. Virgil acknowledged that we were probably right, but we could leave that change for another day.

Progress *Check*

1. How would you change Figure 7.3 to show a separate organization unit performing the inspect work function?
2. Could you model the intermediate error event with a gateway instead? What would that look like?

LO 7-4

Develop business rules to implement controls for the conversion process.

BUSINESS RULES AND SUNSET GRAPHICS' CONVERSION PROCESS CONTROLS

Again, we asked Virgil and Linda B about controls over the conversion process. As with the other processes, we intended to define controls by developing business rules for the process. First, we needed to identify important business events and define Sunset's intention or objective for each event. Then, we determined the appropriate actions to take based on the conditions. For example, we've already listed important business events in the activity models, so let's examine Sunset's conversion process in Figures 7.2 and 7.3 to develop some possible business rules.

Virgil and Linda summarized their objectives for the steps in the process. Of course, their overall goal was to ensure finished products were

Inspecting work and discarding defects.

available to meet expected demand. Because they were not going to directly supervise the process anymore, they wanted to be sure that effective controls were applied.

We outlined some standard controls over the conversion process, suggesting segregation of authorizing, issuing, and conversion work duties. We reiterated that *access controls* limit which of their partners can view and change records in the system and help implement appropriate segregation of duties. We also need *application controls* to ensure data integrity and an audit trail. For example, we need to control the assignment of production authorization and material issue numbers to make sure they are all accounted for. Plus, we need to establish appropriate ranges or limits for each value that partners can add or change in the system.

With Virgil and Linda's direction, we developed an initial set of business rules for the conversion process. They articulated their intentions for every step in the process, and then we set business rules to segregate duties and limit partner authority appropriately. Table 7.1

TABLE 7.1
Using Business Rules to Implement Internal Controls

Process Steps	Intention	Partner Authority/Action	Access Controls	Application Controls
Authorize Production	Partner with proper authority authorizes production to ensure finished goods are available to meet expected demand.	Supervisor must authorize production >$5,000.	Partner authorizing production cannot modify inventory records.	System must provide authorization order number control, default values, and range and limit checks; must also create audit trail.
Issue Raw Material	Issues from raw material according to bill of material recorded accurately.	Partner issuing material must not be same partner who authorized production.	Partner recording issue of material cannot modify bill of material.	System must only allow partner to enter the number of items issued based on bill of material, subject to range and limit checks on quantities; date defaults to current date.
Perform Work	Direct labor costs recorded promptly and accurately.	Partner performing direct labor must not be same partner authorizing production.	Partner recording labor costs cannot modify production authorization.	System must provide control numbers, hours, costs range, and limit checks; date defaults to current date.
Inspect Work and Discard Defects	Inspection ensures that only products meeting quality standards are allowed.	Partner inspecting work must not be a partner performing work.	Partner recording inspection cannot modify inventory records.	System must provide limit checks; date defaults to current date.
Complete Production	Finished product inventory must be updated promptly and accurately.	Partner placing products in finished inventory must not be same partner authorizing production.	Partner recording update of inventory records cannot modify production authorization.	System must default date to current date; inventory update limit is based on authorization.

shows the initial set of business rules for Sunset's conversion process. We noted that we would need to set application controls for almost every attribute updated during data entry.

SUNSET GRAPHICS' STRUCTURE MODELS

LO 7-5
Develop structure models for the conversion process using UML class diagrams.

Now, both Virgil and Linda B looked forward to adding the conversion process features to Sunset's new database. This would mean that their database could handle their entire supply chain encompassing purchasing, making, and selling their products. We proceeded to examine Sunset Graphics' conversion information requirements. As described in Chapter 3, the primary purpose of our UML class diagram of the conversion process is to create a blueprint for the development of a relational database to support the collection, aggregation, and communication of process information. As in Chapters 5 and 6, we follow the **REA** framework (resources, events, and agents) as a proven approach to describing business processes in a way that meets both accounting and broad management information requirements.

Basic UML Class Diagram for Conversion

Based on what Virgil and Linda told us about their conversion process, we thought it was very close to a generic conversion process model shown in Figure 7.4. As indicated by numbers 1 and 2, an employee (**agent**) with supervisory responsibility authorizes production (**event**) of one or more finished good items (**resources**). Next, numbers 3 and 4 denote that an employee (agent) issues (event) the raw material (resource) into **work-in-process inventory** based on the bills of material for the finished goods items. Finally, number 5 shows that production employees perform work to make the finished goods items and their direct labor is recorded (**labor operations event**).

FIGURE 7.4
Generic UML Class Diagram for the Conversion Process

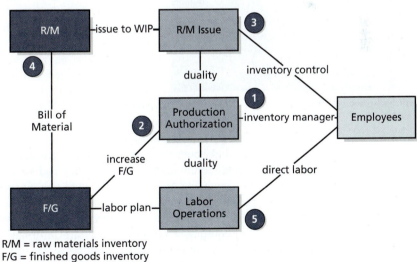

R/M = raw materials inventory
F/G = finished goods inventory
WIP = work-in-process inventory

We explained that the association between finished goods and labor operations indicates the planned labor. The bill of materials association between finished goods and raw material indicates the planned material content of each finished good item. The two duality associations link the raw material issue and labor operations events to the production authorization. Thus, the data structure captures information about both planned and actual conversion activity.

Virgil said that he understood most of the diagram, but where is the work-in-process inventory resource? We explained that we don't need to model a separate work-in-process inventory, because we can calculate that value at any time. For example, the **raw material issue event** records the value of items issued into work-in-process. The labor operations event records the value of direct labor added to work-in-process. The labor plan association establishes standard overhead allocation rates. Until the job is complete, the accumulated material, labor, and overhead costs increase work-in-process inventory. When the job is complete, which would be recorded in the initial **production authorization event,** the cost of goods manufactured increase the finished goods inventory value.

Refining the UML Class Diagram for Sunset's Conversion Process

Virgil thought Sunset's bill of material should be more than an association, although he agreed that the company's conversion process resembled the generic model. For Sunset, the bill of material contains more than a simple link between Sunset's material (raw materials) and its final products (finished goods). He also believed that they really had no defined labor plan. Sunset just recorded direct labor incurred and used a simple overhead allocation scheme.

Updating finished goods inventory.

We replied that it was easy to modify the generic process diagram to reflect Sunset's information requirements for the conversion process. We could "promote" the bill of material association to a **type image** class, because there was more detail involved. Also, the bill of materials association is typically a **many-to-many relationship** between raw materials and finished goods, because each raw material item could be used for multiple finished goods items and vice versa. We would likely create a table to implement that association, anyway. We could also remove the labor plan association between the finished goods resource and the labor operations event. We developed the class diagram shown in Figure 7.5 reflecting those modifications, including multiplicities, and also keeping the association between Sunset Partners and Product Categories from the sales and collection process.

Virgil and Linda both thought that the revised class diagram accurately reflected their information requirements. However, they had some hypothetical questions about modeling the conversion process to make sure they understood it perfectly. For example, they asked how we would modify the model if Sunset used equipment in the conversion process and wanted to record direct equipment costs. We replied that we would simply add an equipment resource to capture information about the equipment, and then we would add an equipment operations event to record the costs of the use of the equipment. They said that made sense; an event records costs applied to work-in-process and a resource captures permanent information about the things available for use in the process. We added that type images can be used to specify the plan for how the resources would be used, and then the plan could be compared to the actual usage recorded in the events.

FIGURE 7.5
Revised UML Class Diagram for Sunset's Conversion Process

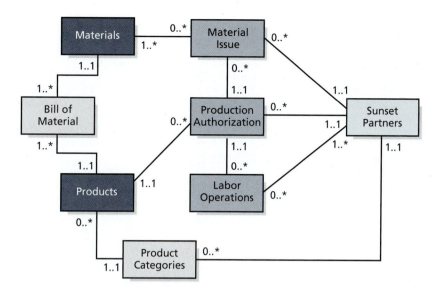

3. Figure 7.5 dropped the labor plan association. Could Sunset instead have "promoted" the labor plan association to a type image? How would that affect the diagram?
4. Add the equipment resource and equipment operations event to the diagram, and define the multiplicities.

LO 7-6

Implement a relational database from the UML class diagram of the conversion process.

SUNSET GRAPHICS' RELATIONAL DATABASE

Virgil and Linda B were both interested in implementing the conversion UML class diagram in a relational database for Sunset. Again, we use Microsoft Access, but the process would be similar for any database-driven system. We encourage students to use the following description to implement a relational database to support information requirements for the conversion process.

Relational Database Planning for Attributes

During the model development process, we again reviewed Sunset's existing documents to determine specific data requirements for each class/table. We then followed the guidance in Chapters 3 and 4 to determine allocation of foreign keys. This resulted in a list of tables, attributes, data types, field sizes and primary and foreign keys as shown in Table 7.2.

Create Database and Define Tables

The next step is to create a new, blank Microsoft Access database and create the tables described in Table 7.2. Then, establish relationships between the tables as shown in Figure 7.6 (on page 161) following the process outlined in Chapter 5. At that point, Sunset's purchases and payments process database is set up.

PK/FK	Attribute Name	Type	Size
	Table: tblBill_of_Material		
PK	BOM_number	Text	10
	Issue_sequence	Double	8
	Standard_quantity	Double	8
FK	Product_number	Text	10
FK	Material_number	Text	255
	Special_handling	Memo	
	Table: tblLabor_Operations		
PK	Labor_Ops_Number	Text	10
FK	Prod_auth_number	Text	10
	Labor_ops_description	Memo	
	Table: tblLabor_Operations_Partners		
PK	Labor_ops_number	Text	10
PK	Partner_number	Text	10
	Actual_direct_labor_hours	Long Integer	4
	Actual_direct_labor_wage	Currency	8
	Table: tblMaterial_Issue		
PK	Matl_Issue_number	Text	10
FK	Issue_date	Date/Time	8
	Issued_by	Text	10
FK	Prod_Auth_number	Text	255
	Table: tblMaterial_Issue_Material		
PK	Matl_issue_number	Text	10
PK	Material_number	Text	10
	Qty_issued	Long Integer	4
	Table: tblMaterials		
PK	Material_number	Text	10
	Material_description	Text	255
	Material_price	Currency	8
	Material_quantity_on_hand	Integer	2
	Material_notes	Memo	
	Table: tblPartners		
PK	Partner_number	Text	10
	Partner_first_name	Text	15
	Partner_last_name	Text	15

PK/FK	Attribute Name	Type	Size
	Partner_hire_date	Date/Time	8
	Partner_SocSecNo	Text	11
	Partner_Address	Text	50
	Partner_Address2	Text	50
	Partner_City	Text	20
	Partner_State	Text	2
	Partner_Zip	Text	10
	Partner_phone	Text	14
	Partner_cellphone	Text	14
	Table: tblProductCategory		
PK	Product_category_number	Text	10
	Product_category_description	Text	255
FK	Product_category_manager	Text	10
	Product_category_notes	Memo	
	Table: tblProduction_Authorizations		
PK	Prod_auth_number	Text	255
	Prod_auth_date	Date/Time	8
FK	Partner_number	Text	10
FK	Product_Number	Text	10
	Sched_qty_to_produce	Long Integer	4
	Actual_qty_produced	Long Integer	4
	Scheduled_completion_date	Date/Time	8
	Actual_completion_date	Date/Time	8
	Overhead_rate	Single	4
	Total_material_cost	Currency	8
	Total_direct_labor	Currency	8
	Total_overhead	Currency	8
	Total_cogm	Currency	8
	Table: tblProducts		
PK	Product_number	Text	10
	Product_description	Text	255
	Product_price	Currency	8
	Product_unit_of_sale	Text	10
FK	Product_category	Text	10
	Product_quantity_on_hand	Integer	2
	Product_notes	Memo	

TABLE 7.2

Sunset Database Tables and Attribute Definitions for the Conversion Process

FIGURE 7.6
Linked Conversion
Process Tables and
with Referential
Integrity Enforced

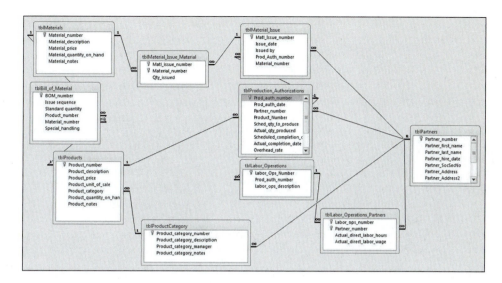

Summary

- From an accounting standpoint, we must account for transfers of raw materials into work-in-process, direct labor, allocated overhead, and the cost of goods manufactured in the conversion process.
- Sunset Graphics provides an ongoing example of how to model the conversion process.
- Activity models can show the basic steps in the process and the collaborations between the company and its customers, as well as exceptions to the process.
- Business rules implement internal control activities.
- There is a standard structure model pattern that allows for collection of accounting information for the conversion process—including issues of raw material into work-in-process and recording direct labor and allocated overhead—such that cost of goods manufactured includes material, labor, and overhead costs.
- The standard pattern is tailored to a specific organization by adding type images to collect management information.
- The structure model provides a blueprint for a relational database that will collect, store, and report sales and collection information.

Key Words

agents (157)   The people or organizations who participate in business events, such as customers and salespeople.

events (157)   Classes that model the organization's transactions, usually affecting the organization's resources, such as sales and cash receipts.

finished goods inventory (153)   For a manufacturing company, the inventory (REA resource) that has completed the manufacturing process and is held for sale to customers.

gateway (154)   Shows process branching and merging as the result of decisions. Basic gateways are depicted as diamonds. Usually, gateways appear as pairs on the diagram. The first gateway shows the branching, and the second gateway shows merging of the process branches.

intermediate error event (154) Occurs between start and end events and affects the flow of the process. Intermediate error events represent interruptions to the normal flow of the process and start the exception flow.

labor operations event (157) In the conversion process, an event that represents the recording of labor (and any associated overhead) costs applied to work-in-process.

many-to-many relationship (158) Exists when instances of one class (e.g., sales) are related to many instances of another class (e.g., inventory) and vice versa. These relationships are implemented in Access and relational databases by adding a linking table to convert the many-to-many relationship into two one-to-many relationships.

production authorization event (158) In a UML class model of the conversion process, an event that records the authorization to produce one or more finished good inventory items.

raw material issue event (158) In a UML class diagram of the conversion process, an event that records the transfer of raw materials into work-in-process.

raw materials inventory (153) For a manufacturing company, the inventory (REA resource) acquired for use (conversion) in the manufacturing process.

REA (157) Resource-event-agent framework for modeling business processes, originally developed by William McCarthy.

resources (157) Those things that have economic value to a firm, such as cash and products.

type image (158) Class that represents management information (such as categorizations, policies, and guidelines) to help manage a business process. Type image often allows process information to be summarized by category.

work-in-process inventory (157) For a manufacturing company, the value of raw materials, direct labor, and manufacturing overhead in production but not yet finished.

Answers to Progress *Checks*

1. You could modify Figure 7.3 by creating an additional swimlane within the Sunset pool for the inspection organizational unit.

2. You could modify Figure 7.3 by adding an additional gateway following the Inspect Work activity with two branches: (a) linking to the Discard Items activity and (b) linking to the Batch Done gateway.

3. An association can be promoted to a type image if it needs to contain more information or link to other classes. Apparently, Sunset's labor operations do not vary according to the specific product. If they did, it could promote the labor plan association shown in Figure 7.5 to a labor plan class as in Figure 7.6. That type image class would link to the products class and the labor operations class.

4. An equipment class would be an additional resource. It would be linked to the products class if the equipment varied according to the specific product. The equipment operations class, like the labor operations class, would record the use of the equipment to add that cost to the costs of production.

Multiple Choice Questions

1. Which of the following is an activity in the conversion process?
    a. Authorize production
    b. Issue raw material
    c. Perform work

    d. Transfer completed work to finished goods

    e. All of the above are activities in the conversion process.

2. Which of the following activities results in work-in-process moving to finished goods inventory?

    a. Authorize production

    b. Inspect work

    c. Complete production

    d. Issue raw material

    e. None of the above

3. Which of the following describes the purpose of a swimlane in BPMN?

    a. Indicate the start of the process

    b. Indicate the end of the process

    c. Identify different activity flow options

    d. Distinguish specific responsibilities for performing different tasks

    e. None of the above

4. Which of the following is not a purpose of using swimlanes to describe the conversion process?

    a. Document the sequence of activities in the process

    b. Expose potential problems in the handoff between organizational units

    c. Show important decision points, and identify responsibility for those decisions

    d. Establish internal control activities, such as segregation of duties

    e. All of the above

5. Which of the following is a business rule implementing access control for the conversion process?

    a. Employee authorizing production cannot modify inventory records.

    b. System must provide control numbers.

    c. Employees preparing quotes cannot modify established prices.

    d. System must create audit trail whenever records are changed.

    e. None of the above

6. Consider a UML class diagram of the conversion process that uses the REA framework. Which of the following events begins a typical conversion process?

    a. Assign employees to departments

    b. Authorize production

    c. Issue raw material into work in process

    d. Sell finished goods

    e. None of the above

7. Review Figure 7.5. Which of the following describes the purpose of the Labor Operations event?

    a. Add the cost of direct labor to work in process inventory

    b. Control the specific labor activities

    c. Ensure that labor is performed

    d. Identify production employees

    e. None of the above

8. Review Figure 7.6. Which of the following is an incorrect posting of a foreign key?

    a. Production Authorization primary key becomes a foreign key in Labor Operations.

    b. Products primary key becomes a foreign key in Bill of Material.

    c. Product Categories primary key becomes a foreign key in Sunset Partners.

    d. Products primary key becomes a foreign key in Product Categories.

    e. All of the above are correct.

9. Review Figure 7.6. Which of the following describes the purpose of the Bill of Material class?

    a. Record the invoices from suppliers for materials purchased

    b. Record the planned raw material contents of each finished good

    c. Record the authorization of production

    d. Describe the labor required for each finished good

    e. None of the above.

10. Compare Figure 7.6 with Figure 7.7. Which of the following describes a reason for the differences between those two figures?

    a. Figure 7.7 includes *tblLabor_Operations_Partners* to implement the many-to-many relationship between *tblPartners* and *tblLabor_Operations.*

    b. Figure 7.7 includes *tblMaterial_Issue_Material* to implement the many-to-many relationship between *tblMaterial_Issue* and *tblMaterials.*

    c. Figure 7.6 includes the minimum multiplicities to specify data integrity requirements.

    d. Figure 7.7 only shows maximum cardinalities between linked tables.

    e. All of the above

Discussion Questions

1. Why should accountants be concerned with the development of bills of material?

2. Describe some businesses that use conversion processes. Do they all use the same sequence of activities? Do they all share the same information structure? Discuss some of the differences in those conversion processes.

3. Think about the UML class diagrams for the sales and collection process described in Chapter 5 and the purchase and payment process described in Chapter 6. If you were asked to prepare an integrated model that shows those two processes as well as the conversion process, where would the models intersect/integrate? Why? What elements are unique to each process?

4. In Figure 7.5, the Labor Operations event tracks direct labor incurred in the conversion process. What event tracks indirect labor?

5. Describe how you would change Figure 7.5 to implement an activity-based costing system with three different cost drivers.

6. Put Figure 7.5 in the context of the overall supply chain that starts with the purchases and payments process (Chapter 6) and ends with the sales and cash receipts process (Chapter 5). How would you expand Figure 7.5 to describe Sunset's supply chain in total?

7. Business rules implement internal controls. Review Table 7.1 and classify each of those business rules listed as access controls as obligatory, prohibited, or allowed as described in Chapter 2. Select two of those business rules and rephrase them, so an obligatory rule is now a prohibited rule, or a prohibited rule is now an allowed rule, and so on.

8. Compare the generic UML class diagram for the conversion process shown in Figure 7.4 with a generic sales and collection diagram, similar to Figure 5.8. Describe the similarities and differences and explain the reasons for those similarities and differences.

Problems

1. The Rubber Duck Brewing Company is a new microbrewery. Rubber Duck's brewing process converts beer raw ingredients—malt extract, malted grain, adjuncts (rice or corn), hops, yeast, and water—into brewed beer. Over time, Rubber Duck has developed a unique recipe for each of its brewed beers. The recipe describes the specific ingredients, the sequence of brewing steps, the specific equipment, and the type of employees required for each step in the brewing process for each beer. Each step in the recipe may involve multiple ingredients (e.g., barley, hops, malts, and yeast) and multiple pieces of equipment, but it only requires one type of employee.

Rubber Duck assigns a unique ingredient number to each ingredient so it can track the quantity on hand. It tracks its brewed beer by the beer name: pale ale, amber ale, porter, stout, lager, pilsner, and so forth. When Rubber Duck decides to brew one of its beers, a supervisor issues a "Brew Order" for that beer, specifying the quantity in gallons to be brewed. Then, the brewing process begins. Several Rubber Duck employees perform each brewing step. Rubber Duck tracks the amount of each raw ingredient actually used in each step as well the time spent by each employee on each step.

Rubber Duck tracks its brewing equipment (e.g., mash tuns, whirlpools, fermenters, and conditioning tanks) by equipment item number, and it also tracks which equipment is used and how long it is used in each brewing step. Each brewing step often requires more than one piece of equipment, and some pieces of equipment are used on multiple brewing steps, although many are used in only one step. For safety, Rubber Duck only allows employees to operate equipment that they are qualified to use.

When the brewing process is complete, the brewed beer is stored in large copper tanks for aging. Ales require relatively little aging (less than 3 weeks), while lagers may require longer aging (up to 5 weeks). The copper tanks are tracked separately from other brewing equipment. Aging of the beer is not part of the brewing process; it takes place after the brewing process.

    a. Prepare a UML class diagram that captures Rubber Duck's brewing process.

    b. Using the preceding information and the following attributes list, prepare a listing of the relational tables, indicating the primary key (PK) and foreign keys (FK) for each table.

Attributes:

Actual aging time to date for the brewed beer in this copper tank

Actual quantity of this ingredient used in this brew step

Actual time for this equipment used in this brew step

Brew order date

Brew order number (brew#)

Brew quantity in gallons

Brew step number (brew step#)

Brew step description

Brewed beer description

Brewed beer quantity on hand (QOH)

Brewed beer name

Brewing recipe step description

Brewing recipe step number (recipe step#)

Copper tank capacity in gallons

Copper tank number (tank#)

Date this employee qualified to operate this equipment

Employee name

Employee number (emp#)

Employee type

Employee type description

Equipment item description

Equipment item number (equip#)

Ingredient description

Ingredient number (ingred#)

Ingredient quantity-on-hand (QOH)

Number of employees of this type

Planned aging time for this brewed beer

Planned time for this equipment in this step

Quantity of beer in this tank (in gallons)

Standard quantity of this ingredient used in this recipe step

Time spent by this employee on this brew step

2. Penny loves pastries. She wanted everyone else to love pastries, too, so she started Penny's Pastries in Orange County about three years ago. After a shaky start, she scored a big contract with **Starbucks** to provide pastries to all stores in southern California. This case describes Penny's daily baking process. Penny's bakery starts preparing fresh pastries every morning about 1:00 a.m. for delivery to local stores by 5:30 a.m. The selection and quantity of pastries varies according to the day of the week as well as the time of the year.

Inventories

Although Penny has a number of her own specialties, she makes many of her baked products according to **Starbucks'** requirements. So, every day she makes some of her own pastries for sale in her bakeries as well as all the pastries for the various **Starbucks** locations. Currently, her finished goods inventory can include more than 50 different kinds of pastries and baked products. Because of the volume that Penny produces, she maintains an extensive inventory of the ingredients that she uses in her baked goods, such as flour, butter, milk, chocolate, and cinnamon.

Baking Plans

Penny carefully plans the contents and preparation of each finished product (pastry and baked good). There are two parts to her formal plans—an ingredient list and a recipe—for each baked product. The ingredient list specifies the quantity of each ingredient required for each finished product. The recipe steps define the sequence of steps that her bakers follow to prepare each finished product. The recipe steps also set the standard number of labor-hours, as well as the specific equipment used, to prepare a standard batch of each finished product.

Daily Baking Process

Early each morning, the supervisor prepares a daily baking order that specifies the quantities of all the different finished products to be prepared that day. As soon as the various products and quantities are known, an inventory clerk uses the ingredient list to issue all the ingredients necessary for the day, moving them from the storeroom to the baking area. In some cases, the clerk may issue ingredients several different times for each daily baking order so that none of the refrigerated items are left out longer than necessary. Penny assigns sequential issue numbers to each issue during the day, and the clerk carefully records the quantity of each ingredient issued.

Penny's bakers prepare the finished products in batches. Each batch produces one finished baked good product. A supervisor (who could be different from the supervisor who issued the baking order) issues a batch order to start the baking process for that batch. The bakers then prepare the ingredients in a series of baking steps according to the recipe for that product using the equipment and ovens specified in the recipe. Penny's bakery has an array of ovens and baking equipment, tracked by equipment number, to keep up with the daily baking production volumes. Because each oven has different characteristics, the baking time for each product can depend on the particular oven used. The baking steps usually involve mixing ingredients, preparing the pastries, placing the prepared items in an oven for baking, and then removing the products and placing them on cooling racks, ready for packing. Each actual baking step may involve the use of multiple pieces of baking equipment and multiple bakers. Penny carefully tracks actual hours of labor and equipment use for each baking step.

General Information

Penny does not separately identify employees as supervisors, inventory clerks, or bakers. There is one employee entity. Information on ingredient lists, recipe steps, finished products, ingredients, and employees is put into the database before those entities are linked to events or type images.

a. Draw a BPMN activity diagram that describes Penny's baking process.

b. Prepare a UML class diagram with classes, associations, and multiplicities.

c. Using the preceding case information and the following attributes list, prepare a listing of the relational tables necessary to support this conversion process. List the tables in the following order: resources, events, agents, type images, and linking tables.

Attributes:

actual baking time for this baking step and this oven	batch#
	employee#
baking order date	employee hours worked on this baking step
baking order#	employee name
baking step#	employee pay rate
batch finish time	equipment description
batch start time	equipment manufacturer

equipment#

finished product description

finished product number of calories

finished product price

finished product QOH

finished product#

ingredient cost

ingredient description

ingredient list#

ingredient list description

ingredient QOH

ingredient unit of issue

ingredient#

issue date/time

issue#

qty of this baked product ordered by this daily baking order

qty of this baked product prepared in this batch

qty of this ingredient issued on this issue#

qty of this ingredient required for this finished product

recipe step#

recipe step description

standard baking time for this recipe step with this oven

standard labor hours for this recipe step

total labor hours for this baking step

Answers to Multiple Choice Questions

1. e
2. c
3. d
4. a
5. e

6. b
7. a
8. a
9. b
10. e

Integrated Project

A look at this chapter

This chapter describes a business analysis and integrated systems development project. It is designed as a group assignment. To complete the assignment, each group must plan and execute a realistic systems design and development project. The finished product will include (1) activity and structure models of a company's business processes, (2) an analysis of the company's existing internal controls, (3) identification of opportunities for effective use of an accounting information system and related information technology to improve the company's performance, and (4) a Microsoft Access relational database system and appropriate queries necessary to prepare financial and managerial accounting reports.

A look back

Chapter 7 completed the comprehensive example describing Sunset Graphics Inc. business processes. It presented basic activity and structure models for the company's conversion process, as well as a description of the database to support that process.

A look ahead

Chapter 9 provides a description of how accounting information systems facilitate management reporting, including using data warehouses, business intelligence, and dashboards. In addition, it also explains the development and emerging use of eXtensible Business Reporting Language (XBRL).

Howard Schultz, Founder, President, and Chief Executive Officer of Starbucks.

After **Starbucks** implemented the **Oracle** E-business Suite, it had the IT backbone necessary to leverage a variety of other applications to support its business processes. As part of the **Oracle** implementation, **Accenture** worked with **Starbucks** to standardize business processes around the world. The **Oracle** ERP system resides on top of **Oracle's** database system, which allows reuse and redistribution of the information collected. **Starbucks'** enterprise data warehouse (EDW) leverages that data to support **Starbucks'** internal business users.

By 2008, thousands of stores could directly access the EDW through web-based dashboards. Using a business intelligence reporting tool from **MicroStrategy Inc.** individual users could develop customized operational performance reports. **MicroStrategy's** reports can even be delivered by e-mail on preset schedules.

Although **Starbucks** closed a number of retail stores in response to the economic downturn, its overall revenues increased from 2008 to 2010. More importantly, its revenue per store is back above $1 million in the United States. Its operating income has almost doubled since 2008, and its operating margin increased from 8.1 percent to 13.8 percent in 2010. Clearly, **Starbucks** has been successful at reducing costs and increasing margins. Without standardized processes and integrated systems providing reliable and timely information for decisions, it is unlikely that it could have achieved this success.

Chapter Outline

Project Background
Client Company Overview
Initial Interviews with Sy's Fish Company Employees
Project Instructions and Deliverables
Prepare Project Plan
Define Business Requirements
Prepare Structure Diagrams
Prepare Activity Models Using BPMN
Import Data in Access, Create Efficient Tables, and Set Relationships
Prepare Queries
Prepare Report
Project Deliverables

Learning Objectives

After reading this chapter, you should be able to:

8-1   Plan and manage a business analysis project.

8-2   Develop an integrated UML class diagram for a business.

8-3   Develop activity models of multiple business processes, and use those models to assess potential risks and opportunities for process improvements.

8-4   Use the UML class diagram to design and implement a relational database system in Microsoft Access.

8-5   Employ the relational database to answer a variety of business performance questions.

PROJECT BACKGROUND

Sy's Fish Company[1] owns a chain of wholesale fish stores. The company has grown rapidly over the past few years and now includes eight different stores. The company is poised to expand further but first needs to develop a better accounting information system (AIS). This project involves a thorough analysis of Sy's Fish Company business processes to assess opportunities for improvement and implementation of a prototype integrated database to provide financial and management information.

Client Company Overview

Sy hired your accounting and consulting firm to design a database accounting system for his business (Sy's Fish Company), construct a prototype system in Microsoft Access, and provide some related accounting/business/systems advice. He recognizes that his current accounting process will not be able to support his rapidly growing business. He also understands the importance of an accounting system that can provide timely management information as well as standard accounting functions. In particular, you are to analyze five processes for Sy's Fish Company. Those processes are selling fish, purchasing fish, paying employees, purchasing miscellaneous supplies and services, and providing refunds to customers. The following interviews with Sy and some key employees describe Sy's Fish Company's business processes. Where information is incomplete, you are to make appropriate assumptions. Your instructor will provide an Excel spreadsheet with all necessary data and any additional instructions. Sy uses accrual accounting and a calendar fiscal year.

Sy's personal Sy's Fish Company hat.

Initial Interviews with Sy's Fish Company Employees

Summary of Interview with Sy

Sy spent most of his adult life fishing. He worked as a deckhand and master on a number of commercial fishing boats. While this work satisfied his quest for adventure, it did not pay well. A few years ago, Sy bought a small wholesale fish store to seek his fortune in a less dangerous but more lucrative occupation. Through hard work, his business, Sy's Fish Company, expanded to other cities on the East Coast. Sy's Fish built a reputation for high-quality fresh fish. Sy guarantees satisfaction or his customers get their money back—no questions asked.

Sy's Fish serves only wholesale customers, such as restaurants and retail stores. Sy's Fish offers its customers more than 20 types of fresh fish, such as sea bass, halibut, salmon, and perch. Each store can carry all types of fish. The stores are basically small warehouses and not retail fish stores. So, Sy's owns a fleet of trucks, with a distinctive logo on the side, used to pick up and deliver fish.

Until recently, all of Sy's recordkeeping was primarily done manually. Each store keeps track of its purchases, inventories, sales, and so forth. Then, they send all the hard-copy documents to Sy, via the accounts payable or payroll clerks when appropriate. Sy prepares his accounting reports from those documents as well as the deposit information he receives

[1]The Sy's Fish Project is based on a project developed by Bill McCarthy, a professor at Michigan State University.

from the banks and the cash disbursement information he receives from the accounts payable and payroll clerks. Recently, Sy's computer crashed and he lost all his records. He has been rebuilding those records from the manual documents using Excel. So far, he has been able to put together his records for early 2013. He wants to move his data from Excel into an Access-based accounting system and prepare financial reports for the first quarter of 2013.

Sy plans to expand his business to multiple cities along the Gulf and West Coasts. So, in addition to providing financial information about his current performance, he wants advice on the risks his business faces and how he can mitigate those risks with cost-effective internal controls. To facilitate recordkeeping and management after the expansion, Sy is considering the installation of computers at each store, as well as the use of iPads to record transactions at the source. He believes that eventually he should use an online accounting system (cloud computing) and have each store submit transactions daily via the Internet. Thus, he also wants an evaluation of the benefits of using of information technology and how that would affect his internal control system.

Summary of Interview with Natalie Merchant, AP Clerk, Boston Store

Natalie prepares checks for payments to fishers and miscellaneous vendors. The stores mail purchase documents for fish to her almost every day. She knows that the fishers need to be paid promptly, so they can pay their crew, buy fuel, and so forth. So, she tries to pay them a week after she receives the documents. If she receives multiple purchases from the same fisher during that time, she will combine payments.

For the miscellaneous purchases—such as phone bills, truck repairs, and gasoline—the stores assign purchase order numbers to the vendor's invoice and mail them to her. She holds the documents for payment at the end of the month. If she receives a bill after she has already prepared checks, she will often hold it until the end of the following month before sending payment. Again, she will combine payments if she receives multiple bills from the same vendor.

Natalie stamps each document with the check number, the check amount, and the date paid. After writing the checks and sending out the payments, Natalie packages all the documents (fish purchase documents and miscellaneous invoices) and delivers them to Sy's office.

Summary of Interview with Rascal Flatts, Supervisor, Portland Store

Rascal is the supervisor for the Portland store, and his duties are similar to supervisor duties at all the stores. Being supervisor is only a part-time responsibility. Most of the time, Rascal is just another employee at the Portland store, buying fish, preparing fish for delivery to customers, and making deliveries.

Customers call to place orders for future fish deliveries. Usually, they order about one week in advance. The store employees know most of the customers by name and also know what types of fish they prefer. They also know what types of fish are likely available, so they try to steer the orders to those fish. They record customer orders in the order log. Then, every morning they look at the log to estimate the types of fish and quantities that they need to buy for the day. They don't buy fish for specific orders; instead, they try to get enough fish of each type to meet all the orders for that day.

Each morning, one employee hops in a truck and drives to the local pier to buy the freshest available fish from fishers to fulfill customers' orders. The employee carefully selects the best fish and loads the fish into the truck. Sometimes, it is not possible to get the specific types and quantities that the customers ordered, but other high-quality fish are available. In that case, the employee will buy the other fish and contact the customers to modify their orders. The purchase document identifies the purchase number (sequential), the fisher number, the purchasing employee, the truck VIN (to track mileage), the type of fish, the quantity purchased (in pounds), and the purchase price. The fish are purchased at the prevailing market price that day. On occasion, one purchase can involve multiple types of fish, although typically one purchase is for one type of fish.

When the truck returns to the store with the purchased fish, all employees unload the truck, clean the fish, and place the fish on ice for delivery to the customers in the afternoon. The employees then prepare the delivery documents. Those documents list the customers' original order number, the order date, the delivery (sale) date, the truck VIN used to deliver the fish (to track mileage), the types and quantities of fish both ordered and sold, and the sale price. Sy sets the sales prices for all stores, and those prices can change every couple of months. One order can (and typically does) involve several types of fish.

Each afternoon, the employees load the truck for the deliveries to customers. One employee then delivers the fish. Each customer receives the fish and the delivery document. They then pay for all their deliveries by the end of the month. Customers send the payment to the address listed on the delivery document (currently the address of the New York store). When the employee returns to the store, all the delivery documents are put in an envelope and mailed to Sy.

Summary of Interview with Bruce Springsteen, Payroll Clerk, Baltimore Store

Bruce maintains the payroll records. Each employee fills out his or her time card each day. At the end of each month, each store supervisor collects employee time cards, checks them for accuracy, and sends them by overnight delivery to Bruce at the Baltimore store. If a time card looks to be incorrect, the supervisor asks the employee to correct it. Bruce then prepares the payroll checks and sends them to the addresses designated for each employee. Once the checks are mailed, Bruce mails the time cards and copies of the checks to Sy.

Summary of Interview with Elton John, Accounts Receivable Clerk, New York Store

Elton receives payments from customers at the end of each month. He assigns sequential cash receipt numbers to each incoming payment, recording the customer number, the receipt date, and the receipt amount. Each day, Elton deposits all checks received in the bank and then mails the list of cash receipts along with a copy of the deposit slip to Sy. Elton says that he is really not an accounts receivable clerk, because he never knows how much the customer owes; he just knows how much he received and deposited.

Summary of Interview with Taylor Swift, Employee, Myrtle Beach Store

Taylor described the customer refund process. Sy's Fish guarantees satisfaction and provides complete refunds if the customer is unhappy with any fish received on an order. The customer calls the local store and reports a problem with the fish. The employee who answers the phone immediately prepares a refund authorization. If the customer hasn't yet paid for that order, the employee instructs the customer to take that amount off his or her bill. In that case, the employee then sends the refund authorization directly to Sy for information. If the customer has paid for that order, the employee notifies the customer that he or she will receive a check within about a week. The employee sends the refund authorization form to the accounts payable clerk in Boston, who sends the customer a check. Then, the refund authorization and the payment information are forwarded to Sy.

PROJECT INSTRUCTIONS AND DELIVERABLES

Figure 8.1 describes a suggested sequence of activities to complete this project. This project represents an "ill-structured" problem. Your group should discuss the problem statement and list its significant parts. You may feel that you don't know enough to solve the problem, but that is the challenge! You will have to gather information and apply concepts,

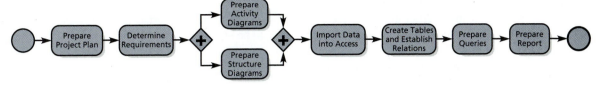

FIGURE 8.1
Suggested Project Steps

principles, or skills that you have learned or need to learn as you engage in the problem-solving process. First, identify what you need to know to solve the problem. Consider the strengths and capabilities of each team member. Respect everyone's input. Your instructor will provide additional information regarding changes to the scope of this project where his or her requirements differ from those listed.

LO 8-1

Plan and manage a business analysis project.

Prepare Project Plan

Develop, and write out, a problem statement and timeline in your own words that comes from the group's analysis of what you know and what you will need to know to solve it. Identify the major steps you will undertake to complete the project, when they need to be completed, and who will perform them. You are encouraged to use project planning tools, such as a Gantt chart. Refer to Chapter 15 for a description of project planning/management elements.

Define Business Requirements

First, understand the details of Sy's business. Review the interview summaries provided earlier. Focus on (1) the structure of data necessary to support those processes in a database system and (2) the sequence of activity in Sy's current business processes. Sy also wants advice on (1) identifying and managing risks as his business grows and (2) better using information technology to make his business more efficient.

LO 8-2

Develop an integrated UML class diagram for a business.

Prepare Structure Diagram

Using the information gained from the interviews and other sources, prepare an integrated UML class diagram that incorporates the data requirements of all of Sy's business processes. Consider updating the REA data model as you proceed with the project so you can submit a professional-looking model with your final report.

LO 8-3

Develop activity models of multiple business processes, and use those models to assess potential risks and opportunities for process improvements.

Prepare Activity Models Using BPMN

After gaining an understanding of Sy's business processes, document each current process with a business process activity diagram using business process modeling notation (BPMN). At this point, you should expect to prepare at least five separate activity diagrams corresponding to known Sy's Fish business processes. Each process should end with the documents being mailed to Sy, who records the information.

LO 8-4

Use the UML class diagram to design and implement a relational database system in Microsoft Access.

Import Data into Access, Create Efficient Tables, and Set Relationships

Using the Excel spreadsheet that Sy prepared, transfer Sy's data to Access, establish efficient tables, and link the tables together on the relationships screen, enforcing referential integrity. You should make your relationships screen look like your REA data model so it can be compared to your UML class diagram. You should assume that the data may contain inefficient tables and occasional typographical errors. You will need to correct those. After importing the data, you will need to set appropriate primary keys, check data types, and modify tables as necessary to be sure that they are efficient. You will need to modify some of the tables to make them efficient for use in a relational database. Then, create the relationships among tables. Be sure to enforce referential integrity or understand why you cannot.

LO 8-5

Employ the relational database to answer a variety of business performance questions.

Prepare Queries

Prepare queries to determine Sy's Fish Company's financial and operational performance as specified in the deliverables. Each deliverable may require multiple queries. Be sure to clearly identify each query according to which deliverable it addresses and whether it is an interim or final query for that deliverable. In preparing the queries, you should remember that Sy's Fish Company operates on a calendar fiscal year, so the first quarter will include activity from January 1 to March 31. There may be transactions that did not occur during the first quarter, so you must handle those transactions appropriately.

Prepare Report

Assemble your final report to Sy's Fish Company addressing its financial and operational performance, risk assessment, and recommendations for use of technology. The final report should be prepared in an executive summary style. Remember that Sy is not an accountant, so you should interpret the accounting results for him. Present important results in the body of the report. Use tables, charts, and graphics whenever possible. Include the financial statements, operating performance information, and diagrams as enclosures to the report.

Project Deliverables

1. Prepare four sets of queries to answer questions that Sy has already asked as follows:
   - *Information for Sy's income statement.* Determine overall sales revenue, gross profit and corresponding gross profit percentage, general and administrative expenses, and net profit for Sy's Fish Company for the first quarter based on the information available.
   - *Information for Sy's balance sheet.* Determine balances in the asset, liability, and equity accounts at the end of the first quarter.
   - *Information for store financial performance.* Determine which store earned the greatest net profit for the first quarter (be sure to show all the stores and sort in descending net profit order).
   - *Information for accounts receivable.* Determine the accounts receivable balance for each customer at the end of the first quarter (show all customers).

2. *Financial performance evaluation.* Perhaps the most important part of the project is to use the prototype Access-based accounting system to report to Sy on his financial and operational performance for the first quarter of the year. The report should describe and evaluate Sy's Fish Company's financial performance in the first quarter using appropriate graphical and comparative information based on your queries. You should use relevant financial ratios to highlight Sy's performance. Include professionally formatted financial statements (income statement and balance sheet) as an appendix to your summary report. Because Sy is not an accountant, you should interpret these results so he can understand them. It is important to convince Sy that you fully understand his financial status.

3. *Risk assessment and recommendations for risk management.* The report should provide a risk assessment and recommendations for risk management. Based on your models and your understanding of his business, describe the threats, vulnerabilities, and risk profile of Sy's Fish. Describe the potential consequences of Sy's risk exposure. Recommend actions to mitigate those risks.

4. *Evaluate information technology.* The report should assess benefits from Sy's plans for use of information technology—based on the process documentation—and provide recommendations for alternatives. Link your evaluation and recommendations to your business process activity diagrams to describe how the use of technology could streamline his processes. In particular, describe which uses of information technology would be cost effective and which would not.

Summary

- This chapter outlines a demanding business analysis project for Sy's Fish Company.
- The project involves
    - The use of project planning and management tools.
    - Defining business requirements.
    - Preparing an integrated UML class diagram.
    - Preparing activity diagrams using BPMN.
    - Importing data into Access from Excel.
    - Cleaning and correcting data and data structures.
    - Preparing queries to provide financial information.
    - Assessing risks and recommending ways to mitigate risks.
    - Assessing potential opportunities for use of technology.

Reporting Processes and eXtensible Business Reporting Language (XBRL)

A look at this chapter

In this chapter, we explain how accounting information systems facilitate management reporting, including using data warehouses, business intelligence, and dashboards. We then explain the development and emerging use of eXtensible Business Reporting Language (XBRL). We also discuss the potential for XBRL and other emerging technologies to address reporting needs.

A look back

Chapter 8 involved a comprehensive business analysis and integrated systems development process. It required students to execute a realistic design and development project, including activity and structure models of a company's business processes. The project involved evaluating internal controls and assessing opportunities for effective use of AIS and information technologies to improve the company's performance.

A look ahead

Chapter 10 examines issues in ethics and internal controls that are addressed by the Sarbanes-Oxley Act of 2002 (SOX) as well as important control and governance frameworks, including the COSO, COBIT, and ITIL frameworks. In particular, those areas that are critical to an organization's efficiency and effectiveness in operations, reliability in financial reporting, and compliance with applicable laws and regulations.

Jake Ruttenberg, Starbucks

2009 Data Warehouse Architect of the Year, *Oracle Magazine*

Starbucks' Jake Ruttenberg doesn't stay awake each night worrying about the data warehouse that delivers 40,000 business dashboards to Starbucks' field leadership team. "Our data warehouse and retail dashboard business intelligence systems are critical to the success of each store and the entire business," says Ruttenberg, Starbucks IT Manager of Application Development, Business Intelligence Solution Delivery. He notes, "Our managers are asking more difficult questions, and we use the data warehouse to provide the data to answer those questions."

With Ruttenberg's and Oracle's help, Starbucks has built a 10-terabyte data warehouse that supports 20,000 users. It is used at least on a daily basis by close to 8,000 Starbucks stores to manage inventory, staffing, and much, much more.

Source: Kelly, David A. Editor's Choice Awards, *Oracle Magazine*, 2009, http://www.oracle.com/technetwork/issue-archive/2009/09-nov/o69awards-100810.html, accessed February 2013.

Chapter Outline

Introduction
Data Warehouses and Data Marts
Business Intelligence
Digital Dashboards
Financial Reporting and XBRL
History and Development of XBRL
How XBRL Works
XBRL Assurance
XBRL GL

Learning Objectives

After reading this chapter, you should be able to:

9-1 Explain how data warehouses are created and used.

9-2 Describe the basic components of business intelligence and how they are utilized in a firm.

9-3 Describe how digital dashboards allow for continuous tracking of key metrics.

9-4 Explain how XBRL works and how it makes business reporting more efficient.

INTRODUCTION

Earlier chapters in this textbook demonstrated how information is gathered and accumulated in a database. We are now interested in the reporting of that information to both internal and external users. We introduce the overall concept of a data warehouse and then specifically explain how data warehouses may be used in business intelligence settings. We also discuss how dashboards are used to manage a company's operations. Finally, we explore the use of XBRL to share financial and nonfinancial information with external users like the Securities and Exchange Commission, the Internal Revenue Service, financial analysts, and current or potential investors.

LO 9-1

Explain how data warehouses are created and used.

DATA WAREHOUSES AND DATA MARTS

Our discussion thus far in this book has been about operational systems primarily designed and optimized to capture business transactions, such as sales and purchases. In contrast, a data warehouse is essentially a new repository (or new system) designed to be optimized for speed and efficiency in data analysis. More specifically, a **data warehouse** is a collection of information gathered from an assortment of external and operational (i.e., internal) databases to facilitate reporting for decision making and business analysis. Data warehouses often serve as the main repository of the firm's historical data (or, in other words, its corporate memory) and will often serve as an archive of past firm performance.

The best way to illustrate is by using a figure. Figure 9.1 shows operational and external databases that are used as inputs into the data warehouse. The operational databases may all come from within the company's enterprise system or various systems throughout the firm. The external databases may come from a variety of places, including purchased data from the Gartner Group, the Federal Reserve, industry organizations, and so forth.

The actual data warehouse may become too big and overwhelming for specific groups within the firm to use. A **data mart** takes a subset of the information from the data warehouse to serve a specific purpose, such as a marketing data mart, an inventory data mart, or

FIGURE 9.1
Model of Data Warehouse Design

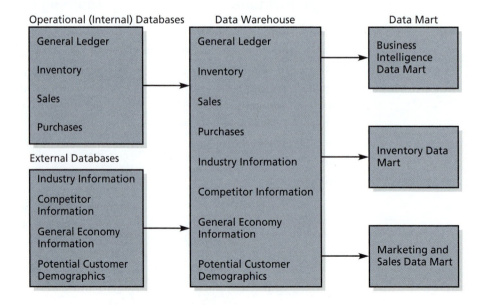

a business intelligence data mart. Whereas a data warehouse is a repository for the overall firm, the data mart is a subset of the data warehouse for a specific purpose or function. In essence, a data warehouse is made up of many data marts.

The opening vignette suggests Starbucks uses a data warehouse and data marts within its organization. Figure 9.2 provides an example of a potential data warehouse design for **Starbucks**. The figure highlights four types of data marts (although the potential number is unlimited) that may be useful to Starbucks: business intelligence, inventory, marketing, and sales and human resources.

The advantages and benefits of using a data warehouse include the following:

- Data warehouses use a common data model for all data in the warehouse, making it easy to compare information all the way from customer invoices, bills of lading, sales journals, purchasing journals, and general ledgers to industry information, competitor information, and the like. We discussed some data models in Chapters 3 and 4. Suffice it to say that before the data are loaded into the data warehouse, any data inconsistencies from the input databases are removed so that the data warehouse has homogenous data that can be readily accessed and analyzed.

- Because the data warehouse is kept separate from the operational database, the information in the warehouse can be stored safely for extended periods of time, and data warehouses can run data queries without affecting the performance (i.e., slowing down) of the company's operational systems.

- When appropriate, data warehouses work together with operational systems to provide necessary insight, particularly in the case of customer relationship management (CRM) and supply chain management (SCM) systems.

- Data warehouses are often designed to facilitate decision making (such as those often used in managerial accounting) and facilitate management by exception (such as variance reports, trend reports, variance analysis reports, and reports that show

FIGURE 9.2
Potential Data Warehouse Design for Starbucks

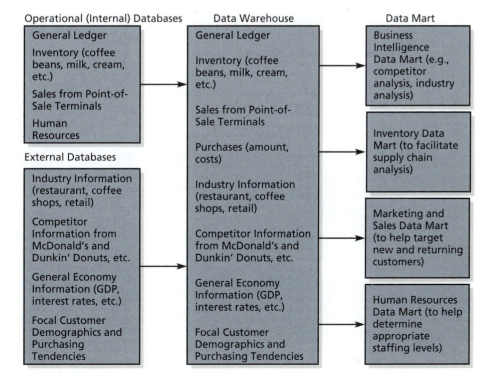

actual performance compared with budgeted information). Often, these types of systems used to support managerial decision making are called **decision support systems (DSSs)**.

It should also be noted that a key disadvantage of a data warehouse is that they quickly become obsolete with outdated data unless there is a mechanism to keep updating the internal and the external databases as time passes.

Progress *Check*

1. Why would **Apple's** marketing department only use a data mart instead of the entire data warehouse?
2. Imagine what might be included in a data warehouse for **Best Buy**. How might it be useful?

LO 9-2

Describe the basic components of business intelligence and how they are utilized in a firm.

BUSINESS INTELLIGENCE

Business intelligence is a computer-based technique for accumulating and analyzing data from databases and data warehouses to support managerial decision making. The term *business intelligence* is often used interchangeably with *competitive intelligence*. While competitive intelligence often deals with the examination of external information regarding competitor strategic and tactical actions, the process of business intelligence can be viewed more generically as including these three steps:

1. Gather information (either internal information, external information or both) from a variety of sources.
2. Analyze (or discern) patterns and trends from that information to gain understanding and meaning.
3. Make decisions based on the information gained.

One way that firms may gather business intelligence is by use of a web crawler, which systematically browses the Internet in a systematic way, collecting information.

There are many different settings where business intelligence is used. Perhaps the best way to explain business intelligence is to consider potential settings where business intelligence might be used.

- Imagine **American Airlines** trying to decide how to price its flights from Dallas to Phoenix. It can use business intelligence to track its competitor's prices over different times, days of the week, and so on. It can also use business intelligence to decide the right mix of first-class, business, and economy passengers to maximize revenue. It can also use business intelligence to decide the costs of canceling a flight based on its mix of first-class and economy-class customers.

- Imagine **Goldman Sachs** trying to price an initial public offering of stock for a firm in the Internet retail industry. It can use business intelligence to assess market conditions, assess how other Internet retail firms are performing in the stock market, and assess how initial public offerings have recently performed.

- Imagine **Dunkin' Donuts** using business intelligence to track information about its potential franchisees and the stages of a franchisee contract (see the opening vignette in Chapter 3 for details).

American Airlines relies on business intelligence to price their flights.

- Imagine **ESPN** trying to figure out the demographics of its audience (e.g., age, gender, net worth, interests outside of sports) watching its various sports offerings (e.g., football, basketball, soccer, auto racing, equestrian events). This will facilitate identifying the potential customers buying commercial spots as well as pricing its commercial breaks and finding other sponsorship opportunities.
- Imagine **e-bags** using business intelligence to track pricing information for its various, assorted luggage and bags at its offline and online competitors, so that the management can price products appropriately to stay competitive in the market.
- Imagine **Ford** using business intelligence to find indicators of quality issues to pinpoint machinery failures in its assembly plants after collecting and analyzing data on its processes. Sorting through the data may help **Ford** predict and prevent failures.
- Imagine **Allstate** or other insurance carriers using business intelligence to forecast claim amounts, medical coverage costs, and important elements that affect medical coverage. Such knowledge can be used to allow the firm to optimize its own insurance coverage and the handling of its medical claims. As the underlying health care requirements change due to recent legislation, such business intelligence will be critical for Allstate's continued success.

Data mining is one technique used to analyze data for business intelligence purposes. Data mining is the process of using sophisticated statistical techniques to extract and analyze data from large databases to discern patterns and trends that were not previously known. Data mining is often used to find patterns in stock prices to assist technical financial stock market analysts, or in commodities or currency trading. Another example of data mining in a retail setting might be analyzing the point-of-sale terminal to find the following trends:

- Items frequently bought in combination (e.g., cereal and milk; wieners, hot dog buns, ketchup, mustard, and relish; ice cream and cones; cayenne pepper and antacid; turkey and stuffing; chips and pop; diapers and baby food).
- Items frequently included in a large $200-plus grocery bill.
- Items frequently purchased by people making relatively small purchases, with "small" perhaps being defined by a dollar amount (i.e., less than $20) or defined by the fact that the customer used the express check-out counter.[1]

The main caveat about data mining is making sure the results are reasonable (or even plausible). While data mining may find a statistical correlation or relationship between two data items, it may or may not have a plausible relationship in the real world. There is a classic example that ice cream sales are correlated with drownings, suggesting that as ice cream sales increase, the number of drownings also increases. That does not mean that ice cream sales cause drownings or that drownings cause more ice cream sales, but rather that warm weather caused both. So it is clear that professional judgment must be used when using data mining techniques.

Progress *Check*

3. How would **Starbucks** use business intelligence to monitor **Dunkin' Donuts** or other competitors (like **McDonald's**)? What sources would they monitor?
4. How would the concepts behind business intelligence and data mining be used by the Miami Heat of the National Basketball Association to best compete on the court with the Oklahoma City Thunder?

[1] www.cs.ubc.ca/nest/dbsl/mining.html, accessed July 2010.

DIGITAL DASHBOARDS

Your car has a dashboard that is easy to read and contains information that is critical to the driver (e.g., engine status, engine heat, rpms, speedometer, odometer, fuel levels, etc.). The original automobile dashboard designers carefully considered the most important metrics of the automobile's performance and conveniently put them in the best place for the driver to see. Figure 9.3 illustrates an automobile dashboard.

FIGURE 9.3
Automobile Dashboard

In accounting information systems (AISs), a **digital dashboard** is designed to track a firm's process or its performance indicators or metrics to monitor critical performance. Examples of the metrics that might be continuously tracked include month-to-date orders, days that receivables are outstanding, budget variances, and days without an accident on the assembly line. While the data on the main dashboard may monitor high-level processes, lower level data can be quickly accessed by clicking through the links. This high-level summary with the lower-level detail allows executives not only to see the summary but also drill down deeper as questions arise. Figure 9.4 presents an example of a digital dashboard (or digital cockpit) for **General Electric**. Sub-business tabs (along the top) and the cockpit map (along the left side) give the user the ability to drill down deeper into the data.

Specialized dashboards may track overall corporate processes and performance or be specialized by function or department. These dashboards may track building projects, customer relationships, sales and marketing, security, operations, and the like.

FIGURE 9.4
**Digital Dashboard
for General Electric**

Source: http://www.ge.com/
annual01/letter/cockpit/.

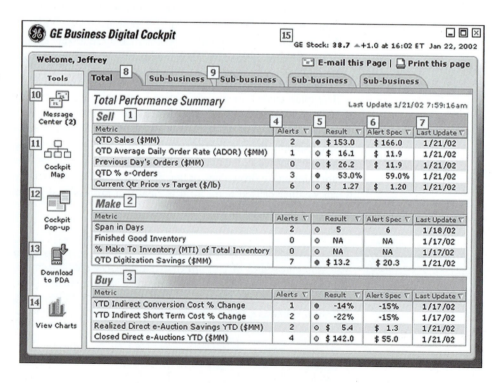

5. What business processes could be on a digital dashboard for your business school?
6. Why is a dashboard needed instead of just a standard report?

LO 9-4

Explain how XBRL works and how it makes business reporting more efficient.

FINANCIAL REPORTING AND XBRL

XBRL stands for e**X**tensible **B**usiness **R**eporting **L**anguage and is based on the **XML** language (**Extensible Markup Language**), a standard for Internet communication among businesses. XBRL is specifically designed to electronically communicate business information and is used to facilitate business reporting of financial and nonfinancial data.

One of the advantages of XBRL is that it greatly enhances the speed and accuracy of business reporting. XBRL International has developed a taxonomy to describe and tag thousands of financial statement items.

XBRL provides major benefits in the preparation, analysis, and communication of business information. Instead of treating financial information as just a block of text that has to be manually reentered into a computer (or digitized) to give it meaning, XBRL gives each financial statement item (both text and numbers) its own unique tag that is computer readable and searchable. Total assets, for example, has its own unique tag telling the database exactly what it is. Accounts receivable has its own tag, and inventory has yet a third tag.

In February 2009, the U.S. Securities and Exchange Commission (SEC) passed a new rule titled, "Interactive Data to Improve Financial Reporting," which required all large domestic and foreign accelerated filers to begin formatting their financial statements using XBRL. The new rule also requires these same public companies to format their financial statements using XBRL on their corporate websites. XBRL US, a division of XBRL International, was chosen to develop a single taxonomy for SEC financial reporting. Details regarding XBRL and the SEC are available at the SEC's XBRL website: http://xbrl.sec.gov/.

Figure 9.5 presents how financial reporting would look under XBRL. The data begin in the AIS. XBRL tags are then assigned to each financial and nonfinancial item either automatically by the enterprise system or manually by a member of the accounting department or its designee. Before the data can be accessed by external parties, assurance must be provided by an external auditor (discussed in more detail later). Once assurance is complete, the database is available for various uses, including reporting on the firm's website, filing to regulators (SEC, IRS, etc.), and providing information to other interested parties (such as financial analysts, loan officers, and investors). Each interested XBRL user can either access standard reports (i.e., 10-K going to the SEC or the corporate tax return going to the IRS) or specialized reports (i.e., only specific data) using what is called an XBRL style sheet (discussed in more detail later). The power of XBRL allows interested parties to either access standardized financial statements and reports or access only the information that is needed most for their own use.

History and Development of XBRL

XBRL has been a few years in the making—from initial concept all the way to SEC adoption. Figure 9.6 provides a brief history of XBRL and highlights the important events in its formation.

How XBRL Works

In this section, we present a description of how the data goes from the AIS to ultimate an XBRL report. Figure 9.7 provides a model of how XBRL works.

FIGURE 9.5
Financial and
Nonfinancial
Reporting Using
XBRL: From the AIS
to the End User

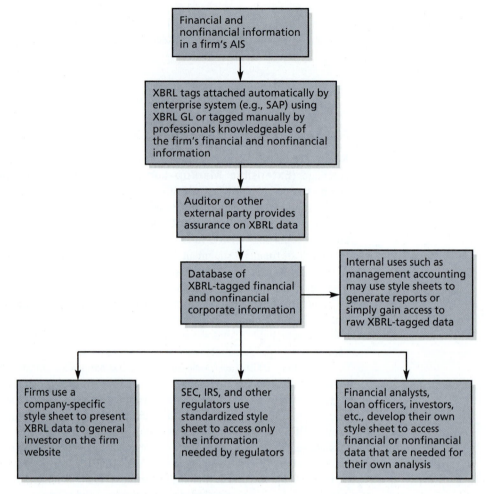

The **XBRL specification** (currently version 2.1) outlines the technical framework for XBRL. It provides the underlying technical details of what XBRL is and how it works.

XBRL Taxonomy

The **XBRL taxonomy** defines and describes each key data element (e.g., total assets, accounts, payable, net income). Because each national jurisdiction may have different accounting rules and regulations, each country may have its own taxonomy for financial reporting. That is why there are different taxonomies for each country: XBRL Australia, XBRL Canada, XBRL Germany, XBRL IASB, XBRL Japan, XBRL-Netherlands, and XBRL-UK.

Taxonomies continue to be developed to enable filings to regulators (such as banks), tax authorities (such as the IRS), and other governmental entities. For example, U.S. banks are required to submit their quarterly report, "Report of Condition and Income," or their Call Report, to the Federal Deposit Insurance Corporation (FDIC) using XBRL. The Federal Financial Institutions Examination Council (FFIEC) is responsible for creating XBRL Call Report taxonomy to facilitate filing call reports.

XBRL Instance Documents

The XBRL for US GAAP has approximately 12,000 element labels or tags.[2]

While the XBRL taxonomy describes the data elements, **XBRL instance documents** contain the actual dollar amounts or the details of each of the elements within the firm's

---

[2]"Staff Interpretations and FAQs Related to Interactive Data Disclosure," Securities and Exchange Commission, www.sec.gov/spotlight/xbrl/staff-interps.shtml, accessed July 2009.

FIGURE 9.6
History of XBRL

Source: www.xbrl.org/
history.aspx. Used with
permission from
XBRL.org.

April 1998	Charles Hoffman, a CPA from the accounting firm Knight Vale and Gregory in Tacoma, Washington, contemplated how XML could be used as a means to electronically deliver financial information.
January 1999	A prototype of XBRL is presented to the AICPA; the AICPA agrees that XBRL is important to the accounting profession.
July 2000	XBRL releases the first XBRL specification for financial statements for commercial and industrial companies in the United States. The committee announces the formation of an international organization to position for rapid global expansion and adoption.
June 2001	XBRL announces an effort to create XBRL for transactions internal to the company. This is often called XBRL GL, which is essentially XBRL on the general ledger.
October 2001	XBRL recognizes that different countries have different reporting needs and divides up the job of developing specifications to different XBRL jurisdictions, such as XBRL-Australia, XBRL-Canada, XBRL-Germany, XBRL IASB, XBRL-Japan, XBRL-Netherlands, and XBRL-UK.
February 2002	The Australian Prudential Regulatory Agency (APRA), one of the world's largest regulatory agencies, announces that XBRL is being used to overhaul data collection from 11,000 super funds, insurers, and banks required to report to it on a regular basis.
December 2003	XBRL 2.1 Specification is released.
May 2004	XBRL-UK releases taxonomy for UK GAAP.
July 2005	XBRL International releases a new version of its GL taxonomy, which allows the efficient handling of financial and business information contained within an organization.
2008 and early 2009	The SEC mandates that operating firms provide their financial statements to the SEC and on their corporate websites in interactive data format using XBRL.

FIGURE 9.7
How XBRL Works

Source: "Interactive Data:
The Impact on Assurance",
Assurance Working Group
of XBRL International,
November 2006, www.
xbrl.org/Announcements/
Interactive-Data-Assur-
ance-2006-11-10.pdf,
accessed July 2009, used
with permission.

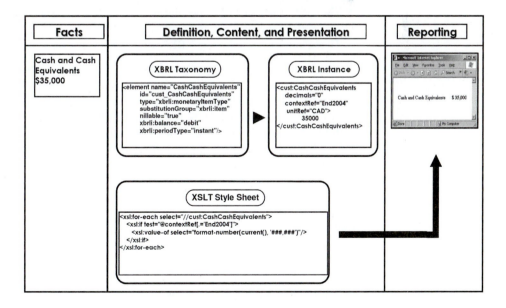

XBRL database. Thus, XBRL instance documents are a collection of data in a computer readable format. It is not until the style sheet is applied that the financial statement information is finally readable by people.

XBRL Style Sheets

XBRL style sheets take the instance documents and add presentation elements to make them readable by people. The data may be presented in a number of formats, including HTML, PDF, Microsoft Word, and Microsoft Excel (among others). The style sheet is made in conformance with a standardized language called Extensible Stylesheet Language (XSL). The official XSL specification for the XSL language is XSLT. This language is not governed by XBRL but is a standard means for taking data from XBRL or XML and presenting computer readable data in a way that is readable to humans. As discussed in Figure 9.4, different users will have different style sheets to access the exact data they are interested in. While the SEC may be interested in a standardized style sheet to retrieve a standardized report, a bank loan officer or financial analyst may be interested in developing his or her own to facilitate analysis.

XBRL Assurance

Before the SEC mandated XBRL submissions, **assurance** on any voluntary XBRL filings generally followed guidance from the Public Company Accounting Oversight Board (PCAOB), which relied on the auditor comparing a paper output of the XBRL-related documents to the information in the official EDGAR (Electronic Data Gathering, Analysis and Retrieval) filing to note any possible differences. Now that the use of XBRL is mandated by the SEC, assuring those XBRL documents is not required. It is expected that investors and other financial statement users will ultimately demand some assurance from an auditor or external party on a firm's use of XBRL.

There is no clear way to predict the future, but we can predict that the assurance afforded to XBRL will be quite different from the common external auditor's report on the auditee's financial statements and more than just matching a paper copy of the financial statements to the output of XBRL reports. However, we do believe that XBRL assurance will include assurance that:

1. The most current, standardized XBRL taxonomy is used.
2. The underlying financial and nonfinancial data that are used in XBRL tagging are reliable.
3. The XBRL tagging is accurate and complete.
4. The reports generated using XBRL are complete and received on a timely basis.

XBRL allows highly disaggregated data, so not only is it possible to know the level of sales, but it is possible to know sales revenue in much more detail. For example, it is possible for firms to apply XBRL tagging to sales by state or by country, by product line, by store or by office, and so on. While the extent of disaggregated data that a company will provide is still in question, the possibility allows opportunities for firms to provide this potentially helpful data to external parties. As firms begin to use XBRL to disclose disaggregated data, assurance will be needed on items that have never before been disclosed to investors. It will be especially critical for these items to receive assurance as mentioned under item 2 to ensure that the underlying financial and nonfinancial data used in XBRL tagging are reliable.

XBRL GL

Thus far, we have focused on XBRL for financial reporting. That type of XBRL is meant to facilitate efficient communication between firms and external parties (e.g., shareholders, regulatory bodies like the SEC and IRS, and the like.) In contrast, **XBRL GL** (also known as **XBRL Global Ledger Taxonomy**) serves as a means to facilitate efficient communication *within a firm.* XBRL GL allows the representation of anything that is found in a chart of accounts, journal entries, or historical transactions—financial and nonfinancial. The ability to tag using XBRL is generally supported by enterprise systems (ERPs) such as SAP, Oracle, and Microsoft.

According to XBRL International, the advantages of XBRL GL include the following:

- XBRL Global Ledger is *reporting independent.* It collects general ledger and after-the-fact receivables, payables, inventory and other nonfinancial facts, and then permits the representation of that information using traditional summaries and through flexible links to XBRL for reporting.
- XBRL Global Ledger is *system independent.* Any developer can create import and export routines to convert information to XBRL GL format. This means that accounting software developers need only consider one design for their XML import/export file formats. Application service providers can offer to supply XBRL import and output so end-users can more easily use their own data. Companies developing operational products, such as point of sale systems or job costing, or reporting tools can link with many accounting products without needing specialized links to each one.
- XBRL Global Ledger permits *consolidation.* Popular low-end products and mid-market solutions are not designed to facilitate consolidating data from multiple organizations. XBRL GL can help transfer the general ledger from one system to another, be used to combine the operations of multiple organizations, or bring data into tools that will do the consolidation.
- XBRL Global Ledger provides *flexibility,* overcoming the limitations of other approaches such as electronic data interchange (EDI). It offers an *extensible, flexible, multinational solution* that can exchange the data required by internal finance, accountants, and creditors.[3]

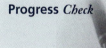

Progress *Check*

7. Using Figure 9.5 as a guide, how will XBRL GL facilitate the process of tagging the data that are generated by the firm's AIS?
8. What are the four predicted assurance needs for XBRL in the near future?

Summary

- Data warehouses serve as a repository of information that is separate from the operating databases of the firm. Data warehouses include data from a number of operational (internal) and external sources that will be helpful in providing information supportive for decision making across a number of functions in the firm. Data marts represent a slice of data from the data warehouse to meet a specific need.
- Business intelligence uses computer-based techniques to accumulate and analyze data that might be helpful to the firm's strategic initiatives.
- Digital dashboards track critical firm performance in a way that is easily accessible to executives.
- XBRL serves as a means to electronically communicate business information to facilitate business reporting of financial and nonfinancial data to users. XBRL greatly enhances the speed and accuracy of business reporting.

[3]www.xbrl.org/GLTaxonomy/, accessed July 20, 2010, used with permission.

Key Words

assurance (*186*) Independent, professional opinions that reduce the risk of having incorrect information.

business intelligence (*180*) A computer-based technique for accumulating and analyzing data from databases and data warehouses to support managerial decision making.

data mart (*178*) A subset of the information from the data warehouse to serve a specific purpose

data mining (*181*) A process of using sophisticated statistical techniques to extract and analyze data from large databases to discern patterns and trends that were not previously known.

data warehouse (*178*) A collection of information gathered from an assortment of external and operational (i.e, internal) databases to facilitate reporting for decision making and business analysis.

decision support system (DSS) (*180*) A computer-based information system that facilitates business decision-making activities.

digital dashboard (*182*) A display to track the firm's process or performance indicators or metrics to monitor critical performance.

XBRL (eXtensible Business Reporting Language) (*183*) An open, global standard for exchanging financial reporting information.

XBRL Global Ledger Taxonomy (XBRL GL) (*186*) Serves as a ledger using the XBRL standard for internal purposes.

XBRL instance documents (*184*) A document containing XBRL elements.

XBRL specification (*184*) Provides the underlying technical details of what XBRL is and how it works.

XBRL style sheet (*186*) Adds presentation elements to XBRL instance documents to make them readable by people.

XBRL taxonomy (*184*) Defines and describes each key data element (e.g., total assets, accounts, payable, net income, etc.).

XML (Extensible Markup Language) (*183*) Open, global standard for exchanging information in a format that is both human- and machine-readable.

Answers to Progress *Checks*

1. Specific functions in a firm, such as marketing, often do not need the whole data warehouse but would prefer a data mart that most closely addresses their needs. **Apple** may be interested in the demographics of the customer segment that purchases iPods and iPhones to best identify those most like to buy an iPad or other **Apple** innovation.

2. To answer this question, we'll use Figure 9.2 as a guide. Among other things, **Best Buy** would be interested in general ledger, inventory, and sales information from its internal databases. The company would also be interested in data from the retail industry, specifically from the retail segment that includes consumer electronics, personal computers and entertainment software, and appliances. General economic information and focal customer demographics would all be useful.

3. **Starbucks** could use business intelligence to monitor websites, news articles, court filings, and the like for **Dunkin' Donuts'** prices, the locations for potential stores, and proposed new products.

4. Business (perhaps better termed as "competitive") intelligence and data mining could be used in the NBA to see which defenses work best, who to foul at the end of the game, who would usually take the end-of-the-game shot, who and when to play tight defense at the three-point line, and so on. This would be particularly helpful in a playoff series of five to seven games, where the team plays its competitor in successive games.

5. A business school might need to monitor the following business processes on its digital dashboard:
    a. Number of students enrolled each semester.
    b. Number of courses offered.
    c. How full each section is to determine if more sections should be offered, etc.
    d. Job placement rates in each major.
    e. GMAT scores of its incoming masters of accounting and MBA students.
6. A dashboard is used to monitor, in a user-friendly way, the critical business processes that most affect firm performance. Standard reports may always be used but may not be as accessible as a digital dashboard.
7. XBRL GL will automatically tag the various financial and nonfinancial elements in the enterprise system software. This makes this step of tagging trivial for the firm to perform.
8. The four predicted assurance needs for XBRL include:
    a. The most current, standardized XBRL taxonomy is used.
    b. The underlying financial and nonfinancial data that are used in XBRL tagging are reliable.
    c. The XBRL tagging is accurate and complete.
    d. The reports generated using XBRL are complete and received on a timely basis.

Multiple Choice Questions

1. A subset of a data warehouse is called a:
    a. Small data warehouse
    b. Data mart
    c. Data martian
    d. Business intelligence
2. A data warehouse may include a:
    a. XBRL style sheet
    b. Competitor information
    c. Digital dashboard
    d. iPad
3. American Airlines may use business intelligence to:
    a. Track the cost of snacks on its airplanes
    b. Monitor the cost of its pilots and flight attendants
    c. Track the cost of its airplane fuel
    d. Monitor prices on competitive routes
4. The computer-based technique to accumulate and analyze data is called:
    a. Business intelligence
    b. Data warehouse
    c. Digital dashboard
    d. XBRL
5. The steps in business intelligence include:
    a. Analyze data for patterns, gather information, make decision.
    b. Create data warehouse, query data warehouse, make decision.
    c. Query data warehouse, create data warehouse, make decision.
    d. Gather information, analyze data for patterns, make decision.

6. Digital dashboard tracks, in a user-friendly way:

   a. Automobile speed

   b. Critical business failures

   c. Critical business processes

   d. Critical business markets

7. XBRL facilitates business reporting of:

   a. Business processes

   b. The XML language

   c. Financial and nonfinancial information

   d. Only financial information.

8. The first person to propose using XML be used as a means to electronically deliver financial information was:

   a. Albert Gore

   b. Charles Hoffman

   c. Robert Byrd

   d. Herb Hackett

9. XBRL GL, or XBRL Global Ledger Taxonomy, is different from XBRL US GAAP because it facilitates:

   a. Efficient communication between the firm and external parties

   b. Efficient communication within a firm

   c. Efficient communication with the supply chain

   d. Efficient communication with customers

10. The stated advantages of XBRL GL do not include:

    a. Reporting independent

    b. System independent

    c. Scalability

    d. Flexibility

Discussion Questions

1. Using Figure 9.2 as a guide, name three internal and three external databases that you think should be included in a data warehouse for **Bank of America**, **Wells Fargo**, or your local bank. Support your answer.

2. Using Figure 9.2 as a guide, name three internal and three external databases that you think should be included in a data warehouse for your university. Support your answer.

3. Name five items that you think would be included in a digital dashboard for **ESPN** or for **Disney**. Why are these critical business processes for that company?

4. Who will rely on XBRL data for decision making? Why is assurance needed on XBRL data? Support your answer.

5. Why is there a different XBRL taxonomy for each country, including XBRL-Australia, XBRL-Canada, XBRL-Germany, XBRL-Japan, XBRL-Netherlands, XBRL-US, and XBRL-UK? What would happen if there was only one XBRL taxonomy for all countries?

6. How would the XBRL style sheets be different for financial analysts as compared to the Securities and Exchange Commission? How would XBRL style sheets be different for a firm's website as compared to bank loan officers?

7. Why is XBRL needed in the financial community? In your opinion, why did the Securities and Exchange Commission mandate its usage? What does it provide that was not available before XBRL?

8. Why would XBRL be used for internal uses such as management accounting? (*Hint:* See Figure 9.5.)

Problems

1. Using Figure 9.1 and 9.2 as guides, name four internal and four external databases that you think should be included in a data warehouse for marketing function of **Procter & Gamble** or the consumer packaged goods company with whom you are most familiar. Procter & Gamble has products like Gillette razors, Tide detergent, and Pampers diapers. Why are these eight databases you recommend critical to the effective functioning of the marketing department to sell more products? Support your answer.

2. Which of the four predicted assurance needs in the near future do you believe is most critical to ensuring XBRL accuracy? Support your answer.

3. XBRL allows disaggregated data to be presented to interested external parties. Financial analysts often predict one-year-ahead earnings and then suggest whether an investor should buy, sell, or hold a stock. Which type of disaggregated data do you think financial analysts would be most interested in receiving when predicting one-year-ahead earnings: detailed sales data, detailed expense data, detailed asset data, and/or detailed liability data? Support your answer. In your opinion, which disaggregated XBRL data would be most useful information in predicting whether an investor should buy, sell, or hold a stock?

4. In the text, we mentioned that data mining is often used to analyze stock prices and stock returns. A *Wall Street Journal* article by Jason Zweig, "Data Mining Isn't a Good Bet for Stock-Market Predictions" (August 8, 2009), mentions that data mining has revealed that you can predict stock returns by tracking the number of 9-year-olds in the United States. Another data mining exercise predicts that stocks are more likely to go up on days when smog is not as bad.[4] While the statistical correlation may be valid, there must be a logical reason that a particular factor will predict stock returns.

    Required:

    a. Give your opinion on whether the number of 9-year-olds in the United States should or should not predict stock returns.

    b. Give your opinion on whether a smoggy day should or should not predict stock market returns.

    c. Give your opinion on what does predict stock returns, if anything.

5. XBRL touts as its primary advantage that it increases efficiency for the firm and those interested in its business reports.

    Required:

    a. How is XBRL more efficient for the firm that reports its business performance? Does the use XBRL GL in a firm's accounting software make XBRL more or less efficient than when XBRL GL is not used?

    b. How is XBRL more efficient for those using its business reports for regulator, investing, or other purposes?

    c. Are there any cases when it is less efficient to use XBRL?

6. How would **Coca-Cola** use business intelligence to monitor **Pepsi Cola's** operations in Russia? What sources of data need to be gathered? How would it be analyzed?

Answers to Multiple Choice Questions

1.	b	6.	c
2.	b	7.	c
3.	d	8.	b
4.	a	9.	b
5.	d	10.	c

[4]http://online.wsj.com/article/SB124967937642715417.html, accessed July 2010.

Part **Three**

Managing and Evaluating AIS Projects

Accounting Information Systems and Internal Controls

A look at this chapter

This chapter provides a general discussion on control issues in accounting information systems. In particular, we examine issues in ethics and internal controls that are addressed by the Sarbanes-Oxley Act of 2002 and important factors in corporate governance. These related areas are critical to an organization's efficiency and effectiveness in operations, reliability in financial reporting, and compliance with applicable laws and regulations. In addition, important control and governance frameworks including COSO, COBIT, and ITIL are covered in this chapter.

A look back

Chapter 9 provided a description of how accounting information systems facilitate management reporting, including using data warehouses, business intelligence, and dashboards. In addition, we also explained the development and emerging use of eXtensible Business Reporting Language (XBRL) in electronic financial reporting.

A look ahead

In Chapter 11, we discuss computer fraud and information security–related issues. The focus includes systems integrity and availability, as well as threats and risks in conducting business.

You probably often visit **Starbucks** for coffee. Have you ever visited www.starbucks.com to learn more about the firm? You might be surprised to find more than just different types of coffee, a menu, store locations, and so on. You can find a lot of information under the tag called "Responsibility— Ethical, Local, Global." **Starbucks** believes businesses should be responsible to the communities they serve. The company is committed to "buying and serving the highest-quality, responsibly grown, ethically traded coffee to help create a better future for farmers." The philosophy and ethical values of a firm is one of the critical factors that form the firm's control environment. The Committee of Sponsoring Organizations (COSO) indicates that without a good control environment, even the best-designed control systems may fail. The control environment sets the tone of a firm and signifies how the firm values integrity and ethics of its employees.

Chapter Outline

Learning Objectives

After reading this chapter, you should be able to:

10-1 Explain essential control concepts and why a code of ethics and internal controls are important.

10-2 Explain the objectives and components of the COSO internal control framework and the COSO enterprise risk management framework.

10-3 Describe the overall COBIT framework and its implications for IT governance.

10-4 Describe other governance frameworks related to information systems management and security.

INTRODUCTION

Ethics, internal controls, and information security are three closely related areas critical to corporate governance. Safeguarding the assets of a firm has always been the responsibility of its management. Given the swift advancements in computing technology and the pervasive use of IT in all aspects of business operations, managers and accountants have to reexamine how to establish and monitor internal controls. For internal and external auditors, it is important to assess the effectiveness of internal controls to meet the mandate of the Sarbanes-Oxley Act.

LO 10-1
Explain essential control concepts and why a code of ethics and internal controls are important.

ETHICS, THE SARBANES-OXLEY ACT OF 2002, AND CORPORATE GOVERNANCE

The Need for a Code of Ethics

Ethical principles are derived from cultural values, societal traditions, and personal attitudes on issues of right and wrong. Integrity and individual ethics are formed through a person's life experience. Ethics plays a critical role when people make choices and decisions. Although individuals have their own values and may behave differently from one another, firms often choose to establish a formal expectation, through a **code of ethics,** on what is considered to be ethical within the group in order to promote ethical behavior. Ethical behavior prompted by a code of ethics can be considered a form of internal control. Given today's diversified and globalized business environment, a firm will have to rely on the ethics of its employees to operate efficiently and effectively. In addition, the importance of a code of ethics should be emphasized because employees with different culture backgrounds are likely to have different values.

In addition, many professional associations have developed codes of ethics to assist professionals in selecting among decisions that are not clearly right or wrong. Some examples include the American Institute of Certified Public Accountants (AICPA), the Information Systems Audit and Control Association (ISACA), the Institute of Internal Auditors (IIA), and the Institute of Management Accountants (IMA). The certification programs of these associations require the knowledge of the codes of ethics in developing professionalism.

WorldCom used shady accounting methods to mask its declining financial condition by falsely professing financial growth and profitability to increase the price of its stock. On March 15, 2005, CEO Bernard Ebbers was convicted of fraud, conspiracy and filing false documents with regulators. He was sentenced to 25 years in prison.

Corporate Governance as Addressed by Sarbanes-Oxley

The impact of public policy on the accounting profession through the enactment of laws and regulations has been well-documented and can be traced back to the 1930s.[1] Among those policies enforced, the **Sarbanes-Oxley Act of 2002 (SOX)** has probably had the most far-reaching effect on public companies and accounting firms. This bill was a response to business scandals such as Enron, WorldCom, and Tyco International. SOX requires public companies registered with the SEC and their auditors to annually assess and report on the design and effectiveness of internal control over financial reporting.

SOX also established the **Public Company Accounting Oversight Board (PCAOB)** to provide independent oversight of public accounting firms. The PCAOB issues

[1]See the Securities Act of 1933, Securities Exchange Act of 1934, and Foreign Corrupt Practices Act of 1977.

auditing standards and oversees quality controls of public accounting firms. PCAOB Auditing Standard No. 5 (AS 5) encourages auditors to use a risk-based, top-down approach to identify the key controls. That is, auditors should start at the financial statement level when analyzing controls, focusing on entity-level controls[2] followed by reviewing significant accounts, disclosures, and management assertions.

SOX is arranged into 11 titles. The first two titles are most relevant to auditors. As far as compliance for public companies, the most important sections within the other titles are considered to be 301, 302, 404, 406, 409, 802, 807, and 906 (see Figure 10.1).

FIGURE 10.1
Titles and Compliance Requirements of Sarbanes-Oxley Act

SOX Titles	Key Sections	Key Compliance Requirements
Title I: Public Company Accounting Oversight Board (PCAOB)	101	Establishment
	103	Auditing, quality control, and independence standards and rules
	104	Inspections of registered public accounting firms
Title II: Auditor Independence	201	Services outside the scope of practice of auditors
	203	Audit partner rotation
	204	Auditor reports to audit committees
	206	Conflicts of interest
Title III: Corporate Responsibility	301	Public company audit committees
	302	Corporate responsibility for financial reports
Title IV: Enhanced Financial Disclosures	404	Management assessment of internal controls
	406	Code of ethics for senior financial officers
	409	Real-time issuer disclosures
Title VIII: Corporate and Criminal Fraud Accountability	802	Criminal penalties for altering documents
	807	Criminal penalties for defrauding shareholders of publicly traded companies
Title IX: White-Collar Crime Penalty Enhancements	906	Corporate responsibility for financial reports

Do you consider SOX helpful to improving corporate governance? Is SOX relevant to a company's social responsibilities? You can find online that some public companies provide a sustainability report on their websites. What is the purpose of the sustainability report?

Corporate governance can be defined as a set of processes and policies in managing an organization with sound ethics to safeguard the interests of its stakeholders. Corporate governance also promotes accountability, fairness, and transparency in the organization's relationship with its stakeholders. At the Global Corporate Governance Forum held by World Bank (2000), Mr. Adrian Cadbury stated that: "Corporate governance is concerned with holding the balance between economic and social goals and between individual and communal goals. The corporate governance framework is intended to encourage the efficient use of resources and to require accountability for the stewardship of those resources. The aim is to align as nearly as possible the interests of individuals, corporations and society."

[2]According to the PCAOB Release 2007-005, examples of entity-level controls include internal control environment, risk assessment and management, management override, centralized processing, and monitoring.

Progress *Check*

1. Why does a firm need a code of ethics? Is it important to corporate governance?
2. The Sarbanes-Oxley Act was enacted in 2002 and established PCAOB. What are the functions of PCAOB?

CONTROL AND GOVERNANCE FRAMEWORKS

Overview of Control Concepts

Internal control involves the processes that an organization implements to safeguard assets, provide accurate and reliable information, promote operational efficiency, enforce prescribed managerial policies, and comply with applicable laws and regulations. Appropriate internal controls support organizations' objectives through accountability and transparency for good corporate governance. According to SOX, the establishment and maintenance of internal controls is a management responsibility.

Firms use internal controls as a means of preventing errors and deterring fraud. The three main functions of internal control are prevention, detection, and correction. **Preventive controls** deter problems before they arise. Preventive controls require compliance with preferred procedures and thus stop undesirable events from happening. For example, a transaction should be authorized to ensure its validity. Hence, a signed source document should be required before recording a transaction. **Detective controls** find problems when they arise. These controls are procedures and techniques designed to identify undesirable events after they have already occurred. For example, bank reconciliations and monthly trial balances are prepared to catch mistakes. **Corrective controls** fix problems that have been identified, such as using backup files to recover corrupted data. Detective controls are often linked to accompanying corrective controls to remediate any issues that are discovered.

In a computerized environment, internal controls can also be categorized as general controls and application controls. **General controls** pertain to enterprisewide issues such as controls over accessing the network, developing and maintaining applications, documenting changes of programs, and so on. **Application controls** are specific to a subsystem or an application to ensure the validity, completeness, and accuracy of the transactions. For example, when entering a sales transaction, use an input control to ensure the customer account number is entered accurately.

Given SOX, the SEC requires management to evaluate internal controls based on a recognized control framework such as the frameworks developed by the **Committee of Sponsoring Organizations (COSO)** of the Treadway Commission.

LO 10-2

Explain the control objectives and components of the COSO internal control framework and the COSO enterprise risk management framework.

Commonly Used Frameworks

COSO is composed of several organizations: American Accounting Association (AAA), AICPA, Financial Executives International (FEI), IIA, and IMA. The purpose of COSO is to study the causal factors that lead to fraudulent financial reporting and to develop recommendations for public companies, independent auditors, the SEC and other regulators, and educational institutions to improve the quality of financial reporting through internal controls and corporate governance.[3] COSO developed two frameworks to improve the quality of financial reporting through accountability, effective controls, risk management, and corporate governance. The Committee issued the "Internal Control—Integrated Framework" in 1992, and the "Enterprise Risk Management—Integrated Framework" in

---

[3]See www.coso.org.

2004. The COSO internal control framework is one of the most widely accepted authorities on internal control, providing a baseline for evaluating, reporting, and improving internal control. Given the dramatic changes in the business environments, COSO has updated the internal control framework (COSO 2.0) to codify the principles for effective internal control, to address changes in the business and operating environments, and to respond to expectations from stakeholders.

As a future business professional, do you think you need to know so much about control frameworks? Why is this knowledge critical to your success in the future career?

The COSO enterprise risk management (ERM) framework expanded the original COSO internal control framework to provide guidance in defining, assessing, managing, and transferring risk in order to maximize firm value. The COSO ERM focuses on the strategic alignment of the firm's mission with its risk appetite. Although most firms in the United States already use the COSO internal control framework in establishing and evaluating their internal control systems, many are still applying the concepts in COSO ERM as the basis for developing risk-based internal control systems. AS No. 5 encourages the top-down risk assessment approach in evaluating internal controls. Therefore, the focus of both management and external auditors has become more in line with the COSO ERM framework.

The **control objectives for information and related technology (COBIT)** framework is an internationally accepted set of best IT security and control practices for IT management released by the IT Governance Institute (ITGI). It is a control framework for the governance and management of enterprise IT. COBIT provides management with an understanding of risks associated with IT and bridges the gap between among risks, control needs, and technical issues.

The **Information Technology Infrastructure Library (ITIL)** is a set of concepts and practices for IT service management. COBIT defines the overall IT control framework, and ITIL provides the details for IT service management. ITIL is released by the UK Office of Government Commerce (OGC) and is the most widely accepted model for IT service management. ITIL adopts a lifecycle approach to IT services, focusing on practices for service strategy, service design, service transition, service operation, and continual service improvement.

The **International Organization for Standardization (ISO) 27000 series** is designed to address information security issues. The ISO 27000 series, particularly ISO 27001 and ISO 27002, have become the most recognized and generally accepted sets of information security framework and guidelines.

COSO Internal Control Framework

The updated COSO internal control framework (COSO 2.0) defines internal control as a process—affected by an entity's board of directors, management, and other personnel—designed to provide reasonable assurance regarding the achievement of objectives in effectiveness and efficiency of operations, reliability of reporting, and compliance with applicable laws and regulations. Accordingly, the COSO 2.0 framework indicates that:[4]

1. Internal control is a process consisting of ongoing tasks and activities. It is a means to an end, not an end in itself.
2. Internal control is affected by people. It is not merely about policy manuals, systems, and forms. Rather, it is about people at every level of a firm who affect internal control.
3. Internal control can provide reasonable assurance, not absolute assurance, to an entity's management and board.
4. Internal control is geared toward the achievement of objectives in one or more separate but overlapping categories.
5. Internal control is adaptable to the entity structure.

[4]See www.coso.org/resources.htm.

According to the COSO 2.0 framework, an effective internal control system should consist of three categories of objectives and five essential components. The three categories of objectives are:

1. Operations objectives: effectiveness and efficiency of a firm's operations on financial performance goals and safeguarding assets.
2. Reporting objectives: reliability of reporting, including internal and external financial and nonfinancial reporting.
3. Compliance objectives: adherence to applicable laws and regulations.

To support a firm in its efforts to achieve internal control objectives, COSO 2.0 suggests five components of internal control:

1. Control environment—sets the tone of a firm, influences the control consciousness of its employees, and establishes the foundation for the internal control system. Control environment factors include the management's philosophy and operating style, integrity and ethical values of employees, organizational structure, the role of the audit committee, proper board oversight for the development and performance of internal control, and personnel policies and practices.
2. Risk assessment—involves a dynamic process for identifying and analyzing a firm's risks from external and internal environments. Risk assessment allows a firm to understand the extent to which potential events might affect corporate objectives. Risks are analyzed after considering the likelihood of occurrence and the potential loss. The analysis serves as a basis for determining how the risks should be managed. This component will be discussed later in the chapter.
3. Control activities—occur throughout a firm at all levels and in all functions. A firm must establish control policies, procedures, and practices that ensure the firm's objectives are achieved and risk mitigation strategies are carried out. This component will be discussed later in the chapter.
4. Information and communication—supports all other control components by communicating effectively to ensure information flows down, across, and up the firm, as well as interacting with external parties such as customers, suppliers, regulators, and shareholders and informing them about related policy positions. Relevant information should be identified, captured, and communicated in a form and timeframe that enables employees to carry out their duties.
5. Monitoring activities—the design and effectiveness of internal controls should be monitored by management and other parties outside the process in an ongoing basis. Findings should be evaluated, and deficiencies must be communicated in a timely manner. Necessary modifications should be made to improve the business process and the internal control system.

The three objectives and five components of the COSO internal control framework are part of the COSO ERM framework.

Progress *Check*   3. What is the definition of internal control?
                         4. What are the three main categories of internal control?

COSO ERM Framework

All firms encounter uncertainty in daily operations. Uncertainty presents both risk and opportunity, with the potential to reduce or enhance the firm's value. For example, Paul Walsh, CEO of Diageo, indicated that

> Managing risk can be one of the most overlooked areas within a business' structure. It is critical, particularly for global companies such as Diageo, for risk management processes and strategies to be imbedded with its operations. At Diageo, we have an exclusive-level Audit and Risk Committee which is tasked with overseeing and implementing effective risk management and control in the business. Whether it's navigating the global financial crisis or contingency planning for global health epidemics such as avian flu, these are significant issues which can impact your business performance and sustainability.[5]

The COSO enterprise risk management framework (2004) defines **enterprise risk management (ERM)** as "a process, affected by the entity's board of directors, management, and other personnel, applied in strategy setting and across the enterprise, designed to identify potential events that may affect the entity, and manage risk to be within the risk appetite, to provide reasonable assurance regarding the achievement of objectives."[6] Similarly, COSO indicates that:

1. ERM identifies potential events that may affect the firm.
2. ERM manages risk to be within the firm's risk appetite.
3. ERM provides reasonable assurance regarding the achievement of the firm's objectives.

Note that internal control is an integral part of enterprise risk management. The COSO internal control framework is the basis for existing rules, regulations, and laws. It has been incorporated into this ERM framework. In addition to internal controls, COSO ERM expands the COSO internal control framework to provide a broader view on risk management to maximize firm value (see Figure 10.2). The relationship is depicted in a cube. The four objectives categories—strategic, operations, reporting, and compliance—are represented by the vertical columns, the eight ERM components by horizontal rows, and the firm's units by the third dimension.

The ERM framework takes a risk-based, rather than a control-based, approach to achieving the firm's objectives in four categories:

1. Strategic—high-level goals, aligned with and supporting the firm's mission and vision.
2. Operations—effectiveness and efficiency of operations.
3. Reporting—reliability of internal and external reporting.
4. Compliance—compliance with applicable laws and regulations.

---

[5]M.S. Beasley, Bruce C. Branson, and Bonnie V. Hancock, *Enterprise Risk Oversight—A Global Analysis*, CIMA and AICPA Research Series, September 2010. Retrieved at http://www.aicpa.org/interestareas/businessindustryandgovernment/resources/erm/downloadabledocuments/enterprise%20risk%20v3.pdf, accessed February 2013.

[6]Richard M. Steinberg, Miles E.A. Everson , Frank J. Martens , Lucy E. Nottingham, *Enterprise Risk Management-Integrated Framework Executive Summary*, September, 2004. Retrieved at http://www.coso.org/documents/coso_erm_executivesummary.pdf, accessed February 2013.

FIGURE 10.2
COSO ERM Model

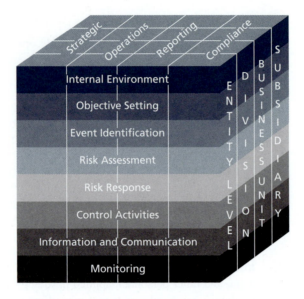

The COSO ERM consists of eight interrelated components. ERM is not strictly a serial process; it is a multidirectional, iterative process in which each component can influence the others. These components are:

1. Internal environment—provides the discipline and structure for all other components of enterprise risk management. It encompasses the tone of a firm, influences the risk consciousness of its people, and sets the basis for how risk is viewed and addressed by the firm. Internal environment factors include a firm's risk management philosophy and risk appetite,[7] integrity and ethical values, organizational structure, board of directors and the audit committee, human resource policies and practices, assignment of authority and responsibility, commitment to competence, and development of personnel.

2. Objective setting—based on the firm's mission and vision, management sets specific objectives before identifying potential events[8] affecting their achievement. Management should have a process in place to set strategic, operations, reporting, and compliance objectives. Objectives are set at the strategic level, establishing a basis for operations, reporting, and compliance, and the chosen objectives shall support and align with the firm's mission and be consistent with its risk appetite.

3. Event identification—internal and external events affecting achievement of a firm's objectives must be identified. After identifying all possible events, management must distinguish between risks and opportunities. Opportunities are channeled back to management's strategy or objective-setting processes. Identified risks should be forwarded to the next stage for assessment and be managed according to the firm's risk appetite.

4. Risk assessment—the same as in the COSO internal control framework. This component will be discussed later in the chapter.

5. Risk response—management selects risk responses and develops a set of actions to align risks with the entity's risk tolerances and risk appetite. The four options to respond to risks are reducing, sharing, avoiding, and accepting risks. This component will be discussed later in the chapter.

---

[7]A company's risk appetite takes into consideration its risk-taking attitude and how this attitude relates to the expectations of its stakeholders.

[8]COSO defines an event as "an incident or occurrence emanating from internal or external sources that affects implementation of strategy or achievement of objectives. Events may have positive or negative impacts or both."

6. Control activities—the same as in the COSO internal control framework. This component will be discussed later in the chapter.
7. Information and communication—the same as in the COSO internal control framework.
8. Monitoring—the process of evaluating the quality of internal control design and operation and the effectiveness of the ERM model. The ERM components and internal control process should be monitored continuously and modified as necessary. Determining whether a firm's enterprise risk management is effective is a judgment resulting from an analysis of whether the eight components are present and functioning properly. Thus, the components are also criteria for effective enterprise risk management. Monitoring is accomplished through ongoing management activities and conducted by other parties outside the process. ERM deficiencies are reported to top management and the board.

Everyone in a firm is responsible for enterprise risk management. The chief executive officer (CEO) is ultimately responsible and should assume ownership. All others support the firm's risk management philosophy, comply with its risk appetite, and manage risks within their duties. The following comments from Jörg Pässler, group treasurer at Sappi Group Treasury, are about enterprise risk oversight:

> The financial crisis of 2008/09/10 has awakened the need to comprehensively review and manage risk, especially those that seem very remote. If Lehman Bros. can go under, if AIG can go to the brink due to material exposures to a specific market that was deemed "safe," and if government default is viewed as a possibility, then we need to re-assess our risks with a completely different mindset. The comment 'that can never happen' will probably never be used in risk assessments again.[9]

Risk Assessment and Risk Response

Risk assessment is the process of identifying and analyzing risks systematically to determine the firm's risk response and control activities. It allows a firm to understand the extent to which potential events might affect corporate objectives. Given AS 5, risk assessment is also a first step in developing an audit plan to meet the mandate of SOX Section 404. According to COSO ERM, the risks of an identified event are analyzed on an inherent, control, and residual basis. **Inherent risk** is the risk related to the nature of the business activity itself. It exists already before management takes any actions to address it. For example, an inherent risk of a fast food corporation is a high number of competitors in the industry. **Control risk** is the threat that errors or irregularities in the underlying transactions will not be prevented, detected, and corrected by the internal control system. For example, an accounts payable clerk is required to get approval if the total dollar amount on any specific purchasing order (PO) is more than a predetermined limit (such as $1,000). The possibility that a clerk may create multiple purchasing orders for one transaction in avoiding the required authorization is a control risk. **Residual risk** is the product of inherent risk and control risk (i.e., Residual risk = Inherent risk × Control risk). In other words, it is the risk that remains after management's response to the risk or after the controls put in place to mitigate the risk. Firms should first assess inherent risk, develop a response or implement a control, and then assess residual risk.

According to COSO ERM,[10] management assesses risks from two perspectives—likelihood and impact—and uses a combination of both qualitative and quantitative risk assessment methodologies. When sufficient and/or credible data for quantitative assessment are not available, management often uses qualitative assessment techniques that

---

[9]Beasley, Branson, and Hancock, *Enterprise Risk Oversight—A Global Analysis.*
[10]*Enterprise Risk Management-Integrated Framework Application Techniques,* p. 310.

depend largely on the knowledge, experience, and judgment of the decision maker. Regarding risk response, COSO ERM indicates four options:[11]

1. Reduce risks by designing effective business processes and implementing internal controls.
2. Share risks by outsourcing business processes, buying insurance, or entering into hedging transactions.
3. Avoid risks by not engaging in the activities that would produce the risk.
4. Accept risk by relying on natural offsets of the risk within a portfolio, or allowing the likelihood and impact of the risk.

In determining risk response, management should evaluate options in relation to the firm's risk appetite, cost versus benefit of potential risk responses, and degree to which a response will reduce impact and/or likelihood. Selections of responses should be based on evaluation of the portfolio of risks and responses.

The process to assess risks is as follows : (1) identify risks to the firm; (2) estimate the likelihood of each risk occurring; (3) estimate the impact (i.e., potential loss in dollars) from each risk; (4) identify controls to mitigate the risk; (5) estimate the costs and benefits of implementing the controls; (6) perform a cost/benefit analysis for each risk and corresponding controls; and (7) based on the results of the cost/benefit analysis, determine whether to reduce the risk by implementing a control, or to accept, share, or avoid the risk. Figure 10.3 illustrates this process.[12]

FIGURE 10.3
Risk Assessment and Response Approach to Selecting Control Activities

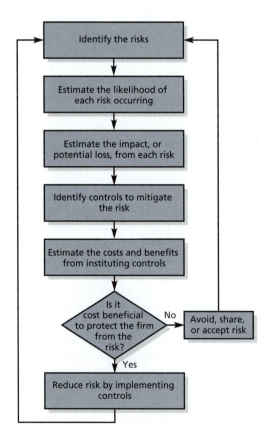

[11]Ibid., p. 55.
[12]Adapted from *Accounting Information Systems,* by M.B. Romney and P.J. Steinbart, 12th ed. (New York: Prentice Hall, 2012), p. 194.

Cost/Benefit analysis is important in determining whether to implement an internal control. The benefits of an internal control should exceed its costs. Costs are easier to measure than benefits. Costs incurred from implementing controls are often for personnel and technology, such as the price of a video camera and the value of additional hours of employee work incurred. They often can be quantified. Conversely, control benefits usually involve qualitative factors—such as increased productivity, improved customer satisfaction, better interaction with suppliers, or enhanced employee loyalty—and are difficult to measure. One way to measure the benefits of a control is using the estimated impact of a risk times the decreased likelihood if the control is implemented:

$$\text{Expected benefit of an internal control} = \text{Impact} \times \text{Decreased likelihood}$$

For example, due to input errors in making sales orders, Carlsbad Bottle Company may ship goods to wrong customers. The company estimates that if this happens, the impact of this type of event will cost about \$15,000, due to lost revenue, rerouting expense, and so forth. The likelihood of this risk is estimated as 10 percent. If Carlsbad Bottle Company implements a data validation step for input control, the likelihood of this risk could be only 0.5 percent. The cost to implement this control is \$200. Given this information, the expected benefit = \$15,000 × (10% − 0.5%) = \$1,425. The expected benefit of implementing the control (\$1,425) is larger than the cost (\$200), with a net benefit of \$1,225 (i.e., the difference between \$1,425 and \$200). Hence, Carlsbad Bottle Company should implement the control.

Progress *Check*

5. What are the four options of risk response?
6. What is the calculation for the expected benefit of an internal control?

Control Activities

Control activities are the policies and procedures that help ensure that necessary actions are taken to address risks to achieving the firm's objectives. There are two categories of control activities: physical controls and IT controls.

Physical controls are mainly manual but could involve the physical use of computing technology. These types of control activities include (1) authorization to ensure transactions are valid, (2) segregation of duties to prevent fraud and mistakes,[13] (3) supervision to compensate imperfect segregation of duties, (4) accounting documents and records to maintain audit trails, (5) access control to ensure only authorized personnel have access to physical assets and information, and (6) independent verification to double check for errors and misrepresentations.

Business environments have continued to increase in complexity with ever-greater reliance on the information produced by IT systems and processes. **IT controls** involve processes that provide assurance for information and help to mitigate risks associated with the use of technology.[14] Firms need IT controls to protect information assets, remain competitive, and control costs in implementing IT projects. IT controls are a subset of a firm's internal controls, and are categorized as IT general and application controls.

---

[13]The general guideline for segregation of duties (SOD) is that transaction authorization, record keeping, and asset custody should be separated from each other.
[14]www.theiia.org.

IT general controls (ITGC) relate to enterprise-level controls over IT:

- IT control environment—sets the tone at the top and forms culture regarding IT service and management.
- Access controls—restrict access to IT facilities, programs, and data. Access controls in IT systems are related to proper authorization and segregation of duties.
- Change management controls—the processes of making sure changes to programs and applications are authorized and documented. Changes should be tested prior to implementation so they do not affect system availability and reliability.
- Project development and acquisition controls—related to the systems development life cycle (SDLC). The controls involve analysis, design, testing, implementation, and evaluation of IT projects. Through management review and approval and user involvement, a firm establishes a formal methodology for developing, acquiring, implementing, and maintaining information systems and related technologies.
- Computer operations controls—involve anti-virus protection, backup and recovery procedures, minimizing system downtime, and patch management.

IT application controls are activities specific to a subsystem's or an application's input, processing, and output. Application controls include configured automated input controls, reports or data generated from the system and used in manual controls or accounting procedures, and automated calculations or data processing routines programmed into the application. The application controls are grouped into three categories to ensure information processing integrity: input, processing, and output controls. Most mistakes in an accounting information system occur while entering data. Control efforts are focused on input rather than processing and output activities.

Input controls ensure the authorization, entry, and verification of data entering the system. Authorization of data entry is accomplished by using an access control matrix. This matrix specifies which portion of the system users are allowed to access and what privilege(s) users have (e.g., view, create, update and delete). Common data entry controls include the following:

- Field checks ensure the characters in a field are of the proper type.
- Size checks ensure the data fit into the size of a field.
- Range checks test a numerical amount to ensure that it is within a predetermined range.
- Validity checks compare data entering the system with existing data in a reference file to ensure only valid data are entered.
- Completeness checks ensure all required data are entered for each record.
- Reasonableness checks ensure the logical relationship between two data values is correct. For example, an hourly rate of $120 may pass the range check on pay rates (between $8.5 and $150). However, it is not a valid input because the data value of the record for position is "intern"—that is, the pay rate of $120 per hour is not reasonable for an intern.
- Check digit verifications prevent the transpositions of numbers such as entering 5168 for a valid number of 5186. A check digit generated by an algorithm is appended to the original number to create a combination. A number and check digit combination that does not satisfy the algorithm reveals an error.
- Closed-loop verifications retrieve and display related information to ensure accurate data entry. For example, when a receiving clerk enters a part number, the inventory system displays the description of the item so that the receiving clerk can verify that the correct part number had been entered.

Processing controls ensure that data and transactions are processed accurately. Important processing controls include the following:

- Prenumbered documents are generated internally to ensure that there is no duplicate or missing record. Prenumbered source documents are used in batch processing[15] to make sure authorized transactions are processed once and once only.
- Sequence checks ensure a batch of data is in sequence for batch processing.
- Batch totals ensure that a batch goes through the processing stages containing the same set of records, no missing or duplicate record. Three commonly used batch totals are:
    1) A record count indicates that the same total records are in the batch.
    2) A control total is the sum of a dollar amount field or a quantity field in the records. Sometimes, the sum of a field containing dollar values is called "financial total."
    3) A hash total is the sum of a numeric field, such as employee number, which normally would not be the subject of arithmetic operations.
- Cross-footing balance tests compare totals provided in multiple methods to ensure accurate processing.
- Concurrent update controls prevent two or more users updating the same record simultaneously.

Output controls provide output to authorized people and ensure the output is used properly. For example, only the required number of copies should be printed. Any additional copies should be disposed of following authorized procedures. Printed output should be delivered promptly to the designated party. Electronic, sensitive material should be encrypted for transmission and data storage.

Progress *Check*

7. Explain the purposes of physical controls.
8. What are application controls?
9. Give a few examples of input controls.

LO 10-3

Describe the overall COBIT framework and its implications for IT governance.

COBIT Framework

Information technology governance is a subset of corporate governance and includes issues regarding IT management and security. IT governance is the responsibility of management and consists of the leadership, organizational structures, and processes that ensure that the firm's IT sustains and extends its business objectives.[16] To achieve effective IT governance, controls should be implemented within a defined control framework for all IT processes to provide a clear link among IT governance requirements, IT processes, and IT controls. COSO is one of the generally accepted internal control frameworks for enterprises. COBIT (control objectives for information and related technology) is a generally accepted framework for IT governance and management.

The most current version of the COBIT framework is COBIT 5. COBIT 5 expands on COBIT 4.1 by integrating other major frameworks and standards, such as ISACA's Val

---

[15]Batch processing, different from real-time processing, has a delay between the time a transaction occurs and the time it is processed. A batch consists of many records that have been accumulated for processing at the same time.

[16]*COBIT 4.1 Executive Summary,* 2007, p. 5.

IT and Risk IT, the Information Technology Infrastructure Library (ITIL), and related standards from the International Organization for Standardization (ISO). COBIT 5 assists firms in creating value from IT by maintaining a balance between realizing benefits and optimizing resource use. COBIT 5 enables IT to be governed and managed in a holistic manner for the firm by taking in the end-to-end IT functional areas of responsibility and considering the IT-related interests of internal and external stakeholders. COBIT 5 defines "governance" as ensuring that firm objectives are achieved by evaluating stakeholder needs; setting direction through decision making; and monitoring performance, compliance, and progress. In most firms, the board of directors is responsible for governance. Per COBIT 5, "management" includes planning (i.e., aligning, planning, and organizing), building (i.e., building, acquiring, and implementing), running (i.e., delivering, servicing, and supporting), and monitoring (i.e., monitoring, evaluating, and assessing) activities in alignment with the direction necessary to achieve the firm's objectives.[17] In most firms, management is the responsibility of the executives under the leadership of the CEO. Figure 10.4 presents the principle of COBIT 5 in separating governance from management.

COBIT provides a supporting tool set that bridges the gap among IT control requirements, technical issues, and business risks. The COBIT framework:[18]

- Provides a business focus to align business and IT objectives.
- Defines the scope and ownership of IT process and control.
- Is consistent with accepted IT good practices and standards.
- Provides a common language with a set of terms and definitions that are generally understandable by all stakeholders.
- Meets regulatory requirements by being consistent with generally accepted corporate governance standards (e.g., COSO) and IT controls expected by regulators and auditors.

FIGURE 10.4
COBIT 5 Governance and Management Key Areas

Source: *COBIT 5,* Figure 30, p. 73.

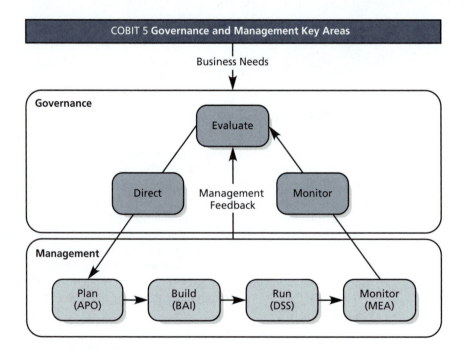

---

[17]*COBIT 5.0,* 2012, p. 31.
[18]*COBIT 4.1 Executive Summary,* 2007, p. 8.

COBIT control objectives provide high-level requirements to be considered for effective control of IT processes. The overall control objectives are to increase business value or reduce risk; to establish and maintain policies, procedures, and organizational structures related to IT; and to provide reasonable assurance that business objectives will be achieved. According to COBIT, the key criteria of business requirements for information are as follows.

- Effectiveness—relevant and timely information.
- Efficiency—information produced economically.
- Confidentiality—protection of sensitive information.
- Integrity—valid, accurate, and complete information.
- Availability—information available when needed.
- Compliance—information produced in compliance with laws and regulations.
- Reliability—reliable information for daily decision making.

COBIT 5 supports IT governance and management by providing a framework to ensure that IT is aligned with the business; IT enables the business and maximizes benefits; IT resources are used responsibly; IT risks are managed appropriately. In summary, COBIT 5 has five key principles for governance and management of enterprise IT: meeting stakeholder needs, covering the enterprise end-to-end, applying an integrated framework, enabling a holistic approach, and separating governance from management.

Progress *Check*

10. What are the IT resources and business requirements of information identified in the COBIT framework?

LO 10-4

Describe other governance frameworks related to information systems management and security.

Information Technology Infrastructure Library

The IT Infrastructure Library (ITIL) was developed by the UK government in the mid 1980s and has become a de facto standard in Europe for best practices in IT infrastructure management and service delivery. The ITIL has evolved as a result of firms' increasing dependence on IT. In recent years, there has been growing global recognition and adoption of ITIL.[19]

ITIL's value proposition centers on providing IT service with an understanding of the business objectives and priorities and the role that IT services has in achieving the objectives. Figure 10.5 illustrates the structure of ITIL. ITIL adopts a life-cycle approach to IT services and organizes IT service management into five high-level categories:[20]

1. Service strategy (SS)—the strategic planning of IT service management capabilities and the alignment of IT service and business strategies.
2. Service design (SD)—the design and development of IT services and service management processes.
3. Service transition (ST)—realizing the requirements of strategy and design and maintaining capabilities for the ongoing delivery of a service.

---

[19]C. Davis and M. Schiller, *IT Auditing Using Controls to Protect Information Assets,* 2nd ed. (New York: McGraw-Hill, 2011), p. 407.
[20]UK Office of Government Commerce, *Executive Briefing: The Benefits of ITIL* (2010).

FIGURE 10.5
Overview of ITIL
Version 3

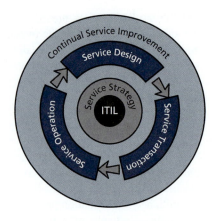

4. Service operation (SO)—the effective and efficient delivery and support of services, with a benchmarked approach for event, incident, request fulfillment, problem, and access management.
5. Continual service improvement (CSI)—ongoing improvement of the service and the measurement of process performance required for the service.

The ITIL life cycle starts with service strategy. In this phase, IT personnel should identify the customers or users of the IT services.[21] Then, IT personnel and business personnel (i.e., business strategists) should collaborate to develop IT service strategies that are aligned with and support the business strategy. The service design phase ensures that new and changed IT services are designed effectively to meet customer/user expectations in a cost-effective manner. Through the service transition phase of the life cycle, the IT service design is built, tested, and moved into production in order to ensure that the customer/user can achieve the desired value. This phase involves managing changes, controlling the assets and configuration items (e.g., hardware, software, etc.), service validation, testing, and transition planning to ensure that users, support personnel, and the production environment have been prepared for the changed IT assets to function properly. Once transitioned, the service operation phase delivers and supports the service on an ongoing basis. This process includes managing disruptions to service through rapid restoration of incidents, determining the root cause of problems and detecting trends associated with recurring issues, handling daily routine end user requests, and managing service access. The last phase of the IT service life cycle is continual service improvement. During this phase, a firm should offer a mechanism for IT to measure and improve the service levels, the technology, and the efficiency and effectiveness of IT processes.

ISO 27000 Series

The ISO 27000 series of standards are designed to address information security issues. Despite the evolving names and scope, the ISO 27000 series, particularly ISO 27001 and ISO 27002, have become the most recognized and generally accepted sets of information security framework and guidelines. ISO 27001/27002, ISO 17799, and BS 7799 are, essentially, the same core set of standards dealing with various aspects of information security practices and information security management. The ISO 27001 and 27002 standards were published in October 2005, replacing and enhancing BS 7799-1, BS 7799-2, and ISO 17799 standards with harmonization of other generally accepted international standards. Figure 10.6 presents a summary of the major operational standards in the ISO 27000 series.

[21]V. Arraj, *ITIL White Paper: The Basics,* May 2010. Retrieved from http://www.best-management-practice.com/gempdf/itil_the_basics.pdf, accessed February 2013.

FIGURE 10.6
Summary of the major standards in the ISO 27000 Series

ISO 27001	ISO 27002
This standard replaces BS 7799-2, providing specification for information security management systems (ISMSs).	This standard was called ISO 17799, which was formerly known as BS 7799-1.
ISO 27003	**ISO 27004**
A new standard offers guidance for implementing ISMSs.	This standard covers ISMS measurement and metrics; includes suggested ISO 27002–aligned controls.
ISO 27005	**ISO 27006**
This standard provides the methodology for information security risk management.	This standard provides guidelines for accreditation of ISMS certification.

The main objective of the ISO 27000 series is to provide a model for establishing, implementing, operating, monitoring, maintaining, and improving an information security management system (ISMS). The ISMS standard emphasizes using a "process approach," which is defined as "the application of a system of processes within an organization, together with the identification and interactions of these processes, and their management to produce the desired outcome."[22] It also employs the plan-do-check-act model (PDCA), which is used to structure the process approach. In the "plan" stage, an ISMS is established. Then, the IT personnel maintain and improve the ISMS in the "act" stage. The established ISMS is reviewed and monitored in the "check" stage, followed by the "do" stage to implement and operate the ISMS.

ISO 27001 and 27002 address 11 major areas with regard to information security and outlines 133 security controls within those 11 areas:

1. Security policy.
2. Organization of information security.
3. Asset management.
4. Human resources security.
5. Physical and environmental security.
6. Communications and operations management.
7. Access control.
8. Information systems acquisition, development, and maintenance.
9. Information security incident management.
10. Business continuity management.
11. Compliance.

Figure 10.7 presents the basic steps required to set up an information security management system in accordance with ISO 27001/27002.

COMPARING CONTROL/GOVERNANCE FRAMEWORKS

As we know, COSO 2.0 provides a general internal control framework that can be applied to all firms on various systems. COBIT 5 is a comprehensive framework for IT governance and management and provides management and auditors with control objectives, risk and value drivers, best practices regarding information security, and a performance measurement matrix to maximize the benefits from IT. ITIL is a framework focusing on IT infrastructure and IT service management. The ISO 27000 series is a framework for information security management. One of the biggest advantages in adopting COBIT 5 is that

---

[22]The ISO 27000 Directory, www.27000.org/index.htm.

FIGURE 10.7
Steps to Establishing an ISMS Following ISO 27001/27002

Source: http://iso-27000-series
.blogspot.com/2008_06_01_
archive.html

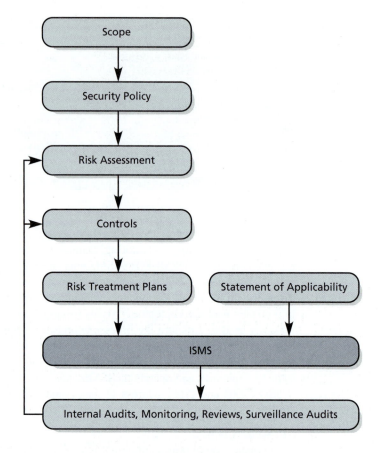

it is a general control/security framework for information technology. Because COBIT 5 includes other widely accepted standards, frameworks, and guidance for building effective IT governance and practices, a firm can implement a wide range of desirable IT processes and controls, as well as achieve its business objectives regarding IT security and service management, by using it.

Summary

- Given the mandate of the Sarbanes-Oxley Act of 2002, management is responsible for designing internal controls and evaluating the effectiveness of the controls based on a control framework. COSO is the most commonly accepted internal control framework. COBIT is a generally accepted framework for IT governance and management. Most American firms use COBIT for IT governance and to evaluate IT controls for SOX Section 404 compliance.
- There are three general categories of internal controls. Preventive controls deter problems before they arise. Detective controls find out problems when they arise. Corrective controls fix problems that have been identified. In a computerized environment, internal controls can be categorized as general controls and application controls.
- General controls are those applicable to enterprisewide issues. Application controls are specific to a subsystem or an application including input, processing, and output controls.
- COSO publishes two control frameworks: COSO internal control integrated framework and COSO enterprise risk management (ERM) integrated framework. The COSO

internal control framework is a widely accepted authority on internal control, providing a foundation for evaluating, reporting, and improving internal control. The COSO ERM framework expanded the COSO internal control framework to provide guidance in defining, assessing, managing, and transferring risk in order to maximize firm value. The COSO ERM focuses on the strategic alignment of the firm's mission with its risk appetite.

- The COBIT framework is a control framework for IT governance and management to ensure the integrity of information and information systems. Two additional governance frameworks related to information technology are the ITIL and the ISO 27000 series. ITIL provides best practices in IT infrastructure management and IT service delivery. The main objective of the ISO 27000 series is to provide a model for establishing, implementing, operating, monitoring, maintaining, and improving an information security system.

Key Words

application controls (*198*) Specific to a subsystem or an application to ensure the validity, completeness, and accuracy of the transactions.

code of ethics (*196*) What is considered to be ethical within an organization to promote ethical behavior.

Committee of Sponsoring Organizations (COSO) (*198*) Composed of several organizations (AAA, AICPA, FEI, IIA, and IMA); studies the causal factors that lead to fraudulent financial reporting and develops recommendations for public companies, independent auditors, the SEC and other regulators, and educational institutions to improve the quality of financial reporting through internal controls and corporate governance.

control objectives for information and related technology (COBIT) (*199*) An internationally accepted set of best IT security and control practices for IT management released by the IT Governance Institute (ITGI).

control risk (*203*) The threat that errors or irregularities in the underlying transactions will not be prevented, detected, and corrected by the internal control system.

corporate governance (*197*) A set of processes and policies in managing an organization with sound ethics to safeguard the interests of its stakeholders.

corrective controls (*198*) Fix problems that have been identified, such as using backup files to recover corrupted data.

cost/benefit analysis (*205*) Important in determining whether to implement an internal control.

detective controls (*198*) Find problems when they arise.

enterprise risk management (ERM) (*201*) A process, affected by the entity's board of directors, management, and other personnel, applied in strategy setting and across the enterprise, designed to identify potential events that may affect the entity, and manage risk to be within the risk appetite, to provide reasonable assurance regarding the achievement of objectives.

general controls (*198*) Pertain to enterprisewide issues such as controls over accessing the network, developing and maintaining applications, and documenting changes of programs.

Information Technology Infrastructure Library (ITIL) (*199*) A set of concepts and practices for IT service management.

inherent risk (*203*) The risk related to the nature of the business activity itself.

input controls (*206*) Ensure the authorization, entry, and verification of data entering the system.

International Organization for Standardization (ISO) 27000 series (*199*) This series contains a range of individual standards and documents specifically reserved by ISO for information security.

IT application controls (*206*) Activities specific to a subsystem's or an application's input, processing, and output.

IT controls (*205*) Involve processes that provide assurance for information and help to mitigate risks associated with the use of technology.

IT general controls (ITGC) (*206*) Enterprise-level controls over IT.

output controls (*207*) Provide output to authorized people and ensure the output is used properly.

physical controls (*205*) Mainly manual but could involve the physical use of computing technology.

preventive controls (*198*) Deter problems before they arise.

processing controls (*207*) Ensure that data and transactions are processed accurately.

Public Company Accounting Oversight Board (PCAOB) (*196*) Established by SOX to provide independent oversight of public accounting firms.

residual risk (*203*) The product of inherent risk and control risk (i.e., Residual risk = Inherent risk × Control risk).

risk assessment (*203*) The process of identifying and analyzing risks systematically to determine the firm's risk response and control activities.

Sarbanes-Oxley Act of 2002 (SOX) (*196*) A response to business scandals such as Enron, WorldCom, and Tyco International; requires public companies registered with the SEC and their auditors to annually assess and report on the design and effectiveness of internal control over financial reporting.

Appendix

ERP Architecture and Control Issues

Enterprise resource planning (ERP) systems have been steadily growing in popularity since the 1980s. Many firms have come to see integrated systems as an essential competitive edge; the ability to combine all of an enterprise's operations into a single system allows for greater visibility and control over its business concerns.

ERP architecture is generally planned in a way that will meet the needs of the organization from an operational standpoint. The company will need to determine what business processes it needs to put into an ERP system and then determine the proper modules to purchase to begin that process. Most ERP systems will utilize a financial accounting module to record accounting transactions and contain the enterprise's general ledger. Some companies will also need specialized modules (like manufacturing) to track all of the materials and processes needed to produce finished goods.

Modules within an ERP system generally tie together to promote easy integration. For instance, an intercompany sale should easily allow for purchasing and selling legal entities to transact a sale within the system. In a trade sale, costs associated with creating a product in the manufacturing module should easily flow into the cost of sales in the finance module. This easy integration and transferability of data is one of the major advantages granted by an ERP system. However, in some cases, companies still prefer to combine multiple systems to accomplish their business goals. One popular example of this is using a separate customer relationship management system to take customer orders and manage customer-facing interactions. In this case, data must flow from the CRM tool into the ERP system to create an order and then process that order to invoicing and cash collections. This added layer of systems produces more risk because it creates another location—the middleware that manages the flow of data between the systems, where controls must be put in place to protect the confidentiality and integrity of data.

The physical architecture of an ERP system must also be assessed to create a control structure to manage risks. Risk areas include:

1. Where will the servers be hosted?
2. Will there be a client/server or a web-based architecture?
3. How will data flow between the servers and the users, and are those lines of communication controlled by the company and secure?
4. Does the company need to utilize encryption or other controls to protect confidential data?
5. How will the company recover from a critical hardware failure or disaster?
6. How will the company maintain services during a primary systems outage?

Businesses must ensure that their systems comply with relevant laws and regulations and contain safeguards to ensure the reliability of their financial reporting. One of the most important controls over an ERP is the assurance of proper change management. Proper change management mandates the creation of at least three separate ERP system instances, referred to as "environments." The lowest environment with the least number of controls is the development environment. This is the only environment where code changes and configurations can be executed. From this environment, changes are migrated to the quality assurance environment for testing. Full testing should be executed in this environment before any changes can be moved to the final environment: production. Change management is designed to prevent disruptions to service or unauthorized code changes that could be used to commit fraud. All steps in the change management process should be monitored and well documented to ensure that all changes are authorized.

ERP systems should be planned with consideration of the control structure of the business that they are designed for. Control activities like segregation of duties and access controls should be utilized in the system security plan to limit the opportunities for fraud in a company's transactions. The company should use the control frameworks that it has adopted to govern its control structure to plan specific control activities. Controls should be considered for all steps of the system's management process:

1. Plan: Controls should first be considered in the planning stages of any ERP implementation. Business processes and risks should be assessed and controls should be designed to mitigate the risks that are discovered.
2. Build: Controls need to be implemented properly in the build phase of the ERP's life cycle. This includes both initial implementation and any changes that are made through the change management process.
3. Run: Once implemented, controls will help to reduce risks to the business while the ERP system is operational. During this time, support needs to be provided to ensure that the control structure continues to function. An example of this activity is that new users must be properly trained and set up within the confines of the control structure.
4. Monitor: Once a company has set up an ERP system and integrated the enterprise's control structure, it should continue to monitor the implementation to ensure that the controls are effective. This includes activities such as monitoring for users with segregation of duties conflicts and providing internal audits of risk areas within the enterprise.

An ERP system's architecture and control structure are linked out of necessity. As the architecture of the ERP changes due to the addition of modules, middleware, or additional environments, control risk must be assessed and addressed to ensure the integrity of the system.

1. Ethics plays a critical role when people make choices and decisions. To promote ethical behavior, firms often choose to establish a formal expectation on what is considered to be ethical within the group. Ethical behavior prompted by a code of ethics can be considered a form of internal control, so a code of ethics is part of corporate governance.

2. PCAOB was established by Congress to oversee the audits of public companies in order to protect investors and the public interest by promoting informative, accurate, and independent audit reports. In addition, auditors of U.S. public companies are subject to external and independent oversight by PCAOB. It also issues audit standards.

3. According to a COSO report, an internal control is "a process, affected by an entity's board of directors, management and other personnel. This process is designed to provide reasonable assurance regarding the achievement of objectives in effectiveness and efficiency of operations, reliability of financial reporting, and compliance with applicable laws and regulations."

4. Prevention, detection, and correction.

5. Reduce, share, avoid, and accept risks,

6. Expected benefit of an internal control = Impact (potential loss) × Decreased likelihood (due to control implementation).

7. a. Authorization to ensure transactions are valid.

   b. Segregation of duties to prevent fraud and mistakes.

   c. Supervision to compensate imperfect segregation of duties.

   d. Accounting documents and records to maintain audit trails.

   e. Access control to ensure authorized personnel have access to assets and information.

   f. Independent verification to double check for errors and misrepresentations.

8. Application controls are input, processing, and output controls specific to a subsystem or application.

9. Field check, range check, closed-loop verification, reasonableness check, and so on.

10. IT resources are applications, information, infrastructures, and people. The business requirements for information are effectiveness, efficiency, confidentiality, integrity, availability, compliance, and reliability.

Multiple Choice Questions

1. Based on SOX, which of the following sections is about internal controls?

   a. 302

   b. 401

   c. 404

   d. 906

2. SOX requires companies to use COSO or COSO ERM as the framework in evaluating internal controls.

   a. True

   b. False

3. Controls that are designed to prevent, detect, or correct errors in transactions as they are processed through a specific subsystem are referred to as:

   a. General controls

   b. Application controls

   c. Physical controls

   d. Two of the above are correct.

   e. None of the above is correct.

4. Which of the following is *not* a COSO ERM control objective?
    a. Risk assessment
    b. Compliance
    c. Reporting
    d. Operations
    e. Strategic

5. Prenumbering of source documents helps to verify that
    a. Multiple types of source documents have a unique identifier
    b. All transactions have been recorded because the numerical sequence serves as a control
    c. No inventory has been misplaced
    d. Documents have been used in order

6. A field check is:
    a. Preventive control
    b. Detective control
    c. Corrective control
    d. General control
    e. Output control

7. Which is not an example of a batch total?
    a. Record count
    b. Financial total
    c. Hash total
    d. Exception total

8. Backup is a preventive control.
    a. True
    b. False

9. The computer sums the first four digits of a customer number to calculate the value of the fifth digit and then compares that calculation to the number typed during data entry. This is an example of a
    a. Field check
    b. Parity check
    c. Check digit verification
    d. Batch total

10. Which of the following statements is correct?
    a. SOX requires all public companies to use the COSO ERM framework to meet the requirements of Section 404.
    b. Regarding IT control and governance, the COBIT framework is most commonly adopted by companies in the United States.
    c. ITIL is the best internal control framework for the high-tech industry.
    d. ISO 27000 series are best practices for IT service management.

Discussion Questions

1. How has the Sarbanes-Oxley Act affected the audit profession and corporate governance of public firms?

2. What are the objectives and components of the COSO ERM framework?

3. COSO developed two frameworks: the COSO internal control framework 2.0 and the COSO ERM framework. Why did COSO develop the ERM framework? What are the differences between the two frameworks?

4. Use a few sentences to describe IT general controls and application controls. Give a few examples of these two types of controls.

5. Why is the COBIT framework ideal to guide IT governance and management?

6. The ISO 27000 series serves different purposes than ITIL. Which one could be more important to accounting professionals?

7. Segregation of duties is an important internal control. What functions must be separated? If ideal segregation of duties is not economically feasible, what could be done to help compensate this problem?

8. Use a diagram to explain the risk assessment process.

9. Compare the following three types of controls: preventive, detective, and corrective. Give two examples of each type of control. Which one do auditors usually focus on more in an audit?

10. Describe the control activities in the COSO framework. Why are these control activities important for most firms?

Problems

1. The global economic crisis of 2008–2010 has stimulated many boards of directors and executives to reevaluate how they assess and manage risks. Use a diagram to describe the process of risk assessment.

2. A newly hired internal auditor discovered that immaterial thefts by employees are pervasive in the company; employees take books from the company's library, tools from the company's laboratories, supplies, products, and so forth. By interviewing some of the employees, the internal auditor discovered that most employees thought their behavior was not detrimental to the company because none of the items had significant value. What should the company do to prevent this type of employee behavior?

3. The sales department of a company received several claims from its customers that their payments were not credited to their accounts. Investigation uncovered that the accounts receivable clerk has been stealing some customer payments. What are some of the internal control procedures that could prevent and detect the problem?

4. The information system of Carlsbad Bottle Inc. is deemed to be 90 percent reliable. A major threat in the procurement process has been discovered, with an exposure of $300,000. Two control procedures are identified to mitigate the threat. Implementation of control A would cost $18,000 and reduce the risk to 4 percent. Implementation of control B would cost $10,000 and reduce the risk to 6 percent. Implementation of both controls would cost $26,000 and reduce the risk to 2.5 percent. Given the information presented, and considering an economic analysis of costs and benefits only, which control procedure(s) should Carlsbad Bottle choose to implement?

5. Which internal control(s) would you recommend to prevent the following situations from occurring?

   a. Authorization of a credit memo for a customer's account (on receivables) when the goods were never actually returned.

   b. Theft of funds by the cashier, who cashed several checks and did not record their receipt.

   c. Inventory was stolen by receiving dock personnel. The receiving clerk claimed the inventory was sent to the warehouse but the warehouse clerk did not record properly.

   d. Writing off a customer's accounts receivable balances as uncollectible in order to conceal the theft of subsequent cash collections.

   e. Billing customers for the quantity ordered when the quantity shipped was actually less due to back-ordering of some items.

6. Which controls would best mitigate the following threats?

   a. Posting the amount of a sale to a customer account that does not exist.

   b. A customer entering too many characters into the five-digit zip code while making an online purchase, causing the server to crash.

c. An intern's pay rate was entered as $150 per hour, not $15 per hour.

d. Approving a customer order without the customer's address so the order was not shipped on time.

e. Entering the contract number of a critical contract as 13688 instead of 16388, which is a serious mistake for the company.

Answers To Multiple Choice Questions

1. c	6. a
2. b	7. d
3. b	8. b
4. a	9. c
5. b	10. b

Information Security and Computer Fraud

A look at this chapter

Given today's business environment, computers are at the center of most firms' accounting information systems. Awareness of computer fraud is critical to accountants and auditors. In this chapter, we provide examples of computer fraud and illustrate how AIS can be misused in order to achieve personal gains. We also discuss common vulnerabilities and how to manage and assess such vulnerabilities. These topics are related to information security, which has been a critical technology issue for business professionals in the accounting field.

A look back

In Chapter 10, we discussed internal controls and important factors in corporate governance that are critical to an organization's efficiency and effectiveness in operations, reliability in financial reporting, and compliance with applicable laws and regulations. We also provided detailed information on important control frameworks such as COSO and COBIT.

A look ahead

Given the complicated information systems and the tremendous amount of data to be analyzed and reported, accountants must evaluate the design and monitor the integrity of an accounting information system. In Chapter 12, we examine the risks in accounting information systems and how auditors validate that systems are well designed with embedded internal controls and that the systems process data with integrity.

Today, before going to work, you drop by **Starbucks** to grab a cup of coffee. Even early in the morning, **Starbucks** already has a long line of customers waiting, looking at the menu, and deciding what they want to order. Perhaps they visit **Starbucks** regularly and have a specific drink they want to order. For example, you already have your drink in mind: ice caramel macchiato, nonfat milk, one extra shot of expresso, light ice, light caramel to start off the day.

During these 10 minutes while you are waiting, **Starbucks** cafés all over the world—perhaps with even more customers during this time frame—are also serving their customers, each with drinks possibly as unique as the one that you will order. Throughout the course of an entire day, all the individual

Starbucks stores have made countless transactions, which all must be recorded accurately to provide reliable information for decision making to keep **Starbucks** competitive. The integrity of the systems and the quality of information are critical to companies such as **Starbucks** in supporting daily operations, as well as providing consolidated data for year-end financial reporting.

Chapter Outline

Introduction

Systems Integrity and Information Security

Information Security Risks and Attacks

Encryption and Authentication

Computer Fraud and Abuse

Computer Fraud Risk Assessment

Computer Fraud Schemes

Computer Fraud Prevention and Detection

Vulnerability Assessments and Management

Types of Vulnerabilities

An Overall Framework for Vulnerability Assessment and Management

System Availability

Disaster Recovery Planning and Business Continuity Management

Learning Objectives

After reading this chapter, you should be able to:

11-1 Describe the risks related to information security and systems integrity.

11-2 Understand the concepts of encryption and authentication.

11-3 Describe computer fraud and misuse of AIS and corresponding risk-mitigation techniques.

11-4 Define vulnerabilities, and explain how to manage and assess vulnerabilities.

11-5 Explain issues in system availability, disaster recovery, and business continuity.

INTRODUCTION

Rapid development in digital technologies has been a driving factor of consumer demand, employee training, and efficient use of firms' resources. As a result of the maturing digital economy, firms across different industries will continue to be reshaped through the application of information technology. In this chapter, we present a discussion of one of the most critical impacts of technology on firms' operations—information security. We first introduce concepts and risks regarding information security and then provide examples of computer fraud and how AIS can be misused in achieving personal gains. We then explain common vulnerabilities and how to manage and assess those vulnerabilities. Frameworks for vulnerability assessment and management, as well as for business continuity management, are also presented in this chapter.

LO 11-1

Describe the risks related to information security and systems integrity.

SYSTEMS INTEGRITY AND INFORMATION SECURITY

The AICPA conducts a survey each year to identify the top 10 technology issues for certified public accountants (CPAs). The purpose of the survey is to indicate the CPA's unique perspectives on how much each technology will affect financial management and the fulfillment of responsibilities such as safeguarding assets, overseeing business performance, and compliance with laws and regulations. Since 2003, information security management has been ranked as the top technology issue for CPAs. According to AICPA, information security management is "an integrated, systematic approach that coordinates people, policies, standards, processes, and controls used to safeguard critical systems and information from internal and external security threats."[1]

Information security is a critical factor in maintaining systems integrity. If users can perform the intended functions of a system without being degraded or impaired by unauthorized manipulation, the system has maintained its integrity. Good information security ensures that systems and their contents remain the same for integrity. In general, the goal of information security management is to protect the confidentiality, integrity, and availability (CIA) of a firm's information.

- Confidentiality—information is not accessible to unauthorized individuals or processes.
- Integrity—information is accurate and complete.
- Availability—information and systems are accessible on demand.

Information Security Risks and Attacks

Given the popularity of the Internet and mobile devices and the complexity of computer technologies, important business information and IT assets are exposed to risks and attacks from internal (such as disgruntled employees) and external parties (such as hackers, foreigners, competitors, etc.). Some of the more common information security risks and attacks include:[2]

- Virus—a self-replicating program that runs and spreads by modifying other programs or files.
- Worm—a self-replicating, self-propagating, self-contained program that uses networking mechanisms to spread itself.

---

[1] http://infotech.aicpa.org/Resources/Top+Technology+Initiatives/2009+Top+Technology+Initiatives+and +Honorable+Mentions.htm.

[2] Definitions of information security risks and attacks are quoted from National Institute of Standards and Technology (NIST), *Glossary of Key Information Security Terms* (Washington, DC: U.S. Department of Commerce, 2006).

Do you know that mobile devices such as Android phones, tablets, and iPhones/iPads are often the targets for hackers to attack? In addition, mobile apps have emerged as a new attack vector for various security issues.

- Trojan horse—a non-self-replicating program that seems to have a useful purpose in appearance, but in reality has a different, malicious purpose.
- Spam—sending unsolicited bulk information.
- Botnet (bot)—a collection of software robots that overruns computers to act automatically in response to the bot-herder's control inputs through the Internet.
- Denial-of-service (DoS)—the prevention of authorized access to resources (such as servers) or the delaying of time-critical operations.
- Spyware—software that is secretly installed into an information system to gather information on individuals or organizations without their knowledge; a type of malicious code.
- Spoofing—sending a network packet that appears to come from a source other than its actual source.
- Social engineering—manipulating someone to take certain action that may not be in that person's best interest, such as revealing confidential information or granting access to physical assets, networks, or information.

Progress *Check*

1. What are the general goals of information security?
2. Give an example of social engineering.

LO 11-2
Understand the concepts of encryption and authentication.

Encryption and Authentication

Encryption is a preventive control providing confidentiality and privacy for data transmission and storage. It refers to algorithmic schemes that encode *plaintext* into nonreadable form or *cyphertext*. The receiver of the encrypted text uses a "key" to decrypt the message, returning it to its original plaintext form. The key is the trigger mechanism to the cryptographic algorithm. The main factors in encryption are key length, encryption algorithm, and key management. Longer key length provides for stronger encryption. In general, a key length of 56 bits or less is insufficient for sensitive data; 128-bit and longer key lengths are more than sufficient for secure data transmission. In addition, using a strong encryption algorithm and establishing a policy on key management are essential for information security.

In general, cryptographic algorithms are grouped into two categories: symmetric-key and asymmetric-key encryption methods. **Symmetric-key encryption** is fast and suitable for encrypting large data sets or messages. However, key distribution and key management are problematic because both the sender and the receiver use the same key to encrypt and decrypt messages. If a firm has many employees and trading partners at different geographical locations, it is very difficult to always distribute keys in a secured way. In addition, managing one key for each pair of users, which results in exponential growth of the number of keys for each additional party, is not cost-effective given the large number of users among the firms. Conversely, **asymmetric-key encryption** is extremely slow and is not appropriate for encrypting large data sets. However, because each user has a pair of two keys—the **public key** and the **private key**—asymmetric-key encryption solves the problems in key distribution and key management. The public keys are widely distributed and available to other users. The private key is kept secret and known only to the owner of the key. Hence, to transmit confidential information, the sender uses the receiver's public key to encrypt the message; the receiver uses his or her own private key for decryption upon receiving the message. Two common names for asymmetric-key encryption are *public-key encryption* or *two-key encryption*.

Authentication is a process that establishes the origin of information or determines the identity of a user, process, or device. It is critical in e-business because it can prevent repudiation while conducting transactions online. Using asymmetric-key encryption, authentication can be achieved for electronic transactions. For example, to authenticate the receiver (B), the sender (A) e-mails a challenge message to B. B will use his or her private key to encrypt the challenge message and send it to A. If A is able to use B's public key to decrypt and get the plaintext of the challenge message, A has authenticated B successfully. Please notice that only the pair of one user's two keys is used for encryption and decryption. In this example, B used his or her private key to encrypt the message, and A used B's public key to decrypt the message. Keys from different users cannot be mismatched for encryption and decryption purposes. Please note that this process would need to be repeated in reverse to authenticate both parties involved in the transaction.

To conduct e-business, most firms use a hybrid combination of both methods:

1. Both the sender and receiver use the asymmetric-key encryption method to authenticate each other.
2. Either the sender (or the receiver) generates a symmetric key (called a **session key** because it is valid for a certain timeframe only) to be used by both parties.
3. Asymmetric-key encryption is used to distribute the session key. (For example, the sender uses the receiver's public key to encrypt the session key and sends it to the receiver. The receiver uses his or her own private key to decrypt to get the session key.)
4. After both parties have the session key, the session key is used to transmit confidential data/information. This is done because using symmetric key encryption allows faster data transmission.

A **digital signature** is a **message digest (MD)** of a document (or data file) that is encrypted using the document creator's private key. An MD is a short code (e.g., 256 bits long) resulting from hashing[3] a plaintext using an algorithm. Popular hashing algorithms such as SHA-256 use every bit in the plaintext file to calculate the MD. Changing any character in the original document being hashed produces a different MD. Therefore, digital signatures can ensure **data integrity.** In addition, to create a digital signature, the document creator must use his or her own private key to encrypt the MD, so the digital signature also authenticates the document creator. Given the significant attributes of a digital signature (maintaining data integrity and authenticating the document/data creator), it serves a critical role in e-business: No one can enter into an electronic transaction and then subsequently repudiate that he or she had done so. The process should be performed as follows:

1. Both the sender (A) and receiver (B) use asymmetric-key encryption method to authenticate each other.
2. A makes a copy of the document and uses SHA-256 to hash the copy and get an MD.
3. A encrypts the MD using A's private key to get A's digital signature.
4. A uses B's public key to encrypt the original document and A's digital signature (for confidentiality).
5. A sends the encrypted package to B.
6. B receives the package and decrypts it using B's private key. B now has the document and A's digital signature.
7. B decrypts A's digital signature using A's public key to get the sent-over MD. B also authenticates that A is the document creator (to assure nonrepudiation).

---

[3]Different from encryption, hashing is not reversible. A specific hashing algorithm creates same-length MDs, regardless the length of the original documents or data.

8. B makes a copy of the received document and uses SHA-256 to hash the copy and get a calculated MD.
9. If the sent-over MD is the same as the calculated MD, B ensures data integrity (no changes made to the document).

To ensure the asymmetric-key encryption method is functioning well, several key factors must be considered:[4]

1. A **Certificate Authority (CA)** is a trusted entity that issues and revokes digital certificates.
2. A **digital certificate** is a digital document issued and digitally signed by the private key of a Certificate Authority that binds the name of a subscriber to a public key. The certificate indicates that the subscriber identified in the certificate has sole control and access to the private key.
3. A **public-key infrastructure (PKI)** refers to a set of policies, processes, server platforms, software, and workstations used for the purpose of administering certificates and public-/private-key pairs, including the ability to issue, maintain, and revoke public-key certificates.

PKI is an arrangement that issues digital certificates to users and servers, manages the key issuance, and verifies and revokes certificates by means of a CA. Because authentication and nonrepudiation are accomplished by using public keys in decryption, CA plays the most significant role in assuring the effectiveness of asymmetric-key encryption.

Progress *Check*

3. Can we use symmetric-key encryption method to authenticate users? Why?
4. What is a digital signature? Why do we need it?

LO 11-3
Describe computer fraud and misuse of AIS and corresponding risk mitigation techniques.

COMPUTER FRAUD AND ABUSE

The International Professional Practices Framework[5] (IPPF) of the Institute of Internal Auditors (IIA) defines fraud as: "Any illegal act characterized by deceit, concealment, or violation of trust. These acts are not dependent upon the threat of violence or physical force. Frauds are perpetrated by parties and organizations to obtain money, property, or services; to avoid payment or loss of services; or to secure personal or business advantage."[6] In addition, the Statement of Auditing Standards (SAS) No. 99: "Consideration of Fraud in a Financial Statement Audit," states that an entity's management has primary responsibility for establishing and monitoring all aspects of the entity's fraud risk-assessment and prevention activities and has both the responsibility and the means to implement measures to reduce the incidence of fraud.

Some of the most valuable items desired by individuals committing computer fraud are the digital assets maintained by the firm. Most firms gather, create, utilize, store, and discard data that have value to others outside the firm. Such data can be in the form of employee or customer personal information such as government-issued identification numbers, bank account numbers, credit card numbers, and other personal information. Whether the perpetrator is an individual with authorized access to the data or a hacker, these data

---

[4]Definitions are quoted from NIST, *Glossary of Key Information Security Terms.*
[5]The IPPF is the conceptual framework that provides authoritative guidance promulgated by IIA.
[6]Global Technology Audit Guides (GTAG), *Fraud Prevention and Detection in an Automated World* (2009).

Fraud cases bring negative publicity to many companies.

can be sold to others or used for personal gain for crimes such as identity theft, unauthorized purchases on stolen credit cards, or stealing or diverting money from a bank account.[7]

Insiders, having legitimate access to their firms' data, systems, and networks, pose a significant risk to their firms. Employees experiencing financial problems may tend to use the systems they access at work to commit fraud such as stealing confidential data, proprietary information, or intellectual property from their employers. According to the **fraud triangle,** three conditions exist for a fraud to be perpetrated. First, there is an *incentive* or pressure that provides a reason to commit fraud. Second, there is an *opportunity* for fraud to be perpetrated (e.g., absence of controls, ineffective controls, or the ability of management to override controls.) Third, the individuals committing the fraud possess an attitude that enables them to *rationalize* the fraud. Because research indicates that more than half of the malicious incidents in IT security are caused by insider abuse and misuse, firms should implement a sound system of internal controls to prevent and detect computer frauds perpetrated by insiders. However, the reality seems to be that threats from inside have been overlooked by many firms.[8] We address this gap by introducing computer fraud risks, typical fraud schemes, and strategies/techniques to prevent and detect computer frauds.

Computer Fraud Risk Assessment

According to Global Technology Audit Guides (GTAG) provided by IIA, common computer frauds include the following:

1. The theft, misuse, or misappropriation of assets by altering computer-readable records and files.
2. The theft, misuse, or misappropriation of assets by altering the logic of computer software.
3. The theft or illegal use of computer-readable information.
4. The theft, corruption, illegal copying, or intentional destruction of computer software.
5. The theft, misuse, or misappropriation of computer hardware.

Concerning computer fraud risks, management should first review potential risk exposures. Given an identified possible fraud, exposures are management's estimates of the potential loss from the fraud. Computer fraud risk assessment is a systematic process that assists management and internal auditors in discovering where and how fraud may occur and identifying who may commit the specific fraud. A computer fraud risk assessment is often a component of a firm's enterprise risk management (ERM) program.

Similar to an enterprise risk assessment, a computer fraud risk assessment focuses on fraud schemes and scenarios to determine whether the controls exist and how the controls can be circumvented. According to GTAG, computer fraud risk assessments usually include the following key steps:[9]

1. Identifying relevant IT fraud risk factors.
2. Identifying potential IT fraud schemes and prioritizing them based on likelihood and impact.

---

[7]Global Technology Audit Guides (GTAG), *Fraud Prevention and Detection in an Automated World* (2009).
[8]K.C. Brancik, "Insider Computer Fraud—An In-depth Framework for Detecting and Defending Against Insider Attacks," *ISACA Journal Online,* 2 (2009).
[9]GTAG, *Fraud Prevention and Detection in an Automated World,* p. 2.

3. Mapping existing controls to potential fraud schemes and identifying gaps.
4. Testing operating effectiveness of fraud prevention and detection controls.
5. Assessing the likelihood and business impact of a control failure and/or a fraud incident.

Computer Fraud Schemes

It is important to identify potential fraud schemes related to computers and include them in the enterprisewide risk assessment plan. The following scenarios are provided to help you understand general computer fraud schemes regarding unauthorized access to systems/data and unauthorized changes to systems programs/data for personal gains. The following general scenarios should be considered and addressed if applicable to the firm:

1. An employee of a telecommunications firm's payroll department moved to a new position within the department and no longer has privileged access to payroll accounts. However, when changing positions, her access rights to the payroll accounts were left unchanged. An associate told her that he was starting a financial service business and needed some contact information. Using the privileged access rights that she had retained, the employee provided her associate with confidential information of 1,500 employees, including 401(k) account numbers, credit card account numbers, and Social Security numbers, which he then used to commit more than 100 cases of identity theft. The insider's actions caused more than $1 million worth of damages to the firm and its employees.[10]
2. A database analyst of a major check authorization and credit card processing company went beyond his authorized computer access rights. The employee obtained his firm's consumer information of 8.4 million individuals. The stolen information included names and addresses, bank account information, and credit and debit card information. He sold the data to telemarketers over a 5-year period. A U.S. district judge sentenced him to 57 months' imprisonment and $3.2 million in restitution for conspiracy and computer fraud.[11]
3. An IT consultant working under contract for an offshore oil platform company was denied an offer for a permanent job with the same company. He then accessed the firm's computer systems without approval and caused damage by impairing the integrity and availability of data. He was indicted on federal charges, which carry a maximum statutory penalty of 10 years in federal prison.[12]
4. Adding a fictitious vendor to a vendor master file in an accounts payable system is the first step toward committing a cash disbursement fraud. Unless a fraudster can ensure that the vendor exists in the system, it will not be possible to process bogus invoices for payment to the vendor. But once established, invoices can be entered for payment either directly by the perpetrator or by another individual in collusion.[13]
5. Fictitious services could be billed, or employee, customer, or company confidential data could be misappropriated for personal gain by an independent contractor or an offshore programmer.[14]
6. Employees or contractors may copy or download files illegally, causing copyright violations and loss of intellectual property.[15]

---

[10]U.S. Secret Service and CERT Coordination Center/SEI, 2 *Insider Threat Study: Illicit Cyber Activity in the Information Technology and Telecommunications Sector* (2008).

[11]U.S. Department of Justice, Computer Crime and Intellectual Property Section, http://usdoj.gov/criminal/cybercrime.

[12]Ibid.

[13]AICPA Fraud Schemes webpage, www.aicpa.org/InterestAreas/ForensicAndValuation/Resources/FraudPreventionDetectionResponse/Pages/Other%20Fraud%20Schemes.aspx.

[14]GTAG, *Fraud Prevention and Detection in an Automated World.*

[15]Ibid.

7. Third-party service providers that process employee, customer information, or other company confidential information may misappropriate the firm's data.[16]

In addition, the U.S. Secret Service and CERT Coordination Center have also identified computer fraud in the systems development life cycle (SDLC). Figure 11.1 is a summary of such frauds and the corresponding oversights.[17]

One of the main reasons computer fraud is possible is weak access control. The best control over unauthorized access to sensitive information is to require passwords for accessing individual files or subsystems. Logon user IDs should be automatically locked out if the wrong password is entered a predefined number of times. Once locked, a logon user ID should be activated only by appropriate personnel, such as a system administrator. A system itself should enforce password changes on a regular basis (i.e., every 30, 60, or 90 days) and should not permit previous password(s) to be used again for a certain period of time.

FIGURE 11.1
Fraud Schemes in Systems Development Life Cycle

Phase	Scenario	Oversights
Requirements Definition Phase	195 illegitimate drivers' licenses are created and sold by a police communications officer who accidentally discovers she can create them.	Lack of authentication and role-based access control requirements. Lack of segregation of duties
System Design Phase	A special function to expedite handling of cases allows two caseworkers to pocket $32,000 in kickbacks. An employee realizes there is no computerized control in his firm's system, so he entered and profited from $20 million in fake health insurance claims.	Insufficient attention to security details in automated workflow processes Lack of consideration for security vulnerabilities posed by authorized system access
System Implementation Phase	An 18-year old former web developer uses backdoors he inserted into his code to access his former firm's network, spam its customers, alter its applications, and ultimately put the firm out of business.	Lack of code reviews
System Deployment Phase	A computer technician uses his unrestricted access to customers' systems to plant a virus on their networks that brings the customers' systems to a halt. A software engineer did not document or back up his source code intentionally, and then deleted the only copy of the source code once the system was in production.	Lack of enforcement of documentation practices and back-up procedures Unrestricted access to all customers' systems
System Maintenance Phase	A foreign currency trader covers up losses of $691 million over a 5-year period by making unauthorized changes to the source code. A logic bomb sits undetected for 6 months before finally performing a mass deletion of data on a telecommunications firm.	Lack of code reviews End-user access to source code Ineffective backup processes

[16]Ibid.
[17]U.S. Secret Service and CERT Coordination Center/SEI, *Insider Threat Study: Illicit Cyber Activity in the Information Technology and Telecommunications Sector* (2008).

Computer Fraud Prevention and Detection

A fraud prevention program starts with a fraud risk assessment across the entire firm, taking into consideration the firm's critical business divisions, processes, and accounts and performed by management. Management is responsible for fraud risk assessments, while the audit committee typically has an oversight role in this process.[18] The audit committee often works with the internal audit group to ensure that the fraud prevention and detection program remains an ongoing effort. The audit committee also interacts with the firm's external auditor to ensure that fraud assessment results are properly communicated.

Inappropriate use of IT resources by users exposes an enterprise to fraud risks as well as other information security risks. Making employees aware of their obligations concerning fraud and misconduct begins with practical communication and training. Communicating the firm's policy file to employees is one of the most important responsibilities of management. Before new employees receive access to information systems, they should be required to sign an acknowledgement called an acceptable use policy (AUP) or an end-user computing policy. The AUP should explain what the firm considers to be acceptable computer use, with the goal of protecting both the employee and the firm from any illegal act.

A fraud detection program should include an evaluation by internal auditors on the effectiveness of business processes, along with an analysis of transaction-level data to obtain evidence of the effectiveness of internal controls and to identify indicators of fraud risk or actual fraudulent activities.[19] An effective approach is to have a continuous monitoring system with embedded modules to create detailed logs for transaction-level testing.

Progress *Check*

5. Given your understanding of computer fraud, do you think it happens often? Why or why not?
6. Use the fraud triangle to explain one of the fraud schemes.
7. Search over the Internet to find a recent computer fraud scheme. Given the scenario, identify the oversights of the firm.

LO 11-4
Define vulnerabilities, and explain how to manage and assess them.

VULNERABILITY ASSESSMENT AND MANAGEMENT

The Information Systems Audit and Control Association (ISACA) defines vulnerability as "the characteristics of IT resources that can be exploited by a threat to cause harm."[20] The GTAG considers vulnerabilities as weaknesses or exposures in IT assets or processes that may lead to a business risk, compliance risk, or security risk.[21] Vulnerability management and risk management have the same objective: Reduce the probability of the occurrence of detrimental events. The subtle difference between risk management and vulnerability management is that risk management is often a more complex and strategic process that may take many months or years and is mostly conducted using a top-down, risk-based approach, whereas vulnerability management is often a tactical and short-term effort that may take weeks or a few months and is frequently conducted using an IT asset-based approach. The purpose of an asset-based approach is to categorize and prioritize further investigation efforts on each asset and to identify appropriate control measures based on meaningful criteria, such as a monetary value of assets and significance of the corresponding risks. To use this approach, it is important to properly maintain asset inventory on an ongoing basis.

---

[18]KPMG, *Fraud Risk Management: Developing a Strategy for Prevention, Detection, and Response* (2006).
[19]GTAG, *Fraud Prevention and Detection in an Automated World.*
[20]ISACA, *Certified Information Systems Auditors Examination Review Manual* (2009).
[21]GTAG, *Managing and Auditing IT Vulnerabilities* (2006).

Types of Vulnerabilities

Because vulnerabilities are the weaknesses or exposures in IT assets or processes, gaining an understanding of existing controls is important to identifying vulnerabilities. In general, vulnerabilities are categorized based on where they commonly exist: within a physical IT environment, within an information system, or within the processes of IT operations. Figures 11.2, 11.3, and 11.4 provide examples of different types of vulnerabilities.

FIGURE 11.2
Examples of Vulnerabilities within a Physical IT Environment

Threats	Vulnerabilities
Physical intrusion	• External parties entering facilities without permission and/or providing access information • Unauthorized hardware changes
Natural disasters	• No regular review of a policy that identifies how IT equipment is protected against environmental threats • Inadequate or outdated measures for environmental threats
Excessive heat or humidity	• Humidity alarm not in place • Outdated devices not providing information on temperature and humidity levels
Water seepage in a data center	• Server room located in the basement • Clogged water drain
Electrical disruptions or blackouts	• Insufficient backup power supply • No voltage stabilizer

FIGURE 11.3
Examples of Vulnerabilities within an Information System

Threats	Vulnerabilities
System intrusion (e.g., spyware, malware, etc.)	• Software not patched immediately • Open ports on a main server without router access • Outdated intrusion detection/prevention system
Logical access control failure	• Work performed not aligned with business requirements • Poor choice of password • Failure to terminate unused accounts in a timely manner
Interruption of a system	• Improper system configuration and customization • Poor service level agreement (SLA) monitoring of service providers

FIGURE 11.4
Examples of Vulnerabilities within the Processes of IT Operations

Threats	Vulnerabilities
Social engineering	• Employee training not providing information about social engineering attempts
Unintentional disclosure of sensitive information by employee	• Inappropriate data classification rule • Poor user access management allows some users to retrieve sensitive information not pertaining to their roles and responsibilities
Intentional destruction of information	• Approval not required prior to deleting sensitive data • Poor employee morale • Writable disk drive containing data that shall not be deleted, such as transaction logs
Inappropriate end-user computing	• Ineffective training as to the proper use of computer • End-user computing policy not reviewed • Poor firewall rules, allowing users to access illegitimate websites

An Overall Framework for Vulnerability Assessment and Management

There are two prerequisites for vulnerability management. First, a firm should deter-mine the main objectives of its vulnerability management because the firm's resource for managing vulnerabilities is limited. In some cases, a primary purpose of vulnerability management could be to comply with applicable laws, regulations, and standards—in which case, the firm should determine which laws, regulations, and standards it should comply with.

Second, a firm should assign roles and responsibility for vulnerability management. Management may designate a team (i.e., internal audit group, risk management commit-tee, etc.) to be responsible for developing and implementing the vulnerability manage-ment program. When assigning roles and responsibilities (i.e., assigning an owner of each IT asset and/or process, implementing a control self-assessment program, etc.), it is important to note that management's commitment and support, as well as the integra-tion of vulnerability management efforts within all levels of the firm, are critical success factors.

Figures 11.5 and 11.6 provide the overall view and main components of vulnerability management and assessment, as well as brief descriptions of the each component.[22]

FIGURE 11.5
Main Components of Vulnerability Management and Assessment

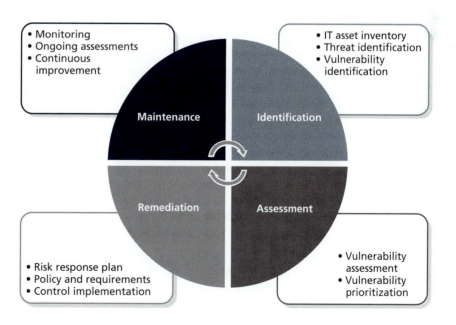

- Monitoring
- Ongoing assessments
- Continuous improvement

- IT asset inventory
- Threat identification
- Vulnerability identification

Maintenance

Identification

Remediation

Assessment

- Risk response plan
- Policy and requirements
- Control implementation

- Vulnerability assessment
- Vulnerability prioritization

[22]GTAG, *Managing and Auditing IT Vulnerabilities.*

VULNERABILITY ASSESSMENT		VULNERABILITY MANAGEMENT	
I. Identification	**II. Risk Assessment**	**III. Remediation**	**IV. Maintenance**
IT Asset Inventory Ensure that all critical IT assets are identified. Ensure IT assets identified are grouped and prioritized. Ensure IT assets are identified and updated periodically.	**Vulnerability Assessment** Identify the approach and criteria to be consistently used for assessing the identified vulnerabilities throughout the organization. Quantify and/or qualify the identified vulnerabilities.	**Risk Response plan** Understand the firm's risk appetite. Conduct a cost/benefit analysis. Select controls and policies to implement.	**Monitoring** Ensure IT assets are maintained in a standardized format to help track logical and physical elements of the IT asset such as model, applications installed, and patches. Ensure change and incident management are integrated with configuration management.
Threat Identification Identify the threats related to each IT asset. If a network scanning or monitoring tool is used, ensure that the tool reflects updated threats and is used periodically.	**Vulnerability Prioritization** Ensure business impact is included as a measurable priority identifier. Prioritize vulnerabilities based on the significance of risks in an area of focus.	**Policy and Requirements** Policy and procedures for remediation should be consistent across the organization. The following five policies are generally of high importance of vulnerability management: • Change management • Configuration management • Incident management • Patch testing • Contingency plans	**Ongoing Assessment** Conduct monitoring on an ongoing basis to verify whether controls are operating effectively as initially implemented. Automatically scan the systems and devices to detect new vulnerabilities and to meet the changes in regulatory requirements.
Vulnerability Identification Identify vulnerabilities associated with each identified threat and IT asset.		**Control Implementation** Analyze whether controls are effective to identified vulnerabilities. Any changes of control should be authorized and tested prior to implementation. Changes of control should cause minimal disruptions to business.	**Continuous Improvement** Continuously improve processes to reach best practice, based on prior findings, ongoing assessment, and the benchmark in the industry.

FIGURE 11.6

Brief Descriptions of the Main Components of Vulnerability Management and Assessment

LO 11-5

Explain issues in system availability, disaster recovery, and business continuity.

SYSTEM AVAILABILITY

A key component of IT service delivery and support is making sure the data are available at all times or, at a minimum, in the moment the data are needed. Even a short period of system downtime on an e-commerce application can result in a loss of e-commerce sales and, potentially, a loss of trust in the provider. For example, in 1999, eBay's system was down for the entire auction site for 22 hours. The company not only lost millions in transaction fees from auction sales, but also billions in stock market value as many investors decided to sell their shares.

Firms continue to monitor system availability. Backups are used to alleviate problems of file or database corruptions. An **uninterruptible power supply** is a device using battery power to enable a system to operate long enough to back up critical data and shut down properly during the loss of power. **Fault tolerance** uses redundant units to provide a system with the ability to continue functioning when part of the system fails. Many firms implement a redundant array of independent drives (RAID) so that if one disk drive fails, important data can still be accessed from another disk.

Virtualization and **cloud computing** are often considered good alternatives to backup data and applications. Cloud computing uses redundant servers in multiple locations to host virtual machines. A virtual machine contains system applications and data backups. If the server hosting a virtual machine fails, the virtual machine can be installed to any other redundant server immediately. Using virtualization and cloud computing for system availability could be cost-effective.

Recently, cloud computing has become a popular model for business operations. In general, cloud computing refers to a service model that a third-party service provider offers computing resources including hardware and software applications to cloud users over the Internet, and the service provider charges on a per-use basis. A cloud user company often shares the computing resources with other user companies, and a cloud provider bears the responsibility for managing and maintaining the resources. A recent survey result shows that 43 percent of 2,014 IT leaders in 50 countries indicate that their companies are projected to have most of their IT efforts running in the cloud by 2015.[23] However, a user company must evaluate a cloud provider's credibility, controls, and security of the systems and networks and its financial viability carefully before using the cloud provider. It is important that a cloud user company obtains and reviews a service organization control (SOC) report from the cloud provider prior to signing an agreement for the service. If the business operations are critical to the cloud service user company (such as storing its confidential data and hosting critical applications), the user company should consider requiring an SOC 1 or SOC 2 report. SOC 2 reports provide the evaluations on a broader set of controls implemented by the service provider.

Connection with Practice

Recovering from 9/11

Although Cantor Fitzgerald lost 700 employees in the 9/11 terrorist attacks, its computer systems were up and running within 2 days, thanks to Recall Corp.

Before the attacks, and on a daily basis, Recall Corp.'s 22 trucks would circle Manhattan 24 hours a day, collecting data tapes and storing them in its New York vaults. About 4 hours after the attack, Recall staff began using bar-code scanners to find thousands of tapes from the 2 million in storage, sifting out the records of the 25 clients they thought would be in the disaster area. Workers spent the next 5 hours pulling backup files, cross-checking them against its database of owners, and guessing which ones were most likely to have been destroyed. Some clients would need data going back a full month, while others needed to go back just one day.

By the time the first calls from the clients came in on Wednesday morning, Recall was ready. That day, the New York office handled its highest volume ever. Its drivers worked 12-hour shifts to deliver 30,000 tapes to Cantor and the two dozen other clients that had been based near Ground Zero. In a normal day, Recall handles just a few rushed deliveries to clients to restore corrupted data, charging $2 per tape for pickup or delivery.

The 30,000 tapes went to "hot sites" selected by clients—big server sites ready to take over any time a company's main facility fails. Cantor Fitzgerald received all of its data on Wednesday afternoon. By Thursday morning, Cantor Fitzgerald was ready for business, trading from Rochelle Park, New Jersey.

Source: T. Kellner, "Total Recall," *Forbes*, October 15, 2001.

[23]Gartner Inc., *Reimagining IT: The 2011 CIO Agenda.* January 2011. Retrieved at: http://www.gartner .com/id=1524714

DISASTER RECOVERY PLANNING AND BUSINESS CONTINUITY MANAGEMENT

Adverse events happen in every daily business environment. For any firm, it is essential to establish and maintain a proper plan to recover from a disaster or any disruptive event and to continue its business operations. In 2011, the severe experience of natural disasters (such as the tsunami in Japan and the tornados in the United States) reinforces the importance of disaster recovery planning and business continuity management.

Disaster recovery planning (DRP) is a process that identifies significant events that may threaten a firm's operations and outlines the procedures to ensure that the firm will resume operations when the events occur. DRP must include a clearly defined and documented plan that covers key personnel; resources, including IT infrastructure and applications; and actions required to be carried out in order to continue or resume the systems for critical business functions within planned levels of disruption. A disaster recovery plan should be reviewed and tested periodically to analyze weaknesses and explore possible improvements.

While DRP is the process of rebuilding the operations and/or infrastructure after a disaster has occurred, **business continuity management (BCM)** refers to the activities required to keep a firm running during a period of displacement or interruption of normal operations. DRP and BCM are the most critical corrective controls, and DRP is a key component of BCM.[24] BCM is broader than DRP and is concerned about the entire business processes, rather than particular assets such as IT infrastructure and applications. To achieve business objectives, a firm must continue to perform its critical business processes, as well as IT functions that support the business processes.

British Standard (BS) 25999 is the generally accepted standard for BCM. It establishes the process, principles, and terminology of continuity management for business and its IT functions. BS 25999 is suitable for any firm and is particularly relevant for firms operating in high-risk environments such as health care, finance, and telecommunications, where the ability to continue operations is paramount for the firm itself and for its customers and stakeholders.[25] As shown in Figure 11.7, BCM often includes the following

> Both DRP and BCM are important to firms because it is about whether they can continue their business or not.

FIGURE 11.7
Components in Business Continuity Management Lifecycle

Source: BCM Institute, BCMPedia, www.bcmpedia .org/wiki/File:BS25999_ BCM_lifecycle.jpg.

[24]R. Muthukrishnan, "The Auditor's Role in Reviewing Business Continuity Planning," *Information Systems Control Journal*, 2005.
[25]Business Continuity Institute, www.thebci.org/certificationstandards.htm.

components: (1) understanding the firm; (2) determining BCM strategy; (3) developing and implementing plans for the BCM; and (4) exercising, maintaining, and improving the firm's BCM practices.

Summary

- Proper use of encryption, authentication, and digital signature technology are important to maintaining information security. Most firms use both symmetric-key and asymmetric-key encryption methods for e-business. Authentication ensures transactions are valid. Encryption maintains confidentiality during data transmission. Digital signatures achieve data integrity and confirm nonrepudiation while conducting e-business.
- Disaster recovery planning (DRP) identifies significant events that may threaten a firm's operations, outlining the procedures that ensure the firm's smooth resuming of operations in the case this event occurs. DRP must include a clearly defined and documented plan that covers key personnel, resources, and actions required to be carried out to resume the systems for critical business functions within planned levels of disruption. DRP is an essential component of business continuity management (BCM), which refers to the activities required to keep a firm running during a period of interruption of normal operations. BCM is broader than DRP and is concerned about the entire business processes, rather than particular assets such as IT infrastructure and applications. To achieve business objectives, a firm must continue to perform its critical business processes, as well as IT functions that support the business processes.

Key Words

asymmetric-key encryption (*223*) To transmit confidential information, the sender uses the receiver's public key to encrypt the message; the receiver uses his or her own private key for decryption upon receiving the message. Also known as public-key encryption or two-key encryption.

authentication (*224*) A process that establishes the origin of information or determines the identity of a user, process, or device.

business continuity management (BCM) (*234*) The activities required to keep a firm running during a period of displacement or interruption of normal operations.

Certificate Authority (CA) (*225*) A trusted entity that issues and revokes digital certificates.

cloud computing (*233*) Using redundant servers in multiple locations to host virtual machines.

data integrity (*224*) Maintaining and assuring the accuracy and consistency of data during transmission and at storage.

digital certificate (*225*) A digital document issued and digitally signed by the private key of a Certificate Authority that binds the name of a subscriber to a public key.

digital signature (*224*) A message digest of a document (or data file) that is encrypted using the document creator's private key.

disaster recovery planning (DRP) (*234*) A process that identifies significant events that may threaten a firm's operations and outlines the procedures to ensure that the firm will resume operations when the events occur.

encryption (*223*) Using algorithmic schemes to encode plaintext into nonreadable form.

fault tolerance (*233*) Redundant units providing a system with the ability to continue functioning when part of the system fails.

fraud triangle (*226*) Three conditions exist for a fraud to be perpetrated: incentive, opportunity, and rationalization.

message digest (MD) (224) A short code, such as one 256 bits long, resulting from hashing a plain-text message using an algorithm.

private key (223) A string of bits kept secret and known only to the owner of the key.

public key (223) A string of bits created with the private key and widely distributed and available to other users.

public-key infrastructure (PKI) (225) A set of policies, processes, server platforms, software, and workstations used for the purpose of administering certificates and public-/private-key pairs, including the ability to issue, maintain, and revoke public-key certificates.

session key (224) A symmetric key that is valid for a certain timeframe only.

symmetric-key encryption (223) Both the sender and the receiver use the same key to encrypt and decrypt messages.

uninterruptible power supply (232) A device using battery power to enable a system to operate long enough to back up critical data and shut down properly during the loss of power.

virtualization (233) Using various techniques and methods to create a virtual (rather than actual) version of a hardware platform, storage device, or network resources.

Answers to
Progress *Checks*

1. The general goals of information security are to safeguard critical systems and to maintain confidentiality, integrity, and availability of information from internal and external security threats.

2. Social engineering could be an attempt to trick someone into revealing information, such as a password, that can be used to attack systems or networks. For example, a hacker may find a phone number of a salesperson from the company's website. The hacker then pretends that he is one of the IT staff working at the helpdesk and calls the salesperson to ask for the salesperson's password in "fixing" a problem on accessing certain files. If the salesperson gives his or her password to the hacker, the hacker can obtain access to the company's network.

3. We cannot use the symmetric-key encryption method to authenticate users because both the sender and the receiver are using the same key. This method does not provide a unique key for each user when transmitting information among different parties.

4. A digital signature is a message digest encrypted using the sender's private key. We use a digital signature to achieve two purposes. The main purpose is to maintain data integrity. The second purpose is to authenticate the sender. If the receiver can use the sender's public key to decrypt the digital signature, the receiver authenticates the sender. The receiver compares the calculated message digest with the sent-over message digest to confirm data integrity.

5. Computer fraud includes a variety of illegal acts that involve a computer or network. If the internal control of a company is not adequate, the wide use of technologies, computers, and other electronic devices in the business world provide an environment for frequent occurrences of computer fraud.

6. Scenario one: The loose access control of the company's information system provided the employee an opportunity to obtain confidential information after leaving the position. The associate lured the employee to disclose the confidential information for his business by providing financial benefits to the employee. The employee committed the identity theft. She rationalized her behavior—because her position had changed, she was no longer responsible for keeping employees' account information confidential.

7. David Nosal used to work for Korn/Ferry, an executive search firm. Shortly after he left the company, he convinced some of his former colleagues who were still working for Korn/Ferry to help him start a competing business. The employees used their login credentials to download source lists, names, and contact information from a confidential database on the company's computer, and then transferred that information to Nosal. (Source: http://www.ca9.uscourts.gov/datastore/opinions/2012/04/10/10-10038.pdf)

8. The Internet Engineering Task Force (IETF) defines vulnerability as a flaw or weakness in a system's design, implementation, or operation and management that could be exploited to violate the system's security policy. The European Network and Information Security Agency (ENISA) defines vulnerability as the existence of a weakness, design, or implementation error that can lead to an unexpected, undesirable event compromising the security of the computer system, network, application, or protocol involved. The Committee on National Security Systems of United States of America defines vulnerability as weakness in an IS, system security procedures, internal controls, or implementation that could be exploited.

9. Examples for each type of the vulnerabilities:

   a. Vulnerabilities in physical IT system

   Threats: Fire

   Vulnerabilities:

   - Nonsensitive automatic fire detection response systems
   - Improper storage of combustible materials
   - Use of malfunctioning heating devices
   - Insufficient training of people about fire prevention and reaction

   b. Vulnerabilities in an information system

   Threats: System intrusion

   Vulnerabilities: No virus scanner on each computer

   c. Vulnerabilities within the process of IT operations

   Threats: Unintentional deletion of information

   Vulnerabilities:

   - Employee mistakes caused by inadequate training about operation
   - Lack of a backup of data and information

Multiple Choice Questions

1. (CISA exam, adapted) Authentication is the process by which the

   a. System verifies that the user is entitled to enter the transaction requested

   b. System verifies the identity of the user

   c. User identifies him- or herself to the system

   d. User indicates to the system that the transaction was processed correctly

2. (CMA exam, adapted) Data processing activities may be classified in terms of three stages or processes: input, processing, and output. An activity that is not normally associated with the input stage is

   a. Batching

   b. Recording

   c. Verifying

   d. Reporting

3. (CISA exam, adapted) To ensure confidentiality in an asymmetric-key encryption system, knowledge of which of the following keys is required to decrypt the receive message?

    I. Private

    II. Public

    a. I

    b. II

    c. Both I and II

    d. Neither I nor II

4. To authenticate the message sender in an asymmetric-key encryption system, which of the following keys is required to decrypt the receive message?

    a. Sender's private key

    b. Sender's public key

    c. Receiver's private key

    d. Receiver's public key

5. To ensure the data sent over the Internet are protected, which of the following keys is required to encrypt the data (before transmission) using an asymmetric-key encryption method?

    a. Sender's private key

    b. Sender's public key

    c. Receiver's private key

    d. Receiver's public key

6. Which of the following groups/laws was the earliest to encourage auditors to incorporate fraud examination into audit programs?

    a. COSO

    b. COBIT

    c. PCAOB

    d. SAS No. 99

    e. Sarbanes-Oxley Act

7. Motive to commit fraud usually will include all of the following, except:

    a. Inadequate segregation of duties

    b. Financial pressure

    c. Personal habits and lifestyle

    d. Feelings of resentment

    e. Alcohol, drug, or gambling addiction

8. (CPA exam, adapted) An information technology director collected the names and locations of key vendors, current hardware configuration, names of team members, and an alternative processing location. What is the director most likely preparing?

    a. Internal control policy

    b. System hardware policy

    c. System security policy

    d. Disaster recovery plan

    e. Supply chain management policy

9. A message digest is the result of hashing. Which of the following statements about the hashing process is true?

    a. It is reversible.

    b. Comparing the hashing results can ensure confidentiality.

    c. Hashing is the best approach to make sure that two files are identical.

    d. None of the above is true.

10. Which one of the following vulnerabilities would create the most serious risk to a firm?
    a. Using open source software (downloaded for free) on the firm's network
    b. Employees recording passwords in Excel files
    c. Employees writing instant messages with friends during office hours
    d. Unauthorized access to the firm's network

Discussion Questions

1. Phishing is a type of social engineering. Give two examples of phishing.
2. If social engineering is a common reason that confidential information was revealed, what needs to be done to prevent this from occurring?
3. Payment Card Industry Data Security Standards (PCI-DSS) and the Health Insurance Portability and Accountability Act (HIPPA) are examples of the laws related to information security. Discuss the major requirements of these legislations.
4. Give an example of employee fraud, and identify reasons it may occur.
5. What are the differences between authentication and authorization?
6. Explain how to use the asymmetric-key encryption method to maintain confidentiality in transmitting a business document electronically.
7. What is hashing? Does it serve the same purpose as encryption? Why?
8. How can data integrity be ensured when conducting e-business? Why is it critical to e-business?
9. Both COBIT and ISO 27000 series are security frameworks. Are there significant differences between the two frameworks?
10. Compare disaster recovery planning (DRP) and business continuity management (BCM).

Problems

1. Compare and contrast symmetric-key and asymmetric-key encryption methods in conducting e-business. Why do companies prefer one method over the other? If a company chooses to use both methods, what might be the reasons? How can the company truly use both methods for e-business?
2. Many internal auditors and IT professionals believe wireless networks and mobile devices pose high risks in a firm's network system. Collect information to examine whether this concern is valid. If so, identify the risks and the general controls to help reduce these risks.
3. Under PKI, Certification Authority (CA) plays a critical role in the success of maintaining information security. Search over the Internet to find a few public firms who are CAs. Compare these firms, and provide suggestions on how to choose a CA as part of information security management.

Answers to Multiple Choice Questions

1. b
2. d
3. a
4. b
5. d

6. d
7. a
8. d
9. c
10. d

Monitoring and Auditing AIS

A look at this chapter

In today's business environment, almost all firms rely on computerized systems in daily operations, in particular, to perform accounting functions. The swift advances in technologies have changed business models and the approaches to collecting data and communicating business information. Given the complicated information systems and the tremendous amount of data to be analyzed and reported, it is challenging for managers, accountants, and auditors to validate that the systems are well designed with embedded internal controls and that they process data with integrity. Accountants' role in the business world is to provide quality information for decision making. Hence, they must understand and be involved in monitoring and auditing accounting information systems.

A look back

In Chapter 11, we provided examples of computer fraud and illustrated how AIS can be misused in order to achieve personal gains. We also discussed common vulnerabilities and how to manage and assess such vulnerabilities.

A look ahead

As managers of IT systems and business partners, accountants are often involved in helping formulate and implement company strategies. Chapter 13 explains how the Balanced Scorecard might be used to formulate, implement, and monitor strategic performance on information technology and information systems.

If you visit the website of **Starbucks**, and click on "Investor Relations," you can access the company's annual reports. You can find two audit reports, both titled "Report of Independent Registered Public Accounting Firm," on pages 89 and 91 of **Starbucks'** 2012 annual reports. The first audit report is the auditor's opinion on whether the financial statements of **Starbucks** fairly represent the company's financial conditions; the second audit report examines the internal control over financial reporting of **Starbucks**. The external auditors from **Deloitte & Touche LLP** conducted audits on the information systems, internal controls, and financial information of **Starbucks** before they rendered the audit opinions. External auditors need to understand a firm's information systems and examine the reliability of the systems before they audit the financial information that is produced by the systems.

Chapter Outline

Introduction
Computer Hardware and Software
The Operating System
Database Systems
LANS and WANS
Wireless Networks
Computer-Assisted Audit Techniques
Continuous Auditing

Learning Objectives

After reading this chapter, you should be able to:

12-1 Understand the risks involved with computer hardware and software.

12-2 Understand and apply computer-assisted audit techniques.

12-3 Explain continuous auditing in AIS.

INTRODUCTION

In Chapters 10 and 11, we provided a general discussion of control, security, and fraud issues in accounting information systems with regard to managing threats and risks in conducting business. In Chapters 5, 6 and 7, we indicated specific internal controls for each major business process—such as sales, cash collections, purchases, cash disbursement, and conversion/manufacturing. This chapter discusses important concepts of monitoring and auditing controls and verifying the accuracy and completeness of the information produced by the systems. We introduce fundamental concepts of critical computer hardware and software, including the operating system, the database, local area networks and wide area networks, and wireless networks. More importantly, we discuss computer-assisted audit techniques (CAATs) and continuous auditing in AIS.

LO 12-1

Understand the risks involved with computer hardware and software.

COMPUTER HARDWARE AND SOFTWARE

Chapter 11 discussed information technology–related frauds and vulnerabilities. To enhance the understanding of those concepts, we discuss important computer hardware and software in this section: the operating system (OS), database systems, local area networks (LANs) and wide area networks (WANs), wireless networks, and remote access.

The Operating System

The **operating system (OS)** is the most important system software because it performs the tasks that enable a computer to operate. The operating system is comprised of system utilities and programs that:[1]

- Ensure the integrity of the system.
- Control the flow of multiprogramming and tasks of scheduling in the computer.
- Allocate computer resources to users and applications.
- Manage the interfaces with the computer.

To consistently and reliably perform these tasks listed, the operating system must achieve five fundamental control objectives:[2]

- *The operating system must protect itself from users.* User applications must not be able to gain control of or damage the operating system.
- *The operating system must protect users from each other.* One user must not be able to access, destroy, or corrupt the data or programs of another user.
- *The operating system must protect users from themselves.* A user's application may consist of several modules stored in separate memory locations, each with its own data. One module must not be allowed to destroy or corrupt another module.
- *The operating system must be protected from itself.* The operating system is also made up of individual modules. No module should be allowed to destroy or corrupt another module.
- *The operating system must be protected from its environment.* In the event of a power failure or other disaster, the operating system should be able to achieve a controlled termination of activities from which it can later recover.

Operating system security should be included as part of IT governance in establishing proper policies and procedures for IT controls that determine who can access the operating system, which resources (e.g., files, programs, printers, or servers) they can use, and what

---

[1]Information Systems Audit and Control Association (ISACA), *CISA Exam Review Manual* (2011), p. 260.
[2]F.M. Stepczyk, "Requirements for Secure Operating Systems," *Data Security and Data Processing*, 5 (1974).

actions they can take.[3] With an ever-expanding user community sharing greater levels of computer resources, operating system security becomes one of the most important IT control issues.

It should be noted that many firms are now turning toward virtualization of their computer resources. In this architecture, hardware resources are split among multiple separate operating systems that exist only as separate environments on the server. In this situation, additional care must be taken to govern and secure the IT environments used.

Database Systems

In today's competitive business environment, data are often the core assets of many companies. In our electronic world, all or most accounting records are stored in a database. A **database** is a shared collection of logically related data that meets the information needs of a firm. Understanding a **database system** is crucial to accounting professionals. Because they have superior knowledge of risks, controls, and business processes, accountants increasingly participate in designing internal control systems and improving business and IT processes in a database environment.

A **data warehouse** is a centralized collection of firmwide data for a relatively long period of time. The data in a data warehouse are pulled periodically from each of the operational databases (ranging from a couple of times a day to once a year), and the data are maintained in the data warehouse for 5 to 10 years. Firms use **operational databases** for daily operations. An operational database often includes data for the current fiscal year only. The data in an operational database are updated when transactions are processed. Such updates do not happen in a data warehouse, so the data in a data warehouse are nonvolatile. Periodically, new data are uploaded to the data warehouse from the operational databases for analysis. The purpose of a data warehouse is to provide a rich data set for management to identify patterns and to examine trends of business events.

Data mining is the process of searching for patterns in the data in a data warehouse and analyzing these patterns for decision making. Data mining is often used to identify patterns in predicting customers' buying behavior for making better selling and production decisions. The tools used in data mining are called online analytical processing (OLAP). Typical approaches in OLAP include drill-down, consolidation, time series analysis, exception reports, and what-if simulations.

Data governance, a discipline that has emerged in recent years, has an evolving definition. It is the convergence of data quality, data management, data policies, business process management, and risk management surrounding the handling of data in a firm.

Connection with Practice

JPMorgan Chase's IT Failure: An Apology and Some Informed Speculation

Customers whacked by JPMorgan Chase's information system debacle—the bank's online banking site was down for three days—finally got an apology, but it's still a little fuzzy about what exactly went wrong. JPMorgan Chase's online site crashed Monday night and stayed offline through Wednesday. On Thursday, the bank said:

> We are sorry for the difficulties that recently affected Chase.com, and we apologize for not communicating better with you during this issue. Giving you 24-hour access to your banking is

(continued)

[3]J.A. Hall, *Information Technology Auditing and Assurance,* 3rd ed. (Cincinnati, Ohio: South-Western College, 2010), p. 69.

of the utmost importance to us. This was not the level of service we know you expect, and we will work hard to serve you better in the future and to communicate with you better if a situation like this should arise again.

Online Bill Payments scheduled for September 13, 14 or 15 were processed by Wednesday night, September 15. It is not necessary to reschedule these payments. If you scheduled a payment during those dates, but do not see it reflected in your payment activity by September 16, please contact us. We will refund any late fees that you may have incurred as a result of our delay in processing your payment.

Thank you for your patience and for the opportunity to work harder to serve you in the future.

Online banking.

The big question here is what exactly went wrong. *Computerworld* notes that JPMorgan Chase blamed a third-party database company's software. That third party is Oracle. Curt Monash, principle of Monash Research, offered some informed speculation in a blog post. Citing tips from readers of his DBMS 2 blog, Monash said:

- A corruption in the Oracle database led to the outage.
- The Oracle database stored user profiles.
- Portals, ACH transactions, loan applications, and trading portfolio access for private clients (i.e., the wealthy types) were affected.

The overall conclusion from Monash is that JPMorgan Chase wasn't to blame. More details are likely to emerge. Let's hope JPMorgan Chase does a thorough post mortem. These days banks are their online sites.

Source: Larry Dignan, *ZDNet.com*, September 17, 2010.

Details of the JPMorgan Chase Oracle Database Outage

After posting my speculation about the JPMorgan Chase database outage, I was contacted by—well, by somebody who wants to be referred to as "a credible source close to the situation." We chatted for a long time; I think it is very likely that this person is indeed what s/he claims to be; and I am honoring his/her requests to obfuscate many identifying details. However, I need a shorter phrase than "a credible source close to the situation," so I'll just refer to him/her as "Tippy." According to Tippy:

- The JPMorgan Chase database outage was caused by corruption in an Oracle database.
- This Oracle database stored user profiles, which are more than just authentication data.
- Applications that went down include but may not be limited to:
  - The main JPMorgan Chase portal.
  - JPMorgan Chase's ability to use the ACH (Automated Clearing House).
  - Loan applications.
  - Private client trading portfolio access.

- The Oracle database was back up by 1:12 Wednesday morning. But on Wednesday a second problem occurred, namely, an overwhelming number of web requests. This turned out to be a cascade of retries in the face of—and of course exacerbating—poor response time. While there was no direct connection to the database outage, Tippy is sympathetic to my suggestions that:
  - Network/app server traffic was bound to be particularly high as people tried to get caught up after the Tuesday outage, or just see what was going on in their accounts.
  - Given that Tippy said there was a definite operator-error contributing cause, perhaps the error would not have happened if people weren't so exhausted from dealing with the database outage.

Tippy stressed the opinion that the Oracle outage was not the fault of JPMorgan Chase (the Wednesday slowdown is a different matter), and rather can be blamed on an Oracle bug. However, Tippy was not able to immediately give me details as to root cause, or for that matter which version of Oracle JPMorgan Chase was using. Sources for that or other specific information would be much appreciated, as would general confirmation/disconfirmation of anything in this post. Metrics and other details supplied by Tippy include:

- The Oracle database was restored from a Saturday night backup. 874K transactions were reapplied, starting early Tuesday morning and ending late Tuesday night.
- $132 million in ACH transfers were held up by the JPMorgan Chase database outage.
- Somewhere around 1000 each auto and student loan applications were lost due to the outage.
- The Oracle cluster has 8 biggish Solaris boxes (T5420 with 64 GB of RAM).
- EMC is the storage provider. In early trouble shooting, EMC hardware was suspected of causing the problem—specifically in a SAN controller—but that was ruled out at some point Monday night.
- JPMorgan Chase's whole fire drill started at 7:38 Monday night, when the slowdown was noticed. Recognition that the problem was database related was very quick (before 8 pm).
- Before long, JPMorgan Chase DBAs realized that the Oracle database was corrupted in about 4 files, and the corruption was mirrored on the hot backup. Hence the manual database restore starting early Tuesday morning.
- And by the way, even before all this started, JPMorgan Chase had an open project to look into replacing Oracle, perhaps with DB2.

One point that jumps out at me is this—not everything in that user profile database needed to be added via ACID transactions. The vast majority of updates are surely web-usage-log kinds of things that could be lost without impinging the integrity of JPMorgan Chase's financial dealings, not too different from what big web companies use NoSQL (or shared MySQL) systems for. Yes, some of it is orders for the scheduling of payments and so on—but on the whole, the database was probably over-engineered, introducing unnecessary brittleness to the overall system.

Source: Curt Monash, *DBMS2.com*, September 17, 2010.

The above example on the IT failure of JPMorgan Chase indicates how complicated the IT infrastructure of a company could be as well as how things could get worse if proper actions were not taken to detect and correct the problems quickly.

LANs and WANs

A **local area network (LAN)** is a group of computers, printers, and other devices connected to the same network and covers a limited geographic range such as a home, small office, or a campus building. LAN devices include **hubs** and **switches.** A packet, which is a formatted, small unit of data, is part of the message or data set that is transmitted over the networks.

A hub contains multiple ports. When a data packet from a computer arrives at one port of a hub, it is copied to *all* other ports so that all other equipment connected to the LAN can receive the arrived packet (like a broadcast). A switch is an intelligent device that provides a path for each pair of connections on the switch by storing address information in its switching tables. From a security perspective, switches provide a significant improvement over hubs because each device connected via the network only sees traffic that has been directed to it via

Sample Local Area Network

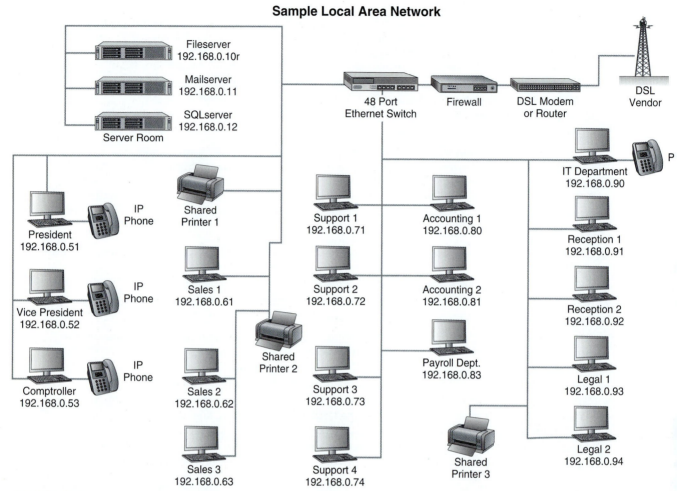

FIGURE 12.1

A Local Area Network Sample

Each computer on a network needs an IP (Internet Protocol) address to be able to communicate and transmit data over the Internet. Notice that 192.168.xxx.xxx are addresses for internal networks only.

Source: Moen and Associates, www.jonmoen.com/Download/Sample%20LAN.pdf.

its designated **MAC (media access controls) address** and cannot eavesdrop on network traffic intended for other recipients. Figure 12.1 illustrates a sample local area network.

Wide area networks (WANs) link different sites together; transmit information across geographically dispersed LANs; and cover a broad geographic area such as a city, region, nation, or an international link. The three main purposes for a WAN are (1) to provide remote access to employees or customers, (2) to link two or more sites within the firm, and (3) to provide corporate access to the Internet.[4] In general, WANs are slower than LAN communication in transmitting data but are often implemented over connectivity that offers guaranteed data rates. Enterprises are often willing to pay for these connections because of the guaranteed quality of service (QoS) and security offered by the point-to-point dedicated connection. WAN devices include **routers** and **firewalls.** Figure 12.2 illustrates a sample wide area network.

A router connects different LANs. Routers are software-based intelligent devices that choose the most efficient communication path through a network to the required

[4]R. Panko, and J. Panko, *Business Data Networks and Telecommunications,* 8th ed. (Upper Saddle River, NJ: Prentice Hall, 2011).

Sample Wide Area Network

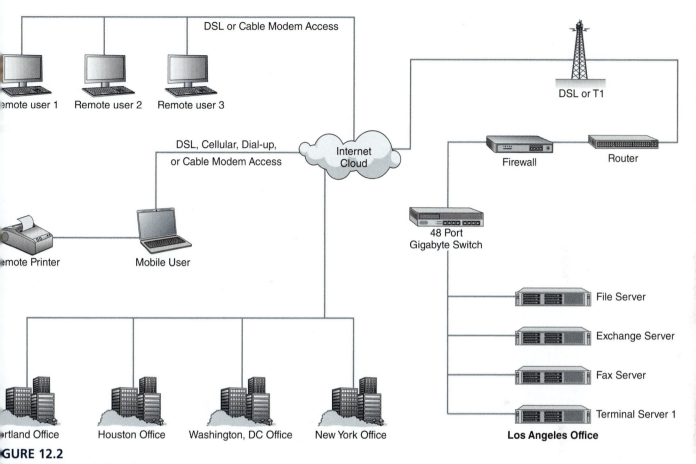

GURE 12.2
Wide Area Network Sample

rce: Moen and Associates, www.jonmoen.com/Download/Sample%20WAN.pdf.

destination. A router examines the Internet Protocol (IP) address of senders and recipients and makes decisions to direct the packet to its recipients' IP address through the most efficient communication path. Routers can also divide and interconnect network segments or link two more physically separate network segments, similar to a switch.

In a computer network, a firewall can be defined as a security system comprised of hardware and software that is built using routers, servers, and a variety of software.[5] Whenever a data packet arrives, the firewall examines each incoming and outgoing data packet to determine whether a data packet should be allowed to continue in the transmission process. Also, a firewall allows individuals on the corporate network to send/receive a data packet from the Internet.

A **virtual private network (VPN)** securely connects a firm's WANs by sending/receiving encrypted packets via virtual connections over the public Internet to distant offices, salespeople, and business partners. Rather than using expensive dedicated leased lines, VPNs take advantage of the public Internet infrastructure with encryption and authentication technology to create a virtual private network that provides users with secure, **remote access** to their firm's network using the Internet. VPNs are a cheaper

In today's business environment, VPN is an important technology. Many firms need to provide secure access for employees who are traveling and for those who work from home.

[5]Panko and Panko, *Business Data Networks and Telecommunications.*

alternative to leased lines, yet they carry the disadvantage of not having guaranteed QoS. VPNs allow for companies to utilize a widely dispersed workforce without losing the productivity provided by a LAN.

Progress *Check*

1. Identify one LAN and one WAN that you have been using.

Wireless Networks

Wireless technologies, which use radio-frequency transmissions and electromagnetic signals as the means for transmitting data, enable devices to communicate without physical connections. According to the Institute of Electrical and Electronics Engineers (IEEE) 802.11 standard, a **wireless network** is comprised of two fundamental architectural components: access points and stations. An **access point** logically connects stations to a firm's network. Access points can also logically connect wireless stations with each other in an ad hoc wireless network.[6] A **station** is a wireless endpoint device equipped with a wireless network interface card (NIC). Common benefits of using wireless technology include:[7]

- Mobility—convenient online access without a physical network using cables for connections.
- Rapid deployment—time saved on implementing networks because of reduction in using physical cables/media.
- Flexibility and scalability—freely setting up or removing wireless networks at different locations.

General security objectives for both wired LANs and wireless LANs include:

- Confidentiality—ensure that communication cannot be read by unauthorized parties.
- Integrity—detect any intentional or unintentional changes to the data during transmission.
- Availability—ensure that devices and individuals can access a network and its resources whenever needed.
- Access control—restrict the rights of devices or individuals to access a network or resources within a network.

Most threats with regard to wireless LANs involve an attacker with access to the radio link between a station and an access point, or between two stations. The most common security threats for wireless LANs include:[8]

- Eavesdropping—the attacker passively monitors wireless networks for data, including authentication credentials.
- Man-in-the-middle—the attacker actively intercepts communications between wireless clients and access points to obtain authentication credentials and data.
- Masquerading—the attacker impersonates an authorized user and gains certain unauthorized privileges to the wireless network.
- Message modification—the attacker alters a legitimate message sent via wireless networks by deleting, adding to, changing, or reordering it.

[6]National Institute of Standards and Technology (NIST), "Establishing Wireless Robust Security Networks: A Guide to IEEE 802.11i," SP 800-97 (2007), p. 22.
[7]Cyber Security Malaysia, *Wireless Local Area Network (WLAN) Security Guideline* (2010), p. 12.
[8]NIST, "Establishing Wireless Robust Security Networks: A Guide to IEEE 802.11i," pp. 27–28.

- Message replay—the attacker passively monitors transmissions via wireless networks and retransmits messages, acting as if the attacker was a legitimate user.
- Misappropriation—the attacker steals or makes unauthorized use of a service.
- Traffic analysis—the attacker passively monitors transmissions via wireless networks to identify communication patterns and participants.
- Rogue access points—the attacker sets up an unsecured wireless network near the enterprise with an identical name and intercepts any messages sent by unsuspecting users who log onto it.

Security controls for wireless networks can be categorized into three groups: management, operational, and technical controls.[9] Management controls are security controls that focus on management of risk and information system security. Management controls include, but are not limited to, assigning roles and responsibilities, creating policies and procedures, and conducting risk assessment on a regular basis. Examples include determining which parties are authorized and responsible for installing and configuring access points and other wireless network equipment; types of information that may or may not be sent over wireless networks; and how transmissions over wireless networks should be protected, including requirements for the use of encryption and for cryptographic key management.[10]

Operational controls in wireless networks typically include protecting a firm's premises and facilities; preventing and detecting physical security breaches; and providing security training to employees, contractors, or third-party users. For example, a firm should define and document the security roles and responsibilities of employees, contractors, and third-party users based on the firm's policies, procedures, and security requirements. It is also important to produce terms and conditions of employment that state the employees', contractors', and third-party users' responsibilities for the firm's wireless network. They should agree and sign the terms and conditions of their employment contract prior to beginning work. In addition, conducting appropriate awareness training on wireless networks and providing regular updates on organizational policies and procedures to employees, contractors, and third-party users can strengthen a firm's security control.

Technical controls are security controls that are primarily implemented and executed through mechanisms contained in computing-related equipment, including access point management and encryption setup. A firm should immediately change the default configuration of all access points that have been deployed, including service set identifier (SSID), administrator credentials, radio signal strength, remote web-based configuration (e.g., administrator's username and password), and Internet protocol service configuration.[11] Regarding data transmission security, all access points should be configured with encryption to maintain confidentiality and data integrity. Using the wired equivalent privacy (WEP) algorithm is not recommended because it is not secure enough. It is better to use the wi-fi protected access (WPA) or the WPA2 algorithm as the cryptography technique to provide more effective authentication and for encryption.

Progress *Check*   2. Do you own a laptop, a cell phone, or an iPad? Can you identify a few security issues while using these devices over a wireless network?

---

[9]Federal Information Processing Standards (FIPS), "Minimum Security Requirements for Federal Information and Information Systems," Publication 200 (2006).
[10]NIST, "Guide to Securing Legacy IEEE 802.11 Wireless Networks," SP 800-48 Rev 1 (2008), p. 29.
[11]Cyber Security Malaysia, *Wireless Local Area Network (WLAN) Security Guideline,* p. 12.

COMPUTER-ASSISTED AUDIT TECHNIQUES

For most large and medium-sized enterprises, there are few business processes that are not driven by computers.[12] Almost all the data needed while conducting an audit are digital. Given today's business environment, it is very difficult to audit effectively and efficiently without using technology, such as **computer-assisted audit techniques (CAATs).**

CAATs are essential tools for auditors to conduct an audit in accordance with heightened auditing standards. Generally accepted auditing standards (GAAS) are broad guidelines regarding an auditor's professional responsibilities in three areas: general standards, standards of fieldwork, and standards of reporting. GAAS requires auditors to gather sufficient and appropriate evidence in the course of audit fieldworks. The Information Systems Audit and Control Association (ISACA) issues Information Systems Auditing Standards (ISASs) that provide guidelines for conducting an IS/IT audit. Recently, ISASs were renamed as IT Standards, Guidelines, Tools, and Techniques for Audit and Assurance and Control Professionals. In "Performance of Audit Work" (S6), ISACA indicates that "during the course of the audit, the IS auditor should obtain sufficient, reliable, and relevant evidence to achieve the audit objectives. The audit findings and conclusions are to be supported by appropriate analysis and interpretation of this evidence."[13] In addition, according to the Institute of Internal Auditors' (IIA) professional practice standard section 1220.A2, internal auditors *must* consider the use of computer-assisted, technology-based audit tools and other data analysis techniques when conducting internal audits.[14]

The term "computer-assisted audit techniques" refers to any automated audit techniques that can be used by an auditor to perform audits in achieving audit objectives. In particular, CAATs enable auditors to gather and analyze audit evidence to test the adequacy and reliability of financial information and internal controls in a computerized environment. Some common areas in which auditors can use CAATs include the following:

- Test of details of transactions and balances.
- Analytical review procedures.
- Compliance tests of IT general and application controls.
- Operating system (OS) and network vulnerability assessments.
- Application security testing and source code security scans.
- Penetration testing.

Auditors may use two CAAT approaches in auditing systems: **auditing around the computer** (or **black-box approach**) and **auditing through the computer** (or **white-box approach**). Using the black-box approach, auditors test the reliability of computer-generated information by first calculating expected results from the transactions entered into the system. Then, the auditors compare these calculations to the processing or output results. If they prove to be accurate and valid, it is assumed that the system of controls is effective and that the system is operating properly. That is, auditors do not need to gain detailed knowledge of the systems' internal logic. The advantage of this approach is that the systems will not be interrupted for auditing purposes. The black-box approach could be adequate when automated systems applications are relatively simple.

The white-box approach requires auditors to understand the internal logic of the system/application being tested. Using this approach, auditors need to create test cases to verify specific logic and controls in a system. The auditing through the computer approach

---

[12]S.A. Sayana, "Using CAATs to Support IS Audit," *Information Systems Control Journal,* 1 (2003).

[13]ISACA, *IT Standards, Guidelines, Tools, and Techniques for Audit and Assurance and Control Professionals* (2010), www.isaca.org.

[14]Institute of Internal Auditors (IIA), *International Standards for the Professional Practice of Internal Auditing (Standards)* (2010), www.theiia.org.

embraces a variety of approaches: the test data technique, parallel simulation, integrated test facility (ITF), and embedded audit module.[15]

The **test data technique** uses a set of input data to validate system integrity. When creating the test data, auditors need to prepare both valid and invalid data to examine critical logics and controls of the system. **Parallel simulation** attempts to simulate the firm's key features or processes. Under this approach, the auditors write a computer program to reprocess the firm's actual data for a past period to generate simulated results. The simulated results are compared with the actual results to determine the validity of the system. The **integrated test facility (ITF)** approach is an automated technique that enables test data to be continually evaluated during the normal operation of a system. The auditor creates fictitious situations and performs a wide variety of tests over the system. This approach requires more computer expertise and is time-consuming and expensive. The **embedded audit module** is a programmed audit module that is added to the system under review. Hence, the auditors can monitor and collect data over online transactions. The collected data are analyzed by auditors in evaluating control risks and effectiveness. The application of this approach requires auditors to have good knowledge and skills in computer programming.

In addition to the aforementioned techniques in auditing controls in a system, one widely used tool in auditing a system is **generalized audit software (GAS).** GAS is frequently used to perform substantive tests and is used for testing of controls through transactional data analysis.[16] GAS refers to standard software that has the capability to directly read and access data from various database platforms. GAS provides auditors with an independent means to gain access to data for analysis and the ability to use high-level, problem-solving software to invoke functions to be performed on data files.[17] Features include mathematical computations, stratification, statistical analysis, sequence checking, duplicate checking, and re-computation. Two of the most popular software packages are Audit Command Language (ACL) and Interactive Data Extraction and Analysis (IDEA). GAS is ideal for investigating large data files to identify records needing further audit scrutiny.

LO 12-3

Explain continuous auditing in AIS.

CONTINUOUS AUDITING

A **continuous audit** occurs when audit-related activities are performed on a continuous basis. With continuous auditing, theoretically, an audit report/opinion can be issued *simultaneously* with, or shortly after, the occurrence of the events under review.[18] Testing in continuous audits often consists of continuous controls monitoring and continuous data assurance.[19] Using automated audit procedures, the audit activities related to continuous auditing range from continuous control assessment to continuous risk assessment and include internal control assurance, financial attestation, fraud examination, identifying audit scope and objectives, audit records follow-ups, and developing annual audit plans. For management, related activities are control and performance monitoring, using the Balanced Scorecard for total quality management, and enterprise risk management. Because continuous auditing is highly dependent on automated audit procedures, technology plays a key role in analyzing trends and patterns of transactions, identifying exceptions and anomalies, and testing controls.[20] Figure 12.3 illustrates the concepts and hierarchy of continuous auditing.

[15]Hall, *Information Technology Auditing and Assurance.*

[16]M.V. Cerullo, "Impact of SAS No. 94 on Computer Audit Techniques," *Information Systems Control Journal,* 1 (2003).

[17]ACL and IDEA are the most widely used GAS applications for data analysis.

[18]Global Technology Audit Guides (GTAG), *Continuous Auditing: Implications for Assurance, Monitoring, and Risk Assessment* (2005), p. 7.

[19]M.G. Alles, A. Kogan, and M.A. Vasarhelyi, "Putting Continuous Auditing Theory into Practice: Lessons from Two Pilot Implementations," *Journal of Information Systems* 22, no 2 (2008), pp. 195–214.

[20]Global Technology Audit Guides (GTAG), *Continuous Auditing: Implications for Assurance, Monitoring, and Risk Assessment* (2005).

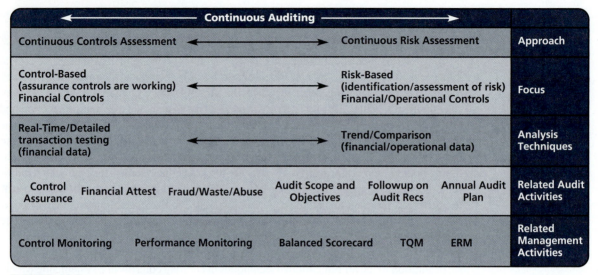

FIGURE 12.3
Concepts in Continuous Auditing

Source: GTAG, *Continuous Auditing* (2005), p. 8.

There are many benefits of conducting continuous audits. Most firms can reduce errors and frauds, increase operational effectiveness, better comply with laws and regulations, and increase management confidence in control effectiveness and financial information. In addition, continuous auditing allows internal and external auditors to monitor transaction data in a timely manner; better understand critical control points, rules, and exceptions; perform control and risk assessments in real time or near real time; notify management of control deficiencies in a timely manner; and reduce efforts of routine testing while focusing on more valuable investigation activities. However, if costs outweigh benefits, continuous auditing should not be implemented.

A 2006 study by Kuhn and Sutton analyzes the particular frauds that WorldCom's management used to deceive investors and assesses whether the "continuous auditing alarms" would have caught the frauds. This study provides guidance to auditors who are establishing continuous auditing initiatives to leverage the lessons learned from the WorldCom debacle and ensure that their continuous auditing routines are able to identify the type of financial fraud that occurred at WorldCom.[21]

Figure 12.4 summarizes the Kuhn and Sutton study and indicates the fraud schemes and the corresponding proposed alarms under continuous audits that would have flagged the activity for further review.

Although the concept of continuous auditing was introduced more than 20 years ago, it was not widely implemented by firms before the proliferation of information technologies in recent years. Today's advanced data analytics, ERP systems, and web-based programming languages such as Extensible Markup Language (XML) and Extensible Business Reporting Language (XBRL) make the implementation of continuous auditing more feasible and less costly than before.

Common IT techniques needed to implement continuous auditing include database management systems, transaction logging and query tools, data warehouses, and data mining or computer-assisted audit techniques (CAATs). Using these techniques, some key

[21]J.R. Kuhn and S.G. Sutton, "Learning from WorldCom: Implications for Fraud Detection through Continuous Assurance," *Journal of Emerging Technologies in Accounting* 3, no. 1 (2006), pp. 61–80.

WorldCom Fraud Scheme	Proposed Continuous Auditing Alarm
Operating expenses were illegitimately reclassified as capital expenditures, which improved the "expenditure-to-revenue" [E/R] ratio by reducing the amount of expenses recorded in current fiscal year.	Create an alarm that simultaneously identifies (1) *reductions* in operating expenses that exceed the industry average and (2) *increases* in capital expenditures that exceed the industry average.
Book values of acquired entities were illegitimately reclassified as goodwill on the books. Which improved the E/R ratio by increasing the effective amortization period of the amounts in question.	Create an alarm that identifies increases in plant, property, equipment, and goodwill that differ significantly from historical averages.
"Taking a bath" by excessively writing down the assets included in the corporate acquisitions gave "the false Impression that expenses were declining over time in relation to revenue (i.e., reducing the E/R ratio and increasing net income from operations)."	Benchmark key ratios (e.g., E/R) against industry averages, and generate an alarm when there is a significant discrepancy between the two.
Allowance for doubtful accounts was underestimated (along with the corresponding expense entry, bad debts expense) to falsely improve the E/R ratio.	Generate an alarm if the allowance for doubtful accounts differs significantly from the last month's ratio (i.e., to Accounts Receivable).

FIGURE 12.4
Continuous Auditing Alarms and the WorldCom Fraud Schemes

functions of continuous audits can be performed, such as accessing and normalizing data from across the enterprise, extracting large transactional volumes without having a negative impact on operational system performance, and testing data and reporting results in a timely manner.

The most significant nontechnical barriers[22] and technical challenges[23] encountered in implementing continuous auditing include:

- Perceived negative impact of continuous auditing on the firm, such as the cost of initial investments, changes in internal audit group's head count, and the quality of audits.
- Priority of implementation in determined key areas, such as which controls should be monitored on a continual basis and which audit activities could be automated.
- Readiness of the internal audit group to develop and adopt continuous auditing.
- Unrealistic expectations of the benefits of continuous auditing.
- Access to all relevant data in a timely manner.
- Accumulating and quantifying the risks and the exposures that have been identified.
- Defining the appropriate analytic that will effectively identify exceptions to controls.
- Developing a suitable scoring/weighting mechanism to prioritize exceptions.
- Balancing the costs and efforts of reviewing large volumes of exceptions against the exposures of the exceptions themselves.

Although there is no universal, well-accepted approach to implementing continuous auditing, there is a general template that a steering team or the internal audit function can use.[24] When a firm considers whether or not to implement continuous auditing, it should first evaluate the overall benefit and cost of having continuous auditing as part of the firm's overall governance, risk, and compliance (GRC) effort. After careful evaluations to rationalize the decision, the firm should develop a strategy in identifying and prioritizing

[22]Deloitte & Touche, *Continuous Monitoring and Continuous Auditing: From Idea to Implementation* (2010), p. 10.
[23]ACL, *Building and Implementing a Continuous Controls Monitoring and Auditing Framework* (2005), p. 3.
[24]Deloitte & Touche, *Continuous Monitoring and Continuous Auditing*, p. 10.

potential areas for continuous audits. Once the strategy is developed, the firm should plan and design how to implement continuous auditing, such as determining the scope of the audit objectives, designing the continuous auditing processes, allocating resources, and creating a reasonable timeline for implementation. Once the resources are approved and in place, the firm can implement continuous auditing followed by periodic performance monitoring on the implementation.

Summary

- Essential concepts of critical computer hardware and software are introduced in this chapter, including the operating system, the database, local area networks, wide area networks, and wireless networks.
- There are two approaches to auditing an information system: auditing around the computer (the black-box approach) and auditing through the computer (the white-box approach).
- Most auditors would like to use computer-assisted audit techniques (CATTs) in auditing a system, such as the test data technique, parallel simulation, and the embedded audit module. CATTs are often used in continuous auditing. Performing audit-related activities on a continuous basis may narrow the gap between daily operations and the required improvements resulting from an audit.

Key Words

access point (248) Logically connects stations to a firm's network.

audit around the computer (or black-box approach) (250) Auditors test the reliability of computer-generated information by first calculating expected results from the transactions entered into the system. Then, the auditors compare these calculations to the processing or output results.

audit through the computer (or white-box approach) (250) Requires auditors to understand the internal logic of the system/application being tested.

computer-assisted audit techniques (CAATs) (250) Essential tools for auditors to conduct an audit in accordance with heightened auditing standards.

continuous audit (251) Performing audit-related activities on a continuous basis.

data governance (243) The convergence of data quality, data management, data policies, business process management, and risk management surrounding the handling of data in a firm.

data mining (243) A process of using sophisticated statistical techniques to extract and analyze data from large databases to discern patterns and trends that were not previously known.

data warehouse (243) A collection of information gathered from an assortment of external and operational (i.e. internal) databases to facilitate reporting for decision making and business analysis.

database (243) A shared collection of logically related data for various uses.

database system (243) A term typically used to encapsulate the constructs of a data model, database management system (DBMS), and database.

embedded audit module (251) A programmed audit module that is added to the system under review.

firewall (246) A security system comprised of hardware and software that is built using routers, servers, and a variety of software.

generalized audit software (GAS) (251) Frequently used to perform substantive tests and used for testing of controls through transactional data analysis.

hub (245) Contains multiple ports.

integrated test facility (ITF) (*251*) An automated technique that enables test data to be continually evaluated during the normal operation of a system.

local area network (LAN) (*245*) A group of computers, printers, and other devices connected to the same network that covers a limited geographic range such as a home, small office, or a campus building.

MAC (media access controls) address (*246*) A designated address that is connected to each device via the network and only sees traffic.

operating system (OS) (*242*) Performs the tasks that enable a computer to operate; comprised of system utilities and programs.

operational database (*243*) Often includes data for the current fiscal year only.

parallel simulation (*251*) Attempts to simulate the firm's key features or processes.

remote access (*247*) Connection to a data-processing system from a remote location e.g., through a virtual private network.

router (*246*) Software-based intelligent device that chooses the most efficient communication path through a network to the required destination.

station (*248*) A wireless endpoint device equipped with a wireless network interface card.

switch (*245*) An intelligent device that provides a path for each pair of connections on the switch by storing address information in its switching tables.

test data technique (*251*) Uses a set of input data to validate system integrity.

virtual private network (VPN) (*247*) Securely connects a firm's WANs by sending/receiving encrypted packets via virtual connections over the public Internet to distant offices, salespeople, and business partners.

wide area network (WAN) (*246*) Links different sites together; transmits information across geographically dispersed LANs; and covers a broad geographic area such as a city, region, nation, or an international link.

wireless network (*248*) Comprised of two fundamental architectural components: access points and stations.

Answers to Progress *Checks*

1. Two or more computers in a small office connected to the same printer form a local area network. The Internet is the most popular and largest wide area network.

2. Mobile devices are subject to man-in-the-middle attacks when using unsecured wi-fi networks. Also, if an iPad user gets applications from any apps store, he or she is at risk of getting malicious applications from the store.

Multiple Choice Questions

1. A local area network (LAN) is best described as a(n):
   a. Computer system that connects computers of all sizes, workstations, terminals, and other devices within a limited proximity
   b. System that allows computer users to meet and share ideas and information

    c. Electronic library containing millions of items of data that can be reviewed, retrieved, and analyzed

    d. Method to offer specialized software, hardware, and data-handling techniques that improve effectiveness and reduce costs

2. Which of the following network components is set up to serve as a security measure that prevents unauthorized traffic between different segments of the network?

    a. Switch

    b. Router

    c. Firewall

    d. Virtual local area networks (VLANs)

3. Unauthorized alteration of records in a database system would impair which of the following components of the CIA tripod?

    a. Confidentiality

    b. Integrity

    c. Availability

    d. Authorization

4. Which of the following is not a task performed by an operating system?

    a. Translate high-level languages to machine-level language

    b. Manage job scheduling and multiprogramming

    c. Support applications and facilitate their access to specified resources

    d. Provide controlled access to data and processes data

5. Managers at a consumer products company purchased personal computer software from only recognized vendors and prohibited employees from installing nonauthorized software on their personal computers by enforcing a new end-user computing policy. To minimize the likelihood of computer viruses infecting any of its systems, the company should also:

    a. Restore infected systems with authorized versions

    b. Recompile infected programs from source code backups

    c. Institute program change control procedures

    d. Test all new software on a stand-alone personal computer

6. Unauthorized alteration of records in a database system can be prevented by employing:

    a. Key verification

    b. Computer matching

    c. Regular review of audit trails

    d. Database access controls

7. An organization is planning to replace its wired networks with wireless networks. Which of the following approaches provides the most secured wireless network?

    a. Implement wired equivalent privacy (WEP) protocol

    b. Allow access to only authorized media access control (MAC) addresses

    c. Disable the network interface card (NIC)

    d. Implement wi-fi protected access (WPA2)

8. The vice president of human resources has requested an audit to identify payroll overpayments for the previous year. Which would be the best audit technique to use in this situation?

    a. Test data

    b. Generalized audit software

    c. Integrated test facility

    d. Embedded audit module

9. Which of following statements about CAATs is not correct?

    a. Parallel simulation attempts to simulate or reproduce the firm's actual processing results.

    b. The test data technique uses a set of hypothetical transactions to examine the programmed checks and program logic in programs.

    c. The integrated test facility is a programmed module or segment that is inserted into an application program to monitor and collect data based on daily transactions.

    d. The embedded audit module may require the auditor to have a good working knowledge of computer programming and a solid understanding of IT risks that may exist in a system.

10. Which of the following audit techniques should an IS auditor use to detect duplicate invoice records within an invoice master file?

    a. Test data

    b. Generalized audit software

    c. Integrated test facility

    d. Embedded audit module

Discussion Questions

1. What are the main reasons for using a VPN?
2. What is a data warehouse? Is it related to cloud computing?
3. We often use regression analyses in data mining. Are accountants required to understand data mining? Why?
4. Use a search engine to identify a few computer-assisted audit techniques (CAATs).
5. Compare and contrast continuous monitoring and continuous auditing.
6. What is the main purpose of using firewalls?
7. Are there differences among hubs, switches, and routers?
8. Identify a few critical security issues in using a wireless network.

Problems

1. (CIA adapted) As an internal auditor, you have been assigned to evaluate the controls and operation of a computer payroll system. To test the computer systems and programs, you submit independently created test transactions with regular data in a normal production run. Identify advantages and disadvantages of this technique.

2. Auditing an accounting information system requires knowledge and skills in both accounting and computers. However, most auditors may not have sufficient expertise in the technical side of computing and information systems. Given today's business environment, how much computer- and information systems–related knowledge and skills must an auditor have to be effective in performing auditing?

3. As the CFO of a small, private retail company in Los Angeles, you often hire interns from the universities near you as accounting clerks throughout the year. In general, the interns are not hired as full-time employees. Are you concerned about security knowing that almost all interns love to use instant messaging, Facebook, Google+, or Twitter at work? Why or why not?

4. (CMA adapted) As chief executive auditor, Mallory Williams heads the internal audit group of a manufacturing company in southern Texas. She would like to purchase a CATT tool to assist her group in conducting internal audit functions. As an intern, you are asked to evaluate and prepare a report describing the audit purpose facilitated and the procedural steps followed for the following CATTs:

    • Generalized audit software.

    • Integrated test facility.

    • Flowcharting (such as Microsoft Visio).

    • Parallel simulation and modeling.

Answers to Multiple Choice Questions

1.	a	6.	d
2.	c	7.	d
3.	b	8.	b
4.	d	9.	c
5.	d	10.	b

AIS Development and Management

The Balanced Scorecard and Business Value of Information Technology

A look at this chapter

As managers and designers of IT systems as well as business partners, accountants are often involved in helping formulate and implement company strategy. The Balanced Scorecard is a well-known strategic performance management system that many companies use to formulate, implement, and monitor strategic performance. In this chapter, we explain concepts embodied in the Balanced Scorecard and describe how information technology supports a company's strategic objectives from a Balanced Scorecard viewpoint.

A look back

Chapter 12 explained the accountants' role in the business when monitoring and auditing accounting information systems.

A look ahead

Chapter 14 presents a process for assessing the business value of IT initiatives. As users, managers, designers, and evaluators of the firm's IT systems, accountants are important members of the team that will develop business case for AIS initiatives. Additionally, as users, managers, and evaluators, they can also be asked to review business cases for IT initiatives in general.

According to an August 2009 article in *The Wall Street Journal,* **Starbucks** is adopting "lean Japanese techniques" in a quest for greater efficiency in its 11,000 U.S. stores. Scott Heydon, Vice President of Lean Thinking at **Starbucks**, has been known to challenge store managers to assemble and disassemble Mr. Potato Head toys in less than 45 seconds. This challenge is intended to get them to think about wasted steps in their processes.

An Oregon City, Oregon, **Starbucks** store was among the first to adopt lean techniques. The store manager first took more than 2 minutes to put Mr. Potato Head together and then take him apart. After reducing extra steps, she reduced the time to about 15 seconds. Then, she examined the steps that her partners took to fill drive-through window orders, including moving and reaching for different ingredients. After streamlining the process, the store reduced the time to fill an average drive-through order to 25 seconds, one of the fastest times in the company.

Starbucks' management believes that reducing waste will give its store partners more time to interact with customers and allow them to improve service. This is important for a couple of reasons. First, the recent economic downturn has reduced customer traffic and forced **Starbucks** to close almost 900 stores. Second, personnel costs amount to 24 percent of **Starbucks'** revenue, one of its largest operating expenses. While reducing waste is important, it won't deliver real value unless **Starbucks'** partners can improve customer service and increase customer traffic. This chapter describes how a company's investment in people and technology can affect the business process performance and how business process performance affects the company's customer value proposition and, subsequently, its financial performance.

Chapter Outline

Learning Objectives

After reading this chapter, you should be able to:

13-1 Describe the Balanced Scorecard framework.

13-2 Explain the purpose of strategy maps.

13-3 Describe different types of IT and why IT initiatives can be difficult to evaluate.

13-4 Define the Balanced Scorecard management process.

13-5 Describe how an AIS system contributes to a Balanced Scorecard management process.

LO 13-1
Describe the Balanced
Scorecard framework.

BALANCED SCORECARD FRAMEWORK

According to a recent survey by the Financial Executives Institute,[1] more than 40 percent of responding financial officers reported that their company's investments in IT are providing little or no return on investment. When existing IT systems and new IT initiatives fail to deliver expected returns, companies have a management problem—not an IT problem. According to a recent article in *IndustryWeek* magazine,[2] "A formal, structured approach that links IT investment to business performance can help companies avoid many of these problems by providing a focus to the investment that is often missing." This chapter offers a framework that describes the potential value of IT relative to a company's strategic objectives. The next chapter describes methods for evaluating return on investment for individual, or portfolios of, IT investments.

Investments in information technology, such as AIS, take on value only in the context of the company's strategy. Executives should analyze each proposed investment as part of a portfolio of potential investments that help to implement a strategy.[3]

The Balanced Scorecard provides a tool that can describe the contribution of IT to the company's strategy. The Balanced Scorecard is a performance measurement framework that allows managers to measure the firm's performance from multiple perspectives that follow from the firm's mission, strategy, and objectives. According the Balanced Scorecard Institute (www.balancedscorecard.org),

> The balanced scorecard is a strategic planning and management system that is used extensively in business and industry, government, and nonprofit organizations worldwide to align business activities to the vision and strategy of the organization, improve internal and external communications, and monitor organization performance against strategic goals.

The **Balanced Scorecard framework** describes performance from four different perspectives based on the firm's strategy to achieve shareholder value. Objectives for each perspective describe the strategy in a series of cause-and-effect relationships (see Figure 13.1).

FIGURE 13.1
Relationships between Balanced Scorecard Perspectives

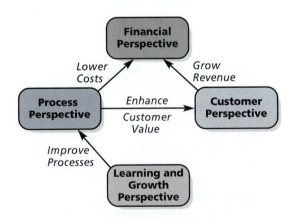

[1]Computer Sciences Corporation and Financial Executives Research Foundation, *Technology Issues for Financial Executives,* Financial Executive Institute (2008).
[2]D. Schrock, J. Cole, and J. Shaffer, "Getting IT Right: How to Plan, Manage and Deliver on Technology's Promise," *IndustryWeek,* December 16, 2010, www.IndustryWeek.com.
[3]See, for example, Deloitte, *Value Matters: Getting Back to What's Really Important in Planning, Budgeting, and Forecasting,* Deloitte Consulting, LLP (2010).

Connection with Practice

Bain and Company, a prominent consulting company, conducts an annual survey of almost 1,500 international executives. The survey asks about the use of the 25 most popular management tools and techniques. For 2009, more than 50 percent of the respondents were using some form of the Balanced Scorecard for strategic management.

Learning and Growth Perspective

The **learning and growth perspective** describes the firm's objectives for improvements in tangible and intangible infrastructure. The firm addresses its goals for investments in human capital, information capital, and organizational capital to make sure that the firm is strategically ready to continuously improve its process performance. Managers use metrics to focus investments, such as employee training or new systems development, to achieve the firm's learning and growth objectives and also link those changes to process objectives.

Customer management process in action.

Process Perspective

The **process perspective** describes the firm's objectives for its business processes so that the firm operates efficiently while delivering products and services that meet its customers' requirements. In their book, *Strategy Maps,*[4] Kaplan and Norton describe four types of business processes:

1. Operations management processes, such as supply, production, distribution, and risk management.
2. Customer management processes, such as those involved with the selection, acquisition, and retention of customers and growth of the firm's market.
3. Innovation processes, such as identifying opportunities, research and development, product design and development, and product launch.
4. Regulatory and social processes, such as financial reporting, accounting, and those that manage environmental, safety and health, employment, and community issues.

Firms invest in learning and growth to improve business process performance, which in turn affects customer and financial performance objectives. Process performance can be measured generally in terms of cost, time, quality, and throughput. Process cost directly

[4]R.S. Kaplan and D. Norton, *Strategy Maps: Converting Intangible Assets into Tangible Outcomes.* (Boston: Harvard Business School Press, 2004).

affects financial productivity measures as shown in Figure 13.2. Time measures, such as cycle time and on-time delivery, directly affect customer service. Process quality affects product quality and customer service and thus drives customer satisfaction and retention. Throughput describes the quantity of products and services that the process can deliver. Financial perspective productivity measures, such as return on assets or return on sales, relate costs to throughput. In general, companies seek to lower process costs, lower cycle times, improve process quality, and increase process throughput to deliver their value proposition to their customers and achieve financial objectives.

Customer Perspective

Within the **customer perspective,** customer satisfaction is considered a leading indicator of firm performance. By operating its business processes, the firm creates a **value proposition** that differentiates it from its competition. The value proposition includes attributes of the firm's products, such as price, quality, and selection, as well as attributes of its relationship with its customers, such as the level of service and efforts to build long-term relationships, and its brand image (see Figure 13.2). When the firm's value proposition meets or exceeds customers' requirements, customer satisfaction results in customer retention and new customer acquisition, which drives sales growth.

Financial Perspective

The final measure is the **financial perspective.** Accounting-based performance measures are considered lagging indicators of firm performance. They confirm the success of the firm's investments in learning and growth, process performance, and ability to deliver value to customers. Balanced Scorecard financial objectives usually relate to firm productivity and long-term growth, both of which drive shareholder value.

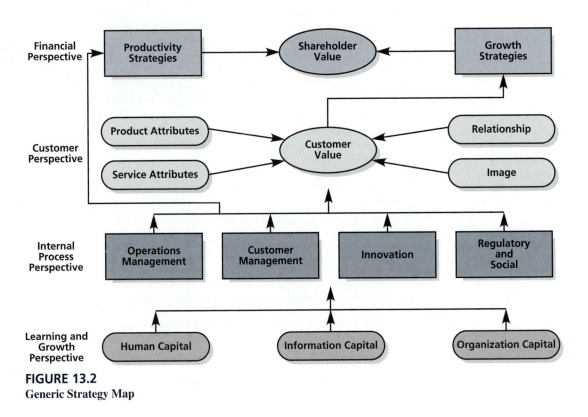

FIGURE 13.2
Generic Strategy Map

Perspective	Performance Objectives	Critical Success Factors	Key Performance Indicators
Financial	How does the firm's performance drive shareholder value?	Demonstrate productivity and growth necessary to create shareholder value.	Return on assets/equity/sales, earnings per share growth rate, sales growth rate, market value added
Customer	How does the firm deliver value to its customers to create long-term growth?	Create customer value necessary to drive revenue growth.	Market share, new customer acquisition rate, repeat purchase rate, satisfaction
Process	How do the firm's processes deliver value to customers while operating efficiently?	Conduct business processes to create customer value and achieve profitable growth.	Process cost, quality, timeliness, and outputs
Learning and growth	How do investments in the employee, organizational, and information systems capabilities support continuous improvement of the firm's business processes and customer relationships?	Invest in human capital, organizational capital, and information capital to improve processes and deliver strategic objectives.	Assessments of employee knowledge, skills, and values; employee change readiness and strategic awareness surveys; readiness ratings of software applications; levels of spending

TABLE 13.1
Balanced Scorecard Perspectives, Objectives, Sample Critical Success Factors, and Key Performance Indicators

LO 13-2
Explain the purpose of strategy maps.

One important feature of strategy maps is the identification of expected cause and effect links among perspectives.

FRAMEWORK INTEGRATING STRATEGY, OPERATIONS, AND IT INVESTMENT

The Balanced Scorecard provides a useful integrating framework to examine a company's strategy/operations management system as well as the potential contributions of IT to company success. A Balanced Scorecard strategy map illustrates the various components of a company's strategy across the four perspectives described in the preceding section.

A **strategy map** is a one-page representation of the firm's strategic priorities and the cause-and-effect linkages among those strategic priorities.[5] It illustrates the firm's strategic objectives (also called critical success factors as shown in Table 13.1) for each perspective as well as the cause-and-effect links among perspectives. A strategy map allows firms to assess and prioritize gaps between their current and desired performance levels.

LO 13-3
Describe different types of IT and why IT initiatives can be difficult to evaluate.

ROLE OF AIS/IT IN A BALANCED SCORECARD FRAMEWORK

A Balanced Scorecard framework allows companies to assess the value of IT investments in terms of contribution to strategic objectives, regardless of whether they employ a Balanced Scorecard performance management system. A Balanced Scorecard framework recognizes the difference between investments in tangible information technology and the capabilities provided by that technology. **Information capital** is an intangible asset that reflects the readiness of the company's technology to support strategic internal processes. In other words, information capital includes:

- Computing hardware, such as individual computers.
- Infrastructure, such as communications networks.
- Applications, such as accounting and decision support software.
- Employees' abilities to use the technology effectively.

To understand the value of IT in a Balanced Scorecard framework and the importance of portfolios of IT investments rather than individual investments, it is helpful to consider different ways to characterize the nature of IT. The following classifications (see Table 13.2)

[5]R.S. Kaplan and D. Norton, *Strategy Maps: Converting Intangible Assets into Tangible Outcomes.* (Boston: Harvard Business School Press, 2004).

TABLE 13.2
Three Categories of Information Technologies

IT Category	Description	Characteristics
Function IT	Assists execution with discrete tasks.	Does not require complements but impact can increase with users' skill.
Network IT	Facilitates interactions.	Does not require complements but impact increases with users' skill and extent of teamwork.
Enterprise IT	Specifies the nature of business processes and requires interactions.	Requires complements and impact often depends on users' skills, teamwork, changes to the way work is performed, and changes in the way decisions are made.

characterize the nature of information technologies and can indicate which initiatives could be harder to implement and evaluate.[6]

1. **Function IT (FIT)**—those that perform a single function, such as enhancing worker productivity for stand-alone tasks. Examples of FIT include word-processing and spreadsheet applications and computer-aided design applications. Function information technologies can improve the productivity of skilled workers, but they can be used without affecting the remainder of the organization.
2. **Network IT (NIT)**—those that allow people to communicate with one another. Examples of NIT include e-mail, instant messaging, network technologies, and blog applications. Network information technologies allow collaboration, foster teamwork, and improve information exchange within the organization, but they do little to change the way that work is performed or decisions are made.
3. **Enterprise IT (EIT)**—those that restructure interactions within the organization as well as with external partners. Examples of EIT include customer relationship management (CRM) and supply chain management (SCM) applications. Enterprise information technologies often change the way business processes are performed as well as the way decisions are made.

Compared to function and network IT, enterprise IT provides more capabilities but requires more complementary resources to achieve its potential benefits. Enterprise IT can provide the following organizational capabilities.

- Transaction automation—the EIT can automate transaction processing, replacing personnel while ensuring that each transaction is performed in a uniform and controlled manner. This allows—and forces—standardized work flow and applications of business rules.
- Process management automation—the EIT can automate administrative processes, incorporating business rules and decision heuristics and reducing the need for administrative specialists.
- Process integration—the EIT can integrate processes previously managed separately, reducing the need for separate systems and separate administration.
- Customer service—the EIT can provide general and customized service to both internal and external clients, thereby reducing the need for customer service agents.
- Performance monitoring and decision support—the EIT can record various process performance indicators and more timely summarize information on **key performance indicators** for management use.

After enterprise IT is implemented, its performance becomes embedded in one or more organizational processes, making it difficult for firms to evaluate the benefit of the IT investment separately from the performance of the process. However, the performance of business processes usually depends on a variety of factors. For example, when an EIT

[6] A. McAfee, "Mastering the Three Worlds of Information Technology," *Harvard Business Review*, November 2006, pp. 141–149.

improves decision support, the impact on business value depends on the decisions, and it can take 3 to 5 years for managers to learn how to use better and timelier information.

IT systems provide relative few business benefits on their own. The value of IT can depend on the existence of complementary organizational capabilities, such as skilled workers, teamwork, the way that work is performed, and the authority to make decisions. Furthermore, the level of these complementary resources can change over time after an IT system is implemented.

Progress *Check*

1. Describe how you think IT creates value for **Starbucks**, whose CIO is now also general manager of digital ventures. Based on what you know about the company, what category of IT best describes **Starbucks'** digital ventures?
2. From your own experience, describe examples of function IT and network IT.

LO 13-4
Define the Balanced Scorecard management process.

USING A BALANCED SCORECARD MANAGEMENT PROCESS

While the relationships among Balanced Scorecard perspectives shown in the generic strategy map (Figure 13.2) shows how information capital contributes to critical business processes, which in turn contribute to customer acquisition and retention and result in financial performance, the strategy map does not describe how companies go about implementing their strategy. According to the creators of the Balanced Scorecard, companies can plan, implement, and monitor performance using the following **Balanced Scorecard management process.**[7] The steps in the process can be thought of as continuous, with the last step feeding back to the first step as shown in Figure 13.3.

1. *Formulate*—the company examines its competitive environment and identifies ways in which it can best compete consistent with its mission, vision, and values.
2. *Translate*—the company establishes specific objectives, measures, targets, and initiatives and develops capital, initiative, and other long-term budgets to guide resource allocation and action according to its strategy.

FIGURE 13.3
**Balanced Scorecard
Management Process**

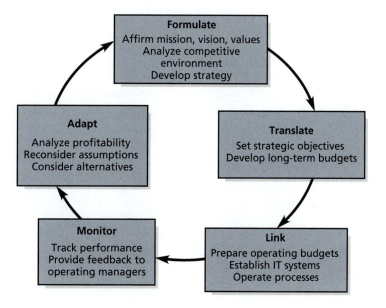

[7]R.S. Kaplan and D. Norton, *The Execution Premium* (Boston: Harvard Business Press, 2008).

3. *Link to operations*—the company prepares operating budgets, prioritizes business process improvements, and key performance indicators. At this point it establishes necessary IT systems to support strategic business processes as well as management reporting and review capabilities.
4. *Monitor*—the company monitors performance to ensure processes are meeting objectives and provides feedback to operating managers to continuous improvement.
5. *Adapt*—the company evaluates the effectiveness of its strategy, conducts profitability analytics, tests the cause-and-effect assumptions of the strategy, and identifies potential alternatives.

LO 13-5

Describe how an AIS system contributes to a Balanced Scorecard management process.

Think about how the models that you prepared in Chapters 5, 6, and 7 would support the information requirements outlined here.

ROLE OF AIS/IT IN THE BALANCED SCORECARD MANAGEMENT PROCESS

IT also has an important role in implementing and managing a Balanced Scorecard management process or similar planning, forecasting, and budgeting processes. Beginning with strategy formulation, companies rely on a variety of information technology systems and capabilities to support their strategy execution and management process. Table 13.3 provides some examples. Business intelligence and financial reporting systems provide data to support strategy development, and business analytics systems provide forecasts and analysis to support senior executives' decisions. Those broad strategic decisions are translated into objectives that guide the capital budgeting process, supported by a variety of systems. Strategic objectives then link to operations. Specific budgets are set, and the company conducts operations, supported by appropriate enterprise IT, such as ERP systems. The enterprise IT performance monitoring and decision support capabilities then assess operational performance against the strategic objectives. Operational managers adjust operations based on feedback. Finally, senior executives use information from business intelligence and financial reporting systems to reevaluate the strategy and consider alternatives.

The use of structured strategic management processes, such as the Balanced Scorecard, ties the effective use of supporting technologies, as described in Table 13.3, to successful performance. Standardized, integrated, and networked technology enhances decision making and performance management. While the capabilities of function IT systems, such as

TABLE 13.3
AIS/IT Contributions to the Balanced Scorecard Management Process

Process Step	Information Technology Capabilities
1. Formulate	Enterprise IT (business intelligence systems, financial reporting systems)
	Function IT (business analytics, executive dashboards)
	Network IT (communication and collaboration)
2. Translate	Function IT (Balanced Scorecard systems, business analytics)
	Enterprise IT (budgeting systems, performance monitoring and decision support)
	Network IT (communication and collaboration)
3. Link to operations	Enterprise IT (budgeting systems, transaction processing, process management, customer service, process integration)
4. Monitor	Integrated Enterprise IT (performance monitoring and decision support)
	Function IT (operational dashboards with key performance indicators)
	Network IT (communication and collaboration)
5. Adapt	Enterprise IT (business intelligence systems)
	Function IT (business analytics, executive dashboards)
	Network IT (communication and collaboration)

business analytics and executive dashboard applications, are important, companies need to gather data from multiple sources, linking dashboards to an integrated view of operating processes. A complete picture of the company's value chain enhances data analysis and accelerates decision making and planning.

Summary

- The Balanced Scorecard provides a framework that allows managers to measure firm performance from multiple perspectives using both financial and nonfinancial measures.
- The four Balanced Scorecard perspectives are as follows:
    - Learning and growth.
    - Business Processes.
    - Customer.
    - Financial.
- Strategy maps illustrate the components of a company's strategy across the four Balanced Scorecard perspectives.
- Investments in AIS/IT create information capital.
- Three classes that describe the nature of information technologies are as follows:
    - Function IT supports individual employees.
    - Network IT allows collaboration among employees.
    - Enterprise IT structures interactions within the organization and with external partners.
- The Balanced Scorecard management process involves the following:
    - Formulating ways to improve competitiveness.
    - Translating objectives into specific targets and initiatives to attain those targets.
    - Linking objectives and initiatives to operations.
    - Monitoring performance.
    - Adapting to continuously improve performance.

Key Words

Balanced Scorecard framework (*262*)   Provides an integrating framework that describes organizational performance relative to its strategic objectives across four perspectives: learning and growth, process, customer, and financial. Objectives for each perspective describe the strategy in a series of cause-and-effect relationships.

Balanced Scorecard management process (*267*)   The process by which companies plan, implement, and monitor performance. It consists of five steps: formulate the strategy, translate the strategy, link the strategy to operations, monitor performance, and adapt.

customer perspective (*264*)   The Balanced Scorecard perspective that describes the organization's customer-related objectives and corresponding customer measures; it views organization performance from the customers' perspective.

enterprise IT (EIT) (*266*)   A type of information technology that restructures interactions within an organization and with external partners, such as customer relationship management systems.

financial perspective (*264*)   The Balanced Scorecard perspective that describes the organization's financial objectives and corresponding financial measures of performance; it views organizational performance from the shareholders' perspective.

function IT (FIT) (*266*)   A type of information technology that performs/supports a single function, such as spreadsheet applications.

information capital (*265*)   An intangible asset that reflects the readiness of the company's technology to support strategic internal processes. It includes computing hardware, infrastructure, applications, and employees' abilities to use technology effectively.

key performance indicator (266) Those measures that the organization feels best indicates the performance of a particular activity.

learning and growth perspective (263) The Balanced Scorecard perspective that describes the organization's objectives and corresponding measures related to improvements in tangible and intangible infrastructure, such as human, information, and organizational capital.

network IT (NIT) (266) A type of information technology that allows people to communicate with one another, such as e-mail and instant messaging.

process perspective (263) The Balanced Scorecard perspective that describes the organization's internal, process-related, objectives and corresponding measures; it views organizational performance from an internal perspective.

strategy map (265) A one-page representation of the firm's strategic priorities and the cause-and-effect linkages among those strategic priorities.

value proposition (264) Represents the product and service characteristics, such as price, quality, selection, and brand image, that the firm attempts to deliver to customers to meet or exceed its customers' expectations and thereby result in customer retention and new customer acquisition.

Answers to Progress *Checks*

1. At the least, IT creates value by supporting operations management processes, including supply chain management. It also creates value in the regulatory and social process by supporting internal and external financial reporting and compliance with myriad local laws, regulations, and tax requirements. **Starbucks'** digital ventures are most likely an example of network IT because they will support content delivery.

2. The answers can vary, but function IT includes individual tax preparation software and other personal applications. Network IT includes e-mail, local wireless networks, and perhaps social media.

Multiple Choice Questions

1. Which of the following is not a Balanced Scorecard perspective?
   a. Learning and growth
   b. Customer
   c. Business process
   d. Financial
   e. All of the above are Balanced Scorecard perspectives.

2. Which of the following is not a type of business process in the Balanced Scorecard framework?
   a. Operations management
   b. Customer management
   c. Innovation
   d. Regulatory and social
   e. All of the above are types of business processes.

3. Which of the following describes the purpose of a strategy map?
   a. A graphical description of expected cause-and-effect linkages among Balanced Scorecard perspectives
   b. A list of the company's mission, vision, and values

c. A representation of the company's strategic priorities

d. Both a and b

e. Both a and c

4. Which of the following does not describe a step in the Balanced Scorecard management process?

a. Formulate the strategy

b. Translate the strategy into strategic objectives

c. Link objectives to operations

d. Monitor performance and provide feedback

e. All of the above describe steps in the Balanced Scorecard management process.

5. Which of the following do not describe characteristics of enterprise IT?

a. Enhance individual worker productivity

b. Automate transaction processing

c. Integrate processes

d. Provide general customer service

e. Monitor performance and support decision making

6. Which of the following would be an example of network IT?

a. Spreadsheets

b. E-mail

c. ERP systems

d. CRM systems

e. None of the above

7. Which of the following is an example of function IT?

a. Spreadsheets

b. E-mail

c. ERP systems

d. CRM systems

e. None of the above

8. Which of the following is not a role of IT in the Balanced Scorecard management process?

a. Strategy development support

b. Long-term budget forecasting

c. Transaction processing

d. Reporting

e. All are roles of IT in the Balanced Scorecard management process.

Discussion Questions

1. Consider a company that competes on price, such as **Walmart**, in comparison to a company that competes on other factors, such as **Starbucks**. Describe how their Balanced Scorecard objectives and the corresponding measures would differ across the four perspectives.

2. One criticism of the Balanced Scorecard is that it can lead to information overload by measuring too many performance indicators. Do you agree with this criticism? Why or why not?

3. If a company does not want to implement a formal Balanced Scorecard performance management system, is it still beneficial for the company to develop a strategy map? Why or why not?

4. Some companies create a Balanced Scorecard by taking some current objectives and key performance indicators (KPI) and assigning them to the four Balanced Scorecard perspectives. Describe the advantages and disadvantages of that approach.

5. Does the Balanced Scorecard framework provide a performance measurement system or a performance management system? Why?

6. A biotech company is considering developing an IT system that will track the progress of its drug compounds through the **Food and Drug Administration (FDA)** approval process. Describe, as specifically as possible, how that IT initiative might affect performance across all four Balanced Scorecard perspectives.

7. A company is developing KPI for the information capital aspect of its learning and growth. It is considering measuring the amount spent on information technology hardware and software as its measure. What advice would you give them about that choice?

8. Outline a Balanced Scorecard for your business school. How would using your Balanced Scorecard system affect the management of the school?

9. Describe likely differences in a Balanced Scorecard between a for-profit company and a not-for-profit (or governmental) organization. Which perspective is likely to be the most different?

10. The CEO of a midsized company is considering purchasing an ERP system but may not have fully considered the other changes that the company needs to make to achieve full value from the system. Using a Balanced Scorecard framework, create a strategy map that describes how the ERP system could benefit company performance with the right set of complementary changes.

Problems

1. Select a prominent public company, such as **Apple**, **Google**, or **Microsoft**. Obtain recent annual reports and news articles about the company. Using that information, develop a strategy map that describes the company's performance. Start by defining its value proposition, and then identifying key business processes that deliver that value proposition.

2. Use the company that you selected for Problem 1. Identify examples of its learning and growth efforts and explain how those might affect its business process performance.

3. Select a prominent company that experienced problems during the recent (2008–2010) economic downturn, such as **Bank of America**, **Goldman Sachs**, or **AIG**. Use recent annual reports and news articles to develop a strategy map that describes the elements that caused the company's financial problems.

4. Using the following objectives, create a strategy map that places them at the proper perspective and links them together. For each objective, develop two possible measures.

   a. Manage the product portfolio for superior innovation.

   b. Acquire new customers.

   c. Improve fixed asset utilization.

   d. Lower cost of serving customers.

   e. Grow revenue.

   f. Create a climate of knowledge sharing.

   g. Implement an IT infrastructure necessary to support growth.

   h. Improve return on assets.

   i. Increase market share.

   j. Achieve just-in-time supplier capability.

5. A company has elected to pursue the initiatives listed in part a. For each initiative, describe which Balanced Scorecard perspectives the initiative will address and, specifically, which of the performance measures in part b it will affect.

   a. Initiatives

   Purchase new, more efficient, production equipment.

   Train employees.

   Renovate older retail stores.

Implement a business intelligence/business analytics system.

Create new advertising campaign.

b. Performance measures

Sales growth percentage.

Percent of repeat customers.

Employee turnover.

Percent of defective products.

Number of new customers.

Number of product warranty claims.

Employee satisfaction.

Answers to Multiple Choice Questions

1.	e	5.	a
2.	e	6.	b
3.	d	7.	a
4.	e	8.	e

Evaluating AIS Investments

A look at this chapter

In this chapter, we describe the process by which firms economically justify IT initiatives. Accounting information systems and information technology initiatives in general often involve substantial costs. As users, managers, designers, and evaluators of the firm's IT systems, accountants are important members of the team that will develop the business case for AIS initiatives. Additionally, as users, managers, and evaluators, they can also be asked to review business cases for IT initiatives in general.

A look back

Chapter 13 described the Balanced Scorecard framework and explained how information technology delivers value by supporting a company's strategic objectives. It also outlined a Balanced Scorecard management process whereby companies plan, implement, monitor, and adjust strategic objectives and showed AIS/IT roles in that context.

A look ahead

Chapter 15 highlights project management considerations. It also describes constraints to successful AIS project implementations and tools that are used to overcome them. Additionally, it discusses a model that indicates whether a new system will actually be useful to the intended AIS users.

Imagine driving up to the drive-through window at **Starbucks** and seeing a **Starbucks** senior executive, wearing a standard-issue green apron, handing you your beverage. If you visited the Mercer Island, Washington, store last year, it was not your imagination. **Starbucks'** new CIO and General Manager of Digital Ventures, Stephen Gillette, worked at the store for a week to better understand customer-facing processes. One of Gillette's first tasks was to align **Starbucks'** IT activities with its customer experience strategies, and a week on the front lines gave him a new perspective on this task.

After years of expansion, **Starbucks** faced a harsh economic climate in 2008. It was forced to close about 10 percent of its almost 7,000 U.S. stores and lay off 12,000 employees. Its stock dropped from more than $38 per share in 2006 to a low of under $8 per share in late 2008.

At their biennial Analyst Conference in December 2008 and the subsequent annual shareholders meeting in early

2009, **Starbucks** executives outlined plans to reduce operating costs by $400 million in fiscal 2009, improve operating efficiencies at remaining stores, and deliver value to its customers. **Starbucks** planned to target technology investments to achieve those goals by (1) leveraging the core enterprise ERP and SCM systems to deliver better analytics and (2) using innovation to enhance its customers' experience. The goal of **Starbucks'** new line of business—digital ventures, led by Gillette—is to expand **Starbucks'** presence in the digital space to create new revenue streams for the company. This chapter focuses on how firms evaluate and justify major information technology initiatives, such as those necessary for **Starbucks** to expand its presence in digital space.

Chapter Outline

Large IT Projects Require Economic Justification

The Business Case for IT Initiatives

Assessing Business Requirements for IT Initiatives

Estimating Benefits

Estimating Costs

Acquisition Costs

Operating Costs

Assessing Risks

Developing the Value Proposition

Test the Sensitivity of Estimates to Changes in Assumptions

Prepare the Value Proposition

Learning Objectives

After reading this chapter, you should be able to:

14-1 Articulate similarities and differences between major IT initiatives and other capital investments.

14-2 Explain the major steps in the economic justification of an IT initiative.

14-3 Explain potential benefits of IT initiatives and how to evaluate them.

14-4 Assess potential costs of IT initiatives and how to evaluate them.

14-5 Describe potential risks of IT initiatives and corresponding risk-mitigation techniques.

14-6 Apply capital budgeting techniques to assess the value of an IT initiative.

LO 14-1
Articulate similarities
and differences
between major IT
initiatives and other
capital investments.

LARGE IT PROJECTS REQUIRE ECONOMIC JUSTIFICATION

IT projects involve substantial costs and offer important **benefits** to organizations. According to the U.S. Census Bureau, businesses in the United States spent more than $250 billion on technology in 2007, including $170 billion in capital investments. Additionally, most investments that are aimed at sustaining, growing, or transforming the business include a central IT component. When managed well, these investments offer organizations significant opportunities to create value. However, **Gartner Inc.**, a prominent consulting firm, estimates that 20 percent of all IT spending is wasted.[1]

Most organizations have developed specific techniques for evaluating IT projects for several reasons:

1. IT projects often require large amounts of capital, and for most firms, capital resources are limited.
2. Selecting one investment often means foregoing other investments.
3. IT projects often involve changes in business processes that will affect substantial portions of the organization.

Capital budgeting techniques provide a systematic approach to evaluating investments in capital assets. Yet, many organizations find it difficult to evaluate IT projects using traditional capital budgeting techniques. To understand why IT projects can be difficult to evaluate, managers need to consider the different characteristics of IT.

LO 14-2
Explain the major
steps in the economic
justification of an
IT initiative.

THE BUSINESS CASE FOR IT INITIATIVES

"A goal without a plan is just a wish."
—Antoine de Saint Exupéry, French writer and aviator

Good governance requires that all significant investments be justified. Therefore, information technology planning requires thorough consideration of alternative approaches and justification of the value of the selected alternative. According to the International Federation of Accountants, a global organization committed to the development of the accounting profession, organizations should create a **business case** for an IT investment. That business case should answer the following questions:[2]

1. Why are we doing this project?
2. How does it address key business issues?
3. How much will it cost, and how long will it take?
4. What is the return on investment and the payback period?
5. What are the risks of doing the project?
6. What are the risks of not doing the project?
7. What are the alternatives?
8. How will success be measured?

As users, managers, designers, and evaluators of the firm's IT systems, accountants are important members of the team that will develop business cases for AIS initiatives. Additionally, as users, managers, and evaluators, they can also be asked to review business cases for IT initiatives in general.

So, how do firms create a business case to justify their IT initiatives? Figure 14.1 describes this **economic justification process**.[3] First the project team assesses the

---

[1] The Gartner Group. *The Elusive Business Value of IT,* 2002.
[2] International Federation of Accountants *Managing Information Technology; Planning for Business Impact,* Information Technology Committee Guideline 2 (December 1999).
[3] See Microsoft Corporation's *Rapid Economic Justification, Enterprise Edition, 2007,* for additional information.

Developing an economic justification.

business requirements for the IT initiative. Next, the team identifies potential solutions that will address those business problems. Then, for each alternative solution, the team evaluates potential benefits, costs, and risks. Finally, that information is combined to form the estimated value propositions for the alternatives and the team formalizes their business case recommendations. The following sections describe each step in this process.

FIGURE 14.1
Economic Justification Process

Note: The gateway symbol with the plus sign indicates that the process takes all three paths.

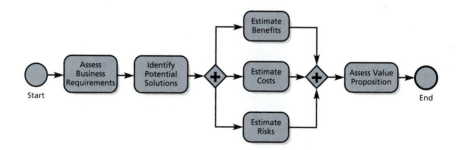

Assessing Business Requirements for IT Initiatives

To align with business requirements, IT initiatives should reduce one or more gaps between the firm's current and desired performance levels as indicated by the firm's strategy map. Therefore, the project team must explicitly link the proposed technology with performance improvements for one or more selected critical success factors. IT alone is usually not sufficient to achieve important changes, so the project team must also consider other enabling changes that, in conjunction with the technology, will accomplish substantial business change as shown in Figure 14.2.

Examples of complementary changes include providing training, redefining job descriptions, reconfiguring tasks, or offering incentives. For each critical success factor to be addressed by the IT initiative, the project team identifies (1) the specific business

FIGURE 14.2
Benefit Dependency

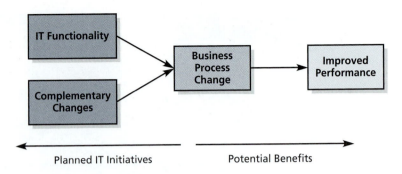

Planned IT Initiatives   Potential Benefits

processes that affect that critical success factor, (2) problems with those business processes, (3) opportunities to address those problems, and (4) the specific technology that would enable changes.

Progress *Check*

1. Think back to the discussion of the Balanced Scorecard framework in Chapter 13. Like other firms, **Starbucks'** value proposition includes attributes of its products, such as price, quality, and selection; attributes of its relationship with its customers, such as the level of service and efforts to build long-term relationships; and its brand image. Which of those attributes are most important to **Starbucks** customers' satisfaction? How does that relate to **Starbucks'** financial problems in 2008?
2. What elements of the value proposition are **Starbucks'** digital ventures likely designed to improve? Why?

LO 14-3
Explain potential benefits of IT initiatives and how to evaluate them.

ESTIMATING BENEFITS

Once the opportunities for improvement are identified, the project team next assesses the potential benefits of each alternative. A benefit is a positive consequence—such as a reduction in the performance gaps for a critical success factor—of an IT investment. Benefits should be measurable in financial terms:

Ultimately, benefits must be measured in terms of the financial impact of the project.

1. Revenue enhancement—creating new sales opportunities, such as using e-commerce capabilities to expand the firm's market.
2. Revenue protection—protecting existing revenue streams. For example, a data encryption system protects the loss of customer data and encourages customers to share data.
3. Cost savings—opportunities to modify business processes to reduce low value-added or manually intensive activities, to improve capabilities to manage assets to increase efficiencies, or to reduce errors. For example, improving inventory management information allows reduced inventory investments.
4. Cost avoidance—opportunities to modify business processes to avoid cost increases in the future, such as installing current software that will accommodate changes to international financial reporting standards when required.

Note that the benefits should be measured in comparison to the revenues and costs that will occur if the IT initiative is not implemented. These revenues and costs can be different than current levels of revenues and costs. Often, the project team must estimate the amount and timing of future benefits for a number of reasonable alternative situations without complete information. There are several possible approaches that can be used to quantify expected benefits:

- Simulation—using simulation software to test the impact of a change in a key performance indicator on the firm's financial statements under a variety of assumptions to establish the likely benefit.
- Expert opinion—consulting with experts to establish the likely benefit or the probability of achieving a particular level of benefit.
- Real option theory—using sophisticated financial techniques that compare the probability of achieving benefits with an investment against the benefits of not making that investment.
- External benchmarks—using the actual experience of other firms that made similar investments in similar contexts to estimate the likely benefit.

These approaches start with an assessment of the effectiveness of current performance based on the current outputs and inputs for the process or processes under consideration as shown in Figure 14.3. Then, they consider the potential impact of the change and forecast the long-term benefit.

FIGURE 14.3
Forecasting Effects of Change

LO 14-4
Explain potential costs of IT initiatives and how to evaluate them.

ESTIMATING COSTS

Relevant costs include the incremental expense of developing, implementing, and operating the proposed IT initiative over its life cycle. The total **acquisition cost** includes all direct and indirect costs required to acquire and deploy the technology. The total **operation cost** includes all direct and indirect costs of operating, maintaining, and administering the technology over its expected life. Technology consulting firms, such as Gartner Inc. and International Data Corporation, publish widely used total cost of ownership figures for various technologies, and Gartner has developed an extensive chart of accounts to classify IT initiative costs.[4]

Acquisition Costs
Direct Costs

The direct acquisition costs include all costs necessary to acquire and implement the IT initiative:

Hardware

Software

Networking and communications

Development

Project management

Consulting

Training

---

[4]Gartner Inc., *Distributed Computing Chart of Accounts* (2003), available at www.gartner.com/4_decision_tools/modeling_tools/costcat.pdf.

Indirect Costs

The indirect acquisition costs include costs not directly related to the acquisition and implementation, such as business disruption and employee downtime.

Operating Costs

Direct Costs

The direct operating costs include all costs necessary to operate, maintain, and administer the technology:

- Hardware replacements
- Software upgrades
- Maintenance contracts
- Help desk support
- Ongoing training
- Administration
- Decommissioning

Indirect Costs

The indirect operating costs include costs of user downtime and lost productivity, such as time spent on self-training, peer support, and end user data management.

The project team must also estimate the amount and timing of the direct and indirect costs of acquisition and operation of IT initiatives without complete information. The various approaches to quantifying benefits, outlined earlier, also apply to estimating costs. Additionally, there are several commercial software products designed to help firms estimate total cost of ownership.

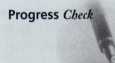

Progress *Check*   3. Do you own a personal computer, a cell phone, an iPod, or an iPad? What is your total cost of ownership for each of those? Do you have any indirect costs of owning those products?

LO 14-5
Describe potential risks of IT initiatives and risk-mitigation techniques.

ASSESSING RISKS

Each alternative IT initiative carries risks of failing to achieve the prospective benefits and exceeding the estimated costs. To help identify risks, it is usually helpful to consider the following categories of risks. One classification scheme is as follows:[5]

- **Alignment risk**—the solution is not aligned with the strategy of the firm.
- **Solution risk**—the solution will not generate projected benefits.
- **Financial risk**—the solution will not deliver expected financial performance.
- **Project risk**—the project will not be completed on time within budget.
- **Change risk**—the firm or part of the firm will not be able to change.
- **Technological risk**—the technology will not deliver expected benefits.

After identifying relevant risks, the project team should assess the financial impact on the firm if the risk scenario occurs, the probability that the risk scenario will occur, and costs of mitigating the risk. Some of the risk assessment can be done during the

[5]Risk categories taken from Microsoft Corporation, *Rapid Economic Justification, Enterprise Edition, 2007.*

Systems implementation problems kept Hershey's from accepting Halloween orders.

quantification of costs and benefits, and the estimated costs and benefits can be adjusted for risk. Risk-mitigation techniques include considering portfolios of IT initiatives, rather than single initiatives, and considering outsourcing where contracts can protect against certain risks. Table 14.1 describes examples of risk-mitigation techniques for each risk category.

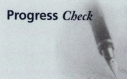

Progress *Check*

4. A few years ago, **Hershey's Corp.**, a leading manufacturer of chocolates, confectionaries, and beverages, implemented SAP's R/3 enterprise resource planning software using a big bang approach, where all the software was implemented at once. Because of problems with the implementation during a busy period, **Hershey's** could not take orders or deliver products for Halloween. By the time the problems were corrected, they cost **Hershey's** more than $100 million. What risks were involved? Was this the fault of the software? Do you think **Hershey's** planning allowed for this contingency when it justified the IT initiative?

TABLE 14.1
Examples of Risk-Mitigation Techniques

IT Initiative Risks	Risk-Mitigation Examples
Alignment risk	Use the Balanced Scorecard framework (Chapter 13) to assess the link to strategy.
Solution risk	Use sensitivity analysis to consider likely alternative benefit levels.
Financial risk	Interview other users of similar IT; follow a structured Balanced Scorecard management process (Chapter 13).
Project risk	Ensure active top management support for the project.
Change risk	Conduct training, and create employee incentives for successful use of the new IT.
Technological risk	Require hardware and software vendors to demonstrate that their systems can meet requirements.

LO 14-6

Use capital budgeting techniques to assess the value proposition for an IT initiative.

The business case establishes the value proposition for the preferred alternative or alternatives.

DEVELOPING THE VALUE PROPOSITION

The last step in the IT economic justification process is to combine the information developed in the previous steps to describe the **value proposition** for the preferred alternative. This value proposition is unrelated to the term used in Chapter 13. The firm's senior executives need to understand the financial implications of the IT initiative so they can decide whether to allocate resources to it. The project team will employ capital budgeting techniques using the expected cash flows for each alternative:

1. Determine the relevant time frame for costs and benefits.
2. Select appropriate discount rates to apply.
3. Prepare capital budgeting financial metrics.
4. Assess the sensitivity of results to the assumptions.

The relevant time frame for most IT initiatives is 3 years or less because technology changes rapidly. The appropriate discount rates usually run from 5 to 15 percent, depending on the firm's cost of capital and the riskiness of the particular project. Financial metrics commonly used include the following and are summarized in Table 14.2:

- **Payback period** and **breakeven analysis**—both compare the costs with benefits of an IT project. The breakeven point is where the total value of benefits equals that of total costs. The payback is the number of periods needed to recover the project's initial investment.

$$\text{Payback period} = \text{Initial investment/Increased cash flow per period}$$

Assume an IT project is expected to cost $20,000 up front, and it will provide net benefits that average $16,000 per year for the next 3 years.

$$\text{Payback period} = \$20,000/\$16,000 = 1.25 \text{ years}$$

- **Net present value (NPV)**—sum of the present value present value of all cash inflows minus the sum of the present value of all cash outflows. Each cash outflow/inflow is discounted to its present value.

$$\text{Present value} = CF_t/(1 + r)^t$$

where:
CF = cash flow for period t
r = discount rate (typically the firm's weighted average cost of capital)

Again, assume an IT project that is expected to cost $20,000 up front and return $16,000 per year for 3 years. Assume a discount rate of 10 percent. Then, the NPV is calculated as follows.

Year 0	Present value $= -\$20,000/(1.10^0)$	$-\$20,000$
Year 1	Present value $= \$16,000/(1.10^1)$	$\$14,545$
Year 2	Present value $= \$16,000/(1.10^2)$	$\$13,223$
Year 3	Present value $= \$16,000/(1.10^3)$	$\$12,021$
NPV	Sum of present values	$\$19,790$

- **Internal rate of return (IRR)**—the discount rate that makes the project's net present value equal to zero. There is no solvable formula for internal rate of return. Instead, financial calculators and spreadsheet software, such as Microsoft Excel, use an iterative technique for calculating IRR. Starting with guess, they cycle through the calculations

Financial Metric	Strength	Weakness
Payback period	Easy to calculate and understand. Widely used.	Ignores the time value of money as well as both costs and benefits occurring after the payback period.
Accounting rate of return	Relates estimates to standard accounting ratios using accrual accounting. Shows impact on operating income.	Ignores the time value of money. Assumes cash flows in all periods are similar.
Net present value	Considers the time value of money. Incorporates cash flows over the life of the IT initiative. Compares the dollar value of the benefits from an IT initiative to the initial investment.	Larger projects tend to have larger net present values. Does not show rate of return on investment. Sensitive to discount rate applied.
Internal rate of return	Considers the time value of money. Incorporates cash flows over the life of the IT initiative. Computes the unique rate of return for the initiative. Not sensitive to a selected discount rate.	Fails to consider the size of the project. Sensitive to timing of the cash flows.

TABLE 14.2
Financial Metric Strengths and Weaknesses

until the result is accurate. The IRR and NPV functions are related in that if you use the IRR as the discount rate (r) in calculating NPV, your NPV is zero.[6]

- **Accounting rate of return (ARR)**—the average annual income from the IT initiative divided by the initial investment cost.

ARR = (Average annual income from IT initiative)/(Total IT initiative investment cost)

Again, using the same assumed initial outlay and subsequent net cash flows described earlier, the accounting rate of return would be calculated as follows.

$$ARR = \$16,000/\$20,000 = 80\%$$

Table 14.3 shows an example of the financial metrics applied to an IT initiative with an implementation cost of $20,000 and positive net cash flow for the subsequent 3 years.

TABLE 14.3
Example Comparing Payback, NPV, and IRR

Discount Rate	10%					
Project 1	**Year 0**	**Year 1**	**Year 2**	**Year 3**	**Total**	**Average**
Benefits		$20,000	$20,000	$30,000	$70,000	$23,333
Costs	$20,000	$7,500	$7,500	$7,500	$42,500	$10,625
Cash flow	−$20,000	$12,500	$12,500	$22,500	$27,500	$15,833
Payback	1.26					
NPV	$16,908					
IRR	52%					
Project 2	**Year 0**	**Year 1**	**Year 2**	**Year 3**	**Total**	**Average**
Benefits		$30,000	$20,000	$20,000	$70,000	$23,333
Costs	$20,000	$7,500	$7,500	$7,500	$42,500	$10,625
Cash flow	−$20,000	$22,500	$12,500	$12,500	$27,500	$15,833
Payback	1.26					
NPV	$18,342					
IRR	71%					

Note that total cash flow is equal, but NPV and IRR are not, due to time value of money.

[6]Note that Excel assumes that the cash flows occur at the end of the year, so the initial outlay would be assumed to be for year 1. Try this by entering the data and using the Excel NPV and IRR functions.

The two projects have equal payback periods, but project 1 has a higher net present value (NPV), and project 2 has a higher internal rate of return (IRR). This illustrates how risks resulting in increased costs and reduced benefits can affect the value of the IT initiative, especially when considering the time value of money.

Test the Sensitivity of Estimates to Changes in Assumptions

Before prioritizing the alternative IT initiatives based on the financial metrics, the project team should test the impact of changes in assumptions on the various financial metrics. These tests can be performed using spreadsheet or simulation software. The assumptions can also be reviewed by subject matter experts. Because each financial metric has both strengths and weaknesses, IT initiatives should be evaluated using several metrics (see Figure 14.4).

FIGURE 14.4
Project Value

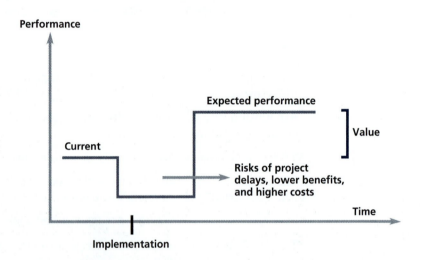

Prepare the Value Proposition

The final step is to assemble the analysis for each alternative IT initiative and recommend the preferred alternatives. The value proposition must address the business case questions listed earlier in the "Business Case for IT Initiatives" section, especially focusing on these five areas:

1. The change and technology proposed.
2. The anticipated benefits (related to the firm's critical success factors).
3. The group(s) within the firm that will benefit.
4. The timing of the benefits.
5. The likelihood of achieving those benefits as planned.

Summary

- Large projects require economic justification comparing the costs against the benefits.
- One step in the economic justification process is the preparation of the business case that identifies the purpose of the project, costs, expected return on investment, risks of doing the project, risks of not doing the project, alternatives considered, and how success will be measured.

- The economic justification process occurs in a series of steps:
  - Assess business requirements.
  - Identify potential solutions.
  - Estimates costs, benefits, and risks.
  - Assess the overall value proposition for each potential solution.
- IT initiatives must also include complementary changes in business processes to improve performance.
- Estimated benefits involve revenue enhancement, revenue protection, cost savings, and cost avoidance.
- Estimated costs involve direct and indirect acquisition and operating costs over the life cycle of the project.
- Relevant risks can be categorized as alignment, solution, financial, project, change, and technological risks.
- The business case should identify ways to mitigate relevant risks.
- The value proposition depends on capital budgeting financial metrics that consider the time value of money and the anticipated timing of the costs and benefits

Key Words

accounting rate of return (ARR) (283)   The average annual income from the IT initiative divided by the initial investment cost.

acquisition costs (279)   All direct and indirect costs necessary to acquire and implement the IT initiative.

alignment risk (280)   The risk that an IT initiative is not aligned with the strategy of the organization.

benefits (276)   The positive consequences to the organization of an IT investment.

breakeven analysis (282)   Determines the breakeven point, where the total value of benefits equals that of total costs.

business case (276)   Economic justification for an IT investment or other major project.

change risk (280)   The risk that the organization will be unable to make the changes necessary to implement the IT initiative successfully.

economic justification process (276)   The process by which an organization creates a business case for an IT investment or other major project.

financial risk (280)   The risk that the IT investment will not deliver expected financial benefits.

internal rate of return (IRR) (282)   The discount rate (return) that makes a project's net present value equal to zero.

net present value (NPV) (282)   The sum of the present value of all cash inflows minus the sum of the present value of all cash outflows related to an IT investment or other capital investment.

operation cost (279)   The recurring cost necessary to operate, maintain, and administer an IT initiative.

payback period (282)   The amount of time necessary to recoup a project's initial investment.

project risk (280)   The risk that the project will not be completed on time or within budget.

relevant costs (279)   Those costs that will change as a result of an IT initiative or other major project.

solution risk (280)   The risk that the proposed solution will not generate expected benefits.

technological risk (280)   The risk that the technology will not perform as expected to deliver the planned benefits.

value proposition (282)   Summarizes the costs and benefits of a preferred alternative IT investment, describing (1) the relevant time frames that the costs will be incurred and benefits realized, (2) the corresponding discount rates to apply to future cash flows, and (3) the sensitivity of the results to assumptions.

Multiple Choice Questions

1. Which of the following is a question that companies should answer when preparing the business case for an IT investment?
   a. How much will it cost?
   b. What are the risks?
   c. What are the alternatives?
   d. How will success be measured?
   e. All of the above

2. What is the first step in the economic justification process?
   a. Identify potential solutions.
   b. Assess the value proposition.
   c. Assess business requirements.
   d. Estimate costs.
   e. All of the above.

3. Which of the following is a not an example of a complementary change necessary to allow an IT initiative to achieve its goals?
   a. Outsource the IT initiative.
   b. Retrain employees.
   c. Redefine job descriptions.
   d. Provide incentives for employees to make the change successfully.
   e. None of the above

4. Which of the following is not an example of benefits of an IT investment?
   a. Increased revenues from access to new markets
   b. Decreased costs from automating manual tasks
   c. Facilitating employee work-from-home arrangements
   d. Allowing compliance with new federal regulations
   e. Reducing the number of inventory count errors

5. Which of the following can be used to quantify benefits on an IT investment?
   a. Gathering expert opinions
   b. Benchmarking against competitor performance
   c. Comparing against the probability of future benefits if investment is foregone
   d. Conducting simulations
   e. All of the above

6. Which of the following are examples of direct costs of acquiring and implementing an IT investment?
   a. Hiring consultants to assess system requirements
   b. Personnel costs of the project team
   c. Training costs of employees who will use the system
   d. Cost of new computer hardware necessary to run the system
   e. All of the above are direct costs of acquiring and implementing an IT investment.

7. Which of the following are not examples of operating costs for an IT investment?
   a. Costs of routine hardware replacements over time
   b. Cost of contract for help desk support
   c. Costs of disposal of electronics at end of life
   d. Costs of software license renewals
   e. All of the above are examples of operating costs.

8. Which of the following is not a category of IT initiative risk?
   a. Alignment
   b. Technological
   c. Financial misstatement
   d. Solution
   e. All of the above are examples of IT initiative risk.

9. If an IT project costs $150,000 and returns net cash flows of $100,000 per year, what is the payback period?
   a. 1 year
   b. 1.5 years
   c. 2 years
   d. 2.5 years
   e. None of the above

10. If an IT project costs $150,000 and returns net cash flows of $100,000 per year, what is the accounting rate of return?
   a. 33%
   b. 50%
   c. 67%
   d. 75%
   e. None of the above

Discussion Questions

1. An important first step in the economic justification process is to assess business requirements. How would the Balanced Scorecard framework presented in Chapter 13 help companies assess their business requirements for IT?

2. Chapter 13 described three types of IT: function, network, and enterprise IT. Consider the diagram shown in Figure 14.2. Which type of IT is likely to have the greatest impact

on business performance? Which type of IT would require the most complementary changes? Why?

3. The benefits of an IT initiative should be measured in comparison to the revenues and costs that will occur if the IT initiative is not implemented. What issues would a project team face when making this comparison? How does it affect the team's assessment of risks?

4. Use Microsoft Excel to assess the NPV of an IT initiative. The initiative will require an initial investment of $250,000 and is expected to return $150,000 per year for the next 3 years. Assume a discount rate of 10 percent. What is the NPV? How does the NPV change if the discount rate is 15 percent? Describe how changes in the discount rate assumption can affect the NPV.

5. Use Microsoft Excel to assess the internal rate of return for an IT initiative. Suppose the initial investment is $70,000. The returns on investment in dollars for the following 5 years are (a) $12,000, (b) $15,000, (c) $18,000, (d) $21,000, and (e) $26,000. Use the IRR function to compute the internal rate of return after 2, 3, and 5 years. Next, assume that the loan for the initial $70,000 is at 8 percent and you are earning 15 percent on the annual returns. Use the MIRR function to calculate the internal rate of return. Is the annual rate of return higher when using the MIRR function than the IRR function? Under what circumstances would it be lower?

6. Consider two projects. Project 1 costs $272,000 and returns $60,000 per year for 8 years. Project 2 costs $380,000 and returns $70,000 per year. Project 2 is determined as less risky, so your company only requires an 8 percent minimum annual return compared to 10 percent for project 1. What is the NPV of each project? What is the absolute maximum that the company should consider investing in each project?

7. Your company has just completed a major IT initiative and is reviewing the outcome. It notes that the project took 3 months longer than expected. As part of the project, the company wanted to use some automatic bar code readers, but the rate of correct bar code reads was below the expected rate. Although managers were worried about employee acceptance of the new system, it appears that the employees have embraced it and, as a result, are making it work better than expected. Refer to Table 14.1 and identify how these results address the risk categories listed in the table.

8. Congratulations. You've won the state lottery. You have a choice of three options: (a) $12 million 5 years from now, (b) $2.25 million at the end of each year for 5 years, or (c) $10 million 3 years from now. Assume you can invest at 8 percent, which option would you prefer?

9. Moore's law essentially suggests that computing power for the same cost doubles every two years. Typical computers that cost $2,000 a few years ago are now available—with substantially greater processing power—for $500. How does this affect planning for major IT projects?

10. **Google** invested heavily in the Android operating system. Yet, it offers the software as open source. In other words, it receives no direct payment from all those cell phone companies that sell smartphones with Android operating systems. How does **Google** justify this IT initiative in economic terms?

Problems

1. SlowRider Inc. had a rudimentary business intelligence (BI) system. Analysts at SlowRider Inc. pulled data from three different ERP systems, loaded the data into Excel spreadsheets, and e-mailed those spreadsheets to the senior managers each month. However, some managers complained that they didn't understand how to get the information they needed, others complained that the data were not accurate, and still others ignored the spreadsheets. SlowRider established a project team to look at acquiring a state-of-the-art business intelligence system. After several interviews with all the managers, the project team was ready to develop the business case.

The project team estimated benefits of the new BI system as follows:

- 5 percent increase in sales through better-focused sales campaigns, which should increase gross margins by $200,000 in year 1 and $300,000 in years 2 and 3.
- 10 percent increase in inventory turnover through better purchasing, which should reduce inventory carrying costs by $100,000 in year 1 and $150,000 in years 2 and 3.

The project team estimated costs over an expected 3-year life as follows:

Cost Element	Year 0	Year 1	Year 2	Year 3
Acquisition cost (new software and implementation)	$400,000			
Operating cost (annual licenses, upgrades, support)		$50,000	$50,000	$50,000
Training	$10,000	$5,000	$5,000	$5,000
Lost productivity during implementation	$20,000			
Total	$430,000	$55,000	$55,000	$55,000

After interviewing managers at other firms that have already implemented similar BI systems, the project team then estimated that the initiative would have the following risks.

Risk Description	Probability	Mitigation Steps
Managers will not use the system, resulting in:		Top management support; incentives to use the system
Revenue growth of 3%	25%	
Inventory turnover increases 5%	25%	

a. Disregarding the risk, calculate the following for the BI investment:
   (1) The payback period
   (2) The NPV (assume 10% percent discount rate)
   (3) The IRR
   (4) The accounting rate of return

b. Recalculate the payback period, NPV, IRR, and ARR considering the risk.

c. Prepare a value proposition for the BI investment. Should SlowRider pursue the investment? What other issues should they consider?

2. The Beach Dude Inc. (BD) sells surf gear and clothing to retail stores around the country. It outsources the production of most of its items, so its warehouse is very busy receiving incoming shipments and preparing deliveries to customers. After a thorough review of its warehouse processes, the company determined that it could save substantial employee time and improve its on-time delivery rates if it adopted a warehouse management system using RFID chips and readers. RFID (radio-frequency identification) is a technology that uses radio waves to automatically identify people or objects. RFID tags are applied to packages, and then RFID readers can be used to track the location and movement of the inventory.

BD estimates that the RFID system—including fixed and mobile scanners, software, servers, installation, and integration with its existing AIS—will cost $400,000. The system has an expected useful life of 5 years and is expected to have a negligible value at that time. Training for the warehouse, IT, and accounting employees is expected to cost an additional $25,000. Additionally, the company's estimate for the cost of RFID tags is $30,000 per year based on the current $0.15 cost per tag. However, it believes there is a 50 percent probability that the cost per tag will decrease to $0.10 per tag in 2 years.

BD estimates that it will save $150,000 per year in reduced employee overtime, fewer priority shipments, reduced inventory losses, and improved inventory turnover. Assume that BD has a cost of capital of 6 percent.

   a. Calculate the following for BD's investment, assuming there is no reduction in the cost of RFID tags:

      (1) The payback period

      (2) The NPV

      (3) The IRR

      (4) The accounting rate of return

   b. Recalculate those values, assuming that the cost of RFID tags does decrease in 2 years as expected.

   c. Identify some potential risks and possible omissions in BD's planning. Provide examples of situations that would lead to the risks that you identify.

3. Refer to the **Starbucks** vignette at the beginning of this chapter. **Starbucks** has aggressively pursued digital ventures to improve the customer experience and increase the amount of customer transactions per visit. Among other things, **Starbucks** mines the data from customer loyalty cards to examine buying patterns to predict what customers will buy in the future. It is looking for an increased "wallet-share."

   a. Describe why it is difficult to evaluate **Starbucks'** digital ventures investments using traditional capital budgeting techniques.

   b. What are some other ways that **Starbucks** could evaluate the benefit of its digital ventures?

4. Sunset Graphics is considering two mutually exclusive projects. Both require an initial investment of $100,000. Assume a marginal interest rate of 10 percent and no residual value for either investment. The cash flows for the two projects are expected to be the following:

Year	Project 1	Project 2
1	$30,000	$0
2	$30,000	$20,000
3	$30,000	$20,000
4	$30,000	$50,000
5	$30,000	$75,000

   a. Compute the NPV, payback, and IRR for both projects. Which is most desirable?

   b. Assume straight-line depreciation is used for both projects; compute the accounting rate of return. What do you think of the ARR criterion?

   c. Assume a change in interest rate to 15 percent. Does that change your views on which project the company should adopt?

   d. Assume a change in interest rate to 6 percent. Does that change your views on which project the company should adopt?

   e. For investments in technology, which cash inflow projection is most likely?

5. Sunset Graphics is considering moving to a cloud-based accounting system because its current system only runs on outdated computers. The cloud-based system is very similar to the current system, so there would be no additional training required. The cloud-based system will cost $1,500 per month for the next 36 months. The company will write off its old equipment and record a corresponding loss of $2,000. It will buy five new computers to access the cloud at a total cost of $2,200.

Their alternative is to purchase a new local accounting system. If it pursues this alternative, the company will also spend $2,200 on five new computers and write off the old hardware and software. The new software will cost $40,000. Sunset Graphics uses a discount rate of 10 percent.

a. Which alternative is the best solution? Why? What factors would influence your decision?

b. Assume the local accounting system is expected to last 5 years but will require a major upgrade costing $15,000 at the end of year 3. Also assume that the cost of cloud-based system will fall to $1,200 per month for months 37–60. Neither alternative will have any residual value. Compare the two alternatives again.

Answers to Multiple Choice Questions

1.	e	6.	e
2.	c	7.	e
3.	a	8.	c
4.	c	9.	b
5.	e	10.	c

The Systems Development Life Cycle and Project Management:
Addressing the Challenges of Building AIS Systems

A look at this chapter

This chapter highlights the systems development life cycle and project management. We make the case that management needs to understand how AIS systems are developed and describe the roles of the project manager and project sponsor. We also highlight the constraints to successful AIS project implementations and the tools that are used to overcome them. Finally, we discuss a model to determine whether a new system will actually be useful to the intended AIS users.

A look back

Because accounting information systems and information technology initiatives in general often involve substantial costs, Chapter 14 discussed ways firms economically justify IT initiatives and ensure that those initiatives align with objectives of the overall business.

Starbucks certainly seems to control one corner of the retail market. But **Walmart** has to be viewed as the 10-ton gorilla in retail. **Walmart** initially relied entirely on home-grown internal systems, and its technology has helped it lead the market in many respects, including supply chain management, RFID tags, and electronic commerce. However, in 2008 **Walmart** chose SAP to help it with its accounting information system. With more than $450 billion dollars in global sales annually and more than 2,000,000 employees, the project management of a new accounting information system for **Walmart** has to be carefully and meticulously completed. Choosing the right people to serve as project manager, project sponsor, project team members is just the beginning of ensuring a successful AIS implementation.

Chapter Outline

Introduction

Description of the Systems
  Development Life Cycle

Effective Information Technology
  Planning

Projects, Project Management, and
  Project Sponsors

Challenges of IT Project
  Management

Constraining Factors of IT Projects

Scope

Cost

Time

The 15-15 Rule

Project Management Tools

Will the System Be Used, and Will It
  Be Useful?

Addressing Perceived Usefulness

Addressing Perceived Ease of Use

Learning Objectives

After reading this chapter, you should
be able to:

15-1 Describe each phase in the systems
development life cycle.

15-2 Explain the core principles of
information systems planning.

15-3 Define *project management,* and
describe the positions of those
who lead the project.

15-4 Explain why IT projects are
challenged and the tools that
are used to overcome these
challenges.

15-5 Explain why users do or do not
want to use a new information
system designed for them.

LO 15-1
Describe each phase
in the systems
development life cycle.

INTRODUCTION

We have learned about many of the processes and components of an accounting information system (AIS) thus far in this book. Another key component in understanding the accounting information system is to know how these AIS systems are developed and brought into operation. In an organization, accountants play a key user role in telling systems developers what information is needed in an accounting information system and often play an important role in implementing projects. Managing and carrying out the systems development life cycle to achieve an intended outcome is called **project management** and is the topic of this chapter.

DESCRIPTION OF THE SYSTEMS DEVELOPMENT LIFE CYCLE

To best understand the design, use, management and evaluation of an accounting information system, it is important to understand the systems development life cycle. The **systems development life cycle (SDLC)** is the process of creating or modifying information systems to meet the needs of its users. The SDLC is generally viewed as the foundation for all systems development that people use to develop such systems. The SDLC has five phases: planning, analysis, design, implementation, and maintenance.

1. The **planning phase** of the SDLC begins with a business need for a new or better information system. This phase involves summarizing the business needs with a high-level view of the intended project. A feasibility study is often used to evaluate economic, operational, and technical practicability. This includes making a business case for the system. It is also used as a basis to get buy-in and funding from upper management.
   - *Example:* Let's suppose that the **Starbucks** marketing department wants to analyze what type of pastries sell best with its various hot and cold drinks. In order to do so, it will need to change the software on its POS (point-of-sale) terminals and develop an easy system for the marketing department to run what-if analyses with its data. A feasibility analysis suggests that it is operationally and technically practical to make this change, and if this information is captured, the chief marketing officer of **Starbucks** will be much more successful when she presents her case for potential marketing promotions featuring drinks and pastries. The marketing officer expects the payoff in profits for such systems to be greater than the approximately $63,000 needed to plan, design, and implement this system.
2. The **analysis phase** of the SDLC involves a complete, detailed analysis of the systems needs of the end user. The analysis phase further refines the goals of the project into carefully specified functions and operations of the intended system. This step may involve looking at the entire system in different pieces and drawing various flowcharts and diagrams to better analyze the situation and project goals.
   - *Example:* **Starbucks** systems analysis team meets with all of the desired users of the enhanced system (including the chief marketing officer). The users want to make sure that considerable flexibility is built into the system in order to address both current and potential data analysis needs.
3. The **design phase** of the SDLC involves describing in detail the desired features of the system that it uncovered in the analysis phase. These features may be described using screen layouts, process and event diagrams (such as we learned earlier in this book), and other documentation. A **systems analyst** is responsible for both determining the information needs of the business and designing a system to meet those needs.
   - *Example:* The **Starbucks** systems designers take the requested business requirements from the analysis stage and begin to design how the new what-if **Starbucks** analysis system would look on a screen and the business rules and process diagrams needed to make such a change in the system.

4. The **implementation phase** of the SDLC involves development, testing, and implementation of the new proposed system. Development is the process of transforming the plan from the design phase into an actual, functioning system. The testing of the system involves testing for errors, bugs, and interoperability with other parts of the system. It also serves to verify that all of the business requirements from the analysis phase are met. Implementation involves placing the system into production such that users can actually use the system that has been designed for them.

   - *Example:* The **Starbucks** systems developers write the computer code and test it. Once testing is complete and the business requirements are met, the users are trained and the new software is put into actual use. At this point, the users can begin to perform what-if analyses using the new software.

5. The **maintenance phase** of the SDLC is the final phase and includes making changes, corrections, additions, and upgrades (generally smaller in scope) to ensure the system continues to meet the business requirements that have been set out for it. The maintenance phase continues indefinitely because the system must continue to evolve as the underlying business evolves.

   - *Example:* The **Starbucks** system undergoes continuous and regular maintenance to ensure that it meets the underlying business requirements. Specifically, as new products are introduced and new information is needed, the system continues to be modified and upgraded.

During the maintenance phase new, substantive changes are often needed to meet the changing, evolving needs of the firm. The systems development life cycle starts again and the planning phase begins anew in a recursive manner to assess whether a new or upgraded system needs to be developed. This recursive nature is a reason why it is called a life cycle. The recursive nature of the systems development life cycle is illustrated in Figure 15.1.

FIGURE 15.1
The Recursive Nature of the Systems Development Life Cycle

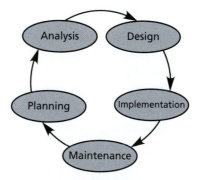

Connection with Practice

The Information Systems Audit and Control Association (ISACA) and the IT Governance Institute (ITGI) developed Control Objectives for Information and Related Technology (COBIT) to serve as a set of best practices for information technology (IT) management. COBIT provides managers, auditors, and IT users with a set of generally accepted measurements, processes, indicators, and best practices to assist them in maximizing the benefits derived through the use of information technology. COBIT's guidance corresponds to the SDLC, namely, plan and organize, acquire and implement, deliver and support, and monitor and evaluate.

LO 15-2

Explain the core principles of information systems planning.

EFFECTIVE INFORMATION TECHNOLOGY PLANNING

As the title of this chapter suggests, we want to emphasize the importance of effective IT planning. During the first phase of the SDLC, the planning phase, an information technology plan should be developed to support the overall firm strategy. The plan should provide a roadmap of the information technology required to support the business direction of a firm. This should include an outline of the required resources and the expected benefits that will be realized when the IT plan is implemented. While each information technology plan is unique to the needs and circumstances of a firm, the International Federation of Accountants suggests that these 10 core principles be followed to ensure effective information technology planning:[1]

- Alignment—the planning phase should support and complement the business strategy of a firm.
- Relevant scope—the overall scope of the planning phase should be established to facilitate formulation of effective ways to address the business needs.
- Relevant timeframe—the appropriate planning horizon should be formulated that provides both short- to medium-term deliverables as well as long-term alignment with the business strategy.
- Benefits realization—costs of implementation should be commensurate with the tangible and intangible benefits that are expected to be realized. The expected benefits should be bigger than the costs.
- Achievability—the planning phase should recognize the capability and capacity of the firm to deliver solutions within the stated planning timeframe.
- Measurable performance—the planning phase should provide a means to measure and monitor project performance and as a means of communicating success to both stakeholders inside and outside the firm.
- Reassessment—the plan should be periodically reassessed to ensure it is relevant to the evolving business strategy of the firm.
- Awareness—the resulting plan that comes out of the planning phase should be communicated widely.
- Accountability—identification of those responsible for implementing the plan should be explicitly clear.
- Commitment—management commitment to the plan's implementation should be clear and evident.

Each of these core principles is important to effective information technology planning.

Progress *Check*

1. Why is the systems development life cycle recursive? Will systems development ever be completed?
2. Why is measurable performance important to consider in the planning phase of the systems development life cycle?

The Sarbanes-Oxley Act of 2002 (SOX) highlights the importance of accounting information system controls by requiring management and auditors to report on the effectiveness of internal controls over the company's accounting information system.

[1]International Federation of Accountants, *Managing Information Technology Planning for Business Impact* (January 1999).

Consider these two excerpts taken from two auditors' SOX 404 reports. In both cases, the firms revealed a material weakness that may have allowed a material misstatement in the financial reports.

The first is from the 10-K filing of Oneok Inc. (2005):

> . . . The Company's third party software system associated with accounting for derivative hedging instruments was inadequately designed to appropriately account for certain hedges of forecasted transactions and thus did not facilitate the recognition of hedging ineffectiveness in accordance with generally accepted accounting principles. The software system incorrectly reversed previously recognized hedging ineffectiveness when additional derivative instruments (basis swaps) were incorporated into the Company's hedging strategy related to the forecasted transactions. As a result, misstatements were identified in the Company's cost of sales and fuel account and accumulated other comprehensive income (loss) . . .

Oneok Inc. is in the business of oil and natural gas production. To minimize the risks associated with the rise and fall in the prices of crude oil and natural gas, Oneok uses a hedging strategy to buy and sell oil and gas futures. However, the material weakness in the accounting information system suggests that the software was not designed correctly to account for this hedging, which resulted in misstatements. Had the software been designed correctly, it would not have caused a misstatement.

This one is from Barrett Business Services Inc.'s 2008 10-K filing:

> Our Company did not maintain effective controls over information technology ("IT"); specifically, general IT controls over program changes and program development were ineffectively designed and/or operating as of December 31, 2008.

Barrett Business Services presents another case of ineffective design of the accounting information systems, which resulted in a material weakness. As accountants understand the design of accounting information systems, they are better equipped to address potential weaknesses in the accounting information system.

Connection with Practice

Segregation of Duties

In nearly all accounting textbooks, the importance of segregation of duties (SOD) is discussed. The general rule is that accounting controls, whether they be manual or computerized, should be set up to separate (1) custody of assets, (2) authorization of transactions, and (3) record-keeping responsibilities.

In a recent SOX 404 report published in TRC Companies' 2006 10-K, it is disclosed that "the Company did not adequately design controls to maintain appropriate segregation of duties in its manual and computer-based business processes which could affect the Company's purchasing controls, the limits on the delegation of authority for expenditures, and the proper review of manual journal entries."

Segregation of duties is not just a concept you read in a textbook. It continues to be a real issue at companies today.

In both examples, the design of the information system was ineffective and was the source of a potential material weakness in the accounting information system. This highlights the real need for accountants to understand the design and development of accounting information systems, which is the topic of this chapter.

LO 15-3
Define *project management*, and describe the positions of those who lead the project.

Can you imagine merging the databases of customers, flights, accounting information, and frequent flyer miles for the combined merged firms of United Airlines and Continental Airlines? Now that's a big project!

PROJECTS, PROJECT MANAGEMENT, AND PROJECT SPONSORS

Projects are a series of tasks that are generally performed in a defined sequence to produce a predefined output. The history of project management has its roots in engineering and construction projects. In an information technology setting, a project might include the creation of a new, unique IT product or service such as replacing old computers, moving data to a different cloud computing environment, installing a new financial reporting database, or merging financial reporting databases. For example, can you imagine merging an accounting information system from two different systems into one? We'll highlight this IT project management setting throughout the rest of this chapter.

As defined earlier in the chapter, project management is the planning, organizing, supervising, and directing of an IT project. A **project manager** is the lead member of the project team and is responsible for the project. The project manager's mission is to coordinate the entire project development process to successfully complete the project. A project manager must also be able to analyze the project charter, a document that details the objectives and requirements of the project.

The third important concept surrounding a project is the presence of a project (or executive) sponsor. The **project sponsor** will often be a senior executive in the company who takes responsibility for the success of the project. The project sponsor is generally a different person than the project manager but often serves as the project champion. In addition, this person takes critical roles in the project, including the following:

- Supporting the project manager in managing the project.
- Advocating for the project to the company management and also to those outside the company (e.g., vendors, suppliers, shareholders, etc.).
- Obtaining necessary resources for successful completion.
- Monitoring overall scope for the project to ensure successful completion and work to prevent scope creep (as discussed later).
- Accepting responsibility for issues and problems that arise that the project manager cannot handle alone.

All IT projects move through these five phases of the project management life cycle: initiating, planning, executing, monitoring and controlling, and closing. These phases contain the needed processes to move the project from the initial idea to project implementation and subsequent maintenance.

The modern project management concept began with the Manhattan Project, which the U.S. military led to develop the atomic bomb.

Progress *Check*   3. Why is the project sponsor so important?
4. Why should accountants be interested in project management?

LO 15-4
Explain why IT projects are challenged and the tools that are used to overcome these challenges.

CHALLENGES OF IT PROJECT MANAGEMENT

Before we get too far into discussing the details of the challenges of IT project management, it should be noted that IT projects are frequently canceled, late, over budget or don't deliver the intended consequences. To illustrate the problem, here are some statistics on the outcomes of recent IT projects. Every few years, the Standish Group performs a survey to evaluate the outcomes of IT projects. Figure 15.2 provides a summary of its 2009 report.

FIGURE 15.2
Information Technology Project Outcomes

Source: Standish Group, 2009.

	2009	2006	2004	2002	2000	1998	1996	1994
Successful	32%	35%	29%	34%	28%	26%	27%	16%
Challenged	44%	19%	53%	15%	23%	28%	40%	31%
Failed	24%	46%	18%	51%	49%	46%	33%	53%

The report shows that software projects now have a 32 percent success rate compared with 35 percent from the previous study in 2006 and 16 percent in 1994. On the other hand, 44 percent of projects were challenged (i.e., late, over budget, and/or with less than the required features and functions) while 24 percent failed (i.e., canceled prior to completion or delivered and never used). While there seems to be improvement since 1994's low successful outcome percentage, there are still 68 percent (44 percent challenged + 24 percent failed) of the projects that either outright failed or were challenged in 2009. This low success rate can be attributed to poor project management and helps illustrate why project management is so critical in firms today. In the next section, we consider the specific obstacles, or constraining factors, that project managers face and the tools to overcome those challenges.

CONSTRAINING FACTORS OF IT PROJECTS

There are many reasons information technology projects fail to meet expectations. First, there are project management concerns that exist for all projects—such as deadlines, budget constraints, and limited resources (i.e., people) to focus efforts on completing the project successfully. Second, information technology projects face unique challenges because technology continues to change and oftentimes has glitches. These changes and glitches may come from hardware, operating systems, or databases. Third, there might also be security risks or interoperability issues between computer systems.

A project manager is generally told that a project must be completed by a certain date or for a certain cost or both. All information technology and other projects are constrained by three factors: cost, scope, and time constraints. This is often called the Dempster's triangle or the **triple constraint**. For a project to be successful, these three constraints must be held in balance. Once any of the constraints becomes out of balance, the project is likely headed for an unsuccessful outcome. Figure 15.3 provides an illustration of the triple constraint. Notice that in the center of these three constraints is quality. While the triple constraints do need to be carefully addressed, some level of quality must be met to be useful

FIGURE 15.3
The Triple Constraints of Project Management (Dempster's Triangle)

to the firm. As a project manager, you are often told that a project must be completed by a certain date or for a certain amount of money (cost) or both. At the same time, the deliverable (or result) of your project must also meet some minimum specifications (quality) to meet the firm's intended purposes.

Scope

The size or scope of the project is often defined in the initial stages of the project. However, in most projects, the scope begins to expand when additional features are added to the original specifications to add desired functionality. **Scope creep** is the broadening of a project's scope that occurs after the project has started. The change in scope often comes about from small, relatively insignificant change requests that the project team accepts to keep the project sponsor satisfied (e.g., information system available in Spanish or an e-commerce program able to transact with euros as well as U.S. dollars). Eventually, the number of change requests may become numerous enough to become significant, or some of the individual requests may be big enough to require much more work than originally expected.

The larger the scope expands beyond its initial specifications, the more the project will drift away from its original purpose, timeline, and budget. To help control scope creep, the project sponsor must be involved in the process to ensure that scope changes are absolutely needed and to assess if the benefits of the enhanced scope outweigh the costs. If the project scope is expanded, there must be additional time and funding to complete it.

Cost

A major challenge for IT projects is keeping the project within the planned budget. Often, the initial budget at the start of a project may not reflect all of the costs to bring the project to completion. As the IT project manager becomes aware of the costs to date and the expected costs to complete the project, she or he must share this information with the project sponsor and other company leadership. She or he then suggests changes to the allocation of resources or tasks that do not significantly change the scope of the project. This can be a challenge if additional costs are needed to successfully complete the project but additional needed funds are not available.

Time

Due to the rapid evolution of business and technology, most information technology projects are constrained by time. The results of these information systems often serve as a basis for a competitive advantage within the firm. Sometimes, systems implemented quickly can have a first-mover advantage. For this reason, the project manager is often given a deadline by which the project needs to be completed and delivered. Likewise, if software or hardware vendors don't deliver their solutions on time, the project will not be completed on time. To help address these time constraints, there are several project management tools available, including the PERT and Gantt charts which are discussed later.

The 15-15 Rule

Sometimes it is important to know when an IT project will not reach a successful conclusion. At that point, it may make sense to stop investing in an IT project. As some would say, you need to know when to "quit throwing good money after bad" or in a poker game, "to know when to fold." One indicator that the project might have serious difficulty in achieving a successful outcome is called the **15-15 rule**, which states that if a project is more than 15 percent over budget or 15 percent off the desired schedule, it will likely never recoup the time or cost necessary to be considered successful. Of course, to know if the project is 15 percent over budget or 15 percent off the desired schedule requires careful monitoring by the project manager (and possibly the project sponsor).

Progress *Check*

5. What are the triple constraints of project management? How can scope creep cause distortions in cost and time?
6. When should the project manager and project sponsor approve scope changes? When should they deny scope changes?

PROJECT MANAGEMENT TOOLS

The previous section mentioned that one of the triple constraints of projects is time. There are two project management tools to help with this time constraint by scheduling, organizing, and coordinating the tasks within a project. The most popular tools in use today are the PERT and Gantt charts.

PERT is actually an acronym for **Program Evaluation Review Technique**. PERT was originally developed in the 1950s by the U.S. Navy to manage the building of the Polaris submarine missile.

The first step in a PERT chart is to identify all tasks needed to complete a project. This breakdown of all of the project tasks is often called the **work breakdown structure (WBS)**. These tasks generally define all events and deliverables. After the tasks have been identified, the next step is to establish the sequencing of those events. The sequencing suggests which tasks need to precede the other tasks and which are dependent on the other tasks. A key part of making sure the PERT and the Gantt chart work is being able to define all of the tasks—including all internal, external, and interim tasks. This identification of all tasks is sometimes called the **100% rule**. The 100% rule, therefore, requires thorough and complete project planning.

The best way to explain a PERT chart is to see one and explain how it works. Consider the PERT chart in Figure 15.4. A PERT chart is a graphical representation of a project that consists of numbered *nodes* (either circles or rectangles) representing milestones in the project linked together by labeled directional lines representing tasks that need to be completed in the project. The numbers on the various directional lines indicate how much time has been allotted to the task. The sequencing of the tasks is denoted by the direction of the arrows on the lines. Some of the tasks must be completed in a certain sequence, like the set of tasks between numbered nodes 1, 6, 7, and 9 in Figure 15.4. These are called *dependent tasks* because they require that the previous task be completed before they can begin the next task. The tasks between nodes 10 and 11 cannot begin until all the preceding tasks (incoming directional lines) for node 10 are completed, including tasks 5, 8, and 9.

Because these all must be done in order, the longest string of time allotted to dependent tasks must be determined. We call this the critical path. The **critical path** is the longest path for a project and represents the minimum amount of time needed for the completion of the project when sufficient resources are allocated. The critical path helps the project manager figure out how resources should be allocated in order to complete the project within the shortest amount of time. In Figure 15.4, that path is 1, 2, 3, 4, 5, 10, 11, 12.

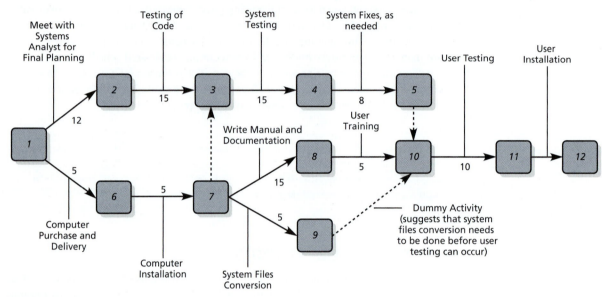

FIGURE 15.4
Example of a PERT Chart

Some tasks are not dependent on the completion of one to start the other, such as the tasks between nodes 7 and 8, and nodes 7 and 9. Tasks 5 and 8 are called *parallel,* or *concurrent tasks* because they can be done at the same time. Tasks that must be completed in a specific sequence but don't require additional resources or a specific completion time are considered to have *task dependency*. These are called *dummy tasks* and are represented by dashed lines with arrows. For example, the dashed lines between nodes 9 and 10 suggest that the software testing and related fixes must be completed before user testing can take place.

Henry Gantt, an American mechanical engineer, is generally credited with inventing the Gantt chart.

Another similar, but complementary project management tool is the use of the Gantt chart. A **Gantt chart** is a graphical representation of the project schedule by mapping the tasks to a project calendar. Gantt charts are especially useful when monitoring a project's progress.

A Gantt chart illustrates the start and finish dates of the various tasks of the project. Some Gantt charts also show the dependency between the tasks. Figure 15.5 shows an illustration of both a PERT chart and a related Gantt chart and how they might work together. Each letter represents a task to be performed. The PERT chart shows the critical path; the Gantt chart also shows the term "margin" and ". . ." to signify the slack time before the next critical path task needs to be completed. As the project progresses through time, the Gantt chart is used to show the current status.

One noted advantage of the PERT chart over the Gantt chart is that it clearly illustrates the dependence of one task on another. At the same time, one disadvantage of the PERT chart is that it can be much more difficult to interpret, especially on complex projects.

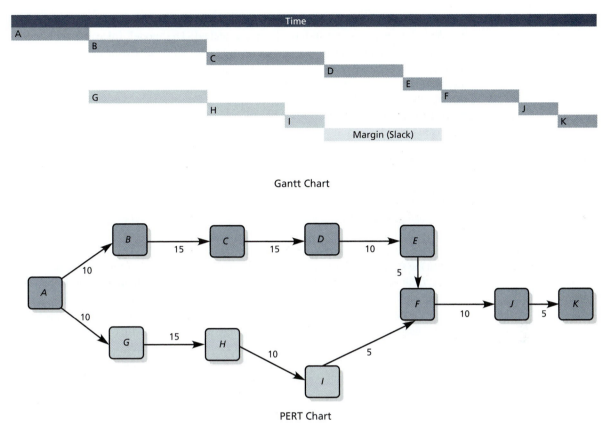

FIGURE 15.5
Example of Gantt Chart and its Relationship to the PERT Chart

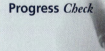

Progress *Check*

7. Why is the 100% rule critical for identifying the work to be done?
8. What is a parallel or concurrent task? Are these tasks required to be done at the same time? If you have to choose, which parallel or concurrent task should be done first?

LO 15-5
Explain why users do or do not want to use a new information system.

WILL THE SYSTEM BE USED, AND WILL IT BE USEFUL?

Outside of the triple constraints is the challenge of whether the system will actually be used by the intended users once it is completed. In other words, even though the system is on time, on budget, and built to the firm's specifications, users may not use the system. There are some systems that are scrapped because the users simply don't want to use them.

Let's assume the systems department sends you an e-mail and tells you they are ready to install a new accounting system's module for accounts payable on your computer. While the old system will still be available for a short time, your boss and the systems department would like you to start to use the system and get used to it. They will even pay you to go to training at a nice hotel and for a nice lunch. But because change is hard for everyone, you wonder "if the new system will work as good as the old," "if you'll ever figure out how to use it," or "if this is the system that will ultimately replace your job".

In a study by Fred Davis[2], a model was proposed that predicts whether systems will be adopted or whether the system will be scratched. The model, titled the **technology acceptance model (TAM)**, suggests that users will adopt a new or modified system to the extent they believe the system will help them perform their job better. TAM would call this **perceived usefulness**. At the same time, TAM defines the extent to which a person believes that the use of a particular system would be free of effort. We call this concept **perceived ease of use**. So if the user believes that the system is easy to learn and use (i.e., perceived ease of use) and will help the user to perform his or her job better (i.e., perceived usefulness), the model predicts the user will make the effort to learn the new system and ultimately adopt it. Figure 15.6 offers an illustration of the technology acceptance model.

Addressing Perceived Usefulness

Project managers and project champions and systems analysts and developers alike all take responsibility for building a system that will be useful to the users. One way to make the perception and reality that the new system will be useful to users is by extensive communication between the systems builders and the user base and by meeting their needs. As the project progresses, feedback on what features will be included and which will not be included will keep all users involved in the process. To achieve the milestone and ensure on-time delivery, project managers usually create a *specification,* which includes a feature list from the feedback of the potential users. The features can be further categorized into "must-have" features, "nice-to-have" features, and "future improvements" to determine their priorities. Based on the features and priorities, system developers implement the most important must-have features within the specified timeframe and continue on to the nice-to-have features. Future improvements are usually more sophisticated and time consuming to implement but cannot be addressed in the allowable timeframe, so they are often considered in the second (or maintenance) phase.

In Figure 15.6, we also note the directional arrow going from perceived ease of use to perceived usefulness. This recognizes the possibility that if the system is perceived to be easy to use, it will also be perceived to be more useful. Likewise, if a new system is fraught with errors and issues and has not been completely tested, it will not be perceived to be useful or easy to use.

In an accounting information system, system features to address new regulatory requirements (e.g., new FASB standards, new SEC disclosures, Sarbanes-Oxley laws, etc.) would be considered "must-have" features. In contrast, an accounting information system that allows the user to track the cost of shipping from China to the United States for each product may be considered a "nice-to-have" feature. However, if management requires this information to adequately manage the business and make critical decisions, it may rise to "must-have" feature status. In either case, we learn that as the new AIS system meets the needs of the users, they will perceive it to be more useful and be more likely to adopt it.

Addressing Perceived Ease of Use

There are many things that can be done to help new users prepare to actually use the system. Systems analysts and developers can mock up the computer screen to show the look and feel of the system well before the new system is written. Project managers can also ensure that users undergo extensive training before the system goes into operation so they feel comfortable with it.

At times, instead of rolling out the computer system for the whole staff at the same time, it may make sense to pilot test the new system with some peer leaders who can ultimately help steer adoption for the rest of the users to the new system. For example, in

---

[2]F. Davis, "Perceived Usefulness, Perceived Ease of Use, and User Acceptance of Information Technology," *MIS Quarterly* 13, no. 3 (1989), pp. 319–340.

August 2010, **Walmart** piloted its new SAP accounting information system at its Asda subsidiary in the United Kingdom before the worldwide rollout. They found that the UK implementation was so successful that the company now plans to roll it out globally. This certainly helps make an AIS implementation at other **Walmart** locations less stressful.

All of these strategies can help users feel confident they can learn and use the new system.

FIGURE 15.6
The Technology Acceptance Model

Source: F. Davis, "Perceived Usefulness, Perceived Ease of Use, and User Acceptance of Information Technology," *MIS Quarterly* 13, no. 3 (1989), pp. 319–340.

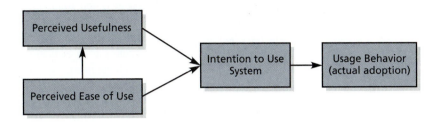

Systems analysts, systems developers, and project managers should all be aware of how a new system is perceived by those who will ultimately be using it. They should consistently communicate with this user group to make sure the system will be useful and easy to use.

Connection with Practice

Perceived Usefulness or Failure?

The London Ambulance Service (LAS) developed a brand-new software system of routing ambulances throughout the London area. The system was put into operation on the morning of October 26, 1992. After just a few hours' use, however, problems began to appear in the routing system. The system was unable to track ambulance location or status. Not knowing the relative location of the trucks, the system then began to send multiple trucks to some locations, but no trucks to others. The problem was further exacerbated when customers kept calling back when their requested ambulances did not arrive. As additional calls, both new and call-backs, were entered into the system, it became further clogged, and the problems increased. The next day, the LAS switched back to the original, manual system to make sure to keep up with demand.

Because of the huge population served only by the LAS network, many people were affected by the failure of this computer system. Forty-six avoidable deaths could be attributed to the failure of the computer system had the requested ambulance arrived on time. One ambulance crew arrived so late that they found that the patient had not only died, but his body had already been taken to the mortician. In a different case, a heart attack patient waited more than 6 hours for an ambulance before finally having her son take her to the emergency room. Almost 4 hours later, the LAS called to see if the ambulance was still needed. Finally, another woman kept calling the ambulance service every 30 minutes for 3 hours before an ambulance finally came. By then, it was too late—her husband had already died.

A useful system? No, this was a failure.

Sources: A. Finkelstein and J. Dowell, "A Comedy of Errors: The London Ambulance Service Case Study," *IWSSD*, 8th International Workshop on Software Specification and Design (1996), p. 2; and D. Dalcher, "Disaster in London: The LAS Case Study," *ECBS*, IEEE Conference and Workshop on Engineering of Computer-Based Systems (1999), p. 41.

Progress *Check*

9. What can be done to address perceptions of usefulness of a new accounting information system?
10. What can be done to address perceptions of ease of use of a new accounting information system?

Summary

- Users and auditors of an accounting information system need to understand the basics of AIS project management to understand how accounting information systems are developed.
- The systems development life cycle is the foundation for all systems development, models, and methodologies that people use to develop such systems. The SDLC has five phases: planning, analysis, design, implementation, and maintenance.
- Effective information systems planning is of critical importance to the firm because it is the stage that the firm uses to evaluate needed changes to the system. Ten core principles of effective information systems planning were highlighted.
- Project managers and project sponsors each play key roles in managing system development.
- Many AIS and IT projects fail to meet expectations. If we can understand the reason these projects fail, we can better design the project management process to address these reasons.
- Scope, time, and cost represent the triple constraints of project management. If any of these constraints get out of control, the project will likely face overwhelming challenges. The project manager and project sponsor use various project management tools to monitor and control the scope, time, and costs.
- AIS developers, project managers, and project sponsors should all be aware of how a new system is perceived by those who will ultimately be using the new system. They should consistently communicate with the end-user group to make sure the system will be (or at least perceived to be) useful and easy to use.

Key Words

100% rule (*301*)   A rule requiring 100 percent planning of all tasks, including all of the internal, external, and interim tasks.

15-15 rule (*301*)   A rule suggesting that if a project is more than 15 percent over budget or 15 percent off the planned schedule, it will likely never recoup the time or cost necessary to be considered successful. At this point a decision needs to be made on if or how to proceed from that point.

analysis phase (*294*)   The phase of the SDLC involves a complete, detailed analysis of the systems needs of the end user as well as a proposed solution.

critical path (*302*)   The longest path for a project and represents the minimum amount of time needed for the completion of the project when sufficient resources are allocated.

design phase (*294*)   The phase of the SDLC that involves describing in detail the desired features of the system that were uncovered in the analysis phase.

Gantt chart (*302*)   A graphical representation of the project schedule that maps the tasks to a project calendar.

implementation phase (*295*)   The phase of the SDLC that involves development, testing, and implementation of the new proposed system.

maintenance phase (*295*)   The final phase of the SDLC that includes making changes, corrections, additions, and upgrades (generally smaller in scope) to ensure the system continues to meet the business requirements that have been set out for it.

perceived ease of use (*304*)   The extent to which a person perceives that the use of a particular system will be relatively free from effort.

perceived usefulness (*304*)   The extent to which users believe the system will help them perform their job better.

planning phase (*294*)   The phase of the SDLC that summarizes the business needs with a high-level view of the intended project.

Program Evaluation Review Technique (PERT) (*301*)   A project management tool used to help identify all tasks needed to complete a project. It is also helpful in determining task dependencies.

project (*298*)   A series of tasks that are generally performed in a defined sequence to produce a predefined output.

project management (*294*)   The process of carrying out the systems development life cycle to achieve an intended outcome.

project manager (*298*)   The lead member of the project team who is responsible for the project.

project sponsor (*298*)   Generally a senior executive in the company who takes responsibility for the success of the project.

scope creep (*300*)   The change in a project's scope after the project work has started.

systems analyst (*294*)   Person responsible for both determining the information needs of the business and designing a system to meet those needs.

systems development life cycle (SDLC) (*294*)   The process of creating or modifying information systems to meet the needs of its users. It serves as the foundation for all processes people use to develop such systems.

technology acceptance model (TAM) (*304*)   A model that predicts when users will adopt a new system to the extent they believe the system will help them perform their job better.

triple constraint (*299*)   Three factors that constrain information technology and other projects: cost, scope, and time. Also known as Dempster's triangle.

work breakdown structure (WBS) (*301*)   The process of identifying all tasks needed to complete a project.

Answers to Progress *Checks*

1. The recursive nature of the SDLC reflects that the firm continues to evolve, always needing new and different information. While a particular system may be completed and put into use, because the business is always changing, a firm's systems development should never be considered complete.

2. It is important to set expectations clearly and measure whether a system has met those expectations (or not). This is particularly important to consider in the earliest planning phases.

3. For a project to be successfully implemented, there must be executive support. A project sponsor ensures that the project has initial and continuing executive support to ensure the necessary and appropriate resources are available. One of the most important responsibilities for the project sponsor is to monitor the overall scope of the project and make sure there is enough support for any scope changes that might occur.

4. Accountants use and audit the information that comes out of an accounting information system. But how was the system designed? Can they trust the numbers that come out of the system? Accountants must understand the design and development of an accounting information system to be able to trust the information coming out of that system.

5. Scope, cost, and time are the triple constraints of project management. If the scope becomes different and/or larger, the cost and time to complete can quickly become overwhelming and become a source of failure.

6. Generally, scope changes are made to satisfy potential users and executives. They may make the system more useable and have desired features. The project manager and project sponsor must assess and balance the costs and benefits of scope changes. If a change has too little impact, costs too much or can easily be done in a future upgrade to the system, the project manager and project sponsor should deny the scope change.

7. In order to plan the project, the work breakdown structure must be complete, or 100% planned. This will help in sequencing the tasks, figuring out which tasks are dependent on other tasks, and allowing for planning of the complete project.

8. A parallel, or concurrent, task is a task that can be done or completed at the same time. All other things equal, the parallel task that is on the critical path should be completed first because subsequent tasks depend on that task being completed.

9. To address perceptions of usefulness by the ultimate user, extensive communication between the systems builders and the user base needs to occur. As the new system assesses and addresses user needs, users will feel more comfortable that the new system will be useful. Accountants who will use the system should be included in the discussion of what the new system needs to have and how the new system will address them.

10. To address perceptions of ease of use by the ultimate user, project managers should ensure that users have extensive training and that those who feel most comfortable with the new system use it first in a pilot test.

Multiple Choice Questions

1. Which phase of the systems development life cycle would include a feasibility analysis?
   a. Analysis phase
   b. Planning phase
   c. Design phase
   d. Implementation phase

2. The IFAC suggested 10 core principles of effective information technology planning. Which of the following is not one of those 10 core principles?
   a. Achievability
   b. Reassessment
   c. Accountability
   d. Justifiable cost

3. Projects are considered challenged if they are
   a. Late, over budget, or do not have the required features and functions
   b. Canceled prior to completion
   c. Delivered, but never used
   d. Completed early

4. The triple constraint of project management does not include the constraint of
   a. Technical issues
   b. Time
   c. Cost
   d. Scope

5. The PERT and Gantt charts primarily address the triple constraint of
   a. Technical issues
   b. Time
   c. Cost
   d. Scope

6. The 100% rule suggests that before a PERT chart is done, a project manager must
   a. Make sure 100 percent of the project is funded
   b. Make sure the project team is devoted solely, or 100 percent, to this project

c. Make sure 100 percent of the project tasks are defined

d. Make sure that each person on the project team got 100 percent on their project management final exam

7. The critical path in a PERT chart represents:

a. The sequencing of tasks

b. The most important tasks of the whole project

c. The longest path of tasks needed for project completion

d. The tasks that must be completed without errors

8. The technology acceptance model does not address:

a. Perceived usefulness

b. Perceived systems quality

c. Perceived ease of use

d. Intention to use

9. The Sarbanes-Oxley Act's 404 reports require management and auditors to report on

a. The financial condition of the firm

b. The quality of the project management planning

c. The academic background and experience of the company's accounting leadership

d. The effectiveness of the internal controls of the company's accounting information system

10. In this chapter, *projects* are defined as

a. A series of tasks performed in a defined sequence

b. Turning raw talent into an NFL quality quarterback

c. Turning blueprints from an architect into a completed building

d. Merging two databases into one

Discussion Questions

1. Rank the 10 core principles of effective information technology planning in order of importance in your opinion. Provide support for your top 5 important principles.

2. Imagine the role of the project sponsor when a leader of the accounting bookkeepers comes to complain that the new information system could possibly result in the loss of five bookkeeper jobs. The bookkeepers argue that they will get the union involved if needed to protect their jobs. What should the project sponsor do?

3. Explain the 100% rule. Assume you are telling your roommate about this rule, and use an example that is relevant to him or her.

4. Your grandmother regularly uses a Sony Walkman (vintage 1989) that has cassette tapes. She is quite pleased with this technology because it lets her go on her evening constitutional and listen to music of her era. And of course, she has listened to this music for many years! What features would you point out to her to ease the "perceived usefulness" and "perceived ease of use" concerns? Use the technology acceptance model as discussed in the chapter to suggest whether she will use a brand new iPod Touch if given to her as a Christmas present.

5. What are the differences between the situation in Question 4 and that of users of a brand-new accounting information system?

6. Compare and contrast a PERT chart and a Gantt chart. How do they complement each other?

7. Using the 15-15 rule as a guide, when would a project manager and/or project sponsor proceed with completion of a project even if it is both 15 percent over budget and 15 percent off the initial schedule?

Problems

1. As part of effective IT planning in the systems development life cycle, a return on investment (ROI) calculation may be performed as part of the economic feasibility analysis. Often, many of the benefits from a new information system may be intangible benefits (e.g., system is easier to use or system enhances customer service, etc.) that are hard to quantify in an income statement. How would you suggest this be included in the economic feasibility analysis?

2. In the chapter, we discussed an example of **Starbucks** using the systems development life cycle to develop the capability to analyze what type of pastries sell best with its various hot and cold drinks. Now, let's suppose that **NASDAQ** requires all of the firms trading on the exchange to report their financial statements not only using GAAP but also International Financial Reporting Standards (IFRS). Because **Starbucks'** current system cannot handle the IFRS requirements, the financial reporting system must be modified. Using **Starbucks** as an example, explain what types of activities would occur in each of the five phases of the systems development life cycle in preparation for reporting financial results according to IFRS.

3. Accountants generally do not have all of the necessary systems analyst and systems development skills needed to develop accounting information systems. Why should you be interested in project management of an accounting information system?

4. For your personal consulting business, you decide to set up an accounting information system to help with taxes as well as to help monitor your revenues and expenses. You've heard that QuickBooks is easy to set up, so you buy it, install it on your computer, enter in recent transactions and begin to use it.

   Required:

   1. Explain one or two ways you could be a user of this accounting information system. (*Hint:* Use the discussion in the text considering the role of accountants in accounting information systems.)

   2. Explain one or two ways you could be a manager of this accounting information system. (*One possibility:* What practices do you employ to make sure your system is safe?)

   3. After a few months, you decide to expand your QuickBooks with additional modules (payroll, inventory, etc.). Access the QuickBooks website (http://quickbooks.intuit.com), and consider one or two ways in which you could be a designer of your accounting information system.

5. Brainstorm a list of reasons why 68 percent (including 44 percent challenged + 24 percent failed) of the information technology projects either failed or were challenged in 2009. Consider specifics of each of the elements of the triple constraints model and any other common delays, including the challenges of working with programmers, software and hardware suppliers and vendors, and the like. What is the best way to overcome these issues and decrease the number of projects failed or challenged?

6. As mentioned in the opening vignette, **Walmart** is implementing its SAP system throughout its worldwide operations. If **Walmart** has the choice, should it implement this system in China before, at the same time, or after the implementation in the United States? Use the technology acceptance model (in particular, perceived ease of use) to explain your answer.

7. The following PERT chart (Figure 15.7) represents the tasks to be done to implement a system. Can you think of other steps that should be included? Is there adequate time for training given the technology acceptance model's recommendation to focus on perceived usefulness and perceived ease of use? What is the critical path for this project?

8. Consider the triple constraint figure in Figure 15.3. Why is quality included in that figure even if it is not a triple constraint? Why is quality a concern (or not a concern, based on your point of view) for the project manager and project sponsor?

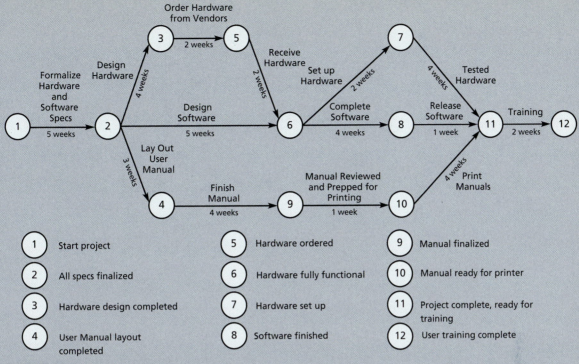

FIGURE 15.7
PERT Chart for Problem 7

Answers to Multiple Choice Questions

1. b
2. d
3. a
4. a
5. b

6. c
7. c
8. b
9. d
10. a

This glossary presents various structure and activity models to show modeling options. It is not intended to be all-inclusive, but rather to provide examples of how to model common situations. For the structure models, the basic assumption is that resources, agents, and type images are added to the database before they are linked to other classes, so the minimum multiplicity is zero. Otherwise, the models show the most common multiplicities.

The glossary presents examples of structure models in the following section and then presents some generic activity models in the last section. The models are presented in the following order: sales and cash receipts process, purchases and cash disbursements process, and the conversion process; for the structure models, it includes miscellaneous and integrated models.

Structure Models Using the REA Framework

1. Sales: Generic Model

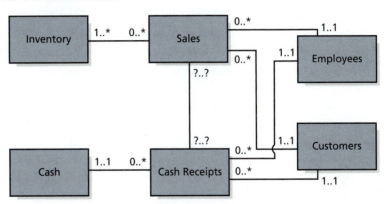

The generic model represents typical economic resources, events, and agents involved in the sales process. This model assumes that inventory items are not tracked individually (like high-value items such as automobiles and houses), but rather by UPC code, such that all products with the same UPC code are considered to be the same item.

2. Sales: With Invoice Tracking

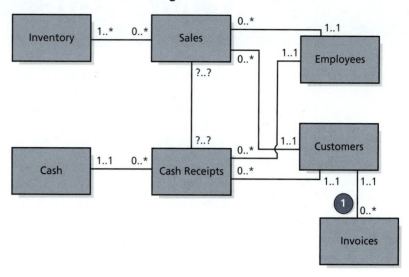

This model extends the generic model to track the invoices issued to each customer as shown in association 1 between Customers (Agent) and Invoices (Type Image).

3. Sales: Employees Assigned to Service Particular Customers

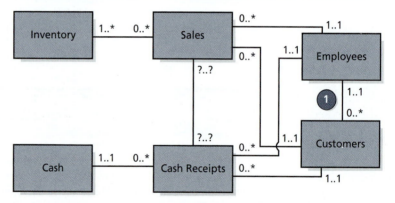

This model extends the generic model to represent assignment of employees to customers. Association 1 links customers to the assigned employee, such as when sales take place on commission. Similarly, employees can be assigned to inventory, when specific employees manage specific inventory items.

4. Sales with Summary

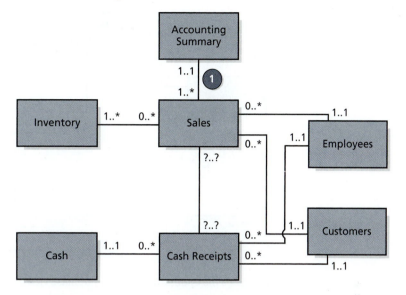

This model presents a simplified example of the summarization of economic activity by fiscal period in order to prepare financial reports. In this case, sales are summarized by fiscal period as shown in association 1 between Accounting Summary and Sales.

5. Purchases: Generic Model

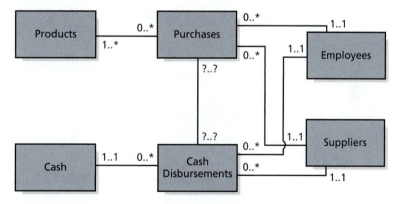

The generic model represents typical economic resources, events, and agents involved in the purchases process. Like the generic sales model, this model assumes that inventory items are not tracked individually, but rather by UPC code or similar identifier.

6. Purchases: With Commitment Event

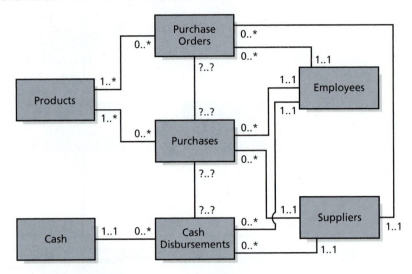

This model adds the commitment event, Purchase Orders, to the generic model. A commitment precedes the economic event. It records anticipated purchases but does not directly affect the financial statements. Note that this model requires tracking both the items ordered and the items received, which is a level of complication that many organizations avoid. Thus, they use a structure that combines the Purchase Orders and Purchases event as shown in the next model.

7. Purchases: With Combined Purchase Orders and Purchases

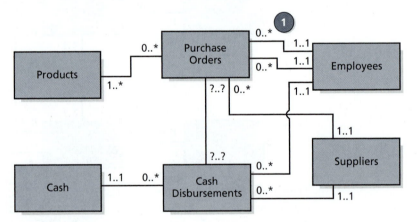

This model shows the combined Purchase Orders and Purchases event (still titled Purchase Orders). The Purchase Order class would track (1) the date of the order and (2) the date of the receipt(s). The organization is now concerned with only one association between Purchase Orders/Purchases and the Products classes. However, there are now two associations between the Employees and Purchase Orders class, representing the requirement to track the two roles (purchasing agent and receiving agent) separately for internal control.

8. Purchases: With Type Images to Manage the Purchases Process

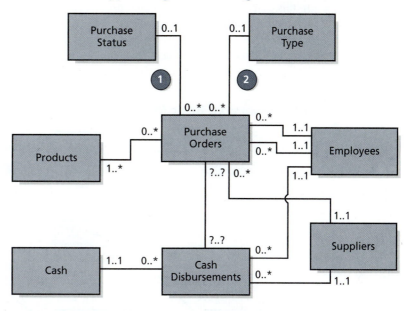

This model shows potential use of two type images to manage the purchase process. The Purchase Status type would summarize information based on the point in the purchase process at the end of a fiscal period (e.g., amounts on order, amounts received, amounts paid). The Purchase Type would summarize information according to the type of purchase (e.g., routine organizational supplies and services, inventory replenishment, and asset acquisition).

9. Purchases: With Type Images Linked for Summary Information

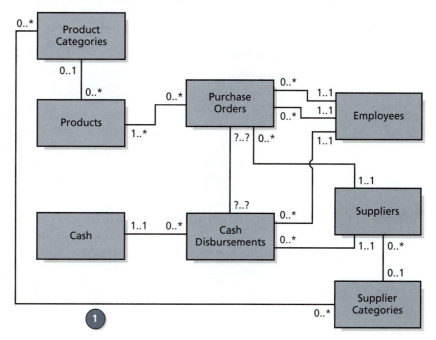

This model provides an example of the use of type images to summarize information. In this case, the organization could use the category classes to obtain summary information about supplier characteristics and activity, about product characteristics and activity, and about the common activity for each product and supplier category combination. For example, annual sales for each supplier category and product category combination would be recorded in the linking table between those two type images.

10. Conversion: Basic Model

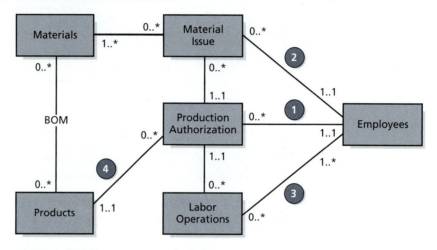

This basic conversion process model shows the structure related to (1) a supervisor authorizing production, (2) raw material issued into work-in-process, (3) labor applied to work-in-process, and (4) finished goods (products) increased when production completes.

11. Conversion: Production in a Series of Steps

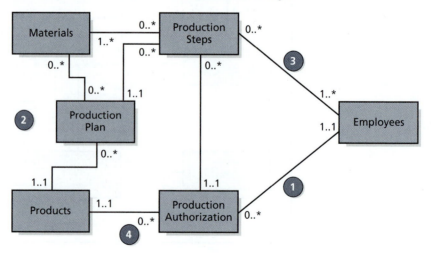

This revised conversion model shows production in a series of steps according to a production plan (a type image). The model shows (1) the supervisor authorizing production, (2) the production plan determining the raw material and labor needed to produce a specific product, (3) employees' work and materials issued into work-in-process, and (4) finished goods (products) increasing when production completes. This model can be expanded to include accounting for equipment (a resource) use in the production steps.

12. Miscellaneous: Recursive Relationships

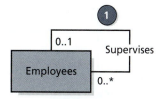

This is an example of a class related to itself. In this case, the association describes the supervisory relationship between an employee and several other employees. Similar common uses include products related to other substitute products and organizational departments that are parts of other organizational departments.

13. Miscellaneous: Associations Indicating Roles

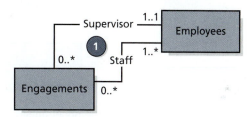

This is an example where two associations link the same two classes to indicate different agent roles in the event. In this case, each engagement (e.g., audit or consulting engagement) has one supervisor as well as several staff members. Placing the name of the role on the association can help clarify the purpose of the associations.

14. Integrated Models: Sales and Purchases

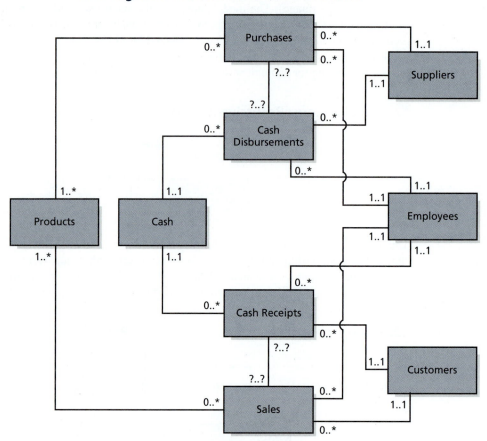

This is a basic example of a model integrating the sales (and cash receipts) and purchases (and cash disbursements) processes. Note that the two duality events (Purchases and Cash Disbursements or Sales and Cash Receipts) as well as the external agents (Customers and Suppliers) are unique to one process. However, the internal agent (Employees) and resources (Products and Cash) are shared across processes.

15. Integrated Models: Sales, Conversion, and Purchases

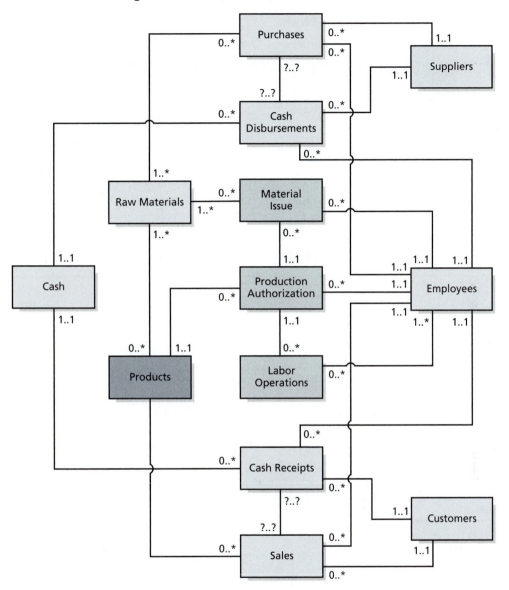

This is an example of a model integrating the sales (and cash receipts), conversion, and purchases (and cash disbursements) processes. In this case, the organization purchases raw materials that are converted into products (finished goods) that are then sold to customers. Again, the duality events (Purchases and Cash Disbursements, Sales and Cash Receipts, Production Authorization and Material Issue and Labor Operations) as well as the external agents (Customers and Suppliers) are unique to one process. However, the internal agent (Employees) and resources (Raw Materials, Products, and Cash) are shared across processes.

Activity Models Using BPMN

16. Sales: Basic Model

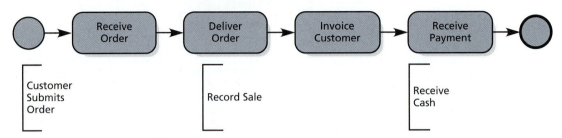

This model shows typical activity flow for a business that takes orders. Note that the steps in the model generally correspond to events in an REA diagram: commitment (receive order), sale (deliver order), and cash receipt (receive payment).

17. Sales: Basic Model with Pools and Swimlanes

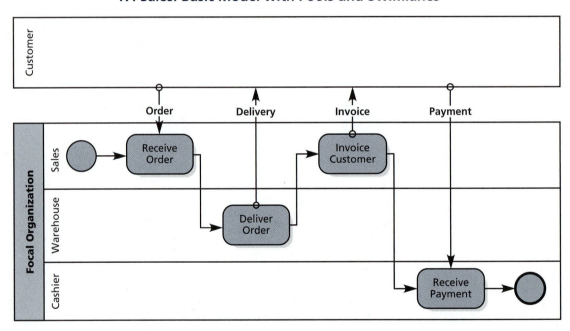

This is the basic model with pools and swimlanes to show responsibility for the various tasks. Note that there are no visible activities in the Customer pool, because we are normally not interested in the specific steps they take. Instead, the focus moves to the interactions between pools, shown as message flows (dashed lines). It is good practice to put labels on the message flows to clarify the nature of the interactions. Within the pool of interest, the sequence flows connect the start and end events without any break.

18. Purchases: Basic Model

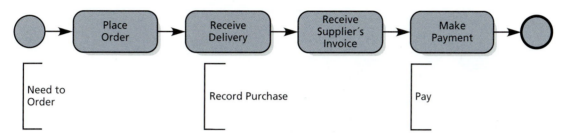

This model shows typical activity flow related to issuing purchase orders. Note that the steps in the model generally correspond to events in an REA diagram: commitment (place order), purchase (receive order), and cash disbursement (make payment).

19. Purchases: Basic Model with Gateway

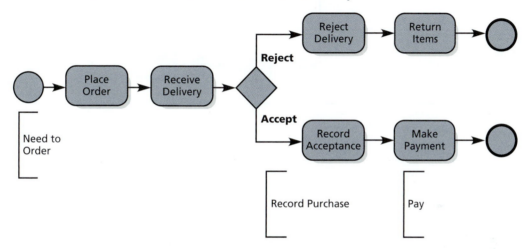

This model is similar to the basic model, except it includes the gateway to show different flow options after the receipt of the delivery: (1) accept and make payment and (2) reject and return the items to the supplier.

20. Purchases: Basic Model with Subprocess and Error Event

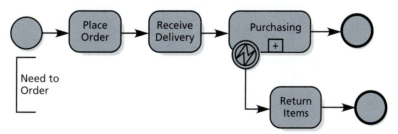

In this model, the purchasing activities are now collapsed into a subprocess. The error event shows flow when the items are rejected. This version of the model would be used when the purchasing process is well-defined and shown elsewhere.

21. Purchases: Basic Model with Intermediate Events

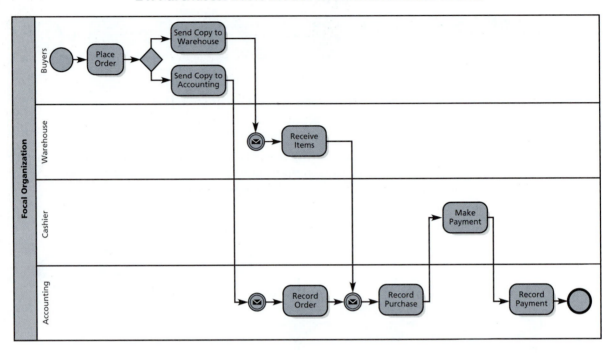

This model focuses on internal flows for the purchases process using swimlanes to show responsibility. In this case, the intermediate events show that documents are mailed between the various organizational elements (i.e., from the buyers to accounting, from the buyers to the warehouse, and from the warehouse to accounting). Thus, the technology (mailed documents) forces sequential processing. This model could then suggest alternative technologies to expedite process flow and allow parallel processing.

22. Conversion: Basic Model with Repeated Activities

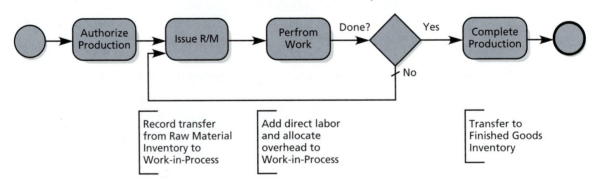

This model describes the basic conversion process and is closely related to the REA model that shows (1) the authorization, (2) raw material issued into work-in-process, (3) labor (and equipment) applied to work-in-process, and (4) completion of production and transfer to finished goods. The gateway routes the flow back until all production to carry out the authorization is complete.

23. Conversion: Basic Model with Repeated Activities and Batches

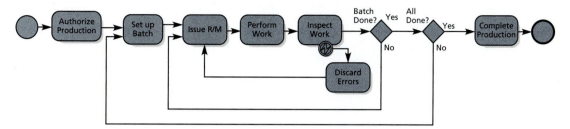

This model expands on the previous model to include batches. In this case, the flow starts with production authorization, to batch setup, to batch activity; it then first repeats until each batch is done, and then repeats until all batches are done. This model also includes an intermediate error event that halts the normal process flow when items fail inspection.

Glossary

A

access controls (*108*)   Limit who can use and change records in the system; for example, passwords control who can use an application.

access point (*248*)   Logically connects stations to a firm's network.

accounting information system (AIS) (*4*)   A system that records, processes, and reports on transactions to provide financial and nonfinancial information to make decisions and have appropriate levels of internal controls for those transactions.

accounting rate of return (ARR) (*283*)   The average annual income from the IT initiative divided by the initial investment cost.

accounts payable (*130*)   Amounts owed to suppliers for goods and services received. In a data modeling context, accounts payable are calculated based on receipts (purchases) from each supplier less the corresponding payments (cash disbursements) to those suppliers.

accounts receivable (*104*)   Monies owed by customers for prior sales of goods or services. In a data modeling context, accounts receivable are calculated as each customer's sales less corresponding cash receipts.

acquisition costs (*279*)   All direct and indirect costs necessary to acquire and implement the IT initiative.

activities (*32*)   In business process modeling, activities represent specific steps in a business process.

activity models (*31*)   Models that describe the sequence of workflow in a business process or processes.

agents (*109, 135, 157*)   The people or organizations who participate in business events, such as customers and salespeople.

aggregation relationship (*53*)   A special-purpose UML notation representing the relationship between two classes that are often considered together, such as when a sports league is made up of a collection of teams.

alignment risk (*280*)   The risk that an IT initiative is not aligned with the strategy of the organization.

analysis phase (*294*)   The phase of the SDLC involves a complete, detailed analysis of the systems needs of the end user as well as a proposed solution.

annotations (*33*)   Model elements that allow the modeler to add additional descriptive information to the model. Annotations are modeled with text inside a bracket connected to other model symbols with a dashed line.

application controls (*108, 198*)   Ensure data integrity and an audit trail; for example, new invoices are assigned sequential numbers; Specific to a subsystem or an application to ensure the validity, completeness, and accuracy of the transactions.

association (*51*)   UML symbol that depicts the relationship between two classes; it is modeled as a solid line that connects two classes in a model.

assurance (*186*)   Independent, professional opinions that reduce the risk of having incorrect information.

asymmetric-key encryption (*223*)   To transmit confidential information, the sender uses the receiver's public key to encrypt the message; the receiver uses his or her own private key for decryption upon receiving the message. Also known as public-key encryption or two-key encryption.

attributes (*52, 60, 69*)   Data elements that describe instances in a class, very much like fields in a database table; Characteristics, properties, or adjectives that describe each class.

audit around the computer (or **black-box approach**) **(*250*)**   Auditors test the reliability of computer-generated information by first calculating expected results from the transactions entered into the system. Then, the auditors compare these calculations to the processing or output results.

audit through the computer (or **white-box approach**) **(*250*)**   Requires auditors to understand the internal logic of the system/application being tested.

authentication (*224*)   A process that establishes the origin of information or determines the identity of a user, process, or device.

automate (*17*)   The use of technology to replace human labor in automating business processes.

B

Balanced Scorecard framework (*262*)   Provides an integrating framework that describes organizational performance relative to its strategic objectives across four perspectives: learning and growth, process, customer, and financial. Objectives for each perspective describe the strategy in a series of cause-and-effect relationships.

Balanced Scorecard management process (*267*)   The process by which companies plan, implement, and monitor performance. It consists of five steps: formulate the strategy, translate the strategy, link the strategy to operations, monitor performance, and adapt.

benefits (*276*) The positive consequences to the organization of an IT investment.

breakeven analysis (*282*) Determines the breakeven point, where the total value of benefits equals that of total costs.

business analysis (*29*) The process of defining business process requirements and evaluating potential improvements. Business analysis involves ascertaining, documenting, and communicating information about current and future business processes using business process modeling and related tools.

business case (*276*) Economic justification for an IT investment or other major project.

business continuity management (BCM) (*234*) The activities required to keep a firm running during a period of displacement or interruption of normal operations.

business intelligence (*180*) A computer-based technique for accumulating and analyzing data from databases and data warehouses to support managerial decision making.

business model (*29*) A simple, abstract representation of one or more business processes. A business model is typically a graphical depiction of the essential business process information.

business process (*29*) A defined sequence of business activities that use resources to transform specific inputs into specific outputs to achieve a business goal.

business process modeling notation (BPMN) (*32*) A standard for the description of activity models.

business rule (*57*) Succinct statements of constraints on business processes; they provide the logic that guides the behavior of the business in specific situations.

business value (*10*) Items, events, and interactions that determine the financial health and well-being of the firm.

C

cardinalities (*60*) *See* multiplicities.

cash (*104, 135*) The organization's monies in bank or related accounts. The instances of the class are individual accounts. This is considered a resource.

cash disbursements (*130*) Record payments of cash to external agents (e.g., suppliers) and the corresponding reduction in cash accounts. This is considered an event.

cash receipts (*111*) Record receipts of cash from external agents (e.g., customers) and the corresponding deposit of those receipts into cash accounts. This is considered an event.

Certificate Authority (CA) (*225*) A trusted entity that issues and revokes digital certificates.

Certified Information Systems Auditor (CISA) (*9*) The CISA designation identifies those professionals possessing IT audit, control, and security skills. Generally, CISAs will perform IT audits to evaluate the accounting information system's internal control design and effectiveness.

Certified Information Technology Professional (CITP) (*9*) The CITP designation identifies accountants (CPAs) with a broad range of technology knowledge and experience.

Certified Internal Auditor (CIA) (*9*) The CIA designation is the certification for internal auditors and is the standard to demonstrate competency and professionalism in the internal auditing field.

change risk (*280*) The risk that the organization will be unable to make the changes necessary to implement the IT initiative successfully.

choreography (*106, 131*) The interaction (message flows) between two participants (modeled as pools) in a process modeled using BPMN.

class (*50*) Any separately identifiable collection of things (objects) about which the organization wants to collect and store information. Classes can represent organization resources (e.g., trucks, machines, buildings, cash, investments), persons (e.g., customers, employees), events (e.g., sales, purchases, cash disbursements, cash receipts), and conceptual structures (e.g., accounts, product categories, budgets). Classes are typically implemented as tables in a relational database, where individual instances of the class are represented as rows in the table.

class diagrams (*50*) Structure models prepared using UML notation.

cloud computing (*88, 233*) Internet-based computing, where shared resources, software, and information are provided to firms on demand; Using redundant servers in multiple locations to host virtual machines.

code of ethics (*196*) What is considered to be ethical within an organization to promote ethical behavior.

collaboration (*106, 131*) A BPMN model showing two participant pools and the interactions between them within a process.

Committee of Sponsoring Organizations (COSO) (*198*) Composed of several organizations (AAA, AICPA, FEI, IIA, and IMA); studies the causal factors that lead to fraudulent financial reporting and develops recommendations for public companies, independent auditors, the SEC and other regulators, and educational institutions to improve the quality of financial reporting through internal controls and corporate governance.

composition relationship (*53*) A special-purpose UML notation representing the relationship between two classes that are often considered together, similar to aggregation relationships, except in composition relationships, one class cannot exist without the other, such as a book and the chapters that compose the book.

computer-assisted audit techniques (CAATs) (*250*) Essential tools for auditors to conduct an audit in accordance with heightened auditing standards.

constraints (*52*) Optional or mandatory guidance about how a process should perform in certain situations.

continuous audit (*251*) Performing audit-related activities on a continuous basis.

control objectives for information and related technology (COBIT) (*199*) An internationally accepted set of best IT security and control practices for IT management released by the IT Governance Institute (ITGI).

control risk (*203*) The threat that errors or irregularities in the underlying transactions will not be prevented, detected, and corrected by the internal control system.

corporate governance (*197*) A set of processes and policies in managing an organization with sound ethics to safeguard the interests of its stakeholders.

corrective controls (*198*) Fix problems that have been identified, such as using backup files to recover corrupted data.

cost/benefit analysis (*205*) Important in determining whether to implement an internal control.

critical path (*302*) The longest path for a project and represents the minimum amount of time needed for the completion of the project when sufficient resources are allocated.

customer (*105*) The external agent in the sales and collection process.

customer perspective (*264*) The Balanced Scorecard perspective that describes the organization's customer-related objectives and corresponding customer measures; it views organization performance from the customers' perspective.

customer relationship management (CRM) (*15*) Software used to manage and nurture a firm's interactions with its current and potential clients. CRM software often includes the use of database marketing tools to learn more about the customers and to develop strong firm-to-customer relationships.

D

data (*6*) Raw facts or statistics that, absent a context, may have little meaning.

data dictionary (*69*) Describes the data fields in each database record such as field description, field length, field type (e.g., alphanumeric, numeric), etc.

data flow diagram (DFD) (*42*) Another type of activity model that graphically shows the flow of data through a system and also incorporates elements of structure models.

data governance (*243*) The convergence of data quality, data management, data policies, business process management, and risk management surrounding the handling of data in a firm.

data integrity (*224*) Maintaining and assuring the accuracy and consistency of data during transmission and at storage.

data mart (*178*) A subset of the information from the data warehouse to serve a specific purpose.

data mining (*181, 243*) A process of using sophisticated statistical techniques to extract and analyze data from large databases to discern patterns and trends that were not previously known.

data models (*50*) A graphic representation of the conceptual contents of databases; data models support communication about database contents between users and designers of the database.

data warehouse (*178, 243*) A collection of information gathered from an assortment of external and operational (i.e, internal) databases to facilitate reporting for decision making and business analysis.

database (*68, 243*) A shared collection of logically related data for various uses.

database administrator (*69*) The person responsible for the design, implementation, repair, and security of a firm's database.

database management system (DBMS) (*68*) A computer program that creates, modifies, and queries the database. Specifically, the DBMS is designed to manage a database's storage and retrieval of information.

database system (*243*) A term typically used to encapsulate the constructs of a data model, database management system (DBMS), and database.

decision support system (DSS) (*180*) A computer-based information system that facilitates business decision-making activities.

design phase (*294*) The phase of the SDLC that involves describing in detail the desired features of the system that were uncovered in the analysis phase.

detective controls (*198*) Find problems when they arise.

digital certificate (*225*) A digital document issued and digitally signed by the private key of a Certificate Authority that binds the name of a subscriber to a public key.

digital dashboard (*182*) A display to track the firm's process or performance indicators or metrics to monitor critical performance.

digital signature (*224*) A message digest of a document (or data file) that is encrypted using the document creator's private key.

disaster recovery planning (DRP) (*234*) A process that identifies significant events that may threaten a firm's operations and outlines the procedures to ensure that the firm will resume operations when the events occur.

discretionary information (*6*) Information that is generated according to one's own judgment.

documentation (*29*) An information transmission and communication tool that explains how business processes and business systems work.

E

economic justification process (*276*)   The process by which an organization creates a business case for an IT investment or other major project.

embedded audit module (*251*)   A programmed audit module that is added to the system under review.

encryption (*223*)   Using algorithmic schemes to encode plaintext into nonreadable form.

enterprise IT (EIT) (*266*)   A type of information technology that restructures interactions within an organization and with external partners, such as customer relationship management systems.

enterprise risk management (ERM) (*201*)   A process, affected by the entity's board of directors, management, and other personnel, applied in strategy setting and across the enterprise, designed to identify potential events that may affect the entity, and manage risk to be within the risk appetite, to provide reasonable assurance regarding the achievement of objectives.

enterprise system (ES) (*12, 86*)   A centralized database that collects data from throughout the firm. Commercialized information system that integrates and automates business processes across a firm's value chain located within and across organizations.

entities (*60*)   The people, things, and events in the domain of interest; in UML notation, entities are modeled as classes.

entity integrity rule (*71*)   The primary key of a table must have data values (cannot be null).

error event (*107*)   An intermediate event in a BPMN model showing processing for exceptions to the normal process flow.

events (*32, 109, 135, 157*)   Important occurrences that affect the flow of activities in a business process. BPMN includes symbols to define start, intermediate, and end events; Classes that model the organization's transactions, usually affecting the organization's resources, such as sales and cash receipts.

F

fault tolerance (*233*)   Redundant units providing a system with the ability to continue functioning when part of the system fails.

15-15 rule (*301*)   A rule suggesting that if a project is more than 15 percent over budget or 15 percent off the planned schedule, it will likely never recoup the time or cost necessary to be considered successful. At this point a decision needs to be made on if or how to proceed from that point.

financial perspective (*264*)   The Balanced Scorecard perspective that describes the organization's financial objectives and corresponding financial measures of performance; it views organizational performance from the shareholders' perspective.

financial risk (*280*)   The risk that the IT investment will not deliver expected financial benefits.

finished goods inventory (*153*)   For a manufacturing company, the inventory (REA resource) that has completed the manufacturing process and is held for sale to customers.

firewall (*246*)   A security system comprised of hardware and software that is built using routers, servers, and a variety of software.

firm infrastructure (*11*)   Activities needed to support the firm, including the CEO and the finance, accounting, and legal departments.

flowcharts (*37*)   Visualizations of a process activity; they are activity models much like models using BPMN.

foreign key (FK) (*53, 70*)   Attribute that allows database tables to be linked together; foreign keys are the primary keys of other tables placed in the current table to support the link between the two tables.

form (*71*)   Forms are utilized by users to enter data into tables and view existing records.

fraud triangle (*226*)   Three conditions exist for a fraud to be perpetrated: incentive, opportunity, and rationalization.

function IT (FIT) (*266*)   A type of information technology that performs/supports a single function, such as spreadsheet applications.

G

Gantt chart (*302*)   A graphical representation of the project schedule that maps the tasks to a project calendar.

gateway (*32, 132, 154*)   Show process branching and merging as the result of decisions. Basic gateways are depicted as diamonds. Usually, gateways appear as pairs on the diagram. The first gateway shows the branching, and the second gateway shows merging of the process branches.

general controls (*198*)   Pertain to enterprisewide issues such as controls over accessing the network, developing and maintaining applications, and documenting changes of programs.

generalization relationship (*53*)   A special-purpose UML symbol that supports grouping of things that share common characteristics; it reduces redundancy because the shared characteristics need only be modeled once.

generalized audit software (GAS) (*251*)   Frequently used to perform substantive tests and used for testing of controls through transactional data analysis.

H

hierarchical data model (*68*)   Organizes data into a tree-like structure that allows repeating information using defined parent/child relationships.

hub (*245*)   Contains multiple ports.

human resource management (*11*)   Activities include recruiting, hiring, training, and compensating employees.

I

implementation phase (*295*)   The phase of the SDLC that involves development, testing, and implementation of the new proposed system.

inbound logistics (*10*)   Activities associated with receiving and storing raw materials and other partially completed materials and distributing those materials to manufacturing when and where they are needed.

informate-down (*17*)   The use of computer technology to provide information about business activities to employees across the firm.

informate-up (*17*)   The use of computer technology to provide information about business activities to senior management.

information (*6*)   Data organized in a meaningful way to the user.

information capital (*265*)   An intangible asset that reflects the readiness of the company's technology to support strategic internal processes. It includes computing hardware, infrastructure, applications, and employees' abilities to use technology effectively.

information overload (*6*)   The difficulty a person faces in understanding a problem and making a decision as a consequence of too much information.

Information Technology Infrastructure Library (ITIL) (*199*)   A set of concepts and practices for IT service management.

information value chain (*6*)   The overall transformation from a business need and business event to the collection of data and information to an ultimate decision.

inherent risk (*203*)   The risk related to the nature of the business activity itself.

input controls (*206*)   Ensure the authorization, entry, and verification of data entering the system.

integrated test facility (ITF) (*251*)   An automated technique that enables test data to be continually evaluated during the normal operation of a system.

intermediate error event (*154*)   Occurs between start and end events and affects the flow of the process. Intermediate error events represent interruptions to the normal flow of the process and start the exception flow.

intermediate event (*133*)   Occurs between start and end events and affects the flow of the process.

intermediate timer event (*133*)   Intermediate events that indicate a delay in the normal process flow until a fixed amount of time has elapsed.

internal rate of return (IRR) (*282*)   The discount rate (return) that makes a project's net present value equal to zero.

International Organization for Standardization (ISO) 27000 series (*199*)   This series contains a range of individual standards and documents specifically reserved by ISO for information security.

IT application controls (*206*)   Activities specific to a subsystem's or an application's input, processing, and output.

IT controls (*205*)   Involve processes that provide assurance for information and help to mitigate risks associated with the use of technology.

IT general controls (ITGC) (*206*)   Enterprise-level controls over IT.

K

key performance indicator (*266*)   Those measures that the organization feels best indicates the performance of a particular activity.

L

labor operations event (*157*)   In the conversion process, an event that represents the recording of labor (and any associated overhead) costs applied to work-in-process.

learning and growth perspective (*263*)   The Balanced Scorecard perspective that describes the organization's objectives and corresponding measures related to improvements in tangible and intangible infrastructure, such as human, information, and organizational capital.

local area network (LAN) (*245*)   A group of computers, printers, and other devices connected to the same network that covers a limited geographic range such as a home, small office, or a campus building.

M

MAC (media access controls) address (*246*)   A designated address that is connected to each device via the network and only sees traffic.

macro (*72*)   Macros are defined by Access users to automate processes such as opening a specific form.

maintenance phase (*295*)   The final phase of the SDLC that includes making changes, corrections, additions, and upgrades (generally smaller in scope) to ensure the system continues to meet the business requirements that have been set out for it.

mandatory information (*7*)   Information that is required to be generated or provided by law or regulation.

many-to-many relationship (*110, 136, 158*)   Exists when instances of one class (e.g., sales) are related to many instances of another class (e.g., inventory) and vice versa.

These relationships are implemented in Access and relational databases by adding a linking table to convert the many-to-many relationship into two one-to-many relationships.

marketing and sales activities (*10*)   Activities that identify the needs and wants of their customers to help attract them to the firm's products and buy them.

message digest (MD) (*224*)   A short code, such as one 256 bits long, resulting from hashing a plaintext message using an algorithm.

message flows (*35*)   BPMN represents exchanges between two participants (pools) in the same process as message flows, which are modeled as dashed arrows.

module (*72*)   Some Microsoft applications come with modules built in that will be automatically added onto Access.

multiplicities (*51*)   UML symbols that describe the minimum and maximum number of times an instance of one class can be associated with instances of another class for a specific association between those two classes; they indicate whether the two classes are part of one-to-one, one-to-many, or many-to-many relationships.

N

net present value (NPV) (*282*)   The sum of the present value of all cash inflows minus the sum of the present value of all cash outflows related to an IT investment or other capital investment.

network data model (*68*)   A flexible model representing objects and their relationships; allows each record to have multiple parent and child records or M:N mapping, also known as many-to-many relationships.

network IT (NIT) (*266*)   A type of information technology that allows people to communicate with one another, such as e-mail and instant messaging.

O

100% rule (*301*)   A rule requiring 100 percent planning of all tasks, including all of the internal, external, and interim tasks.

one-to-many relationship (*110*)   Exists when instances of one class are related to multiple instances of another class. For example, a customer can participate in many sales, but each sale involves only one customer.

one-to-one relationship (*136*)   Exists when instances of one class (e.g., sales) are related to only instance of another class (e.g., cash receipts) and each instance of the other class is related to only one instance of the original class.

operating system (OS) (*242*)   Performs the tasks that enable a computer to operate; comprised of system utilities and programs.

operation cost (*279*)   The recurring cost necessary to operate, maintain, and administer an IT initiative.

operational database (*243*)   Often includes data for the current fiscal year only.

operations (*10*)   Activities that transform inputs into finished goods and services.

orchestration (*106, 131*)   In BPMN, the sequence of activities within one pool.

outbound logistics (*10*)   Activities that warehouse and distribute the finished goods to the customers.

output controls (*207*)   Provide output to authorized people and ensure the output is used properly.

P

pages (*72*)   Access pages allow data to be entered into the database in real time from outside of the database system.

parallel simulation (*251*)   Attempts to simulate the firm's key features or processes.

payback period (*282*)   The amount of time necessary to recoup a project's initial investment.

perceived ease of use (*304*)   The extent to which a person perceives that the use of a particular system will be relatively free from effort.

perceived usefulness (*304*)   The extent to which users believe the system will help them perform their job better.

physical controls (*205*)   Mainly manual but could involve the physical use of computing technology.

planning phase (*294*)   The phase of the SDLC that summarizes the business needs with a high-level view of the intended project.

pools (*34*)   BPMN symbols used to identify participants, actors, or persons that perform activities and interact with other participants in a process.

preventive controls (*198*)   Deter problems before they arise.

primary key (PK) (*52, 69*)   An attribute or a combination of attributes that uniquely identifies an instance of a class in a data model or a specific row in a table.

private key (*223*)   A string of bits kept secret and known only to the owner of the key.

process maps (*37*)   Simplified flowcharts that use a basic set of symbols to represent a business process activity.

process perspective (*263*)   The Balanced Scorecard perspective that describes the organization's internal, process-related, objectives and corresponding measures; it views organizational performance from an internal perspective.

processing controls (*207*)   Ensure that data and transactions are processed accurately.

procurement (*11*)   Activities involve purchasing inputs such as raw materials, supplies, and equipment.

product (*104, 135*) Class representing the organization's goods held for sale, that is, the organization's inventory. This is considered a resource.

production authorization event (*158*) In a UML class model of the conversion process, an event that records the authorization to produce one or more finished good inventory items.

Program Evaluation Review Technique (PERT) (*301*) A project management tool used to help identify all tasks needed to complete a project. It is also helpful in determining task dependencies.

project (*298*) A series of tasks that are generally performed in a defined sequence to produce a predefined output.

project management (*294*) The process of carrying out the systems development life cycle to achieve an intended outcome.

project manager (*298*) The lead member of the project team who is responsible for the project.

project risk (*280*) The risk that the project will not be completed on time or within budget.

project sponsor (*298*) Generally a senior executive in the company who takes responsibility for the success of the project.

Public Company Accounting Oversight Board (PCAOB) (*196*) Established by SOX to provide independent oversight of public accounting firms.

public key (*223*) A string of bits created with the private key and widely distributed and available to other users.

public-key infrastructure (PKI) (*225*) A set of policies, processes, server platforms, software, and workstations used for the purpose of administering certificates and public-/ private-key pairs, including the ability to issue, maintain, and revoke public-key certificates.

purchase discount (*130*) An offer from the supplier to reduce the cost of a purchase if payment is made according to specified terms, usually within a specified time.

purchase order (*130*) A commitment event that precedes the economic purchase event. It records formal offers to suppliers to pay them if the supplier complies with the terms of the purchase order.

purchases (*130*) Records the receipt of goods or services from a supplier and the corresponding obligation to pay the supplier. These are considered events.

Q

query (*71*) Query in Access is a tool used to retrieve and display data derived from records stored within the database.

quote (*105*) Description of the products and/or services to be provided to a customer if ordered.

R

raw material issue event (*158*) In a UML class diagram of the conversion process, an event that records the transfer of raw materials into work-in-process.

raw materials inventory (*153*) For a manufacturing company, the inventory (REA resource) acquired for use (conversion) in the manufacturing process.

REA (*109, 135, 157*) Resource-event-agent framework for modeling business processes, originally developed by William McCarthy.

receipt (*135*) Same as the purchases event.

referential integrity rule (*71*) The data value for a foreign key must either be null or match one of the data values that already exist in the corresponding table.

relational data model (*68*) Stores information in the form of related two-dimensional tables.

relationship (*60*) The business purpose for the association between two classes or two database tables; *see* association.

relevance (*5*) Information that is capable of making a difference in a decision.

relevant costs (*279*) Those costs that will change as a result of an IT initiative or other major project.

reliability (*5*) Information that is free from bias and error.

remote access (*247*) Connection to a data-processing system from a remote location e.g., through a virtual private network.

report (*71*) Reports in Access are used to integrate data from one or more queries and tables to provide useful information to decision makers.

residual risk (*203*) The product of inherent risk and control risk (i.e., Residual risk + Inherent risk × Control risk).

resources (*109, 135, 157*) Those things that have economic value to a firm, such as cash and products.

risk assessment (*203*) The process of identifying and analyzing risks systematically to determine the firm's risk response and control activities.

router (*246*) Software-based intelligent device that chooses the most efficient communication path through a network to the required destination.

S

sales (*104*) Events documenting the transfer of goods or services to customer and the corresponding recognition of revenue for the organization.

sales order (*105*) Event documenting commitments by customers to purchase products. The sales order event precedes the economic event (sale).

Sarbanes-Oxley Act of 2002 (SOX) (*8, 196*) A federal law in the United States that set new and enhanced standards for all U.S. public companies, management, and public accounting firms.; A response to business scandals such as Enron, WorldCom, and Tyco International; Requires public companies registered with the SEC and their auditors to annually assess and report on the design and effectiveness of internal control over financial reporting.

scope creep (*300*)   The change in a project's scope after the project work has started.

sequence flows (*32*)   BPMN symbols that show the normal sequence of activities in a business process. Sequence flows are modeled as solid arrows, with the arrowhead showing the direction of process flow.

service activities (*10*)   Activities that provide the support of customers after the products and services are sold to them (e.g., warranty repairs, parts, instruction manuals, etc.).

session key (*224*)   A symmetric key that is valid for a certain timeframe only.

solution risk (*280*)   The risk that the proposed solution will not generate expected benefits.

station (*248*)   A wireless endpoint device equipped with a wireless network interface card.

strategy map (*265*)   A one-page representation of the firm's strategic priorities and the cause-and-effect linkages among those strategic priorities.

structure model (*50*)   A conceptual depiction of a database, such as a UML class model or an entity-relationship model.

Structured Query Language (SQL) (*80*)   A computer language designed to retrieve data from a relational database.

subprocess (*106, 132*)   Represent a series of process steps that are hidden from view in BPMN. The use of subprocesses in modeling helps reduce complexity.

suppliers (*130*)   In the UML diagram of the purchases and payments process, the external agents from whom goods and services are purchased and to whom payments are made.

supply chain (*13*)   The flow of materials, information, payments, and services from raw materials suppliers, through factories and warehouses, all the way to the final customers of the firm's products.

supply chain management (SCM) software (*14*)   Software that connects the focal firms with its suppliers. It generally addresses segments of the supply chain, including manufacturing, inventory control, and transportation.

swimlanes (*34*)   BPMN symbols that provide subdivisions of pools to show, for example, functional responsibilities within an organization.

switch (*245*)   An intelligent device that provides a path for each pair of connections on the switch by storing address information in its switching tables.

symmetric-key encryption (*223*)   Both the sender and the receiver use the same key to encrypt and decrypt messages.

systems analyst (*8, 294*)   Person responsible for both determining the information needs of the business and designing a system to meet those needs.

systems development life cycle (SDLC) (*294*)   The process of creating or modifying information systems to meet the needs of its users. It serves as the foundation for all processes people use to develop such systems.

T

technological risk (*280*)   The risk that the technology will not perform as expected to deliver the planned benefits.

technology (*11*)   Supports value-creating activities in the value change. These technologies also include research and development to develop new products or determine ways to produce products at a cheaper price.

technology acceptance model (TAM) (*304*)   A model that predicts when users will adopt a new system to the extent they believe the system will help them perform their job better.

test data technique (*251*)   Uses a set of input data to validate system integrity.

timer events (*133*)   Indication of a delay in the flow of a process to a specific date, an elapsed time (for example, 30 days), or a relative repetitive date, such as every Friday.

transform (*17*)   The use of computer technology to fundamentally redefine business processes and relationships.

triple constraint (*299*)   Three factors that constrain information technology and other projects: cost, scope, and time. Also known as Dempster's triangle.

type image (*112, 137, 158*)   Class that represents management information (such as categorizations, policies, and guidelines) to help manage a business process. Type image often allows process information to be summarized by category.

U

uninterruptible power supply (*232*)   A device using battery power to enable a system to operate long enough to back up critical data and shut down properly during the loss of power.

V

value chain (*10*)   A chain of critical business processes at a company that creates value.

value proposition (*264, 282*)   Represents the product and service characteristics, such as price, quality, selection, and brand image, that the firm attempts to deliver to customers to meet or exceed its customers' expectations and thereby result in customer retention and new customer acquisition; Summarizes the costs and benefits of a preferred alternative IT investment, describing (1) the relevant time frames that the costs will be incurred and benefits realized, (2) the corresponding discount rates to apply to future cash flows, and (3) the sensitivity of the results to assumptions.

virtual private network (VPN) (247) Securely connects a firm's WANs by sending/receiving encrypted packets via virtual connections over the public Internet to distant offices, salespeople, and business partners.

virtualization (233) Using various techniques and methods to create a virtual (rather than actual) version of a hardware platform, storage device, or network resources.

W

wide area network (WAN) (246) Links different sites together; transmits information across geographically dispersed LANs; and covers a broad geographic area such as a city, region, nation, or an international link.

wireless network (248) Comprised of two fundamental architectural components: access points and stations.

work breakdown structure (WBS) (301) The process of identifying all tasks needed to complete a project.

work-in-process inventory (157) For a manufacturing company, the value of raw materials, direct labor, and manufacturing overhead in production but not yet finished.

X

XBRL Global Ledger Taxonomy (XBRL GL) (186) Serves as a ledger using the XBRL standard for internal purposes.

XBRL instance documents (184) A document containing XBRL elements.

XBRL specification (184) Provides the underlying technical details of what XBRL is and how it works.

XBRL style sheet (186) Adds presentation elements to XBRL instance documents to make them readable by people.

XBRL taxonomy (184) Defines and describes each key data element (e.g., total assets, accounts, payable, net income, etc.).

XBRL (eXtensible Business Reporting Language) (183) An open, global standard for exchanging financial reporting information.

XML (Extensible Markup Language) (183) Open, global standard for exchanging information in a format that is both human- and machine-readable.

Photo Credits

Chapter 1
Page 2: © Kumar Sriskandan/Alamy; p. 7: © Allison Rocks! Photography; p. 12: Courtesy of Amazon.com; p. 15: George Frey/Bloomberg via Getty Images.

Chapter 2
Page 26: AFP/Getty Images; p. 30: Keith Brofsky/Getty Images.

Chapter 3
Page 48: Purestock/SuperStock; p. 50: Image Source/Getty Images; p. 57: © Prisma Bildagentur AG/Alamy.

Chapter 4
Page 66: Tim Boyle/Getty Images; p. 70: The McGraw-Hill Companies/Ashley Zellmer, photographer; p. 88: JILL JARSULIC/KRT/Newscom.

Chapter 5
Page 102: © James Leynse/CORBIS; p. 105: Ingram Publishing/SuperStock.

Chapter 6
Page 128: Jon Feingersh/Getty Images; p. 133: Digital Vision/Getty Images; p. 139: Todd Wright/Blend Images/Getty Images.

Chapter 7
Page 150: Ingram Publishing/SuperStock; p. 155: Tetra Images/Getty Images; p. 158: Steve Cole/Getty Images.

Chapter 8
Page 168: Kevin P. Casey/Bloomberg via Getty Images; p. 170: Courtesy of Vernon J. Richardson.

Chapter 9
Page 177: Courtesy of Oracle Magazine; p. 180: © Per Andersen/Alamy; p. 182: © Transtock Inc./Alamy.

Chapter 10
Page 194: © MARK/epa/CORBIS; p. 196: © Reuters/CORBIS.

Chapter 11
Page 220: Tom Lasseter/MCT via Getty Images; p. 226: 2007 Getty Images, Inc.

Chapter 12
Page 240: © Mathias Beinling/Alamy; p. 244: © Radius Images/CORBIS.

Chapter 13
Page 261: © Muskopf Photography, LLC/Alamy; p. 263: Plush Studios/DH Kong/Getty Images.

Chapter 14
Page 274: Tom Pennington/Getty Images; p. 277: © Dmitriy Shironosov/Alamy; p. 281: Barry Chin/The Boston Globe via Getty Images.

Chapter 15
Page 292: © Danny Johnston/AP Photo; p. 298: Photo courtesy of National Nuclear Security Administration/Nevada Site Office/DOE.

Index

Bold page numbers indicate definitions or key discussions of terms; page numbers followed by *n.* indicate footnotes or source notes.